THE NEED TO BE WHOLE

The Need to Be Whole: Patriotism and the History of Prejudice

WENDELL BERRY

SHOEMAKER & COMPANY

Library of Congress Control Number: 2022935000

ISBN: 979-8-9856798-0-9
eISBN: 979-8-9856798-1-6

Cover and interior design by Gopa & Ted2, Inc.
Printed in the United States of America

Shoemaker & Company

Distributed by Publishers Group West

10 9 8 7 6 5 4 3 2 1

We can go through the world being half people, and most of us do that most of our lives.
—*Porch Talk with Ernest Gaines*

No one would claim victory, which was no problem for us. A fundamental principle of nonviolence is that there is no such thing as defeat once a conflict is justly resolved, because there are no losers when justice is achieved.

~

I believe the power and the endurance of Martin Luther King Jr.'s vision and leadership was the fact that it extended to all people, regardless of class or race.

~

We are one people, one family, one house.
—John Lewis, *Walking wth the Wind*

In the West our peculiar civilization was based upon regional autonomy, whose eccentricities were corrected and sublimated by the classical-Christian culture which provided a form for the highest development of man's potentialities *as man*. Man belonged to his village, valley, mountain, or seacoast; but wherever he was he was a Christian whose Hebraic discipline had tempered his tribal savagery and whose classical humanism had moderated the literal imperative of his Christianity to suicidal other-worldliness.... The myth of science which undermined this culture and created the modern economic man rooted out the regional economies, and is now creating a world regional economy.... Regionalism without civilization—which means, with us, regionalism without classical-Christian culture—becomes provincialism; and world regionalism becomes world provincialism. For provincialism is that state

of mind in which regional men lose their origins in the past and its continuity into the present, and begin every day as if there had been no yesterday. . . . I am convinced that even the die-hard traditionalist would deny his own shrinking tradition if he refused to act for the remnant of it left because he can't have it all. For this remnant may be useful; there will be a minority with a memory . . .
—Allen Tate, "The New Provincialism"

To think in terms of ideology rather than of geography accorded with inclinations of the American mind.
—John Lukacs, *Confessions of an Original Sinner*

The real science of political economy . . . is that which teaches nations to desire and labour for the things that lead to life: and which teaches them to scorn and destroy the things that lead to destruction . . . The great and only science of Political Economy teaches them . . . what is vanity, and what substance; and how the service of Death, the Lord of Waste, and of eternal emptiness, differs from the service of Wisdom, the Lady of Saving, and of eternal fulness . . .
—John Ruskin, *Unto This Last*

The Indian knows that even the smallest animal has great importance and can teach us great things. So too, all the little things we do every day have great importance. Our life is full of many little things in each day and in every moment. We should not concentrate on some great event that we expect to come in the future, but in the correct performance of all our daily obligations. In this way, we will show respect for all created things and for Acbadadea [the Creator].
—Thomas Yellowtail, *Yellowtail: An Autobiography*

From my experience with leisure I have learned that too much of it is not good. Having not quite as much as you would like gives a greater value to the time you do have, and it gives a drive and conciseness to your productions.

Anyway, I prefer to do my own work, lowly as it may seem to the proud ones for whom the use of arms and legs is to be avoided at all costs. It is a simpler way, and the rewards are independence, and satisfaction of accomplishment, and the pleasure of being out-of-doors when the sun sets.
—Harlan Hubbard, *Payne Hollow*

[L]o, we bring into bondage our sons and our daughters to be servants, and some of our daughters are brought unto bondage already: neither is it in our power to redeem them; for other men have our lands and vineyards.
—Nehemiah 5:5

It is worth noting that our modern notion of the industrial society, in which each seeks a share in the material exploitation of Nature, would not be regarded as a society at all by Plato or Aristotle, but as a form of political degeneration.
—Joseph Milne, "The Heavenly Order and the Lawful Society"

Mencius said: "You can't talk sense to the inhumane. They find repose in risk, profit in disaster, and joy in what will destroy them. If you could talk sense to them, would there be ruined countries and ravaged houses?"
—*Mencius*, translated by David Hinton

The test of a man's freedom is his responsibility as a workman. Freedom is not incompatible with discipline, it is only incompatible

with irresponsibility. He who is free is responsible for his work. He who is not responsible for his work is not free.
—Eric Gill, *A Holy Tradition of Working*

[T]he marvelous advances in technique made during recent decades are improvements in the pump, rather than the well.

In all of these cleavages, we see repeated the same basic paradoxes: man the conqueror *versus* man the biotic citizen; science the sharpener of his sword *versus* science the searchlight on his universe; land the slave and servant *versus* land the collective organism.

The case for a land ethic would appear hopeless but for the minority which is in obvious revolt against these 'modern' trends.

A thing is right when it tends to preserve the integrity, stability, and beauty of the biotic community. It is wrong when it tends otherwise.
—Aldo Leopold, "The Land Ethic"

You work from the heart out, you don't work from the issue down.
—*Conversations with Ken Kesey*

Both grandparents owned land. Like Booker T. Washington, they understood that black folks who had their "forty acres and a mule," or even just their one acre, could sustain their lives by growing food, by creating shelter that was not mortgaged. Baba and Daddy Gus, my maternal grandparents, were radically opposed to any notion of social and racial uplift that meant black folks would lead us away from respect for the land, that would lead us to imitate the social mores of affluent whites.
—bell hooks, *Belonging: A Culture of Place*

Contents

CONTENTS

THE NEED TO BE WHOLE

Introduction

A decade or more ago, bell hooks came to visit me so that we could have a conversation about my book, *The Hidden Wound*. That book was published in 1969. The title refers to my belief, then and still, that white people's part in slavery and all the other outcomes of race prejudice, so damaging to its victims, had also been gravely damaging to white people, a damage too little acknowledged and probably less understood. To know that bell hooks, a fellow Kentuckian, thought my book was worth talking about was of course a pleasure and a relief to me. As I recall, our conversation was completely cordial, but what I have most remembered of that conversation is my dissatisfaction with my own part in it. I felt that I had largely failed a dear opportunity.

My trouble then, as I now believe, was that my thoughts and worries and my sense of the past had outgrown *The Hidden Wound* but had not become shapely enough in my mind to be available to conversation. I was, as I would now say, "only thirty-four" when I wrote *The Hidden Wound*. I would have to do a good deal more reading and thinking and looking around, as well as some preliminary writing, in order to write *The Unsettling of America*, which was published in 1977. Meanwhile, I was understanding more and more clearly the danger of dividing land and people into two thoughts, historically or politically or any other way. I was seeing, and on the basis of accumulating evidence, that a society cannot do for its people what it will not do for its land, and vice versa. A society willing to abuse its land will abuse its people, and vice versa. By the time I sat down with bell hooks, my thinking about "the race problem" had become extremely unwieldy. I was trying to lead a bear by the tail.

And then in 2015 I received a review copy of *Democracy in Black*, by Eddie S. Glaude Jr. It was accompanied by a kind letter from Prof. Glaude, saying that he had been moved by *The Hidden Wound* and he wondered what I might think of his book. He also suggested that he would be glad if I would write a "blurb" recommending his book to readers. Well, I am too slow to be an honest blurb writer, and I graduated myself out of that business long ago. But the book attracted me. I read it slowly, as I had to do, marking passages as I went. As I read, I planned to write Prof. Glaude a careful letter, fully assenting to his book's sense of the gravity of the effects of race prejudice upon black people and upon our society, but also discussing points of difference and similarity that interested me, and about which I wanted to know his thoughts. For instance, he wrote that "fears of black men" had always existed among white people, and I wanted to tell him, for what it was worth, that in the countryside and rural towns where I grew up and where the races knew each other familiarly, I was not taught to fear black men— which I assumed was because we white people knew black people as individuals, not as representatives of a category. And when Prof. Glaude wrote of the decay of "a relatively small African American community" in Chicago, I wanted to say that his description would have served as well for most of America's rural small towns. I would say I thought that this decay had the same reasons for both races though no doubt it was worse for black people because of race prejudice.

Eventually I had a list of a dozen topics for my "letter" to Prof. Glaude, too many to deal with in a letter, and the occasion for just a polite note was long past. Again, in spite of my good intentions, I had failed an opportunity that I valued. Looking back now at my projected letter to Prof. Glaude, I can see that my thoughts had begun to move toward this book that was then unforeseen and is now written. More clearly than ever, I could see that both our people and our country have come close to being ruined by race prejudice, or race prejudices, and the continuing effects. But I was worried also about historical and political generalizations that have become too general and too powerful.

Most immediately, it seemed to me that in our public discussion of racial issues, such as it now is, there was too pronounced an assumption that black people and white people are entirely unlike each other in their history and their problems. This cannot be entirely true, and it obstructs the possibility of thinking together about shared problems. If, for example, the decline of a small black community in Chicago resembles, point by point, the decline of the now nearly all-white small towns in my rural county, then we need to push beyond the problems of racial difference to ask what is the matter now with all of us. If the communities of both races are failing, then the problem cannot be race prejudice, or only that, but a prejudice of another kind. We have got to ask, I think, if we are not faced with a prejudice against community life itself.

I am unsure how changes that are great and gradual are made. But let us suppose that in our history there came a time when the value of human communities was put into one pan of a scale, and into the other pan was placed an immense amount of money to be portioned in large shares among a few people, that pan being further weighted by the principle of economic determinism sometimes expressed as "progress," sometimes as "inevitability," sometimes as "Nothing you can do." And of course, community value, being uncondensable and unpriceable, is stupendously outweighed, and it is sent flying off beyond reckoning. Then, says Shani Smith of the perishing Chicago community, who was Prof. Glaude's informant, "businesses that defined the community . . . have . . . gone." She doesn't say where they went, but I know that they didn't move away intact into other communities that they liked better. They are gone because they were killed by chain stores and shopping malls— and by the defection of onetime community members who, for convenience and bargains, chose to shop away from home. I know because countless small towns in rural America have been killed in the same way. I know too that if those communities were alive and working, they would be, to an extent reasonable and possible, economically independent or self-sufficient, and therefore would have a needed power of self-determination.

There is no doubt that black communities have some problems that originate in racism. There is also no doubt that all communities are now failing or failed for reasons that are not racial. Some of those reasons are public—governmental or economic—and must be addressed by public and political means, including, when necessary, protest movements and marches. But a lot of the blame for the destruction of our communities we must accept individually, for we have almost unanimously consented to the movement of our lives away from home. Whether we depart by way of the automobile, the television set, or the computer makes little difference. The upshot for too many of us is the lamentation from the deceased small community in Chicago: "We don't know each other." And so we lose the social and economic benefits of community membership.

Like a living, functioning household, a living, functioning community enables its members to help one another. This ability to help one another, if we have it, is one of the dearest, largest human freedoms. But it cannot be given to us by any of our great public institutions or agencies of the government. If we want living, functioning communities, we will have to make them ourselves in our own neighborhoods, starting with the means at hand and the nearest problems.

And so I partly began a thought or two in response to *Democracy in Black*, clearly a useful book, needed by me. But I still had my bear by the tail, and I was not able to lead him or her into a letter to Prof. Glaude. I am always surprised, slowly of course, by the slowness of my mind. But finally even I could see that a man who thinks he is leading a bear by the tail is more likely being led. Finally, my worries about the problems of race prejudice, worries that began in my childhood and have continued and ramified ever since, led me into this pondering and ponderous book. I had for sure taken hold of a bear's tail, and before I could turn him or her loose, he or she had already led me off the road, and we were traveling through the hills and hollows and grown-over footpaths of our country present and past. By then I had to hold on to the tail of this bear, who was perhaps my Muse. Now it comes clear! This bear is not "he or she," but certainly a lady bear, my Muse, maybe dangerous but maybe helpful, and I had to hold to her tail not only to keep on her safest end, but also in the hope that she would lead me somewhere I needed to go.

Though I cannot presume that either of them would want it, I have to think of this book, in part, as something owed to bell hooks and Eddie S. Glaude Jr. With the same unwillingness to presume, I am bound to say that this book is also owed in part to my long friendship with Ernest J. Gaines, begun in conversation in 1958, continuing in our shared sense of origin in the talk of old people and our loyalty to the places and communities that nurtured us when we were boys. And from still farther back, this book responds to the kindness and instruction offered me when I was a child by Nick Watkins and Aunt Georgie Ashby, about whom I wrote in *The Hidden Wound*.

I have just named five black people I have had much in mind during my work on this book, but without ever assuming that I knew what any one of them would think of any of my thoughts. I am sure nonetheless that their presence in my mind has exerted an exacting requirement and a shaping pressure. I am sure also that their influence has been remarkably various. Having just put their five names into the same paragraph, I am impressed—and reassured—by their unlikeness to one another. Not from them, or from them plus the several other black people of whom I speak in these pages, can I derive anything remotely like a representative figure or stereotype.

And so I come to another of the difficulties of this book: that of bringing a lifetime's knowledge of particular persons and places into the history of race prejudice, race relations, and race problems that has to be understood and talked about somewhat in general terms. Because I *knew* Georgie Ashby and Nick Watkins, and they come into my memory alive, in living attitudes, scenes, and weathers, for me they can never fade or disappear into the abstract Black Woman and Black Man, who are so often called to our attention. Conversely, the scenes and weathers of my own life are so insistently demanding of my attention that I will never succeed in identifying myself to myself as a White Man, or as an Old White Rural Man, as probably I would now be identified by a young urban black man who might drive by and see me standing in my work clothes beside the road. That does not mean that we cannot talk usefully

6

in general terms. It means that when we use those terms we are estranging ourselves from the particularities of the lives we humans must live in the actual world, and so we must think of those terms as always in search of particular examples, just as a particular event or memory will go looking for the general sense or truth, if any, that it exemplifies. The need especially to keep general terms exact, or to give them a sense as exact as possible, seems to have been one of the sternest demands of this book. My pencil has spent a lot more time in the air than on the paper, and I have done a lot of erasing. The biggest irritation of such writing is the need to use over and over again the always inexact adjectives "black" and "white," thus identifying people by their least interesting attribute.

Another difficulty that I have had to deal with is that I cannot see race prejudice and the sufferings related to it as special or isolatable problems calling for special or isolated solutions. When public causes become specialized in various movements, they become oversimplified by being separated, each one a distraction from every other one. I think it is obvious that race prejudice or white supremacy is the original and fundamental mistake in the European conquest of this country. And this was so great a mistake not only because of the harm it did directly to its victims, but also because it led to and remained involved with other mistakes. From the point of view, rarely taken, of our country itself, our history since 1492 is largely a history of mistakes, relating to one another in an interconnection of causes and influences too complex to diagram.

For instance, our treatment of the native tribespeople and enslaved Africans required a debilitating condescension. Our prejudice against the Indians kept nearly all of us from recognizing in their cultures—*and as a possibility for ourselves*—the necessary sanctity of the bond between people and their homelands. Practically, it kept us from learning from them the right ways of living in and caring for the lands we took from them. The ruling class of the South, by their prejudice against enslaved black people and against the "degrading" work assigned to them, denied themselves the direct experience of their land and the knowledge of its best use and care—a contagious alienation that they finally communicated to just about all the rest of us. Our condescension to things we needed desperately to know foreshortened our imagination and stunted our sense of consequence and responsibility.

And so, for another instance, we have come into the present time more than usually distressed, calling everywhere for expert advice, but never having realized that as a public or as a nation, we have always treated the land and the people of the land with the same abuse. By "the people of the land" I mean all who have needed and wanted to be settled and permanently at home: first the previous inhabitants as we came into their tribal homelands; and then, not the frontiersmen or pioneers, but the settlers, the agrarian smallholders, the would-be homemakers, willing to do the land's work and knowing how; and then the freed slaves, who also knew both the land's work and their need for land, but who then entered their second bondage, sharing the fate of poor white people in subservience to merchants and landlords; and finally the small farmers, of whatever race, who were told in the middle of the last century to "get big or get out," and nearly all of whom by now have got out.

That this book is the work of a resolved pacifist, a would-be follower of the teachings of Jesus and of Martin Luther King Jr., makes it odd in an economy based upon war and the technologies of violence. What probably is even odder is that, in a time of almost total urbanization, this is a book by a rural American, a writer who by birth and choice is a country person. Though I have lived in cities, I have always had the country way of seeing that was carefully given to me by my upbringing. My point of view is from ground-level. I judge things above the ground by their effect or influence on the ground. My thoughts at first were guided by my inherited inclination to see the good care of the land as the highest human obligation, and the good care of the human community as the second highest. These principles of mine were radically amplified, clarified, and set in order by my reading, many years ago, of Aldo Leopold's essay "The Land Ethic." That ethic, to one coming upon it in the midst of our darkened and disordered age, declares itself with the sudden brightness of obvious truth. Leopold wrote it out in a single sentence that has lighted my way from the moment I read it: "The land ethic simply enlarges the boundaries of the community to include soils, waters, plants, and animals, or collectively, the land." When I read that, my two thoughts of the land and the community became one thought. The land ethic, Leopold said, "changes the role of *Homo sapiens* from conqueror of the land-community to plain member and citizen of it." And so we can say that, to make whole sense of any dispute between two merely human sides, the land-community must be represented, not as an equal third side, but as the side whose fate ultimately will decide the fate of the other sides.

From the point of view of the land-community, as I have watched for most of my life the economic landscapes in many places but most continuously here at home, it has long been plain to me that our country is in decline and our people with it. The country is in decline because the people are not properly using it and caring for it. The people are in decline for the same reason. Like every knowledgeable observer, of whom only a few are left, I feel that I am watching a long-worsening, extremely complicated emergency that is unnoticed by almost everybody. The emergency, to define it the shortest way, is that both the land and the people are unhealthy.

We no longer speak of health as the natural or normal condition of our bodies and the world. We speak of health as the hoped-for result of the use of products produced by the health industry, which thrives upon illness. As the land and people languish, the economy prospers (for a while).

Because we have so nearly destroyed the sense of the word "health," we find little use for it. When a pandemic strikes and a lot of people are getting sick and many are dying, the public talk is all of cures and preventions—purchased supplies, the getting and spending of a lot of money. Nobody has much to say about health. This is unhealthy. It also is insane. What was and is the best prevention or preparation against a pandemic? The answer, obviously, is health, natural or normal health. In this world of easy communication, in which disease is easily communicated and pandemics are possible, the best preparation was and is to be a healthy people in a healthy country. The best precaution for the events and effects of climate change, or any other calamity, just as obviously is to be a healthy people in a healthy country. But from that possibility we are now radically and perilously displaced.

To deal with so great a problem, the best idea may not be to go ahead in our present state of unhealth to more disease and more product development. It may be that our proper first resort should be to history: to see if the truth we need to pursue might be behind us where we have ceased to look.

~

In 1940 in the United States there were 6,102,417 farms, of which the average size was 175 acres. In 2012 there were 2,109,303 farms containing an average of 434 acres. If we consider that on every one of those four million lost farms there would have been a farmer and family or a tenant farmer and family, and on some of them one or more hired hands and maybe another family, we see that we are reckoning with a movement of many millions of people off the farms and into the cities, or into city work, in about a single lifetime. One set of numbers I have used says that 25 million people left the farms between 1940 and 1967, or in less than half a lifetime. When we try just to guess at all the personal, social, and economic adjusting that would be involved in so massive a population making so fundamental a change, we know that the problems would be incalculable in numbers, in seriousness, and in longevity. This is social—and economic—mobility, often praised, but common sense tells us that its repercussions and ripple effects will be with us a long time, with most of the social problems afflicting the cities.

From the rural point of view, the view from ground level, those of us who still have it can see consequences that are rural, equally troubling, and in some ways permanently damaging to the country. The removal from the land of so many people removes from the land also those people's love, care, skill, and work. And it removes the same love, care, skill, and work from those people. This is an enormous, an enormously consequential, loss to both the land and the people—which is not something that will be said, because it cannot be said, because it is carefully not seen, by the professors and other urban professionals of agriculture. But mere arithmetic tells us that if so many people who have the most direct and practical reasons to love the country are removed from the country, then the country will be less loved. There will be a great reduction of patriotism, in the true sense of that word. Common sense surely can tell us that one farmer, or one farm family, can pay closer attention and give better care to a farm of 175 acres than to a farm of 434 acres. And it does not require a committee of advanced experts to surmise that a small rural town would be better supported economically by a lot of small farms than by a few big ones.

It is important to understand that this drastic reduction of the farm population had the approval and encouragement of the agricultural powers that be. It has been in effect our farm policy since World War II. The ruling doctrine was that the "inefficient" and otherwise dispensable farmers could be replaced—along with their love, care, skill, and work—by the technologies of war. In 1967, as I have been careful to remember, a presidential commission declared that this country's biggest farm problem was a surplus of farmers.

Probably for every effect there is more than one cause, and there were several reasons for people to leave farming. Some were directly replaced by technologies. Some could not survive one of the recurring farm depressions caused by high costs and low prices. Some preferred city work or city life. The most effective way to get rid of farmers—and to enrich the corporations that supply the expensive "inputs" and purchase the cheapened harvests—is by policy to permit and even encourage overproduction. So long as farmers do not control any part of the farm economy, they cannot mutually thrive. They can only compete against each other, increasing production to take advantage of high prices, or to compensate for low prices, and so driving one another, and themselves, into bankruptcy. For this reason, production control with parity pricing is a fundamental necessity of agricultural policy. The loss of so many farmers—of so much "competition"—has not improved the economic security of the surviving farmers. Year after year, generation after generation, they have continued to go under, until almost none are left. The logical portent is that they will keep failing until none is left, and all the land will be owned by large banks and corporations.

Farmers and the land have been sacrificed to the need for cheap food, just as the miners and the land of the Appalachian coalfields have been sacrificed to the need for cheap energy. These cheapenings have been identified as "needs" only because of the greater need of the ruling powers to disguise the real costs to land and people of the industrial production of these commodities. Industrialism requires dispensable land and dispensable people in order to provide cheap goods—or, more accurately, goods produced at the lowest possible cost to be sold at the highest possible price. Tony Oppegard, a mine safety lawyer in Kentucky, told the Louisville *Courier-Journal*: "The U.S. for far too long has deemed acceptable a certain number of miners to die every year" in mines where profit has overruled safety. With the same justice it could be said that for far too long the United States has deemed acceptable a large number of farm bankruptcies every year. We are here speaking of preventable catastrophes, death in the mines and farm failure often leading to suicide, as acceptable costs of production.

It is true, and much noticed only lately, that more black farmers have failed, in proportion to their total numbers, than white farmers, and that this is largely attributable to racial discrimination in the agencies of the United States Department of Agriculture. That is a correctable wrong and it ought to be corrected. But it would be wrong also to assume that the decline of the black farm population is the result only or mainly of racial discrimination. It is necessary to see operating, beyond race prejudice, a prejudice against farmers, and particularly against small farmers—and to see operating beyond those prejudices the fundamental dependence of industrialism and the industrial economy upon the dispensability of human workers. This principle we know as "labor-saving," and, because we ignore the heartlessness of its application, we classify it as "progress." When we are obliged to acknowledge its cruelty, we call it "creative destruction." But for whatever reasons, the cultural and economic bond between land and people has been broken. The land has lost the work that it needs to have from the people it sustains, and the people have lost the work of the land that would be sustaining to them. Our agrarian ancestors, of all races, understood this mutuality and taught it, but as a people we have failed to learn it.

As a result, we live in and from an abandoned, unloved, toxic, eroded, and degraded country that most of our people have forgotten or never knew. And our people are uprooted, scattered, isolated in their multitude, frightened, angry, and as unhealthy as the land. The army finds only 20 percent of our young people, one in five, to be fit for service. In this condition we confront the present pandemic. Many who contract the virus are already sick. We have so far condemned our land and ourselves by ignoring or defying fundamental laws of nature and of human nature.

The law most dangerous to violate can be stated this way: If the land is to be used by people, then it must be used by people who love it, who are culturally prepared and instructed to use it lovingly, and whose cultures therefore are sustained economically. When that law is disobeyed, then the land will be ruined, as ours is now being ruined. This understanding of our condition comes to us from the agrarian traditions of nearly every race and culture that I have so far read about. Nearly all have held the earth to be a living creature whose life we must choose to share on its terms. We have of course one other choice: We can choose against the earth's life and its terms, which is to choose our death, and this is the choice we now are making.

And so I have given the reason that I do not believe we can solve our great problems one at a time. Our problems do not relate to one another in linear sequence, but rather in something like a network, in which correcting one requires correcting several. The land and the people can recover their health by the same work at the same time. For this reason there is no hope in the idea of a purely urban culture. Hope is hard to measure, and I am unsure how much hope is offered by this book. But the first step toward hope is to withhold approval from "solutions" that are hopeless. I can do that.

Because I write as a rural American, from the point of view of the land and the land-communities, I am obliged in honesty to worry about that point of view as possibly a limitation. But I am equally obliged to take it as a responsibility and even, within limits, as an advantage. The "race problem" began as a rural problem necessarily because it began in response to a supposed agricultural need, and before the growth of large industrial cities and urban civilization. The problem became urban when millions of black people, like millions of white people, moved from the countryside into the cities.

And so it is understandable, and necessary, that the effort for racial equality has been defined and led by urban people. But the urban point of view also has a limitation to worry about. It is more limited than the rural point of view because it is much purer and more self-enclosed than the rural point of view. It has been a long time since America has had anywhere an intact, authentic, functioning rural culture. By now all of us still living in the country have been caught up, willy-nilly and just about completely, into the economy and consumer culture of the cities.

What urban liberals don't see, and undoubtedly can't see, is that our race problem is intertangled with our land and land use problem, our farm and forest problem, our water and waterways problem, our food problem, our air problem, our health problem. That is because this "America" is a country as well as a nation. But urban leaders seem to be specialists constitutionally. Despite their present emphasis on "diversity," they seem unable to see or consider the necessary all-inclusiveness of Leopold's "land-community." They handpick urban problems and favor them one at a time without considering the connections that bind problems into bundles. They don't know or think about or talk about the rural problems that are the causes or the results of urban problems. This makes a great silence into which this book tries to speak.

CHAPTER I

───────── ❧ ─────────

Public Knowledge, Public Language

My interest in the American history of race, racism, and "the race problem," along with my belief in fairness both legal and personal, has been a matter of record for almost fifty years. I am another who believes that it is "self-evident, that all [humans] are created equal; that they are endowed by their Creator with certain unalienable rights; that among these, are life, liberty, and the pursuit of happiness." Just as I know the difference between happiness and the pursuit of it, I know of course that we are not equally endowed with gifts, but I believe that when we enter a voting booth, when we petition the government for the redress of grievances, when we appeal to our elected representatives, when we stand before a judge or confront the police, all that we hold dear depends upon our determination to hold ourselves as equal to one another. I take seriously Jefferson's word "all" and (perhaps more seriously than he did) his affirmation of the divine origin of our rights.

The difficulty, for us modern Americans anyhow, comes with the need to honor rightly both the "all" and the distinct persons and lives within the "all." It is easy to issue a general approval of "all humans" or of all of this or that race or category of humans. But for most of us it is impossible to approve of all the individual members even of our own bunch. It is when we come face-to-face with one another individually and personally that our ethical principles, such as that sentence from the Declaration or "love thy neighbor as thyself," are snatched into the wringer of actual experience. Actual experience subjects and exposes us to the actual world, in which we must make a living under the obligation to be honest, form opinions under the obligation to be just, and in general suffer the mysteries, obscurities, and complexities that make truth difficult and righteousness imperfect. Nobody can naturally or easily love everybody. Neither white liberals nor white supremacists can look with favor upon all white people. Neither white nor black liberals will look with favor upon all black people whom they actually know and are obliged to deal with as individuals. Godly and ungodly conservatives can abide one another only in the half-lit masquerade of party politics. To be obliged to confront one apart from all involves risk; it may become a test or a trial. The difficulty and the dread of this is indicated by our disease of "communication" by cell phone, even between persons in the same place.

Whether because of electronic intervention or political anxiety or personal estrangement, many of us now appear to be sheltering or virtually disappearing into the anonymity of some subdivision of "all." Not long ago I read an article about protesting college students, most or perhaps all of whom identified themselves by their political or racial or sexual category—not, as perhaps by now only some of my own generation would have expected, by name or family or home or vocation. This seems to signify a sense of, or perhaps a need for, personal anonymity, which has depreciated the value of privacy and personal integrity, and which functions as self-protection.

I remember when it was a part of manners to ask any stranger you met, "Where are you from?" But that became pointless or even bad manners when the likely answer came to be "Nowhere" or "Every-where." We have become too "upwardly mobile" or mobile or root-less or homeless or alone to start a conversation by asking "Where are you from?" The ancient, sacred bond between land and people has been broken. And how likely are we to ask a stranger "What is your political party?" or "What is your sexual orientation?" or "How important to you is your racial identity?" It is much easier to be estranged. Or it is much easier to converse, at a safe electronic remove, with people in whose category you feel you belong.

A great many people now seem to have abandoned any willing membership in the great category of "all humans," perhaps because of the difficulty of its implied obligations. Instead, they have with-drawn into subcategories composed of people like themselves. This likeness becomes a kind of etiquette, which one does not violate by obtruding one's personal origin, vocation, opinion, or preference. You know you will not be welcome if you show up like Aeneas carry-ing your aged father on your shoulders. Likeness within a category is enforced by the existence of competing categories. Paradoxically, as people disclaim their individual personhood, it becomes harder to acknowledge the claims of their common humanity.

To those who identify themselves by political category, every per-son is a representative person. To liberals, all conservatives are the same, are committed to the same bad causes, and are describable by the same adjectives. To conservatives, liberals are similarly homo-geneous, and equally objectionable. Each political side readily supposes that everybody on the other side is perfectly in agree-ment, focused entirely on politics, and forever collaborating and conspiring for unconditional victory. This sort of contention lives and thrives upon oversimplification, which in turn leads to and depends upon exaggeration. Exaggeration is a violence of language, which, in politics, is full of the threat of violence of other kinds. Exaggeration—extremities of generalization, language overpowering knowledge—prepared us for the Civil War. My example, necessarily, is the political slogan, any political slogan. A slogan works, and is so intended, as a verbal weapon. It may exaggerate by offering a partial truth as the whole truth; it always enlarges personal feeling into the passion of a crowd.

Now it gives us the large rhetoric of public protests and confrontations. I have observed these events, and participated in them too, for long enough to know that they are sometimes necessary, as when legitimate claims and causes are ignored by those in power. But I know also that such events are about as far as possible from the public discourse or dialogue that might lead to solutions and thus to the domestic tranquility that most of us have always desired. Actually effective public dialogue, I think, is never far from the care and the tone of serious conversation among people of goodwill. What passes now for public dialogue is no such thing.

Serious conversation between persons of goodwill seems to me a model or ideal both social and political. As such it is a standard by which to measure other forms of human encounter. By that standard the public protest or demonstration reveals itself as incomplete. On those occasions there are a few leaders and speakers. The other participants serve merely to incarnate the slogans on the banners and signs and to give body and bulk to the words of the speakers. As individuals they are bodies merely, interchangeable, dispensable, and replaceable. They can become distinctly whole and useful only by going from the public event back to their homes, to serious conversation with friends and neighbors, and to the practice at home of the solutions they have recommended in public.

Prevailing conditions suggest that, on the contrary, most people of the political sides return home mostly as the dispersed fragments of a crowd. Thus they notify themselves and others of their merely statistical worth, and of their worthlessness as the persons they actually are in their unique origin and being.

I don't understand very clearly how this contagion of self-devaluation has come to be, or how it nurtures the self-overevaluation and ostentation of a few public persons. I am sure only of a pattern of mutually reinforcing cultural reductions and distortions to which it belongs:

1. Perhaps because of our acceptance of the reduction of work or life's work from vocation ("calling") to "job," many people now speak with conventional dislike of their working lives, apparently longing through their workdays for quitting time, the weekend, vacation, and retirement. They are thus not willingly living, much less enjoying, the most necessary and significant hours of their lives, but are wishing them away. This surely is a sort of death wish. How can workers think well of themselves if they do not think well of their work?

2. If we have submitted with such a grudging acceptance and self-effacement to the degradation of degrading work, it is no surprise that we accept with the same fatality the misanthropy of industrialism, which from the start has made a principle of substituting technologies for workers. Once accepted, though only *if* accepted, this is technological determinism. But it is now commonly understood that such determinism is a settled reality against which we have no choice. While I was writing this, I heard on the radio an expert witness who testified with perfect assurance: "Technology is taking

THE NEED TO BE WHOLE

them there whether they want to go or not." How can people think well of themselves if they know that their work now is, or soon may be, done allegedly better by a machine?

3. People are encouraged by advertisements, experts, and insinuation everywhere in our consumer culture to believe that what they have is inferior to what they might have, and what they are is inferior to what they might be. So they are lulled and tolled into an economy of replacement without limit, discarding meanwhile all that our cultural heritage has to tell us about our need to be reconciled to the limits imposed upon us by partiality and mortality, and our obligation to live well within those limits. When you have succeeded so far in having a better face, a better body, a better house, a better car, and a better spouse or "partner," then what you have is again inferior to what you might have, and so the cycle must begin again. People thus become ideal consumers. But how can they think well of themselves, whose lives are forever inferior and disposable?

4. Disposability is an "efficiency," which justifies throwing away whatever we can no longer use or no longer want. This is an officially approved principle and practice that has profaned land and sea and "outer space" with once-usable materials, existing once and for all, that we have transformed into "waste" and "trash." But we do not limit such wasting to materials. My friend and fellow writer Scott Sanders told me that he had visited public schools whose state of neglect and disrepair implied unmistakably to the students that they were disposable, that they already had been in effect thrown away. This is an economic and social principle hard to limit even to the presently poor and to disfavored minorities. I am pretty sure that, in the shadows of total efficiency and total war, we in our millions know that the military principles of technological determinism and disposability may be applied to any of us. How can people think well of themselves when they know that to the powerful, and

at foreseeable extremes of progress or national defense, their abilities and their lives will count as nothing?

5. If we read or listen with any alertness at all, we know that many of us, and not just scientific materialists, readily speak of organisms, including humans, as machines, and of minds as computers. This is the sovereign reduction and self-reduction of our reductionist age. In its full extent the reduction is from creatures (created by a Creator) to organisms to machines. A lot of us perhaps have understood that if humans are machines then our replacement by more efficient machines is merely reasonable, a matter of course. But far too few of us, I'm afraid, have understood that as soon as we believe ourselves to be machines we lose, or "free ourselves" from, the legal, moral, and cultural inheritance that comes of our long, unresting, presently failing effort to preserve the humanity of humans. We lose moreover the long regard and respect that our tradition gives to the humblest of individual humans, from Eumaios the swineherd, Ruth the daughter-in-law of Naomi, and Mary Magdalene to Corin the shepherd, Huckleberry Finn, and Lena Grove. To whom, and on what ground, would a machine appeal for justice or mercy? It is remarkable that, as machines, we become subject to the crudest biological determinism: "survival of the fittest." How can people think well of themselves if their lot is only to be predator or prey?

6. Those of us who have been to college have encountered, and too likely have learned to speak, the professional languages by which we partition ourselves within specialties and make ourselves unintelligible to outsiders. These languages enable professionals and experts to speak with the appearance of being unaffected by what they are saying, and to speak as if unaffected is good training for speaking, and being, without affection. In the schools and elsewhere the professional languages are likely to be influenced by a set of principles or "worldviews"—objectivity, optimism, pessimism,

inevitability—that are predetermined and predictable, enabling a "conversation" to be conducted, to no end or purpose, entirely in jargon and clichés. Worse than that, such language enables a sort of intellectual and moral sloth, freeing career-captured professors and professionals from the obligation to form an opinion, complete a judgment, or take a stand in any actual place. How can people think well of themselves when their lives have no extent of thought and responsibility outside their specialties or careers?

Because we live now in such self-diminishment, we seem to have agreed to conduct our public conversation about race and racism in terms highly generalized, unexamined, and trite: bare assertions and accusations, generalizations, stereotypes, labels, gestures, slogans, and symbols. This sort of language is useful only to those who see conversation or dialogue as combat, the aim of which is only to win. This is the combat in which people use prejudice (prejudgment or judgment-before-knowledge) to prove their superior virtue—even, ostensibly, to correct the bad conduct of an enemy—by giving an insult, the more wounding the better.

Here I want to accept the guidance of my late friend, William Hull, who said that the way to prevent disagreement from becoming destructive is to seek "clarity rather than victory." Clarity is what we owe, in honesty and goodwill, to one another. Victory can only divide us again into a party of winners and a party of losers, thus preparing us for further confrontation and combat. But if we hope to have clarity we will have to submit to complexity. Nothing so challenges our need for clarity as the history and the present problems of "race relations." Nothing so urgently asks us what we mean when we say we "know" or we "understand."

Statistics, judging from their vast accumulation in our time and the prominence we give them, may now be what we most confidently know. And we know unavoidably the generalizations and conclusions that can be derived from statistics.

We have also the knowledge of "cases" or "case studies." These come from reporters who go to homes or schools or churches or towns or counties, which are in some way representative, in order to tell us about the setting and to quote the people's answers to pertinent questions. Or these may be long-term studies, by anthropologists or sociologists, of an especially interesting group or community. Case studies, of whatever kind, can be useful, but they give us what I would call visitor's knowledge.

If we are enough interested in it to keep it in mind, we know something, more or less, of history. Some people no doubt will say that they have learned something of history from movies or TV or other electrical sources. Maybe so. My own learning of history, beyond conversation mainly with my elders, has come from books, and I prefer books to, for instance, movies. Reading allows one to think as one reads, to read as slowly and carefully as one must, to mark passages and write marginal notes, and it allows immediate rereading to make understanding as sure as possible. A movie requires everybody to think at the pace of the dialogue and action on the screen, and it allows no immediate second looks or second thoughts. Any discourse prepared for radio or television must be trimmed (or inflated) to fit a "time slot." For a newspaper or magazine, it must be limited to a prescribed space. A public speech, a play, or a movie must observe the limits of human attention. But in a book, discourse is free to continue as long as necessary to meet the needs of fullness and clarity.

If we learn history by reading, we must understand that no definitive or final history will ever be written. History, as we study and write and remember it, is not an autopsy that is performed once and for all upon a cadaver, which is then buried or burned. It is always possible that more facts, artifacts, relics, or documents of significance will come to light. We live and read in an ever-changing present that therefore changes our perspective on the past. Our understanding of the past necessarily changes as we see more and more of what it has led to. Most important, as the historian John Lukacs helps us to understand, historians are participating in history while they are writing it, as are readers of history while they read. In all these ways, history belongs to the living and is alive. As soon as we conceive of history as dead or as concerned with "the dead past," it ceases to be of any use to us.

The ways of knowing I have mentioned so far give us public knowledge. Public knowledge, especially as it is selected and gathered into "the news" and then into "public opinion," tends to solidify into abstraction and various forms of oversimplification. Phrases such as "the Negro" and all of its synonyms, like "the white man" and all of its synonyms, and like all the names of categories, are abstractions, apparently simple, easily spoken, but hopelessly complex and scattered in reference. Such names mean somebody or something different to everybody who speaks or hears them.

Recently I heard on the radio yet another expert witness who spoke of "the black experience," seemingly with not a doubt that every hearer of that phrase will understand it in about the same way. If that is so, which I doubt, such understanding is far oversimplified and of little use. I believe we can say with assurance that in some significant ways the black experience is different from the white experience, and from the history of the last four hundred years we could derive a list of those significant ways. But my own experience, as well as my knowledge of a good many people both black and white, insists to me that the black experience is, and has been, for each individual black person significantly different from that of any other black person. And our cultural and political traditions grant a significant precedence to the individual life and experience over the life and experience of a category. There is no general term or phrase that can refer us adequately to the multitude of our lives as we individually live them. But also, as a subscriber to Mr. Jefferson's wondrous sentence, I want to say, if we must deal in abstractions, that black experience and white experience overlap in human experience, and that this shared experience is greater, more significant, and more promising of good than all the differences.

CHAPTER II

—— ～ ——

Equality, Justice, Love

Among the necessary and the least dispensable words in our language are those by which we name our values. Here is a list (surely not complete) of such words: Truth, Justice, Mercy, Forgiveness, Peace, Equality, Trust, Hospitality, Generosity, Freedom, Love, Neighborliness, Home, Reverence, Beauty, Care, Courtesy, Goodness, Faith, Kindness, Health, Wholeness, Holiness. It is obvious, first of all, how unhappily these words and the thoughts they name must associate with the materialism, the several determinisms, the ideal of mechanical efficiency, and the rule of profit and war, which now intrude so powerfully into their company. And so we need more than ever the words on my list. We need them as abstractions commonly understood, as they appear often in the Bible, in the founding documents of the United States, and in various classics of literature. We need them, that is, as the names of familiar ideals by which to rectify our thoughts and our lives. But we need them also in the particularity of effort as we practice them, or as we try or fail to practice them. The great general principles are like an old tree's trunk and main branches that sway but do not break. People in the days and years of their lives are like the leaves that come and go and are moved by the slightest stirrings of the air.

29

Of the words on my list probably none are more prominent now in public usage than Equality and Justice. Like all the others, these can become too public, can reside for too long in public speech and public places without being brought home to the toil and the testing they will meet in our households, neighborhoods, and communities. I find in myself an impulse, which I am inclined to trust is not mine alone, first to affirm the "all men" (all humans) of the Declaration, and then, not to resist it exactly, but to counter it with what I know of particular men and women. Without a sustained movement of conversation back and forth between the public and the personal, the general and the particular, Equality and Justice decline toward nonsense—like the other words that belong, so to speak, to their family of meanings. Particulars are measured and oriented by generalizations, and generalizations are enlivened and tested by particulars. Among the other things it does, knowledge of particular persons sets a cleansing fire to prejudices and stereotypes, which grow like weeds among our ideals and principles, so that we may see through them to actual human faces.

The principle of equality or "equality before the law," as we have taken it from the Declaration of Independence, and elaborated it in the Constitution and in legislation, is a principle first and last. It is a legal and therefore a general safeguard against prejudice, which is always a generalization. To deny a legally established right to persons or groups because of their category is an offense against the law of the land, and the much older spirit of the law. For those of us kindly disposed toward democracy and our species, the principle of equality, thus far, presents no problem. We approve of it and we accept it.

But when we carry this principle home among our families and our neighbors, where ordinarily and fortunately we are beyond the law, we are immediately confronted with a multiplicity of inequalities—of intelligence, appearance, health, age, strength, education, wealth, talent, fate or fortune, and so on and on. We realize that to treat all persons as equal, ignoring their differences, is at best inconsiderate, at worst foolishness or cruelty. Because people individually are not equal to one another, we need discernment, patience, and good manners: ways of enacting respect or courtesy or kindness or compassion for those we perceive as better off or worse off than ourselves. Our neighbors are not effectively our equals unless we treat them as equally entitled to our regard in spite of the inevitable differences. In the places where we live and work, equality is better enforced by good manners and common decency than by the courts and the police. But if good manners were to be normally expected and practiced in our neighborhoods, we might more reasonably hope to see them emulated in law enforcement.

The principle of equality becomes seriously troublesome, I think, when it obscures really significant differences. If a prejudice causes us to see all the members of a disfavored category simply as "equal," then we abandon our obligation to use good sense and good judgment. We then may fail to identify the exceptionally gifted and the exceptionally virtuous, the exceptionally endangered and the exceptionally dangerous.

This blunted egalitarianism, I think, is as troubling in the politics of sex as in the politics of race. Women are as human as men (if I dared, I would say more so), and they ought not to be denied any civil right. They ought to receive equal pay for equal work. But to say that women and men are equally human is not to say that they are the same, or that they are in all ways "like" each other. I am dealing here with the importance of differences, and so I will assume the risk of generalization to speak of the differences between the sexes that seem to me merely obvious: (1)Women are physically and sexually different from men. (2) Their role in procreation is immeasurably more burdening, painful, and dangerous than that of men. (3) They are sexually attractive to most men—which is another danger to them because (4) most women are physically smaller than most men.

In our self-consciously modernizing and improving way, the combination of the movement for women's rights with "sexual liberation" has encouraged both women and men to regard these inequalities as insignificant or as virtually nonexistent. We are encouraged or urged to think that these differences are excuses for, if they are not parts of, a "patriarchal" oppression of women. As a consequence, the forms of a special respect and regard and helpfulness, that women often expected of men and that men often gave, have fallen into disuse, even as the need for them has fairly demonstrably increased.

Wives and husbands are no longer so economically attached, by their work and care, to households as they once were. As men and women go about at large in the world, women are probably as sexually available and sexually exploitable as they once were only in conquered cities. Maybe most women are as promiscuous by nature and as much in want of "recreational sex" as most men; I don't know, and I am content to bypass the question. But I am entirely sure that many men have welcomed the supposition that women, being equal to men, no longer required of them any special consideration, respect, or deference—that they were easily reducible, in short, to the role of "sex objects."

The trouble and the harm occur in situations, very common now, in which the sexes are, in the most insistently practical sense of the term, not equal. A woman at her job, confronting her would-be seducer who is her boss, with her livelihood at stake, is not his

equal. Nor is a 120- pound girl the equal of a 200-pound boy in the
twilight or darkness of a fraternity party.

In the absence apparently of all cultural restraints, women who
have been assaulted or raped have no recourse but the courts of law
or, by way of scandal, the news. Having been exploited by men, they
then must exploit themselves by making their private humiliation
public. A woman too poor to pay a lawyer, and so unfortunate as
to have been abused by nobody famous, has no recourse at all. In
the news and commentary I have read on sexual abuses by men and
the Me Too movement, I have seen no suggestion that the abusive
men ought to have been taught decent manners and a proper sense
of responsibility when they were boys.

I will be reminded, I am sure, that a good upbringing has often
enough been wasted on some men, as of course on some women.
Or, worse, I will be told that we humans are after all only animals
biologically determined, that sex is therefore a contest or a form of
combat in which the power of men can be limited only by a countervailing power of women.

To the first proposition we may reply with the truth that some
men do not rape or abuse women, and that, if they do not, they are
likely to have been told by their elders that they should not. The
second proposition puts at stake every one of our humane aspirations toward a civilized life. To replace all reliance on good manners, sexual propriety or responsibility, and other cultural means
with reliance on the severely limited means of public retaliation is
to give up the integrity of personal and community life—as well,
of course, as the possibility of prevention. Children are not acci-
dental sexual by-products to be put up with, or commodities to be
acquired and neglected. They come with a responsibility that their
parents must meet face-to-face: They must be brought up to be, in
their turn, responsible.

I don't believe I will offend our forebears, who believed that we are given an "inner light" to guide us in this world, if I say that one's conscience is also to a considerable extent an artifact of culture, and I am not talking about "high culture." I can say, for example, that at various times my own conscience has spoken to me in the voices of certain downright women, from whose counsel and example I learned to consider the differences between women and men, and to believe that because of those differences women deserve, and are right when they require, a responsibility that is different from the responsibility of a man to other men.

It seems to me that this issue of sexual difference is useful, perhaps necessary, to a discussion of racial difference. Sexual difference is older in the ages of the world than racial difference. It is the categorical difference we know most intimately, and it raises most urgently the question of our ability to imagine and care for one another across such differences, as I think we must do. The sexual difference also raises pointedly the issue of the past and presence of equality among white people, and we are going to have to deal with that. The law, within its limits, can make people equal, but it cannot make them alike, and it cannot make them friends. Equality is not a relationship. Strangers and enemies can be equal. We can be both equal and alone.

Right relations between two races or two neighbors can be legally defined and to an extent enforced, but only to an extent. In the history of "the race problem" we come again and again to the strict and narrow limits upon the effectiveness of law alone. The general principle can have no substantial or lasting result if it is not absorbed into the ordinary practice of neighborhood among neighbors.

~

Justice too, I think, must go among us as good manners or fairness or common decency. But when we call it by its high and demanding public name, we had better know clearly and say plainly what we mean by it. It is a word too easy to appropriate for bad purposes. How many wars have not been known by at least one side as "just" even as both sides have invented new kinds and technologies of injustice?

Perhaps a worse danger is that the great name can be used casually or thoughtlessly to mean more or less "righteousness" or "doing good." Some time ago I made a list of eleven kinds of justice, used to name movements or the purposes of movements. Among them were Racial Justice, Social Justice, Climate Justice, Ecological Justice, and Economic Justice. Such terms obviously raise questions, for they are inexact. More troubling, their vagueness may permit the people in those movements to assume that they know already what justice is in any given instance, and that justice might readily be achieved if only the skeptics and resisters would get out of the way.

But public justice is not something that simply is done. It requires time and patience. It requires a hard, strictly disciplined effort of thought. The pursuit of justice becomes dangerous when it is dissociated from the pursuit of truth. Our public system of justice insists upon this. Like any human artifact, our system of justice can be perverted, can fail after all to do justice, but I feel always instructed by its instituted care to discover the truth and to make justice dependent upon the truth. We are comforted, or we ought to be, that under the rule of law and its honest use nobody can be indicted, judged, or punished without evidence of guilt, or without a trial that tests the validity of the evidence, or the possibility that the evidence can be retested "on appeal."

Public justice, the justice rendered by law and courts, is necessarily—justly!—general. Its work is to protect the rights of citizens, of *all* citizens. It must not make exceptions. It is opposed to prejudice. Prejudice is opposed to justice, and defies it, by shortcutting or overruling justice's prescribed dependence on truth and the pursuit of truth.

Apart from this traditional respect for truth, the willingness to pursue it rigorously, and the resolve to stand faithfully by it, we humans are too likely to attempt to do justice by opposing one prejudice with another.

The news has obliged us to imagine a public demonstration—in fact a public allegory—in which the self-denominated side of love has confronted the side of hate, believing that a victory of love over hate will secure equality and justice to people who have been oppressed because of their race. I recommend second thoughts about the possibility of a "side" of love, but current political rhetoric tends toward such an absolute division. The side of hate is composed of avowed racists; avowed racists have espoused an absolute, unexcepting prejudice against a kind of people; and so they may be called "the side of hate" rightly enough. That haters hate is morally as straightforward and uncomplicated as it can be. But they themselves are perceived by the side of love as a kind of people. And the side of love, as perceived by the side of hate, is a kind of people also, another kind. And so we have a confrontation of two opposite kinds of people, lovers and haters, each side as absolute in its identity as it can make itself, and they do not know each other. They cannot imagine each other. For the haters, this situation is wonderfully simple and entirely acceptable. They don't need even a notion of consequence. They are there to oppose. That is all. The lovers, on the contrary, have everything at stake and the situation is clouded by moral danger.

Because the confrontation is between two categories of people who do not know each other, it will be easy for the side of love first to understand love merely as opposite and opposed to hate, and then to generalize this opposition as an allegorical battle of Love versus Hate, exchanging slogan for slogan, gesture for gesture, shout for shout. Then if nature and the rule of battle go unchecked, the side of love begins to hate the side of hate. And then the lovers are defeated, for they have defeated themselves. They have fallen into the sort of trap that Mr. Jefferson set for, among others, himself. If you say, "All are created equal," then adding "except for some," the exception overturns the rule, and a great deal else along with it. Just so, love that hates has cancelled itself. It cannot survive its hatred of hate any more than one can survive minus one. It is no more. Chaos and old night have come again.

With us, love has been reduced mostly to a popular word, easy to use to intensify a frivolous appreciation. "Oh, I *love* it!" we say when told of something really cute. Or it can be used as a handy weapon against the haters of whom we disapprove. Too bad. But love comes into our civilization—the Gospels being the source best known to me—as a way of being in the world. It is a force, extraordinarily demanding and humbling, dangerous too, for those who attempt to take it seriously.

As a force and a way of being, love is never satisfied with partiality. It is compelled, by its own nature and logic, to be always trying to make itself whole. This is why the Sermon on the Mount tells us to love our enemies. That is an unconditional statement. It does not tell us to fight our enemies in order to improve them or convert them by our love.

In practice, this commandment seems to cancel or delete "enemy" as a category of thought. What I most valued, at least what moved me most, in reading the statements of the Southern Christian Leadership Conference in the mid-1960s was the realization that Martin Luther King Jr. was not thinking of white people as "the enemy," even though he and his people had to confront the enmity of many white people. It was clear to me that he saw the freedom he sought for black people as a freedom needed also by white people, and I agreed. No freedom could belong securely to any part of the people that did not securely belong to all of them. Dr. King's movement in this way escaped the specialization that usually afflicts movements. He said, "Justice is love correcting that which revolts against love."

This is a version of love uncommonly serious, deliberately a religious, a Christian, version, readily allied to Jefferson's inspired glimpse of human rights as a divine endowment, as opposed to a gift from the state. This love is not much subject to control or limitation by humans. It was love's impulse, its self-moving, toward wholeness that moved King from concern for black people to concern for poor people to concern at last for all people, their land and culture. So I have understood him.

And here I am remembering also Will Campbell, the Improved Southern Baptist preacher, a white man, who at first helped the black people in their civil rights movement, believing that they were "the least of [Christ's] brethren." But then, realizing that they might not after all be "the least," or if the least not the only ones, Brother Campbell felt that his own work was incomplete. He then troubled to get to know members of the Ku Klux Klan, whom he had considered his enemies. He offered them, instead of correction and retribution, kindness and help, and so he admitted them also into his consciousness and care. He was an embarrassment and a troublemaker, no doubt an actual follower of Jesus.

My theme now requires me to take thought of my long advocacy, which began in love and fear for my own home country and community. By the time I was thirty, I could see that my native place and the life of it, along with my affection for it, was not in favor with the urban-industrial system that had clouded over it after World War II. Such a place—rural, small, "backward," and "underdeveloped"—was, in fact, invisible, virtually nonexistent, to that system, and thus mortally endangered by it. I could see that, as it was, its days were numbered. But I could see also that, as it was, its human community was taking respectable care of itself and of the local countryside that supported it. It was clear to me that this good keeping, if it could survive and be cherished, held the possibility of better keeping. There was nothing in the dominant economy and state of mind, however, that would support such a possibility—let alone the possibility that anything at all in such a place, or in fact in any place, might be cherished.

My concern might reasonably have made me an advocate for "soil conservation." But I was a native. My affection for my place was already established in my heart and unspecialized. It included the people and other creatures along with the soil, and it has become ever clearer to me that you cannot conserve the land unless you can conserve the people who depend on the land, who care for it, and who know how to care for it—the people on whom the land depends.

Without quite knowing what I was doing at that time, I had entered the way of love and taken up its work. It could not be simplified or shortcut, but became ever more inclusive, complex, and difficult. Any violence that intrudes between the land and the people extends its damage both ways. But I could not restrict my understanding of the problem of violence to my own place and people. Violence to one place cannot be dissociated from violence to any place. Violence to some people cannot be dissociated from violence to other people. This is the sort of difficulty that imposes an irremediable amateurism. I finally understood this and approved of it. It meant that my permanent motive would be love; it certainly did not mean that I was a hobbyist. But my commitment was pushing me way beyond my schooling. I would have to deal with issues of science, of art, of religion, of economy, of ecology, and so on, with no foreseeable limit. There can be no set bounds to the work of love when it faces boundless violence. I am not speaking here of the love that thrives only by feeding upon a commensurate hatred, but rather of the love, perhaps more fearful, that draws no boundary around itself.

How might we imagine imposing by mere law the principles of equality and justice and love upon a society dominated in its economic life by the violent principles of individualism, competition, and greed? How might we imagine the loyalty or patriotism that could protect the life of the land and the people of any place under the economic rule of "maximum force relentlessly applied"? What must we do for the success of the personal generosity, the common decency, the good manners that are the ultimate safeguards of equality and justice, now that we apparently have settled into permanent war as the basis of our economy? Our economy, let us not forget, defines "equality" as the "right" of everybody to be as wasteful, violent, destructive, consumptive, lazy, and luxurious as everybody else.

By now a major difficulty of writing this book has pretty fully declared itself. The big problem is that the subject of race prejudice, contrary to the assumptions of political correctness and present racial politics, cannot honestly be simplified or specialized or treated as a single subject. Race prejudice is not fundamentally different from prejudices of other kinds. Prejudice in favor of any category of persons is as false as prejudice against that category. Slavery is lack of choice over one's life and work, and the enslavement of black people before the Civil War is in that way like the kinds of slavery that preceded it and the kinds that have followed. Black Americans and white Americans are different but also alike; they have experienced differently the same history; the individual people in both categories are both different and alike. To make one's language able to deal competently with these likenesses and differences cannot and should not be easy. In order to recognize the unique particularity of every individual person and life, everybody's story, one must relinquish dependence on generalizations and stereotypes. Abuse of people is never far separate from abuse of land and the natural world; to poison rivers and winds, as we perfectly know, is to poison people. Stories come from stories and lead to stories. Every story (like every thing) has a context, and every context has a context. There is no honest escape from this complexity, and the whole truth of such complexity cannot honestly be comprehended and explained, not by one person, not by several universities.

For me, the greatest, most comprehensive difficulty, the one I endlessly return to, is that I do not think of the chattel slavery of the antebellum South as a problem that is isolatable or unique. The more I have read and thought about our history, and the more I have observed of the works and effects of our present economy, the more plainly I have seen that old-time version of slavery as one of a continuum of violent exploitations, including other forms of slavery, that has been with us since the European discovery of America. It is so far our history's dominant theme. A failing too little remembered but nonetheless significant is that the southern planters, using slave labor, cropped their land to exhaustion. The availability of apparently endless tracts of "new" land to the west made the eastward lands dispensable. And so we come to a key word in the story of American development or progress: Anything superabundant or "inexhaustible" can be treated as *dispensable*. One of the cruelest ironies of postbellum history is that emancipation, in freeing the slaves of white proprietorship, freed them also from their market value and made them individually worthless in the "free" economy—like the poor whites whose "free labor" was already abundantly available, and who thus were individually dispensable.

So far, there has been no limit to this equation between apparent abundance and dispensability. The immigrants who work in Tyson's meat factories, where they are ruthlessly exposed to the coronavirus (among other dangers) are extremely poor, having only their bodily labor to depend on; they also are numerous and therefore are considered dispensable. We must remember also the homegrown great corporations that depend upon, and defend, forced labor in China. But this freedom to enslave, use, and use up is not limited to corporations. Because the atmosphere is so far too abounding to be captured and sold, it also is worthless, a kind of slave, useful for disposing of wastes. All of us now pollute it freely, at no cost except to the health of every living thing.

On the contrary: It seems natural to me to think that there is a law of love operating in this world. If you see the world's goodness and beauty, and if you love your own place in it (no deed required), then your love itself will be one of your life's great rewards. That is the law that rules the "sticker," the settler, the actual patriot. The opposite law is that of greed, which sees the goodness and beauty of the world as wealth and power. It says: Take what you want. No individual person is purely a settler or an exploiter, but perhaps every person must submit to the rule of one law or the other. The rule of greed, however, can be made pure by incorporating it as a "business," in which every employee obeys, and can obey, only the one rule.

A further difficulty of this book, therefore, is its attempt to assert or reassert the claim of love upon the world and upon ourselves.

CHAPTER III

∾

Degrees of Prejudice

1. My Old Kentucky Home

Though I have maintained a fairly continuous interest in history from my freshman year in college, I am not a historian. What I say about history in these chapters is not the product of systematic research. I am an amateur. My citations come from books I have at hand. I have also relied on documents mainly of local history that I have saved, my memories from my reading and conversations, and my own experience. I have in mind a scale reaching from the formal historical knowledge stored in books to the informal knowledge of the past that is gathered from conversation and personal experience. I assume that all of these kinds of history are necessary both to one another and to anybody's understanding of life in this world.

The great events of history, with which the historians mainly have been concerned, may serve us in a way like the names of human values that I listed at the beginning of Chapter II. They give us a sort of general orientation to our identity as humans, though the discrepancy between our professed values and the great events of history orients us as well and too often to our record of disappointment, sorrow, and shame.

I can identify myself as a modern American, by saying that I was

born in 1934 in the midst of the Depression, acquired the beginnings of historical consciousness during the years of World War II,
believed childishly that the peace of the five-year "postwar period"
would last, and since 1950 have lived through the Korean War, the
Vietnam War, and on into our mingled and apparently unendable
wars in the Middle East. It is certain that, like the Civil War, the
wars of my time have been profitable for some people, and each has
contributed to technological progress. And so it may be, as Ezra
Pound said of World War I, that they have killed the wrong people.
Beyond the diversity of harms we can call "war damage," I think
it is more than likely that this sequence of wars, along with our
addiction to "national defense," the industry, politics, and business
of war, has kept us distracted from the increasingly urgent need to
learn to live in our country without destroying it. These wars at least
have been the most wasteful and depressing of human artifacts, and
they have imposed upon us all an unremitting effort to maintain in
our hearts, if we can, the terms of kindness and sanity. This, I think,
is the condition and the work that we modern Americans share.

In addition to being a modern American, because I was born and
have mainly lived south of the Ohio River, I am inescapably identified (by other people) as a southerner. I am qualified for that
geographically, and also by my descent from slave owners. The
insufficiency of that designation is that in addition to being a modern American southerner, I am a Kentuckian. No member of my
family whom I have known has ever identified us as "southern," and
I am sure that none of us ever aspired to be a Yankee.

Kentucky, anyhow in some of its parts, probably has much in
common with much of the deeper South, for this state was a sort of

bottleneck or funnel through which migrants passed on their way to the frontiers of the South and Southwest. According to the Kentucky historian Thomas D. Clark—who, I am proud to say, was my teacher and friend—"You can observe the same styles and tastes, aesthetics and values, from Kentucky all the way to west Texas, in a sort of fan-like effect."

But Kentucky was a slave state that did not secede, and that makes it unlike either the South or the North. The Civil War in Kentucky, Shelby Foote says, "was literally a brothers' war" in which "at least two-fifths of her white fighting men wore gray." Moreover, as a "border state," Kentucky had fewer slaves and slave owners than the states farther south. In *A New History of Kentucky*, Lowell H. Harrison and James C. Klotter say:

> The great majority of Kentuckians never owned a slave.... The 1850 census counted 139,920 white families; 28 percent of them owned one or more slaves. Only five of the owners held more than one hundred slaves; 24 percent of the slave-holding families held just one slave. The average slave holder in the state owned 5.4 slaves; only Missouri had a lower figure.

Topographically, much of Kentucky was not suited to the plantation agriculture of the South in which slaves were worked in large gangs. Page Smith says that in the border states slaves "were commonly engaged in small-scale farming, in domestic work, and in trades, [and so] the rate of literacy, the knowledge of the white world, and the capacity to function in it were far higher [than in the Deep South]."

As a result of these differences, enslaved people in Kentucky were likely to be involved closely and familiarly in the domestic life and economy of the families who owned them. In the ordinary workaday economies of farms and households, it was possible and even likely that owners and slaves might work together, thus know one another well, and thus be bound to one another by the non-legal bonds of ordinary human life: interdependence, respect, and affection.

In such circumstances slavery might be understood, and experienced by the white and black people involved, as less a merely legal and economic means of exploiting a captive labor force, and more an everyday human relationship. It might have been possible more or less to forget that this relationship was subject to the laws governing proprietorship and property, and further subject to the economic adversity that has almost customarily afflicted farmers.

When this relationship, affectionate as it might have been, suffered economic misfortune, the result could be tragedy and heartbreak. From the mere letter of the law there could be no reprieve or appeal. To pay a debt or prevent a foreclosure, the sale of slaves could become mandatory. This gives us in general outline the plot of "My Old Kentucky Home, Good Night!" by Stephen Foster. This song tells a tale altogether possible in 1853 when Foster wrote it. Here is the original text:

> The sun shines bright in the old Kentucky home,
> 'Tis summer, the darkies are gay,
> The corn top's ripe and the meadow's in the bloom
> While the birds make music all the day.
> The young folks roll on the little cabin floor,
> All merry, all happy and bright:
> By'n by Hard Times comes a knocking at the door,
> Then my old Kentucky Home, good night!

❦

Weep no more, my lady, oh! weep no more to-day!
We will sing one song
For the old Kentucky Home,
For the old Kentucky Home, far away.

❦

They hunt no more for the possum and the coon
On the meadow, the hill and the shore,
They sing no more by the glimmer of the moon,
On the bench by the old cabin door.
The day goes by like a shadow o'er the heart,
With sorrow where all was delight:
The time has come when the darkies have to part,
Then my old Kentucky Home, good-night!
Chorus
The head must bow and the back will have to bend,
Wherever the darkey may go:
A few more days, and the trouble all will end
In the field where the sugar-canes grow.
A few more days for to tote the weary load,
No matter 'twill never be light,
A few more days till we totter on the road,
Then my old Kentucky Home, good-night!
Chorus

These verses, as I understand them and, I think, as understood by their author, issue from the soul of a slave long ago at home in Kentucky, who has been "sold down the river" and put to work on a sugarcane plantation perhaps in Louisiana.

In the first stanza he is remembering the time before his trouble began. Is he sentimentalizing that time or misrepresenting it? I would say that his memory is selective, as human memory almost necessarily is. But it is false only if we can prove that there could have been no such day as he remembers. No human has ever been without reasons to be unhappy, and so all who have been happy have been unreasonably happy. Just about anybody who has had a home, and has been long away, will remember good days at home. This remembering would be especially poignant for one forced into exile.

In the second stanza he recalls the sorrow the slaves felt after they knew that they would have to leave. Their grief has already overcome their customary pleasures, and their grief naturally finds its terms in those lost pleasures. Had they hunted "for the possum and the coon"? Of course they had, for the diets of slaves in many places had been supplemented by wild foods procured by themselves. Had they sung in the evenings? Of course.

In the final stanza the slave mourns his present lot. In the place he was sold off to, he has been reduced from the human relationships he experienced at his home in Kentucky to the true hardship of a man valued *only* for his work. He has now labored for nearly all the rest of his life in humiliation and under compulsion, a trouble to be ended only by death.

This song, then, is a cruel parable, speaking urgently of the difference between being known and being unknown. A Negro slave before emancipation, as we need always to remember, was a person with the sum of qualities that we call "personality," but who bore also a market price, like a horse or a mule or a bushel of corn. This money-worth as a measure of an enslaved person was a cloud or a veil through which, with association and familiarity, an actual individual person would appear.

On a small Kentucky farm, a slave, even one newly bought, would emerge from the abstraction of market value to become a known person, known moreover as a member of the farm's community of humans and other creatures, belonging to it legally as a property, but now also as somebody personally known, and probably also as somebody who, if absent, would be missed. I doubt that any power of custom or law could have prevented this from happening. But when he is reclaimed by the law and the market, sold, and shipped south to take part only as one more in a large crew of field hands on a large plantation, he is again reduced to his market value, and is known then only to himself as a man once personally known and valued, now missed and mourned, in his old home.

Having so far described the emotional range of Foster's song, we can see that its sorrow comes not only from the slave's forced displacement from his home, but also from an extreme difference in the scale at which life was lived and work was done. Whether or not it was Foster's intention to do so, his song raises most touchingly and pointedly the question of economic limits, a question rarely considered in the course of our history, and one scrupulously ignored by the industrialists and their supporters. By explicitly posing the agrarian small farm against the proto-industrial gang-worked sugarcane plantation, the song clearly urges the question: What scale of living and working permits us to know and value one another as the individual and unique persons we know ourselves to be? Or: What are the limits beyond which we disappear as ourselves into our market value as "labor"? And those questions expand reasonably and naturally to this: At what scale of work are we able to attend to and properly care for everything that is involved? And so a problem manifested early in antebellum slavery in the South has led us, not surprisingly, to a problem now afflicting our whole society. To show what I now have in mind, I will use an example that I have taken some care to understand.

An Amish family long dear to me bases the commercial part of its economy mainly on a dairy herd of forty-five Jersey cows, for which the family's small farm produces the necessary feed. From this modest enterprise the family achieves a "quality of life" that is admirable. They recently built themselves a new house. At the time of my last visit the farmwife and her two daughters, then seven and ten years old, were busy at the evening milking. It was a happy scene. The mother and daughters cooperated perfectly, each doing her share according to her strength. They kept steadily at work without haste or fuss. Each of the cows was known by her looks, character, and name. The family's living was being made within a pattern of familiar relationships. The people and the cows knew, understood, and respected one another, which was why the barn stayed so noticeably quiet. The physical work, to which our society has cultivated an aversion, was done with skill, with care, without stress, without lasting too long or becoming in any way a hardship, and allowing for conversation with visiting friends. This twice-a-day chore was taking place where both the people and the animals were at home, and at a scale permitting a careful line to be drawn everywhere between enough and too much. The work was limited by the size of the farm, which was limited by the practice of neighborly love that prevails among the Old Order Amish. Because of the limits of scale, nothing involved being too big or too expensive, the farm retains always a certain resilience and flexibility. If dairying should at some point cease to pay, the family would still have its farm, its farm buildings that could be converted to other purposes, and its staff of capable family members. It would still have its subsistence; using its own land and knowledge, it would continue to provide itself with food and fuel. And it would still have its neighborhood, its church, of families farming on the same scale, submitting to the same limits, committed to care and support for one another. This farm, so complexly dependent on limits, sells its milk to Organic Valley, which incorporates the principle of limited production, borrowed from the old federal tobacco program.

Now consider that this family dairy lives within a farm economy within a national economy that is, by principle, unlimited. This is a so-called growth economy in which, supposedly in order to prosper, every enterprise must grow bigger. By the law and logic of growth, a forty-five-cow dairy expects and is expected to grow to a hundred and then to five hundred and then to a thousand cows. This is affirmed and approved by everybody, except for those of us who still ask questions. And so we ask: Who can know a thousand cows by looks, character, and name, and thus value and watch over and care for them accordingly? The question is absurd. Probably somewhere between fifty and a hundred cows, we began to leave behind the possibility of familiar relationships among the people and their animals. And somewhere between a hundred and a thousand cows, animals and people alike will begin to be accounted less as creatures and more as identical, expendable, and replaceable *things*. So large an enterprise will have grown well beyond the biological and economic integrity of the small Amish farm, where a homegrown dairy herd lives upon homegrown feed in the care of homegrown workers. It has become instead a specialized industrial system, dependent upon undervalued, probably underpaid, "labor" and "purchased inputs." It has also lost the resilience and diversity of the small dairy. It has grown too big to adapt readily to new circumstances or to be readily converted to another use. Like the one- or two-crop cash-grain "operations" of a thousand or several thousand acres, it has grown too big to change—which is to say too big to be changed except by failure and bankruptcy. Meanwhile, a thousand-cow dairy will have displaced more than twenty family dairies like that of my friends, which would have been more sustainable, more democratic, in every sense more healthful and whole.

By now a 10,000-cow dairy is not unusual, each equivalent to two hundred family dairies of fifty cows. But I have also read about a 30,000-cow dairy, which appropriates the livelihoods of 600 fifty-cow family dairies. Our "food system" is now many a mile farther from home than Louisiana was from Kentucky when Stephen Foster wrote his song.

"My Old Kentucky Home" has been Kentucky's state song since 1928. Now when it is sung, most notably just before the running of the Kentucky Derby, it has been shortened by two stanzas. Most Kentuckians, I think, now know only the first. And in the first "the darkies" have become "the people." Thus reduced and revised by perfunctory political correction, our state song has become a piece of deliberate or unconscious nonsense. Who is it who is speaking or singing these words? Who are "the people"? What hard times have come? All that was needed was a word of two syllables to replace "darkies." If the song were made to state that "the horses are gay," it would be sung by the Derby crowd with the same witless nostalgia as before, supposing that some lady is weeping against advice over something pretty sad.

I take this song, as written, to be as fine, as fully imagined, and as moving as it needs to be. Foster's lyrics lay down his indictment as a series of telling details, one after another, with remarkable economy and completeness of sense, with no hint, as there is no need, of authorial comment. It is the imaginative realization of a white man, too rare and greatly needed, of the mortal finality of legal slavery, from which there could be no appeal, and of the burden in it of immitigable sorrow. The song makes a perfect indictment of slavery by showing that it cannot be justified or redeemed by the kindness with which some slave owners treated their slaves. Slavery was wrong, beyond any amelioration of kindness, because of the wrongs, sometimes extreme, that were potential in it. The same is true of the laws and customs of the race prejudice that justified slavery and survived it. However petty or ignorable this prejudice may sometimes appear to be, extreme wrong is potential in it. Children are forbidden to play with matches because there is nothing playful about a burning house.

We may say that, by the measures of the Christian Gospel and of the original principles of our government, it is wrong for some humans to be made the properties of other humans, and we may look back with revulsion at the sufferings of persons whose humanity has been simply cancelled by their status as legal properties. But I have only begun to deal with the evils of slavery. Equally obvious is the potential in the absolute power deducible from legal ownership to transform some owners into monsters of cruelty. Less obvious or less noticed was the degradation of the character of slave owners by the sins of pride and sloth, which finally has produced, virtually in all of us, a contempt for physical work and for the economic landscapes (our country itself) upon which such work was done. (I will deal with this at length in Chapter VIII.)

And so our state song, as written, can lead us into a critical examination of our history that may be of some use. But "My Old Kentucky Home," as it is presently sung, is an instance of my state's by now characteristic wish to substitute public relations for history, which is made easier by Kentuckians' characteristic ignorance of their history. If we are embarrassed by our past, which in fact is sufficiently embarrassing, we can forget it or ignore it, if we can just get rid of the visible or public reminders of it. Once the reminders are silenced or swept away, they can be replaced by an unembarrassed show of righteousness and modernity, as if we of the twenty-first century have been made vastly superior to our forebears merely by the omnipotence of progress and the passage of time. We are in significant ways worse than our forebears, and as my brother once said to me, "You can't clear your conscience by destroying the evidence."

It is a big problem for us that we have so nearly succeeded in obscuring the real complexities, ambiguities, and enigmas of our history by way of silence, ignorance, and the clichés of progress and self-righteousness. By such means history is reduced to an allegorical battle of Good against Evil, in which "we" of course are now, and always would have been, on the side of Good. If "we" had been born white south of the Ohio during slavery, "we" would have owned no slaves. If "we" quit singing about "darkies" and get the Confederate monuments out of sight, then slavery and the Civil War can be put to sleep like a couple of troublesome old dogs. We can be similarly quiet about the state's domination after the Civil War by the railroads and then by the coal industry and now by the agribusiness corporations, about its failure to develop value-adding industries for any of the products of its land economies, about its poverty, its poor schools, its ongoing export of its young people. Tourism, which we make much of, must depend on the haste and the ignorance of tourists, for we cannot hide the cataclysmic wastes left by the coal companies, the eroded croplands, the tumbledown farmsteads, and the decayed country towns. God help the tourist trade if the tourists ever leave the interstates and the parks and actually see what they are looking at.

My point is that Kentucky, and not Kentucky alone, has a steadily continuing history of ecological and social damage that cannot be identified or measured, let alone corrected, by the lights of political correctness.

One of the worst flaws of the politically corrected version of history may be the assumption that the harms and hurts of racism have damaged only the black people and have only benefited the white people. "My Old Kentucky Home," if we hear what it says, warns us differently, though I think it only hints at the real extent of the damage of racism to white people, and its cost to us. I have argued, and I am arguing again, that our history of racism afflicts us all, however unequally the burdens may have been distributed. Slavery itself was a trap into which white people could fall with the best intentions and only a little forgetfulness. This, from *A New History of Kentucky*, tells the result of "a little folding of the hands to sleep":

> In the mid-1850s a respected white man died in Lexington, and an estate sale was held to satisfy his creditors. He had had two daughters born to a quadroon slave. He had given them every care and sent them to Oberlin College in Ohio for an education. They had remained in Ohio, where they were accepted as white without question. When they returned to Kentucky for their father's funeral, they were seized and sold at auction as part of his property. He had neglected to free them.

Here was the division and the affliction incarnated as one flesh. Who can believe that the suffering of this could be confined, even in Lexington, to the two "slaves"?

❧

The only documentary evidence of my family's ownership of slaves, so far as I know, is a photocopy my father made of the will of his great-grandfather, John J. Berry Sr. The will, signed and recorded on May 5, 1857, makes two mentions of slaves:

> Item 4 "I will that My Negro Woman Mahala go to either of my Children She May Select to live [with] and that the other three Children pay to the one She May live with each fifty Dollars for her Support when ever She Needs it"

> Item 5 "I will that My Negroes be divided amongst My three Children Mary Nuttall, Elvessa Johnston and William Sanford Berry and that John J. Berry Jr. Shall not have any of them So long as his present wife lives."

Item 4, bequeathing to a slave woman whichever of his children she may choose to live with, seems remarkable to me, though I have no idea how often such provisions were made. In our gutter-minded time, some will suspect that Mahala was the testator's mistress. I don't know how smart my ancestor was, but surely he would have had better sense than to will her pick of his children to his mistress. More probably, Mahala was an elderly woman to whom he felt indebted for her faithful service.

Item 5, maybe more remarkably, stipulates that his namesake son was to have none of his slaves "so long as his present wife lives." My father supposed that the old man feared that if he left slaves to that son "his present wife" would be mean to them. That seems a reasonable supposition so far as it might explain the motive. My memories of family talk, however, offer no reason to suppose that John J. Sr. was correct in his estimate of his daughter-in-law. She was Lucinda Bowen Berry, my great-grandmother, a woman, as I do know, of strong character, who clearly had not endeared herself to her father-in-law.

On the evidence of the will, John J. Berry Sr. seems previously to have provided farms to his children, and so he must have owned several hundred acres of land and a fair number of slaves. From what I know of the family of John J. Berry Jr. I feel certain that none of the four children became wealthy by inheritance. John J. Jr. never became wealthy by that or any other means.

The will gives evidence of particular care for the welfare of the slaves, which I take to be evidence that their owner knew and related to them personally. So much may reasonably be supposed. It is also reasonably supposable that the bequest to Mahala and the exclusion of John J. Jr.'s "present wife" made something of a stir among the heirs. But the will is more mysterious than revealing. The paramount supposition must be that my great-great-grandfather's death in November 1857 and the provisions of his will were comparatively small interruptions in the life of this neighborhood that would have remained mostly ordinary until the outbreak of war.

It seems likely to me that the greatest concealer of the life of the past is the ordinariness of it. Life is always trying to make itself livable by making itself ordinary, just as work gets itself done by belonging ordinarily to the course of every day. And so what was recorded of slavery would have tended to be extraordinary: examples of unusual cruelty or unusual kindness. Whatever there may have been of kindness in slavery does not excuse it, and whatever was most cruel does not typify it. What is terrible about it is that its worst was inherent in it. Since the purpose of slavery, as of the use of hired help, was to get work done, I assume that the workdays would have needed to become both customary and ordinary. Extraordinary acts of cruelty would have slowed things down and wasted time. One of the elder John J. Berry's grandsons was my grandfather, who died in about the middle of my twelfth year. I remember him and the ways of his farm fairly well. His farming was not much different in its technology and kinds of work from that of his grandfather, and in all of his working life he depended often on the help of black hired hands. From my own memories and much hearsay, I believe that the work was ruled always by the seasons, custom, habit, and the ongoing effort to do the right work at the right time. What was extraordinary would have had to do mainly with weather and mortality.

In our present life, and among most people, an abhorrence of Negro slavery is prominent, conventional, and often expressed, and so that form of slavery is most likely to be described or represented by its most abhorrent examples. There can be no doubt that the cruelty and violence potential in that kind of slavery would inevitably have been realized. But to speak only of that potential and that realization, leaving out the ordinariness or the dailiness of most people's working lives, is no doubt incomplete and misleading.

Things of the past that were both customary and ordinary are twice veiled. We are talking here about the difficulty of "social history"—the lives, as lived day by day, of unfamous people—as distinct from the history, drawn largely from public records, of great events and people of power. What actually happened in the lives of my great-great-grandfather and his children and their slaves, and in such lives elsewhere, in the final years of slavery is not knowable at all from statistics, and is minimally knowable from legal documents. We have a scattering of personal accounts in letters, diaries, travelers' journals, and the testimony of slaves and freed slaves, but these are too scattered to support a general "truth" applicable to every life in every place all the time. We have a similar scattering of fictional accounts such as that of the Phelps plantation in *Huckleberry Finn* or Faulkner's satirical history "Was" in *Go Down, Moses*. And we have the politically correct history of slavery in which slavery means only wealth and ease for the owners and only unremitting cruelty and horror for the slaves. Finally, I think, we have to acknowledge that the burden of history, even that of great events and famous people, is mystery: a world of experience that is unknown and never to be known—a world of untold, untellable stories. And it is the unknowable, not the knowable and the known, that ought to set the tone of our conversation about the past.

2. *The Civil War in Kentucky*

In an interview conducted late in his long life, Thomas D. Clark spoke of the "serious gaps" in our economic history: "I know of no serious attempts to summarize the economic history of horses, tobacco or whiskey, coal, timber, and farm products." And: "We need studies of livestock and of agriculture in general." He acknowledged that a statewide study of this kind would be extremely difficult because of Kentucky's diversity of regions. (I will add that this difficulty will be increased by the want of agricultural knowledge and experience among academic historians.)

As a rural Kentuckian, I feel very much with Dr. Clark the want of a comprehensive history of the *land* of Kentucky, which is no less than necessary to complete the history of our people. A history of our land would have to take into account the violence done to the land, the land economies, and to the land's people during the Civil War. Kentucky did not suffer so many major battles and troop movements as other states, but the war spawned countless "minor" acts of violence and coercion here, during the sectional conflict and after, that were both immediately damaging and long-lasting in their social and political consequences. During the war the state lost, largely by theft, about one-fourth of its horses and more than one-third of its mules, which alone would have seriously reduced the productivity of its farms. But soldiers and marauders also destroyed fences and farm buildings, including people's houses. Anything that could be burned or used or eaten was subject to the jeopardy of either military necessity or civic disorder and violence.

This is a part of history both little noticed and little knowable. It is little noticed, I think, because histories of the state as a whole are obliged to concentrate on major trends and great events. It is little knowable because the violence of that time was spread all over the state, and most of it happened to people who kept no records.

A somewhat popular saying about Kentucky is that the state waited to secede until the Civil War was over. That is somewhat true, but it has the easy oversimplification of a wisecrack. Kentucky never seceded officially, but it seems probable to me that in much of the state an unofficial secession had shaped itself among the people well before Appomattox.

As the war began, Kentucky was painfully drawn in the opposite directions of commitment to slavery and loyalty to the Union. It sent many thousands of its sons into both of the opposed armies. So hopelessly divided, it attempted the hopeless compromise of remaining officially neutral. The in-state factions set up their own military organizations: the Home Guard (Union) and the State Guard (Confederate). There were always guerilla bands serving both sides. After the Confederate army went south, following its defeat at Perryville, the state was occupied by federal troops until the war's end. This forced people sympathetic to the South into versions of outlawry, stealth, secrecy, and silence, which justified suspicion, fear, accusations true and false, and acts of betrayal and revenge among those loyal to the Union. Government by consent of the governed was impossible. The occupying forces ruled by official tyranny. Habeas corpus was suspended or ignored. There was interference in political activity and elections. People were illegally executed or taken as hostages. If you had an allegiance, an opinion, and a barn, your barn was eligible to be burned. Or your house. Or you might be arrested for disloyalty. "Disloyalty," a highly interpretable charge, was a crime. By 1864 there were a lot of disloyal people in Kentucky, and they voted overwhelmingly for McClellan over Lincoln. This was a rebellion within a rebellion, in response to the piecemeal disorder and violence that probably are endemic to "military control" of a civilian population. The troubles were worse in some places than in others, but the historians seem to agree that no county was spared.

In my childhood, I had a sort of breathed-in sense of the stress and disorder of that time. This came from my Berry grandparents, and mainly from my father's mother, who lived until I was grown and whose memories and memories of memories I listened to for many hours.

Not long after my grandfather's birth on March 4, 1864, "some soldiers" came in the night and more or less kidnapped his father. His father, known to his descendants as "Grandpa," was forty-one years of age in that year. I know that Grandpa and Grandma Berry owned some slaves, not many. The time offered to Kentuckians several political "positions," but I am sure only that my family was not actively political, the proof being that Grandpa had not joined either army or any of the lesser partisan groups or sides. The soldiers who came for him that night were probably either Unionists or members of the Home Guard, and they had come either to recruit or to arrest him. They had an encampment at the top of Bowen Hill, the next ridge to the south. His captors took Grandpa there, but no farther, for Grandma ran after them in her nightgown, freed Grandpa, and brought him home. She did this evidently by force of character, for she was unarmed and alone. Maybe the soldiers had a hard time confronting an angry, resolute woman wearing only a nightgown. She was thirty-seven years old. My grandfather was the youngest of five. Grandpa was not molested after that.

On another night, other soldiers came and took from Grandma "a very fine gun" that had been presented to her by "a gentleman" who was her friend. Again the soldiers were camped at the top of Bowen Hill, and again she pursued them. She took back her gun from the soldier who had it, and then she required him to fire it, for she was afraid to fire it and afraid to carry it home loaded.

Those are good stories, known and told by my family, and in my turn by me, with a sort of awed delight in Lucinda Bowen Berry, our redoubtable grandma. But I think that they cannot have been heard, even by a young boy, without intimation of the unlimited threatfulness of a time when soldiers could go to a citizen's, even a neighbor's, house and help themselves to anything at all that they wanted. I am sure that my mind had not yet become strong enough to make historical associations and connections, but it may have mattered even so that I began consciously hearing and remembering those stories during World War II when in some parts of the world such intrusions and takings were ordinary.

When the Civil War was over, and emancipation had come to Kentucky, Grandma gathered the slaves into the kitchen and told them, "You have your freedom now, and you must go." I feel some uncertainty in understanding this. It surely is explainable as common sense: It would have been more comfortable for everybody if the slaves did not begin to live into their new freedom in the place where they had lived as slaves. But she was not a mild woman. She may in addition have meant that their freedom would be their punishment for wanting it. That moment anyhow has the weight and finality of a story that could have happened only once. In hearing it I felt, as I feel now in remembering it, coming perhaps from the tone of my grandmother's voice as she told it, a solemn sadness. These, after all, were people who at the minimum had known one another, who knew and would know forever many of the same things that now, as if merely by a change of tense, were over and done with.

Though they had behind them the history of slave-ownership, though I think their sympathy must have leaned to the South, and though I know that they inherited the racial prejudice of their time and place, I never heard from my grandparents (from either pair of them) any hint of attachment to the Confederacy or of devotion to any of its leaders. This seems more remarkable to me than the stories. Their disaffection, I assume, was attributable to the predations that our neighborhood had suffered from both sides—or, in fact, from the several sides.

When I was in college and had begun somewhat intelligently my interest in local history, an aunt on my mother's side gave me her copy of George Dallas Mosgrove's *Kentucky Cavaliers in Dixie*, a history of the Confederate Fourth Kentucky Cavalry, in which the cavalrymen are too likely to be described as knights. When I mentioned to my grandmother Berry the names of two Henry County officers who appear in that book, Lieutenant Colonel George M. Jessee and Captain Bart Jenkins, she dismissed them both with contempt. She did not like the men the war had taught them to be. And the aunt who gave me the book had no time for Private Mosgrove, whom she had known.

3. *Mount Drennon During the War*

Also during my college years, I learned of a large collection of letters and other papers stored in a trunk in an old house overlooking
Drennon Springs, a place of some historical reputation, known
locally as "the lick," and less than five miles from my hometown
of Port Royal. This house before and after the Civil War was the
home, then known as Mount Drennon, of George D. Dicken, a
prominent and well-to-do farmer, land speculator, and trader in
livestock and other agricultural goods; his wife, Elizabeth; his
daughter, Anna; and about thirty slaves. I spent a Christmas vacation reading through those papers and making notes. The letters
mostly were to and from Anna, and they document something of
the experience of the war years in my home country.

I am going to extract from the letters a chronology of family
and local events, 1860–65, but it will be useful to say first, as back-
ground, that George Dicken in July 1862 was appointed provost
marshal, in command of the Henry County Home Guard. As
such, he had enemies. He was in jail in Frankfort from sometime in
September until early November 1862. And he was in the federal
military prison in Louisville for several months in 1864. In her letters Anna wrote as one immediately involved both in the life of
the countryside and in the wartime troubles of our neighborhood.
Here is a record of some of the significant events recorded in her
letters. In quoting from them I have made a number of small editorial changes.

In 1860, Anna became engaged, against her parents' wishes, to
Henry M. Rust, a young lawyer and state senator from Greenups-
burg. Many letters passed between them because they lived far
apart and travel in those days was difficult; they did not see each
other often. It is apparent from her letters that the roads in winter

could be nearly impassable. For Anna the surest means of transportation would have been the Kentucky River, not far away, and a steamboat, at that time probably *The Dove* or *The Wren*.

By the end of 1860 she had begun to fear that there would be a civil war.

On January 9, 1861, she writes to Henry of her hope that they can find "redress for our wrongs *in the Union*."

On January 26, she tells him of "a discovered plot among the negroes... to burn down a village, and destroy the inhabitants." They had "arms and ammunition, and they expected their freedom in March during the war." The guilty slaves were "punished," and James G. Leach, a state representative sympathetic to the abolitionists, was twice burned in effigy. For the first time, Anna says, she was afraid of the slaves. At about the same time in New Castle, the county seat of Henry County, between the end of the workday and midnight about fifty slaves made a sort of demonstration at the houses of white people sympathetic to the South, "singing political songs and shouting for Lincoln." That was remarkable in itself, and it was more remarkable that the white people apparently did not interfere.

Anna Dicken writes to Henry Rust on February 10, telling him, "The obstinacy of the Southerners almost makes me wish a few South Carolinians *had been hung* as traitors."

On March 17, after Lincoln's inauguration, she writes Henry that she thinks the duty of Kentuckians is to "fight in the Union for their rights." She hopes that Henry will not become a "disunionist."

On May 4, Henry Rust writes to Anna of his distress that the Lincoln government intends to "subjugate" the South. Henry is "in favor of an armed neutrality in Ky," but he thinks such a position will prove impossible.

He apparently was beginning to feel the disaster, for Kentucky, that was implicit not only in its geographic quandary as a border state between the opposed sections, but also in the multiple divisions within its own boundary. How could the state effectively have armed itself, using the small fraction of its people supposedly neutral against the army of either side?

In a letter to Henry Rust on June 6, Anna speaks of her own continuing sympathy for the South, her opposition to its "subjugation," and her support for Kentucky's neutrality. But her father has returned from a long business trip to New Orleans and New York, convinced of the power of the North to overcome the South. He is now, she says, "I am ashamed to say a coercionist"—by which she means a Unionist. She adds that "Mr. Pryor of our country is creating a great commotion as candidate for the legislature on the State rights ticket." She writes, she says, "within the sound of the fife and drum by which a company of Home Guards are drilling."

On June 13 she tells Henry that her father "has joined a military company" of, evidently, the Home Guards. And she says, "Some noisy men of both parties met at Port Royal a few days ago, and came very near closing in a fight between their military companies, after they were through drilling."

Port Royal, I now need to say, was then, as it always has been, a very small town, a hamlet, the center of a small farming community. The "military companies," I assume of recruits, that came so near to fighting were made up of neighbors who knew one another, had played and worked and loafed and gone to school and church together.

Anna's letter of June 13 also indicates that Henry Rust had joined a military company.

On July 4, Anna tells Henry, the Union party had a picnic a few miles from her house. It drew "an immense concourse of people."

In July she wrote of two other nearby public gatherings at which partisan speakers spoke, some abusively, some reasonably.

Anna's letters to Henry Rust of September 13, 17, 24, and 26 all came back to her, bearing the stamp of the dead letter office. Henry evidently was involved in a movement of his military unit, therefore was not reachable by mail.

Anna's letter of September 24 speaks of "rebel encampments in the State from which a guerilla warfare will be carried on." One of these was in Owen County, across the Kentucky River from Henry County—and from her home farm. This has caused "the most intense excitement in this region."

And in the same letter: "B. W. Jenkins, a notorious desperado of this county, passed along the road a day or two ago with a company and stopped at the houses of those he had visited to take leave of them, saying when he returned it would be with a revolver in one hand, and a firebrand in the other, dealing death and destruction to all who supported the State."

In her undelivered letter to Henry of September 26, Anna writes that the Home Guard had lately gone to Springport, one of the many landings along the Kentucky River, where there may have been a ferry boat, to keep the Owen County Rebels from crossing. Her father, needing to stay at the river with his company and worried about Anna and her mother, arranged for six slave men to guard the house at night, watching "alternately [in shifts] until the danger had passed." She adds: "Five of our men proved themselves willing to stand by us until the last one of them fell in our defense. Dick I am sorry to say is a coward, and will take care of himself first."

I am assuming that the slaves, in such circumstances, would have been armed, for they were guarding against a possible attack by armed guerillas. If I am right, then we have here an instance of slaves recruited as soldiers by a Unionist slaveholder to guard against, and to fight if they had to, a band of Confederate soldiers.

A letter to Anna from Henry Rust, written on September 27, 1861, informs her that he was then in Prestonsburg, in the mountains of eastern Kentucky, which was "full of Rebel troops" who were "fortifying the town." He thought them to be in rebellion against the laws of the state. He "told them the hemp was now growing to hang them with."

This was the last, or near the last, of the correspondence between Anna Dicken and Henry Rust. Their marriage had been planned and put off several times because of events of the war and her father's continuing opposition. And then, by a letter of November 18, 1861, she was informed of Henry's death in the Battle of Jory Mountain in eastern Kentucky. The circumstances leading to his involvement in this battle are unclear.

Anna's personal story during the following months, dramatic enough from her point of view, was in the way of the world fairly unsurprising. For weeks after Henry's death, she was sick with despondency and grief. But she was a healthy, sensible young woman, and she accepted her recovery as it came. Frank Troutman, who would have been Henry Rust's best man, wrote to Anna at first in sympathy. But their correspondence continued and became more intimate, with the result that they were married at Mount Drennon on February 24, 1863.

The difference between Anna's story and many a "love story" in and out of fiction, what made it one of a kind, was of course its involvement in the war and its complicated lines of division. Anna's father, so far as can be known, was an exceptionally prosperous slave owner, unquestionably dependent upon the work of slaves, but he was also a Unionist and commander of his county's Unionist Home Guard. Frank Troutman was also a slaveholding farmer, landowner, and businessman, far better educated and more prosperous by a good deal than his father-in-law. But he, by contrast, was strongly and openly sympathetic to the South, opposed to the policies of the Lincoln administration, and yet he hated the war. He declared emphatically his own neutrality and supported the neutrality of the state. He owned farms in Bourbon County, Kentucky, and also in Illinois and Minnesota. By profession he was a lawyer in Paris, the county seat of Bourbon County, an established public man with a fine reputation. He was a widower, probably a good many years older than Anna. Twice he was instrumental in getting her father released from prison, before their marriage and again after. George Dicken's second incarceration, in the military prison in Louisville, beginning in February 1864, was on a charge, evidently false, of diverting funds from the Home Guard to his own use and of selling a forfeited bond. He was sentenced to a prison term of six months and a $2,500 fine. On May 11 of that year Frank Troutman and a colleague presented Dicken's case on a personal visit to President Lincoln, who "set aside the judgment of the Court Martial" on evidence that they supplied. Thus less than a year from the war's end a Unionist slaveholding provost marshal of the Unionist Home Guard of Henry County, Kentucky, was set free from a Union prison by the President of the Union on appeal by a slaveholder sympathetic to the Confederacy and a proponent of Kentucky's hopeless neutrality.

But also, evidently in early 1863, Anna Dicken, daughter of her Unionist father but, like her fiancé, in sympathy with the South, was herself arrested and forced to take the oath of allegiance to the Union.

After Anna's marriage, because she was no longer living at Mount Drennon, the record of events in that neighborhood, as given by this collection of letters, is not as constant as before. But Anna's father, in a characteristically freely spelled letter of March 21, 1863, informs her that "Rubin" Tingle's house had been burned "and all in it." By "all" I am sure he meant its furnishings. Also burned, his letter says, was "Wm Pollard's and everything on the place except His Hen House and Stable." A letter from her mother, written on the same day, tells her that her horse, heroically named "Storm," has been stolen by Rebels from Owen County, and two or three slaves had run away.

On August 19, 1863, Frank Troutman writes from Charleston, Illinois, to Anna, who was staying at Mount Drennon, that he has been informed that Kentucky is or will be under martial law, and "if so it is best for me to stay here at least so long as I can put in my time profitably."

He writes to her on the 22nd: "I am extremely sorry to learn that your pa's barn is burnt."

On November 22, 1863, George Dicken was arrested and confined to the city limits of Louisville. While her father was a captive and during her husband's frequent absences on business, Anna competently supervised the work of the farm at Mount Drennon.

On November 2, 1864, she writes to a friend:

> If our servants were not tampered with I would fear nothing but men are going through the country to persuade and frighten them into the army.... There are a good many Southern soldiers in this part of the state, and recruits are joining them daily. I presume they will not leave until after the draft as it is well known that men of Southern proclivities will join [the Southern soldiers] rather than be forced into the Federal army, but prefer to wait until they see if they escape the draft.

This fragmentary history of my neighborhood during the Civil War concludes with the following passage of a somewhat confusing letter from George Dicken to Anna and Frank written on May 24, 1865. I have reproduced the writer's language as he wrote it because of my inability to clarify it. It must have made clear sense to Anna and Frank, but it cannot be reliably edited.

> All of our Negroes Has left including Susan and all of hir Children from oldest to youngest Nelson Green & Jerry making ten in all left Emley Grimse [Grimes?] all gone Pollard Lige & Violetts Sam lef 22 [of May?] I followed and done my Best But could not over take them

And so we learn imperfectly some of their names in an interval of a minute or so between their unknown lives in slavery and their unknown lives in freedom. George Dicken, the onetime Unionist and provost marshal of the Home Guard, followed them and did his best to overtake them because their absence had exposed most urgently his dependence on them. If he had caught up with them, what would he have said to them? What would he have offered them to persuade them to come back? Nobody will ever know. May 24, 1865, as I write, was 153 years ago. The oldest of my grandfathers, on that day, was nearly fifteen months old. As we measure historical time, that day with its few answers and many questions was only a while ago. And yet, since then, a hillside here in our neighborhood could have been cleared of its original trees, crops grown and harvested on it, and a stand of big trees grown back again.

To have the record given in the Dicken-Troutman family papers is a part of my good fortune as a native and student of this neighborhood. Discontinuous and fragmentary as the record obviously is, those papers were discovered and saved almost by accident. Anna Dicken Troutman was an extraordinary woman—literate, intelligent, sensible—and unlike just about everybody else in her place and time, she made it possible for us to know her a little. Hundreds of her contemporaries lived and died here, leaving behind them nothing in writing except their signatures (if they could write them) on a few documents and their names and dates on their gravestones.

4. A Prison Journal

When George Dicken was released from the federal military prison in Louisville in May 1864, he brought out with him a fellow prisoner's journal that presumably had been entrusted to him for safekeeping. Eventually it was stored with the family letters and other papers in the attic of the stone ell of the old house once called Mount Drennon, dilapidated by my time and now long gone.

The journal gives a detailed account of life in the prison from February 2 to April 13, 1864. The author of nearly all of it was T. A. Catlett of New Liberty in Owen County, who thus was a near neighbor, maybe previously an acquaintance, of George Dicken. T. A. Catlett was forty-four years old, a married man with children. He was a casual speller and writer, but was otherwise literate and intelligent. Though he had no money to pay lawyers or bribe officials, he clearly was, or had been, a man of some standing. He was a Rebel, certainly in principle and sympathy, also presumably by some active involvement that he never explains, for he says that "this is not the first prison I have been in by six." He had been in this prison, he says on February 10, "for upwards of three months." He was a man of compassion also: Of a prisoner seriously ill he says, "I persuaded him to take my bed," which had the only mattress in the room and was "in the most desirable place." In one of the journal's final entries, another writer writes: "I have just received a letter from my prison mate T. A. Catlett who is now at Camp Chase."

And so the author of the journal appears fortuitously and astonishingly among our questions, for a while he tells us a little of what we want to know, and then he passes again into the silence. Unlike the history of great events, the history of families and small places forces us to recognize the past as a shadow from which shadowy figures now and then emerge into light, take on briefly the substance of a story, a part of a story, a few imaginable details, and merge again into the shadow.

During the federal occupation of Kentucky, given the state's conflicts of allegiance and general disorder, a lot of people ran afoul of federal authority, were arrested, and had to be detained somewhere. Evidently there was a new, large need for prison room. The federal military prison in Louisville seems to have been somewhat hurriedly improvised. The Louisville *Journal*, judging from the outside, thought it exceptionally neat and well regulated—so T. A. Catlett reports. His view of it from the inside leads to the opposite conclusion. According to his account, the prison housed its several hundred inmates not in cells but in large rooms. These were divided by partitions built of unseasoned lumber, so that there were cracks an inch and a half wide between the boards. Catlett and "General" Dicken (thus honored or self-promoted) were in a room containing thirty-two miscellaneous and apparently unthreatening prisoners. The adjoining room held "the chain gang," who seem to have been perpetually in irons. Catlett speaks also of a room occupied by deserters and other offenders from the Union army, and another for "disloyal ladies."

In response to the *Journal*'s favorable review of the outside of the prison, Catlett says that the prisoners ate from a table "scoured off with the same broom used for scouring our neat little privy." The handle of the same broom was used to stir the coffee. The prisoners' bread and meat were not served on plates but on the well-scoured naked tabletop. In Catlett's room the rats were controlled by a "rat company" organized among the prisoners. Nobody controlled the lice. Catlett speaks of "several cases of diphtheria," though this diagnosis is attributed to nobody but himself. At the end of February he says that a third of the prisoners complained that they were "unwell."

The prison's judicial procedures seem to have been about as casual as its sanitation. Cases of false arrest were sometimes corrected immediately, but persons thus detained could be overlooked and forgotten. Accusation, for instance, of being a guerilla or a "bushwhacker" could be tantamount to conviction. A person could be arrested and kept with "no charges preferred," sometimes for weeks. Some were charged, with or without evidence, with what seem to have been actual crimes—stealing horses, for instance, or "smuggling quinine to the South"—but, in the prevalent confusion and among so many, who could have been sure of the justice of the charges?

Most disturbing, because so easy to believe and to "prove," are the charges of disloyalty to the Union or of sympathy for the South. Habeas corpus might be officially suspended, as for a time it was, but that and other rights were suspendable or expendable simply by circumstances. You might be arrested for smiling near the grave of a man killed by a guerilla, for shoeing a stranger's horse, for calling General John Morgan a gentleman, for "using disloyal language," or "through a mistake."

Catlett says that acts of charity, hospitality, or neighborliness had become dangerous: "If one of [the citizenry] takes a stranger into his house, gives him a crust of bread or even permits him to come into his yard, if [the stranger] should be a deserter from the Federal Army . . . [the host] is arrested and thrown into prison perhaps for a year." But acts of ordinary precaution or self-protection might be equally dangerous: "If through fear of doing wrong [a person] refuses to feed a federal soldier and to give him anything he calls for . . . he is immediately pronounced disloyal and a Rebel Sympathizer and is arrested and thrown into prison."

The combination of the unassailable military authority of the occupation and the social and political divisions among the people gave to mere suspicion an inordinate and terrifying power. Nobody could be sure whom to trust, or what neighbor or relative might be a betrayer or an enemy. The journal contains many references to spies and to what, in memory of Judas Iscariot, the prisoners called "thirty dollar detectives," who may, the prisoners believed with reason, have been planted among them in the prison.

The following story from the journal's first entry probably cannot, because of its extremity, be understood as a common experience, but it apparently does show what was possible during the federal occupation of Kentucky. It tells us the sort of abuse that people heard about and feared. It seems to me to be authenticated by its accumulation of details, and by its likeness in many of its details to other stories. As before, I have made some editorial changes for the sake of clarity or readability. Even so, there are some missing links, and we cannot know why Catlett's "old acquaintance" was pursued and arrested.

> On yesterday I chanced to recognize an old acquaintance from Bath County, Kentucky, a high-minded honorable citizen. He informed me that the Federal soldiers had robbed him of nearly everything he possessed. They took of him eighty-odd fat hogs, about the same number of one- & two-year old cattle, two hundred bushels of wheat, one hundred & fifty bushels of old corn, all of his present year's crop of corn, & all of his oats, hay, &

fodder, all of his bacon & beef in his meat house, & then stripped his house of all the clothing in it, also all of the beds & bedding. . . . Up to the time of his capture he had not slept in his or any other house for several months. On one occasion [the Federals] surrounded him, but he broke through their ranks and made his escape, after receiving four wounds, two of which was in the calf of the leg, tearing and making a severe wound. [Of the other two wounds, one was] through the arm, the other in the shoulder. . . . He succeeded in crawling about a half a mile, and crawled into a shock of fodder where he remained for nine days. And then [he] was removed to a friend's house where he remained for several weeks, and received all the care a friend could bestow. Soon after this, one of his sons was taken very ill, so ill that it was thought he would not recover. The father's love was too strong to remain in the woods. At a late hour at night he might be seen approaching his own dwelling, expecting every moment to be halted by a Federal soldier. But the thought of his sick child still lured him on. He entered and found the child in fully as critical a condition as represented. He did not remain in the house many moments, but mounted his horse and started after the doctor to get some medicine. After an elapse of an hour or two he returned with medicine, which he gave to his son. He then concluded as no soldiers had been heard of in the neighborhood he would take a nap & return to his hiding place, but unfortunately he slept until the dawn. As he stepped out of his door he found too late that he had been betrayed by a neighbor and his house was surrounded by Federal troops. This occurred on the

20th of January, 1864. He is not permitted to send home for clothing or money. And as to the result of his arrest, it remains for the future to explain.

Catlett does not often speak of his own predicament, but on March 31 he wrote: "I have just received the news that the town of New Liberty, Owen County, Kentucky, has been destroyed by fire, and my wife and children with seventeen other families are houseless, and I am shut up in this filthy prison."

5. The War-Made Peace in Kentucky

From the Battle of Perryville in October 1862 until the war's end, Kentucky was militarily a sort of backwater. No great objective was here to be fought over. The state was "held" by the Union and had to be occupied and (theoretically) kept under control. But the minds of the Union leaders were necessarily turned elsewhere. The occupation was anxious, perfunctory, and violent. The attempted rule by strict military order produced among the ruled, paradoxically but expectably, an almost limitless disorder. It is impossible to see how the state could have emerged from that experience into any slightest opportunity for interracial reconciliation and amity when its white people were so bitterly at odds among themselves. It is likewise impossible to see how anybody who knows much of this history can think of it as morally simple, with all the good on the side of the North and all the evil on the side of the South.

The Civil War was allegorized in this way, afterwards, by people in need of moral simplification: Chattel slavery was a great evil; the Civil War was fought by the North, from first to last, only to free the slaves; the South fought only to keep the slaves enslaved; the North, because it was the side of virtue, won; the South, because it was the side of evil, lost; the slaves were freed, which was good. Thus we come to a computation that looks simple and sure: So great a triumph of good over so great an evil yields, as a net result, a lot of good. I understand this conclusion, and the need for it, so well that I would believe it if I could. But Lincoln did not say at first that his purpose in the war was to free the slaves. He certainly was no friend to slavery, but in 1862, when he had the Emancipation Proclamation in mind, he said: "My paramount object in this struggle is to save the Union, and is *not* either to save or to destroy slavery." Saving the Union was necessarily paramount. Without union, the federal government would have no say-so over slavery in the seceded states. That complicates the idea that the war was only about slavery, and it is a strong statement of political purpose. But then we have got to reckon with the conclusion of William H. Seward, Lincoln's secretary of state, that the war was an "irrepressible conflict," which seems to mean that the war was a war because it was fated to be so and could have been nothing else. When I think of "irrepressible conflict," I remember that the hardest fight I ever saw had no cause. The two fighters, strong big boys, simply did not like each other. They "hated each other's guts," and they fought as if they did not care if they died. Of "the young bloods of the South," who were "the most dangerous set of men that this war has turned loose upon the world," Sherman said, "They hate Yankees, per se." And "irrepressible" may point us also to Edmund Wilson's metaphor that he apparently could not let go: "the wars fought by human beings are stimulated as a rule primarily by the same instincts as the voracity of the [cannibalistic] sea slug"—"not virtue but at bottom the irrational instinct of an active power organism in the presence of another such organism."

I read Wilson's book, *Patriotic Gore*, soon after its publication in 1962, and I have not forgotten his image of the bigger sea slug who "ingurgitates" the smaller one. I suppose it was meant as offered. But I notice also that it prevents the reduction of the idea of virtue to the winner's expectable conclusion that "it was worth it." The computation leading to a net plus really can be true only mathematically: only with numbers, typically with numbers of dollars. But the originating fantasy of our present economy (and way of life) is that the costs and results of any enterprise can be so quantified as to yield an acceptable net quantity. This willful delusion has survived into our own time as the economists' doctrine of "creative destruction" and the "cost-benefit ratio," which justify, invariably, whatever the great commercial and political forces "need" to do — for example, coal mining by "mountaintop removal," of which the costs in excess of monetary expenditures are unknown because unknowable.

By the grace of such a computation, the Civil War yielded to the North, as Robert Penn Warren put it, a "Treasury of Virtue," a perpetually self-renewing account on which the Virtuous are still writing checks. Anybody with a "southern accent" is likely to know this from experience. But for confirmation, let us consider the following sentences from *The Soul of America* by Jon Meacham: "The clash of arms was over, yes, but the battle between North and South, between Union and rebellion, between nothing less, really, than justice and injustice was not fully resolved [by Lee's surrender]." The next sentence states that the Civil War "was only a chapter in the perennial contest between right and wrong in the nation's soul." The consistent parallelism in these sentences draws a firm geographic line dividing right from wrong, right on the North side and wrong on the South side. These sentences, published in 2018, draw the line exactly as it was drawn by abolitionists in the North a century and a half or two centuries ago. The interesting question here is whether these sentences were so constructed by conscious deliberation or by custom ingrained and unconscious. This question is of interest partly because Prof. Meacham seems a fair-minded man, but partly also because the answer does not matter. As long as that line is drawn, consciously or unconsciously, in people's minds the country is divided. The problem with this line is that it obviously is a falsehood. People of some experience and some self-knowledge know that the contest between right and wrong is perennial in the soul of every human, and that right and wrong cannot be geographically divided. People who are somewhat rational are apt to discern also that southern racism is not categorically worse than northern racism. During the Civil War, in fact, some people were living in the South who were opposed to slavery and secession, and some people were living in the North who sympathized with the South.

The line nevertheless continues to be drawn. As long as it is drawn, it will be a serious impairment of what I guess will have to be called the public mind. This is not a problem I know how to solve, but I will need to return to it.

The violence in Kentucky did not end with the official conclusion of the war. When the lines of political enmity and then of war are drawn through households and neighborhoods, peace cannot be made by official settlement or very soon. Here the most conspicuous freedom granted by the war and the general upset that followed was to night-riding outlaws who did as they pleased. The bloody work of local reprisal simply continued.

In the eastern part of Henry County and in Owen County across the river, "bands of armed men, disguised and masked," and "known as Kuklux," killed a hundred people from 1870 to 1874.

The aim of this Kuklux was to drive out of the state "the negroes . . . but also all Radicals who were in favor of negroes." The victims were both black and white, but most were black. Many who were not killed were whipped. I have taken this information and the quotations from the "Official Report of the Owen County Outrages," written in September 1874 by William Russell, deputy United States marshal, who himself was murdered in July of the next year. His report was published in *The New York Times*. Local law enforcement seems to have been either complicit or useless. Everybody was afraid. Toward the end of his report, Russell says, "The majority of the people are all good citizens, and are at heart violently opposed to those Kuklux, but they are under a reign of terror, and are really afraid to express their opinions."

In the same decade, in the same vicinity, there were "marauders" who disregarded the racist program of the Kuklux in favor simply of murder and robbery. Four of those men, all white of course, were lynched at New Castle in September 1877.

Such bands of outlaws, variously named, were widespread in Kentucky in those years. Their killings and other abuses of people of both races terrorized everybody. Thomas D. Clark thought rightly that "the whole social system was in needless turmoil."

There may be nothing so useless as to propose, looking backward, that the past might have been different: What if there had been no Civil War? What if the South had won? There are better ways to pass the time. Even so, it seems to me that the history of my state and my county cannot be understood without understanding that the war, in its effects and its side effects, damaged us greatly, in some ways permanently. The war produced the most narrowly limited solution to the problem of slavery, and it did not solve at all, but in some ways probably worsened, the problem of racism.

The lynching of Jim Simmons and his fellow marauders in New

Castle in 1877 was a famous event, the subject of a lengthy written account and much talk. As late as my own school days, the bridge where the four men were hanged was known as Simmons' Bridge, and the name was weighted with our knowledge that a hanging had happened there, though we did not know why.

Far less acknowledged or recorded, after that, were the lynchings of four black people in this county of Henry—two of these having been little girls, one of them three years old, the other eight. In a history of bad facts, those surely are two of the worst, and those apparently are the only facts available. Having written them, I feel of course the need to explain, but I have no explanation. I don't understand how such a thing could be done, and I am writing in another age of violence when, again beyond my understanding, gunmen have killed children in their schools and we continue to kill children in war. I can only ask the obvious question: How and how soon, from the high threshold of violence established by the Civil War in the seceded states and Kentucky, might a people be expected to descend to a level even of approximate peace? Or: How might they prevent the militarily acceptable violence of any war from inspiring and excusing unacceptable violence during and after the war?

The end of the legal enslavement of black people, and the constitutional changes that followed, I readily affirm as good. I have been asking how much of that good is net—once we have subtracted the cost in suffering and death and grief, the devastation and the lasting impoverishment of both races in the South, the continuance of white racism and disunion, and the persistence, even the increase, of other kinds of slavery and disorder after the war—because the question should be asked, and because I do not think it is answerable.

Now I will say that a further debit that must be entered into our accounting of the Civil War is its legacy of industrial militarism. The extent to which the Civil War solved the problems that caused it, by any honest accounting, is assuredly limited. It did not stop racism in the South, or in the North. Though it formally ended the Confederacy and secession, it did not end the sectional division, which in fact it ratified and deepened by the further division between winners and losers. Nevertheless, it remains popularly credited as the solution, entirely good, of our worst national problem. So successful were we at solving our own great problem that we have generously undertaken to solve international problems and the problems of other nations also by force of war and with the same assurance of our goodness in doing so. If we have a sort of notion of preventability, we are not long detained by it. We appear never to bother with the question of net good. We went to war in Iraq and Afghanistan as if such questions could not be asked, as if no useless war had ever been fought, and in a nationalist confusion of pride, fear, moral certainty, and (never dismissable) the allure of profits to the war industries. That President Trump would allow a sale of weapons to prevail over an urgent moral issue may have been shocking to the shockable, but it was not a surprise, nor was it the personal eccentricity of a strange man. All of us, and especially those of us who live in rural America, know the rule of profit at any cost. We live daily with its effects. War prevails over peace, I imagine, finally because it brings an apparently simple end to the great burden of civilized thought.

∾

Among the papers left by one of my great-grandfathers, M. B. Perry of Port Royal, there is a torn-out page of a pocket account book inscribed as follows:

> Notice
>
> Mr. Perry
> we . ask . you . to .
> let . this . be . notice
> for . you . enough .
> to . start . your
> nigger . don't . make
> any . trade . with . him
> for . next . year .
> we . mean . business .
> the . next . notice
> will . be . in . another .
> way

This came to M. B. Perry in an envelope addressed to him and post-marked at Port Royal on December 18, 1907. There is no explanation, written or remembered, to go with it, but to some extent this can be understood. In this part of the country, to "trade" with somebody for a year would have meant to arrange for a crop, undoubtedly tobacco, to be grown on the shares or "on the halves," the landlord and the tenant each to take half of the income. My ancestor probably had made such an arrangement with a black hired hand, his share of the crop to be received in addition to wages. This would have been resented by some white tenant farmers ("we"), I suppose, as a mark of esteem or respect for the black man, and as his elevation from hired hand to tenant farmer. Had the black tenant replaced a white tenant? I don't know. Nor do I know what response was given to the threat, but I feel fairly safe in guessing that it was ignored. So far as I know, the relationship of that part of my family to its black hired help was stable, more or less permanent. It was as though, despite the racial difference, the employers and the employees belonged mutually to the place. I am supposing that I knew well one of the sons of the man referred to in the note.

The note, anyhow, is alone among M. B. Perry's papers—there is nothing else remotely like it—and it may have been kept because of its singularity. Do I know what could have caused this perhaps sudden intensification of racism and hate? Yes, I do. In 1907, according to C. Vann Woodward, "the American Tobacco Company was estimated to control . . . a capitalization of $500,000,000." This was the "Tobacco Trust," the monopoly of James B. Duke who, to signify his intent, had moved his headquarters from North Carolina to New York. His mastery was his ability to transform the work of farmers and tenant farmers in neighborhoods such as that of Port Royal into wealth and magnificence for himself. In 1907, a tobacco crop in my region may barely have paid its transportation to market and the commission on its sale. It was thus entirely possible for white small farmers and tenant farmers in my country to see themselves as desperately competing—just before Christmas, after all, when their poverty would have been most noticeable to them—with a favored black tenant farmer for "their" share of little or nothing. This, I think, is one of the ways that race prejudice works: You have been reduced economically to the edge of survival, and *then* you notice that your competitor is a "nigger," and you inject into that word a full dose of venom.

And here perhaps is a lesson that advocates of racial harmony should study with care: People—and, one would reasonably suppose, people of different races—may be most at peace with one another when they are reasonably prosperous. The "race problem" in the United States, as we need to remember, began as a rural problem, and it became an urban problem *because* it was a rural problem. In the South, including Kentucky, before and after the Civil War, most people of both races were country people, mostly farmers. Farmers along with loggers and miners, all country people, were and are the primary producers of the "raw materials" that manufacturers such as James Duke's American Tobacco Company transform into "consumer goods" and sell for plenty of money.

A major asset of the secondary economy of the corporations has always been the enforced cheapness of the goods and the work of the country people. When the bankrupt or starved-out or technologically obsolete country people moved into the industrial cities, they came as cheap labor, people identified and valued solely by their economic classification: cheap. When cheap labor, both poor white people and poor black people, moved from country to city, and when they competed on the "job market," the racial division cheapened their labor. Always around the issues of human culture and character there is the to some extent determining circumstance of economic life.

Kentucky until well into my own lifetime was a state both rural and poor, though poorer in some parts than in others. It is now very little a rural state, strictly speaking, for its country people are now mostly consumers in the economy of consumption, the same as urban people, and most of them have "town jobs," but the state is still poor. The persistence of poverty here may be somewhat owing to geography. Kentucky is divided into half a dozen distinctive "physiographic" regions. I have often driven across the ridgeline that divides the watershed of Cedar Creek in Franklin County from the watershed of Elkhorn Creek in Scott County, which also is the dividing line between the Outer Bluegrass and the Inner Bluegrass. The visual difference in topography and vegetation, in the farms and houses, is abrupt and astonishing. Such divisions have made economic differences that in turn have made a variety of human differences. Even more remarkable is the difference between counties such as mine, which from the time of the frontier were dependent on farming and were reasonably prosperous during the six decades of the New Deal tobacco program, and the mountain counties to the east, which for more than a hundred years have been dominated and plundered by the economy of coal.

Even so, it is clear to me that such differences were originally less significant than they have become. At the beginning of "settlement," virtually the whole state was by nature wealthier than the first-comers could easily believe. It had magnificent forests and prairies, its topsoils were fertile and deep, its climate was welcoming, it was rich in rivers and flowing streams. "Heaven," a frontier preacher famously said, "is a Kentucky of a place." All it needed, as Wallace Stegner said of the American West, was a people worthy of it.

"What if," as I said, can be a pointless game. But it is not pointless to propose that a people worthy of Kentucky—as it was at the founding of its first towns in 1775, or as it was in 1865, or as it is now—would have been and would be people willing to define themselves by the natural endowment and the natural limits of their chosen dwelling places. A people worthy of Kentucky, that is to say, would have been or would be a *polity*, aware of itself as such and determined to preserve itself and its land by its good work, its enlivened intelligence, and its loving care.

Such a polity certainly would have been too much to expect in 1775 and the decades following, amid the displacement, greed, speculation, violence, and false hopes of the frontier and the "new" land. But it was eighty-six years from 1775 to the start of the Civil War, maybe time enough for us to learn something of our where-abouts and what it required of us, a beginning maybe. If so, our education was severely retarded by the Civil War and its aftermath. But surely, a historical fantasist might suggest, that hard experience should have tried and tempered us into one people—if not the war itself, then the two and a half years of occupation by the Union army.

If it should have, then the problem was that it didn't. In some circumstances, for some people, hardship and suffering may be a unifying force. But in Kentucky we were divided by our regions, the war divided us, and occupation and oppression probably divided us worse than the war. It is certain that after the war and the unofficial violence that followed, we were more in pieces than ever. We were divided then, not only by geography and race, but also by politics, old and new allegiances, local grudges, by the crosscurrents and eddies of passionate opinion, by fear of the advantages the war had given to the worst among us. We were divided, weary, and grieved by many losses. We have remained divided, never having become a coherent polity capable of economic self-defense. Our state motto, "United We Stand, Divided We Fall," adopted in 1792, is so far only a description of our failure.

Such consolidating force as the war could supply, it supplied to the industrial and financial interests of the North. The war that impoverished and crippled the South gave a running start to northern money and machines. And presently Kentucky's home-grown vandals were replaced by vandals from afar who knew best the value of our "natural resources" and our homegrown "labor." State government functioned pretty much as a hospitality com-mittee to welcome the gilded potentates and tycoons who bought Kentucky coal, timber, tobacco, and other products of the land at prices that shame us to remember, and hauled all of it away without a pause to add value. The state became not merely a colony but a mine, from which everything of value was taken and nothing given back. Later our leaders have proposed to solve our problems as a backward state, rural and poor, by "bringing in industry," implicitly offering our people to their newly arrived benefactors as cheap labor. Perhaps the economic history of Kentucky was wrought by money deposited in the right hands extended in welcome. Or it may have been accomplished by the power and charm of prestige. Let us imagine the humble Kentucky politician, newly ascended from his birth in a log cabin to the heights of campaign eloquence, who suddenly realizes his full potential as an individual by having his elbow squeezed and his hand pumped by the Real McCoy, northern, urban, urbane, powerful, free with the whiskey, and rich. But we probably should not forget the Lexington lawyer and historian William Townsend's rule of thumb: "When they say 'It's not the money, it's the principle,' it's the money."

6. Remembered History

Now I must come to the wonder, or so it seems to me, that my small native country in Henry County at the time of my boyhood was so livable a place. If my memories of it are at all accurate, this was indeed a wonder, for the county then was divided by degrees or intensities of race prejudice. I spoke several pages ago of the terror imposed, in the eastern end of this county and across the river in Owen County in the 1870s, by bands of "Kuklux" whose aim was to drive out "the negroes [and the white] Radicals who were in favor of negroes." A result, no doubt, of that disturbance and in the same vicinity, were "marauders" whose interest was simply in robbery and murder. This recreational marauding seems not to have survived the lynching of the four marauders in New Castle in 1877. But a virulent racism—lineally descended, I am sure, from the lawlessness in Kentucky during the Civil War and that of the Kuklux in the 1870s—persisted in that area, producing atrocities as bad as any, past the middle of the twentieth century.

And yet, within not many miles from places where black people went in jeopardy of their lives and rarely went at all, the towns I knew best in my boyhood offered no such threat. I have in mind the years from 1939, when I was five years old and had begun to know where I was, until 1950, when I got my driver's license and the Korean War began. For me the significant country of those years, as ever since, was a stretch of ten or so miles from New Castle, the county seat of Henry County, northward to a stretch of the Kentucky River just beyond Port Royal, where I now live. New Castle in the 1940s was inhabited by around six hundred people, of whom maybe one-fourth were black. My father's law office was there. That was where I went to school through the eighth grade, where I made friendships with my contemporaries and a number of the grownups who kept the stores and other workplaces. It was where I conducted adventures in the backways and on the roofs of the town and along the creeks, got myself employed at a variety of jobs, and acquired a rich informal education. Until 1946, both of my father's parents still lived on the farm we called "the home place," about six miles from New Castle and four from Port Royal. The population of Port Royal, I think, could not have been more than 150. There, my mother's parents lived in a large brick house at the northeast corner of town. From there, a sizable tract of farmland and woodland spread away to the river and the creek known as Cane Run.

By the time I started school, when I was six and still blessedly ignorant of letters and numbers, I knew some parts of that country familiarly and felt at home in them. As I grew older, I played and rambled there pretty much at large, alone or with my brother or with friends. I learned farmwork there by watching it done, by playing at it, and finally by doing it myself under the supervision of exacting teachers. What I still consider my native land, including the farms of my family and our neighbors and the countryside around New Castle, was an area of maybe twenty square miles. I grew up learning it and knowing it, in intimacy with it. From it I take my understanding of the word "motherland." This little country, in which I have lived nearly all my life, and my story in it give my mind its basis and much of its significant contents.

World War II was the great event of the time of my growing up, and it was prominent and troubling in all our minds. Even so, it seems to me that my home country was then remarkably settled and quieted within itself, not entirely of course, but in a way that it has not been since.

Though I liked the time of my boyhood and remember it gratefully, I know that all of us were maintaining our quota of human imperfections. The main things wrong with us at that time were these: Race prejudice, institutional and customary and personal, was too much among us, and the white people were not paying it enough attention; we were not respectful enough of nature and the natural world; we were suffering a long-established separation between our economic life and our religion, with effects sometimes tangible and practical, to which we were not paying enough attention; and our people were still sometimes inclined to settle their differences by killing each other. The killings of these years I am remembering were all of white men by white men. One would have been too many, and there were several. At least four boys of my generation in New Castle grew up to be killers.

Always hanging over us, moreover, was the economic jeopardy of our land and people. By the time I was five, we were coming to the end of the Depression. My mother's father remembered meeting an old friend at about that time: "Well, Harry," the friend said, "we made it, and we didn't commit suicide, did we?" And my grandfather thought, "No, but you've thought about it."

But there were also a number of things about our life here at that time that I consider to have been right. Our economy was agricultural and our culture was agrarian. The towns served the farmers; the farmers supported the towns. There were many more farms, therefore many more farmers, than there are now. In 1940 there were 1,501 farms in Henry County; in 2012 there were 809. (In 1940 the state of Kentucky had 252,894 farms, in 2012 only 77,064.) To a native of the county, who knew it familiarly from 1940 to 2012, those numbers confirm a solemn story. We have many learned experts who will gladly assure us that the loss from a small county of 692 farms in sixty-seven years constitutes "progress," but that is another gross progress for which we have no net. It is progress by the subtraction of much that the experts have never properly valued but only dismissed. Or we may say that they have forestalled any need for subtraction by valuing the subtrahend at zero.

If we attempt to reckon honestly with the questions of net progress, we will have to begin by granting a positive value, though it is finally not quantifiable, to the domestic life and the domestic economy lived out day by day on those 1,501 Henry County farms. The positive fact is that in 1945 nearly all the people who lived on those farms, whether owners or tenants or hired help, also lived *from* them, and did so entirely by the employment of various forms of (free) solar energy. This living from the farm involved also the employment of a large set of domestic arts, ranging from the arts of the farm itself—which included the skilled management of workstock and the shares of commercial crops and livestock that went to the home kitchen—to the household arts of food production, preparation, preserving, and cooking. The "consumer goods" they bought for their tables—sugar, spices, coffee, etc.—nearly all were luxuries, things they could have done without. Those people, authentically rural and of the farm, whatever schooling they may have had, however contemptible in the eyes of city people, were in fact highly cultured, knowledgeable, skilled, and capable of using their own minds and hands in their own support. The country arts of self-support were also practiced a good deal in the towns. At that time, in comparison to the present, this county was remarkably self-sufficient. To place a value upon that, though its value can only be approximate, we have only to suggest the possibility—perhaps the probability—that a reasonable measure of local self-sufficiency may be necessary, even now. And so I justify my thought that the agrarian economy, or the economy of the agrarian culture, of Henry County in the time of my boyhood was something right.

That so many people, black and white, were employed at farmwork and the work of supporting themselves directly from farms and gardens meant that many people here not only knew how to do the bodily work necessary to their lives and the keeping of their places, but were reconciled to the difficulties of it. When the work needed to be done, they went ahead and did it, applying their minds to it, without thinking of "something better" that they would rather be doing. A significant number of them were self-employed, unbossed, working on their own initiative in accord with their own standards, and to that extent free. The character and culture of that independent workmanship was handed on even to many people of my own generation by their upbringing. That was something right.

There was far less "mobility" then than there was going to be. There was some moving from house to house or farm to farm within the communities or within the county, and some movement from and to greater distances began with the war. In childhood, in a fairly settled place, we may easily believe that things as they are always were and will always be, and I was blessed by that lovely illusion for a while in my own earliest years, but I believe nevertheless that I can trust my impression that during my young life people were mostly staying put. It was not unusual for people to live all their lives or all their married lives in the same house, or for families to live in the same town or on the same farm for generations. Thus much knowledge of places stayed in place, and that also was something right.

After January 1941 our economy benefitted inestimably from our regional version of the New Deal tobacco program, the Burley Tobacco Growers Co-operative Association, which implemented an entirely salutary and practical combination of production controls and price supports. This gave our farmers, for six decades, an asking price for our staple crop, the one commodity that was produced on every farm. By virtue of that program our farmers' economy was reasonably stable and dependable from year to year; a small farm provided a decent livelihood to its family; and many tenant farmers were able to purchase farms. Because this modest prosperity was the status quo here from early in my life and I took it (mistakenly) for granted, I was slow to see how rare in all the history of farming this program and its practical results were. For a while it supported and confirmed our agrarian identity, which rested upon the art of growing Burley tobacco of high quality. That also was something right. (That program remains a model, despite the stigma that the health issue and addiction finally placed upon tobacco.)

In large part because of "the Burley Program," we mostly were Democrats. We loved Franklin Roosevelt because the New Deal had given us more economic security than we had ever known and, to that extent, "freedom from fear." No doubt we were as much at peace with one another as we were because we were politically so much in agreement. I won't go so far as to call this "something right," but it was a good thing at the time.

The agricultural principles of our tobacco program, production controls and parity pricing, unthinkable now by either political party, operated here as a stabilizing force in the years of my boyhood. The great force of change at the same time was World War II, which began the transformation virtually of everything. It completed and confirmed the dominance of industry and industrial values, which the Civil War had established in manufacturing and in finance, and which other wars had advanced.

World War II vastly increased the demand for military machines, weapons, and munitions, and at the same time of course a corresponding enlargement of the need for factory workers. That raised against the life of the independent, self-sufficient family farmer the bid, often irresistible, of good hourly wages, a limited workday, and freedom from worry or responsibility after quitting time. Factory workers were not going to have to work long anxious days at harvest-time or stake their living against the weather or gamble against markets or be burdened with the care of animals. And so, though our people at home were living lives not yet radically different in artistry, difficulty, or values from the lives of their grandparents, they also were now hearing the siren songs of the cities, the "bright lights" and "good jobs." Their sons and daughters were scattered around the world, becoming accustomed to the violent technologies of industrial war, which soon would be transformed into the technologies of industrial agriculture. The advertisements in newspapers and magazines and on the radio were introducing the theme of "something better." The greatest change in human history since the beginning of commercial farming was upon us. Though we could not yet have understood what was happening to us, we were already becoming a different kind of people. The total industrialization of total war produced a dream of total industrialization that would dominate the national and then the global economy for the rest of that century and on into this one. The manufacture of things soon to be destroyed in war was followed in "peace," according to our by then predestinarian economy, by the manufacture of things to be "consumed": soon to be used up, worn out, outmoded, and thrown away. The American Dream, grown naturally from a "new land" economic democracy, had once been self-employment and self-sufficiency based upon ownership of a family farm or "forty acres and a mule" or a small store or a small shop. From now on it would be first "a good job" in a factory, and then a college degree, sedentary work, and retirement—never mind the submissions implied by the word "employee," or the dependence, virtually total, upon "the economy."

In the years between the end of my boyhood and my conscious acceptance of my vocation, I wandered. I did not, I think, wander pointlessly, for the places I went, and what I saw and learned and thought in those places, became permanently necessary to me, but my wandering at the time was aimless, for I did not yet know what I was going to do. Under the influence of advice, then fairly standard, from teachers and friends whom I respected, I assumed that I was going to wander on from "job" to "job" in support of my "career" as a writer.

My wandering, anyhow, took me long enough and far enough away from home to permit the place I knew as my own and the character of its life as I had known it to declare themselves somewhat fully in my memory and my thoughts. At the end of my wandering, when I had returned home to live, I could see how my local inheritance had been already diminished by the economic-technological-social forces that were subjugating it without the least regard or respect for it. I could see that the industrial system conceded no value at all to the goodness and beauty unique to my rather ordinary rural countryside, or to any of the countless such places in the rest of the world. My understanding of these things has been slow and difficult, but I was coming to see that every good thing my best teachers had taught me to love, along with all of my best inheritance, was now at stake.

My vocation was to be, if I could be, a part of its self-defense—to the extent that it might have a self-defense beyond the goodness and beauty that might be already in it. This involves immediately the question of the difference between defense and salvage, which cannot be avoided or put off or easily answered. I am thinking now, to console myself, of Allen Tate who said, "The task of the civilized intelligence is one of perpetual salvage." That is provocative and useful. To think of my intelligence as "civilized" I would have to resort to more qualification than Mr. Tate might have allowed, but I know that salvage is a part of the process. I don't know—I don't think I need to know—whether the task of salvage is to lead to a survival or restoration of civilization or only to gather to our hearts its remnants to keep them alive during at least one more life-time. But I am comfortable in thinking that I may have, or share in, *domestic* intelligence, for my commitment, really, is to homemaking. I want to gather the precious remnants and carry them home.

7. Two Races in One Place, One Time

In telling, so far, something of my history and of my life within it, I have already shown clearly enough that my past includes two races. My mind, as I know it, descends from both races and the relations between them. I was powerfully influenced by the presence of black people in my community, and particularly by some who were my teachers. That influence was one of my dearest privileges, and I would have missed it altogether if I had been born only a few years later. During and after the war, the black people young enough for city jobs began to move away. The older ones who in their generation had been accomplished farmhands or tenant farmers or farmers went "the way of nature" and disappeared from the farms. When they were gone, farm workmen of their kind, black or white, who possessed the necessary skills and were accepting of the difficulties, were, with some exceptions in the following generation, gone from this world. Most of the younger men, black or white, who for a while took their places, were already oriented to city jobs and were in effect headed elsewhere. People at work in one place with their minds in another were experiencing, though nobody then could have been aware of it, a new and ruinous and ominous subtraction.

As I think back now, I am finding it impossible to make a reliable chronology of this change, but for about a decade past the time of my boyhood there were no more black people at work on the farms where I was at work. It was not until the summer of 1961, when I was twenty-seven, that I worked again, and for the last time, with a black man. This was Jim Henderson, who was then growing a tobacco crop and doing other work on a farm owned by my father. We built a lot of woven wire fence that summer. Jim had my father's entire respect, both for his workmanship and his good sense. I was given to understand that when I worked with Jim I was to take direction from him. My biracial education ended that summer with what was in effect my apprenticeship to Jim. There were several benefits, among them the pleasure of his company. He had a capable, interesting mind, and also a supply of stories, funny and revealing, about people of both races whom both of us knew or remembered.

As I grew up knowing pretty well where I was, I grew up knowing pretty well also a good many people who were here with me. From the time of my birth, the people I knew were of both races. I don't remember not knowing black people just as I don't remember not knowing white people. Black people were employed at farmwork and housework by both sets of my grandparents—not many at either place, but to a child's awakening consciousness they were there, belonging there the same as the white people. When I visited those places, their greetings to me were very much a part of the welcome I received. Between New Castle and Port Royal there were other farms where black people lived and worked, but only a few.

In this country of mine, between New Castle and the river, the black population was concentrated in New Castle. They lived mostly in four distinct neighborhoods, one close to the crossroads in the middle of town, the others on the outskirts. As I remember those neighborhoods, they were racially somewhat mixed.

During my boyhood I don't believe I heard the term "race rela-tions," but throughout those years, though decreasingly, I was *involved* in race relations. In so small a town, populated by two races, the races related. They related all the time, sometimes in some places all day every day. When I walked from home to school in the mornings and from school to somewhere more interesting in the afternoons, I was almost certain to see black people whom I would know.

Race prejudice was publicly instituted among us mainly, if not only, by school segregation. The churches were racially divided, but that was not required by law. Church congregations, after all, had often been racially mixed during slavery. There were other cus-tomary divisions that I think were never deliberately or even very consciously imposed or enforced, but were leftovers from the great division made by slavery. The fundamental rule, not inviolable, was that black and white people did not eat or sleep together. (My wife reminds me, however, that my Port Royal grandmother and her "colored" cook sometimes sat down to eat together after the men had eaten and gone.) Other differences were not so clearly defined. In New Castle, for instance, there were places where white and black men loafed together and places where they did not. That was a difference observed and observable but not, I think, explainable. Some things come about by usage, and for reasons not recoverable. People of the two races, so far as I saw, worked together with no restrictions.

I don't think that what I am calling customary racial prejudice became much of an issue then, for there was never a public con-troversy or scandal to give it prominence. But of course that sort of prejudice lived among us, no doubt on both sides. I assume, on the basis of a good deal of listening, that among white people racial prejudice was felt or manifested in a considerable range of intensities. There were some who would tell you, if in some way prompted, that black people were inferior to white people. There were a good many who used casually the language of prejudice, but also a good many to whom such language amounted to a kind of profanity and who scrupulously avoided it and spoke against it. That is all from the testimony of speech. What people may have thought but did not say is a question of some importance, but unanswerable. Another problem is to know how the prejudgment of either race might weigh against a person who was also known and judged as an individual. I can say that I knew nobody then, and have met very few since then, who hated or feared black people in general, or whose self-esteem appeared to depend on disesteem for black people in general. Not then or later have I known anybody who made race prejudice a political principle in the manner of the twenty-first-century white supremacists and neo-Nazis. In my young life nobody, not the most explicitly prejudiced, ever told me that I should hate or fear black people. Nor, though I have only my own memory to go by, do I remember hearing any black man I knew called "boy."

(I assume that there was some anti-Semitism in the small world of my boyhood, but my own childhood seems to have been unaffected by it. At about the age of nine, I was surprised to learn that I knew a few people who were Jews.)

White children learned the racial differences more or less by absorption as they grew up. That, anyhow, was the way I learned them—except that I was strictly and deliberately instructed to be considerate of black people's feelings. This was enforced to the extent that I recognized my offenses as I made them and remembered them with shame. Black children, I have always assumed, would at some point have had to be instructed about the differences by their elders, and to me this is the realization of those times

that is most painful. The most regrettable cost of school segregation, I think, was the detriment to friendships between black and
white children.

It seems to me generally true to say that, despite the racial differences, people of the place and time I am remembering knew one
another familiarly. The black people, I am pretty sure, knew us better than we knew them. Even so, we knew, and were known by, one
another. There can be of course no generalizing about the relationships of individuals, which varied, as one would expect, from hate
to love, from indifference to respect. And we come to the humbling
thought that any generalization about race relations—or human
relations—may be endlessly qualified.

For me, partly because of my own growing up and continuing
thought and partly because of the history of race relations during
most of my life, a hesitancy has come to bear on my memories of
my early relationships with black people. Because of school segregation, most of those I knew best were grownups. From my own point
of view at that time, those relationships had the character only of
a child's uncomplicated feelings. My affection or love for certain
black people seems to me to have been about as straightforward
and unconditional as my affection or love for certain white people.
But for a long time I have known that I cannot know how my relationships with my black elders may have been qualified, for them,
by racial difference. This cuts the authority of my testimony precisely in half, and I must proceed with a measure of doubt, a measure of caution, and a measure of courtesy. I can say, as I have and
will, that Bill White and Nick Watkins and Aunt Georgie Ashby
were and are yet among my friends, and I can say that their friend-

ship to me was shown by acts of kindness that I vividly remember. But my mind then was new to the world, and their minds had been made by long histories nearly all of which, except for what they told me, I did not and do not know. I feel this strongly as a problem of my racial history now, while I am writing these pages. But of course this limitation applies just as insistently to my relationships with white people and especially with my white elders. My authority in bearing witness, in "speaking for myself," is impaired inevitably by my ignorance of other people, even of people who are dearest to me. I can solemnly swear to tell half the truth, more or less.

I think that the most questionable term in our language may be the verb "to know." Did I know my elders, black and white, whom I knew when I was a child? Well, I reply, not nearly as well as I know them now that I am old. I say that with some confidence, and I feel the tremor of it in my heart. But I am obliged to consider that what I know from childhood is only what I remember, and I am separated now by a lifetime from those elders and that child. How much of what I know of them have I imagined or supposed? It may be that my knowledge of my elders then is made true by the love I have for them now. And so I have come, not for the first time, to the likelihood that we know some things by means of love that we cannot otherwise know, and even that we know in the fullest sense only what we love, and that we love and know in the fullest sense only what we have imagined. I am bearing in mind also John Lukacs's assurance that "there are myriad instances and examples when understanding precedes knowledge, indeed, when it *leads* to knowledge." Yes. Probably we are obliged to concede some of the ground of knowledge to a child's understanding. Children always understand more than they know, which may account for the preference given to them by Jesus.

My impression that the settled life of my small home country in the years I am remembering was shared by the two races is, however, supported to some extent by a few friendships and acquaintances that outlasted that time, and by the interest and pleasure with which I have heard some older black people remembering it. Not long ago I went along on a bus tour of the black people's old schools and graveyards here in my county, and I was much impressed by the pleasure and affection with which the older black members of the tour spoke their memories. One of the principal guides, a black man a little younger than I am, said a number of times, "Those were the good old days." Though he knew well the cost to him and his people of the racial difference, he was remembering the eventful life of the more numerous black community of his early years, and also his participation in the farm life of that time when the farms were thriving.

The truly raw and blatant race prejudice of my childhood was against the Axis of World War II. The boys in my grade at school, if I am remembering us correctly, were little attracted to hatred of the Italians, who did not figure prominently in the comic books we read or the adult conversations we overheard. Our fear and hatred of the Germans, though strong and constant, was less than our fear and hatred of the Japanese. Not one of us had ever seen anybody who was Japanese, and so our prejudice was not modified by the least scrap of knowledge. We found no reason to consider that we and they belonged to the same species. We took their caricature in comic books and cartoons to be photographically true. We thought they were uniformly bucktoothed, slant-eyed, weak-eyed, and as yellow as canaries. At recess we boys played a wargame we called "Japs and Americans." I think we must have designated the Japanese without notifying them, which did not matter for we fought no actual battles. We believed that the Japanese soldiers were naturally cruel, as our own were naturally good-hearted. It is touching now, in view of recent history, to remember how proud we were to think that our soldiers did not torture prisoners. That of course reinforced our prejudice, which was total.

And so in our ignorance and innocence we were at one with our government in its "internment" of a hundred thousand Japanese Americans in concentration camps as a "military necessity," suspending habeas corpus, civil rights, and the best of our humanity—as had happened in our own state during the Civil War, but of course we did not know that. We did not know how frail the best of our humanity might become in the face of some version of "necessity." Knowledge of such things, once we have it, ought to tell us that a personal or a customary prejudice can be brought to a terrible perfection by being made official. Such knowledge also should give us a healthy uncertainty about the location of virtue in politics and war.

Something else that is bothering me in this writing is the question of what to call those nonwhite people who were so much a part of the life of my home country, of my own early life, and of the memories I keep alive. I have been calling them "black people," but uneasily, for in the days when we knew one another that was not what they called themselves. I believe that they would have heard "black" as an insult, the same as "darky." If asked to classify themselves I believe they would have said "Negro," a word that, whoever said it, always seemed to me to be stiffened by almost a technical correctitude. The black people I knew in my boyhood called themselves "colored people" or "coloreds" and well-meaning white people also used those terms. But *every* categorical name is a loose fit and an embarrassment. Nobody, after all, is more than approximately white or black.

And so I feel that I am making a point of particular significance when I say that in the time and place of my boyhood we of the two races knew one another. Despite the customary prejudices and differences that had been with us so long, we knew one another personally—by voice and appearance, by stance and demeanor, by family, by stories. We did not see one another as representatives or specimens of our races. We thought, "That is Helen" or "That is Henry," not "That is a colored person." Thus, to an extent, we were freed from categories and from categorical thought. We judged one another, despite prejudice in various degrees, as we individually were, and on the basis of particular knowledge—not because of any virtue or desire to be virtuous, but necessarily because we lived daily and ordinarily in the same small place. (I am asked, "didn't you categorize strangers?" I don't know. So far as I remember, "stranger" was not a word we often used. We did not often encounter strangers.)

I would not have been so much aware of this old mutuality except for the demise here of small-scale, diversified, year-round farming and its partial replacement by one- or two-crop larger acreages depending, when extra help is needed, on the seasonal labor of migrants, chiefly from Mexico. This dependence on racially designated menial workers obviously repeated our old mistake. But this time we were making use of people with whom we shared almost nothing. In addition to the difference of race, there were differences of language, culture, and history, along with the great personal difference of our strangeness to one another, which could not be amended in brief, temporary, purely economic relationships. When they are here, those people are needed, for they are replacing the great majority of our own people who no longer will or can work with their own hands, and who therefore are not "losing their jobs to immigrants." And so here, as apparently in other farming areas where they are needed, the migrant workers have received some appreciation. Farmers, I think, pretty generally know that the American people would be in danger of starving if it were not for immigrant laborers. It is a measure of our people's ignorance of farming that nationally and politically so many seem easily to look down on migrant workers—as we always easily look down on people we depend on to do the kinds of work we think we are too good, too important, or too smart to do for ourselves. Now, for instance, many of us look down on farmers, and on "rural Americans" in general.

In this place at the time of my boyhood, by contrast, we were not dealing with one another as strangers. Granting even prejudice and difference, we were to a considerable and significant extent one people, who belonged together, even to one another. There is nothing wistful or sentimental in my saying this. Our two races—we both, we all—shared much the same knowledge of the same place. We shared the same language, many of the same memories and stories. There was a necessary sharing of knowledge of the kinds of work that we did. We professed versions of the same religion, read and quoted the same Bible in the King James translation, and sang many of the same hymns. We had come to be as we were and to live as we lived because of 165 years (in 1940) of the same history.

"The same history," I said, and I am fully aware of the duality of that phrase. People who are gathered together by a shared history can at the same time be divided by it. But I think that our sharing a native place, language, knowledge, and experience was good, both for what it was and for the good that was potential in it. That goodness—authenticated by age and wear, little acknowledged then, little valued now—makes obvious by comparison the superficiality of the division by complexion.

If we had stayed together, it seems to me that the old mutuality of our shared life might have been helped fundamentally by school integration following the Supreme Court decision of 1954. I was not much in New Castle at that time, but not long ago an elderly black man (elderly, but younger than I am) told me how naturally, because they were in school together, he had made friends with New Castle white boys. I took pleasure in hearing that, but it made me sad too. For by 1954 the old life of the place was breaking up. A lot of black families had moved away. A lot of the graduates of the integrated school would move away or work away. The local communities were losing their centripetal force.

The one what-if that is irresistible to me—and is necessary to the sense I am trying to make—is this: What if the population of the New Castle community had kept the same racial proportions and remained stable during the eighty-one years since 1940 and the sixty-seven years since 1954? What if, in other words, an aim of the national economy had been the maintenance all over the country of such land- and people-conserving communities as New Castle's was, even imperfect as it was, in 1940? Might we not have done much more, in that event, to heal our racial wounds than we have been able to do in the midst of the prevailing fractures? And might our land and our people be in all ways healthier than they are now?

Those questions are not an exercise in wishful thinking, for they imply another question that is substantive and urgent: How is it possible for us to submit our lives and our shared life to the determinism of unlimited economic competition and unlimited technological innovation and yet preserve the values and rights necessary to the life of a community?

8. *About Several People*

It may have been natural, anyhow more or less expectable, that some time ago hearing a report on the radio of an angry and somewhat violent confrontation after the killing of a black man by a white policeman, I thought, "Those people don't know each other." That thought was reflexive—it just came to me—but it came nevertheless out of my belief, growing over many years, in the importance of people knowing one another, of being willing to know one another, of meeting face-to-face, eye to eye, and speaking to one another, in conversation of course, which I hold to be necessary and precious, but also familiarly in the way of decent manners and goodwill: "How you today?" "Fine. How you making it?"

I thought, "Those people don't know each other." And to test myself I picked up a pad of paper and in about twenty minutes wrote the names of seventy black people I had known mainly in and between Port Royal and New Castle, mainly in the time of my growing up. Those were people I knew by name, by stance and gait, some of them also by family and stories. Some I merely knew, some I liked, some I held in awe and kept a distance from, some I loved. I am going to gather up a collection of things I remember myself, and some I remember that other people remembered and told me. I will never claim to know the whole significance of what has been remembered, but I trust that remembrance itself is a sign of significance. We remember things that have mattered to us, though we may not know why they mattered.

At the top of my list, if I had tried to order it according to affection, would have been Nick Watkins and Aunt Georgie Ashby. I wrote at length about them in *The Hidden Wound* fifty years ago. And so I will say here only enough to suggest their importance to me. Nick Watkins taught me to drive a team of mules and gave me a great deal of knowledge and lore related to that art. Now, a lifetime later, when I speak to a team I speak to them in Nick's language. And so I have often been reminded of him by the presence of his speech in my own mind and mouth, and I remember him with love and gratitude. From Aunt Georgie I received my first explicit instruction in race relations and racial wrong. She had not had, I think, much formal schooling, but she could read the Bible, which she understood literally and vividly. Her instruction carried the force of her character, which was considerable. She is near me yet in this writing, which proceeds directly from what she told me a lifetime ago.

Starting from my memories of Nick Watkins and Aunt Georgie, I have written in my fiction about a black couple named Dick Watson and Aunt Sarah Jane. This has placed my memories in the somewhat greater amplitude and light of imagination. Practically, for example, it has permitted me to write dialogue without fretting too much about the possible dishonesty of approximation. But imagination also has informed me of the limits of what I can responsibly know even with the help of imagination.

Next I want to remember Bill White, who worked all his life for my mother's family in Port Royal. His parents were Bet and Joe who worked for my great-grandparents, M. B. and Nannie Perry. I don't know whether Joe White was born on their place or came there, and I don't know the names of Joe's parents or anything about them. I know that Joe was a man who expected to be taken seriously, and was taken very seriously by a young man who came to court Sallyetta, Joe's daughter. If I am remembering correctly, the young man's departure was inspired by a near-miss on the part of Joe's pistol. My uncle Jimmy told me that Joe tied a broken iron-stone pitcher into the top of a tree at the top of a ridge well away from the farm buildings. He said, "That's where I communicate with my honorable ancestors in the upper elements." My uncle told me that when the Port Royal children put on a backyard circus, one of the acts was Joe White dancing on the top of a table. I believe that those memories are all I heard of Joe, whom I never knew. Of Bet I have one memory: a large woman waving cheerfully through a window of my grandparents' washhouse.* I know that her father was Uncle Al Wing, and that she always wore a frilled cap.

My memory of Bet comes from very early in my life, maybe from my third year. Soon after that, because she was a member of my great-grandparents' generation, her place as household help for my grandmother was taken by Bill's wife, Florence. Florence was a small, good-humored person, always busy and, so far as I knew, always kind. When I went to visit my grandparents I would go straight to the kitchen to be greeted by Florence, who would dependably be smiling and would dependably say, "Why hello there, Wendell Berry." Her help was much needed by my grandmother, who herself stayed steadily busy. That was a large, hospitable house where there was always company: visiting relatives and old friends, visiting preachers who would be conducting a revival at one or the other of the two churches, and sometimes virtual strangers who "turned up." There would be a big breakfast and a big dinner (the main meal, at noon). If there was company, those meals would be served in the dining room. After the family and guests had eaten, in the dining room or kitchen, Florence would set two places at the kitchen table, Bill would come in, and the two of them would sit down together for their own unhurried meal. When the dinner

---

*A small outbuilding for washing clothes.

dishes were washed and put away and the kitchen set to rights, Florence would walk home, down through the large pasture that was reserved for the work mules and the milk cows.

My knowledge of Bill in the time of his strength began with my and my brother's childhood visits, when we would go to the fields or barns with him and other grownups who might be on hand, to play while they worked. So long as we minded and stayed out of the way, we boys were included. At times we were pointedly and generously included. I remember a day before the war when Bill and his brother, Nathaniel, made each of us a sort of kite by tying longish sewing threads to the legs of two June bugs. It was delightful to hold one end of the thread while your June bug flew at the other end. But you had to keep him away from the bushes.

Bill was a man of about medium height, strongly made, without an ounce of fat. He was capable of joking and laughing, but within limits. There was his own kind of fastidiousness in the way he wore his work clothes and set his lips together, in the way he used his hands and handled tools or a pocketknife or a rifle. I know from much that I saw and heard that he was a skilled, versatile, faithful worker. He could work a team. When the tractors came, he could use a tractor. He could use all of the many hand tools of farming. Like many farmers, he was something of a mechanic and something of a carpenter. He kept my grandparents' house supplied with coal for the furnace and drinking water from the cistern at the barn. Night and morning he milked the two or three Jersey cows, brought my grandparents' milk to an enclosed back porch, poured it into the cream separator, and carried his own bucket of milk to his house. He cultivated his own big garden beside my grandfather's. With my family and his, he helped to kill and work up several hogs every fall and had his share of the meat. If a fence was being built and a posthole needed to go through rock to be deep enough, it would be Bill who took the lead in using the hand drill, Bill who measured and fused and tamped in the charge of dynamite, Bill who lit the fuse. In the ongoing care and maintenance of the place, he did not always wait to be told. One day my uncle Jimmy found Bill, old and mortally sick, replacing one of the posts that underpinned the corncrib.

I always knew that Bill was a hunter. When he went to work he sometimes would have his rifle with him. He would then be on the lookout, as I now suppose, for a young groundhog as table fare, or perhaps for a stray dog. The rifle was a .22 that he handled like a musical instrument, its stock and barrel wiped clean with an oiled rag.

He was mainly a hunter of squirrels, which he loved for their ways and their flesh. From the time when the year's young ones would begin poaching corn from the fields' edges and then "cutting hickory nuts," he would know what they were up to and where to find them. From the back door of his small house, he had to walk only a few steps until he would be in the streambed of one of the tributaries of Camp Branch and in the woods. This was his domain and an entry into it that he had made thousands of times since he was a small boy.

After I had grown up enough to have my own .22 rifle and the interests that went with it, Bill took me squirrel hunting with him a number of times. That was when I became his student. Though he never explicitly said so, it was immediately clear to me that he allowed me to go with him on the condition that I came as his student. I was to walk behind him, paying him the closest attention, and do exactly as he said. If we were to walk quietly, which was usually his intention once we were under the trees, I was the last thing he wanted on his mind. When I was a child he might joke with me or befriend me or ignore me. When I presented myself to him as a grownup and a hunting companion, that was a different matter. If I wanted to be his companion I would have to accept him as my teacher. He didn't want to hear me walking. If I stepped on a dry stick or made any other audible mistake, he would turn and with his flattened hand, palm down, make an emphatic downward stroke. And so he taught me to watch where I stepped, an important lesson that I never fully learned. Sometimes too he would see a squirrel who had seen us and was keeping perfectly still, high up in a tree and almost hidden among the leaves. Bill would point, and then watch me with a smile both indulgent and critical until I saw it for myself. And so he taught me, with exemplary patience, to look until I saw, an invaluable lesson that I started then to learn, and have never ceased trying to learn better.

Almost certainly some people now will suggest that Bill and other black people treated me kindly because, as hired help of my family, they were obliged to do so. I can reply by saying that it is no trouble even for a child to tell the difference between obligatory deference and kindness freely given.

In the summer of 1957, the first of my marriage, my grandmother told me that Bill was sick, had not long to live, and I needed to go see him. By then I had experienced maybe my full share of the deaths of people I knew and of loved ones, but not enough, even so, to be accustomed to it or to have the manners for it. I did not at all want to go see Bill, knowing that I would not again see him alive in this world, of which he had been for me so significant a part. But my grandmother had spoken in a way that informed me of my duty and of her expectation that I would do it.

I walked down through the pasture to Bill's house, crossed the porch, and knocked on the door. He called, "Come in," and I went in.

He was lying on a narrow cot that had been placed in front of the chimneypiece on the inner wall of one of the front rooms, where it may have been easier to care for him. But from there also he could look out through the front door at the pasture, the passing animals, and the path going up to the barn. The house and its furnishings bore the marks of long use, but also of long keeping and care. The room where Bill lay was spotless and neat. The bedclothes of his cot were neat, perfectly tucked in and smoothed over his body.

He welcomed me cheerfully, smiling, was glad to see me, comforted me by asking how I was and what I had been doing. His grace and hospitality accepted my awkwardness and discomfort, put me at ease, and were a wonder to me. I don't remember any of the words that passed between us then. I felt, as my grandmother had required me to feel, that I owed him a duty. When I felt I had performed it, I found the words I needed to wish him well and tell him goodbye. He said goodbye to me, smiling still, and let me go as freely as he had invited me to come in.

Looking back so far at my dealings with my elders of Bill's generation, I am sometimes obliged to regard my youth as itself a sort of misdemeanor. Now, I believe I know how to visit Bill on his deathbed. I could have pulled over a chair and sat a while close beside him. I could have said, "Bill, I remember the times you took me hunting, and I'll always thank you." I could have asked, "Is there anything you need that I can do for you?" And now, as always with the dead, there are many other questions I wish I could ask him.

Having renewed my remembrances of Bill White, and given him his due of respect and affection, I want to tell a fragment of his story that says much, and withholds more, of the history and character of race relations in Port Royal. This comes, I believe, from about 1920 or a year or two before. Another man, a white man, who worked for my grandfather at that time was Ed Berry. There were many Berrys in Port Royal then, and Ed was at some remove a relative of mine. I came along just soon enough to remember him. He was a tall, lean man who wore bib overalls and a felt hat with a pushed-up crown. The tall hat, from my lowly point of view, seemed to increase his height by about a third. As he crossed the backyard on his way to or from my grandfather's barn, he looked down upon me with a smile and no doubt an appropriate amusement.

At the time I am recalling, Bill White and Ed Berry were much younger than when I knew them and were pretty seriously at odds. I never heard the reason for their quarrel, but it had acquired some history and was established and recognized in the town. Because of it, each man was carrying a pistol in his pocket, and they were not speaking. I imagine they did not look at each other if they could help it. This became a considerable problem for other people, chiefly perhaps for my grandfather, and mainly when Bill and Ed had to work together: when, for instance, they both needed to go into the mill shed to grind corn for the cattle. The mill was powered by a primitive gasoline engine, with flywheels four or five feet in diameter, and a long belt. It was extremely noisy. In such circumstances, the principled noncommunication between Bill and Ed was about as dangerous as it was unproductive. To solve this problem, my grandfather would send my uncle Morgan, then eight or ten years old, to the mill shed with them to carry messages. If, then, Bill needed to say something to Ed, he would speak to my uncle who would speak to Ed.

That is every bit I know of that story. As I know it and have told it, it certainly raises questions that it does not answer. To me it is nonetheless a valuable story. Because I know that Bill never shot at Ed or Ed at Bill, I see their quarrel and my uncle's message-carrying as comedy, and I laugh when I remember it. It is valuable also as an example of the way knowledge works in a settled community. I think my grandfather pretty thoroughly knew Ed Berry and Bill White. He must have known pretty confidently that their quarrel was not headed for a shooting, or he would not have sent his son as a go-between. It is valuable finally because it shows the inadequacy of the clichés and stereotypes of "southern" race relations in the presence of particular people in a particular place—in, for instance, the freedom of the two participants in this biracial feud to carry pistols, as everybody knew they did.

The same goes, I think, for another story of race relations in Port Royal. According to this one, a black lady teaching in the colored school (long gone by my time) snatched up a white boy, and gave him a good whipping. This story likewise raises a question it does not answer. Not too long ago, when Port Royal still retained a staff of native old men to loaf and talk at the store, I heard the question raised and an answer proposed:

"What you reckon she whipped him for?"

"Well, I imagine he said something disrespectful about black people."

After my parents left my father's home place and settled us into a small rented house in New Castle in 1936, the first person who came to cook for us was Helen Harris. Helen was a young black woman who no doubt was a good helper to my mother, but to me she made herself dear by her company and her conversation. She loved to talk, and she must have talked well or I would not so well remember her or so much of what she said. She was full of stories, songs, riddles, and rhymes, and of what I suppose we might call *lore*. She told of a mother who killed her children and to hide their corpses ground them into sausage, but she could not hide her crime from *herself*, for the souls of her children came to her in the form of a little bird who sang to her of what she had done. Helen told this so that I could *see* it. As extreme as this was, I don't remember being frightened by it. As she told it, it somehow got fitted in with the rest of ordinary reality.

She also taught me this:

> Wendell the bendell the teedledy tendell,
> Teelegged, toelegged, bowlegged Wendell.

You could go on with that endlessly, feeding in the names of everybody you knew or had heard of, names of more than two syllables being sometimes a problem. And from her I learned also this:

> Momma, Momma, have you heard,
> Poppa's gonna buy me a mockin' bird,
>
> And if that mockin' bird don't sing,
> Poppa's gonna buy me a golden ring,
>
> And if that golden ring turns brass,
> Poppa's gonna buy me a lookin' glass,
>
> And if that lookin' glass gets broke,
> Poppa's gonna buy me a billy goat,

And if that billy goat don't trot,
Poppa's gonna buy me a house and lot,

And if that house and lot don't suit,
Poppa's gonna buy me a shoe and a boot . . .

and so on apparently forever, if you could keep finding the rhymes. That, as Helen performed it, was not sung but chanted with heavy stresses, like a rope-jumping rhyme. To us then, those rhymes were funny because of their silliness. To me now, it seems a perfect anthem for the consumer economy: a purchase followed by disappointment followed by a purchase, on and on forever.

Maybe a couple of years after she started working at our house, Helen married Henry Brown. And a year or two after that, when I was five or six years old, she and Henry moved to Dayton, Ohio, I suppose for the sake of industrial jobs. By then the country-to-city migration was not a new thing to my grownups, but it was new to me and also a sorrow. I liked especially Helen, but Henry too, and I missed them. I never saw them again, and I have always wondered what happened to them.

One of the legendary figures of my earliest years in New Castle— and not just to me but to all the town—was a black man named Big Sam Henderson. Big Sam was enormous and enormously strong. I can't remember now how many fried chickens he was said to eat at a sitting, but it was several, and he was famous for that. He was famous also for his work, all the kinds of work he could do and was good at. I know that he was in demand as a plasterer of the inner walls of houses, and also as a slaughterer of animals. I remember hearing that he could wrap one arm about the neck of a big calf and hold it while he knocked it in the head. He also collected junk, I suppose in his going about to his other work.

When my brother and I were small boys, Big Sam would sometimes drive his horse and spring wagon through the alley past our house. If we saw him we would run out, calling to him to stop. He would stop, greeting us and smiling. Our mother would give us a lift, he would reach down a hand, and we would ride with him wherever he was going. I have no idea where he took us or how our mother got us back, but it was a fine ride. Sometimes he would be wearing a bloody apron, and rusty pieces of scrap iron would be lying in the bed of his wagon.

"Big Sam," we would say, "what makes you so fat?"

And he would say, "Mush and milk, boys! Mush and milk!"

Another person distinctly outstanding and upstanding in that world at that time was Miss Hattie Clarkson, the teacher of the New Castle "colored school." She was "Miss Hattie" to white people as well as to black people, the "Miss" attached both as a title of respect and almost as a first name, as if she had been "Miss Hattie" from birth. She was spare, straight, and austerely elegant, her hat set firmly and formally upon her head. Her bearing and demeanor, so dignified and so reserved, made her a sort of monument, even an edifice. I never heard her speak, for I could not have brought myself to speak to her. I regarded her with a distant awe. From about the third grade I was often a bad boy in school. My awe of Miss Hattie had to do with my conviction that in her school I would have behaved myself.

In addition to the other things he was, my father was a lawyer. His office was on the second floor of a building directly across the street from the courthouse. And so I knew him familiarly as my father and also by his reputation in the town. I knew that he was respected because of the frequency with which I was told by men I encountered, "Boy, your daddy ain't no count."

In those days some men would almost customarily greet boys with some egregious untruth. This was both a test and a strategy of conversation. I learned early that "your daddy ain't no count" was a compliment. If I shrugged it off, the compliment would have been received, perhaps to the credit of both my father and his appraiser. But if, by some great good fortune, I agreed, the news of that would have spread all over town, accompanied by much laughter.

But even if I and my fellow boys were sophisticated enough sometimes to resist such baiting by the men, our world was to a remarkable extent superstitious. Some of us at least had achieved a sort of nobility of gullibility. We believed anything that seemed to come to us with authority, even if the authority was mostly our own belief. If Callis Robbison, whose father's name was Lying Robbison, said his father said he had seen the ghost of a white bear, not a one of us asked a question or expressed a doubt. We believed devotedly in the real-world lives of singing cowboys and the superheroes of comic books. We elaborated by mere speculation and enthusiasm a sexual lore that had nothing whatever to do with sex—except for our certain knowledge that the birds and animals "did it," and that our parents had "done it" at least once for every child they had. My own parents in fact had endeavored to give me the facts of the matter, which I found too dull to be believed.

And so when I was seven or eight years old and one of my peers revealed to me that my father, because he was a lawyer, was therefore rich, I simply believed him, and I caught from him the idea that having a rich father was something that I had achieved. I felt so enlarged by this knowledge that I knew I could keep it to myself only by being selfish, and I began looking for somebody to tell it to. I already knew this was wrong. My father had told me and would tell me again that I was not to go about speaking boastfully, or even truthfully, about my advantages, such as getting more presents at Christmas than some of my friends. But I knew less in that moment than I was about to learn.

The first likely audience I came to was three black men of about my father's age who were loafing in front of Dutton's Garage. They were talking, resting, enjoying themselves, standing in a row and leaning back against the brick wall. Maybe I thought that, being black people in New Castle and therefore not rich, they would be impressed.

And so I stopped in front of them and came right out with it: "My daddy's rich."

And one of those men looked straight back at me and in just about the same tick of the clock said, "Well! I believe I just might ought to kidnap you."

They all three laughed, and I was instantly more deeply ashamed of myself than probably I had ever been before and have rarely been since.

I think that this is one of the best examples of what I meant when I said we knew one another. According to the stereotype prevailing now, a black man who openly proposed to kidnap a white child south of the Ohio River in 1941 or 1942 would have put his life at stake. But the man who answered me had not lowered his voice, he and his two companions had openly laughed, and not one of the four of us was the least bit afraid. I knew that my answerer was not going to kidnap me, and he knew I knew it. Probably he also knew pretty exactly what my father would have thought of my boast. All four of us, moreover, knew perfectly and immediately that I would never tell a soul. And in fact I never told a soul until I got sense enough finally to join their laughter.

9. Something Neighborly

I am going to tell a story about my father that is necessary to complete this history of race relations in my home country and my life, and I approach this task with some hesitation. That is because I am aware that, now, the bare facts of my father's life—a white man born in Kentucky in 1900, thirty-five years after the Civil War, into a family that had owned some slaves—will cause him, by some people, to be easily condemned. And so, to begin the story, I want to tell a little about him.

He was, as I have said, a lawyer in "rural America," which makes him subject of course to yet another stereotype or two, and other prejudices. I am remembering now an article in a literary journal that condemned one of its subjects for being "as narrow-minded as a small-town lawyer." My father, however, liked to introduce himself as "a country lawyer," especially when he had a case in Louisville. That would be his ambush if his opponent happened to subscribe to the stereotype.

It took me many years, maybe it has taken me all my life so far, to understand the kind of lawyer and the kind of man my father was. If in his time you were a country lawyer in a country you had lived in all your life, in which you knew at least something about everybody, and if you were resolved to love your neighbor as yourself whether you did or did not, and if you were tender enough under your crust to love them, even if you did not, when they came to you troubled, then you belonged in effect to anybody who knew you and needed your help. And so you would hear yourself saying, because you could not not-say, "Don't worry about it. I'll take care of it." You would hear yourself dispensing legal advice to your neighbor the barber while he was cutting your hair. You would spend hours of your life listening, or not listening but nonetheless waylaid, to people needing to hear themselves tell you what they wanted you to tell them. You would spend other precious hours forever lost in helping a client run up a fee that you already knew you would never collect.

I was talking with my brother, John, not long before his death, about the practice of a country lawyer and all that it entailed. I said I was sure that our father had earned a lot of money that he was never paid. John, also a country lawyer, said that both he and our father had probably collected about half of what more professional lawyers would have charged. He said that our father could never bring himself to charge by the hour. "Suppose I solve a case while I'm shaving." To decide what to charge, he considered what his time and work were worth, and then he considered what he knew his client could afford, and adjusted accordingly.

The largest, most continuous work of his life he performed in collaboration with many others. This was the reorganization under the New Deal and then the maintenance and political defense of the Burley Tobacco Growers Co-operative Association. My father served the Burley Association for thirty-four years, as vice president and as president, until his retirement in 1975, and then informally on the telephone at night, for ten or so years after that.

This organization was expectably the effort of white men. But it gave exactly the same benefit to its black members as to the white. This I think is significant. A farmer became a member of the Co-op by the ownership of the tobacco allotment attached to his farm. It was my father's principle, with him almost an instinct, to look past workers to the quality of their work. In his latter years he spoke with affection and respect of the black farmhands he had known in his boyhood, and with gratitude for all they had taught him about work and other things.

I knew my father for fifty-seven years. He had high standards of work and responsibility. We both were incapable of concealing our faults, and we shared several. During my college years and until I was about thirty, we were often at odds. In his dealings with me he could be both extremely demanding and extremely tender, and he kept me on probation, so to speak, for a long time. But his approval of my work, when he finally gave it, point-blank as usual, was and is more dear to me than any other. He was the most interesting man I have ever known, and I loved him no end.

And now I will tell the story about him that I need to tell.

Maybe fifteen years ago I was signing books in a Louisville bookstore. When a black woman came to my table she did not have a book. She had a question:

"Are you Mr. John Berry's son?"

"Yes, I am."

"Well, I thought so, and I had to come. Your daddy stood behind my daddy and helped him buy our farm. You know it was hard for our people to borrow money, and your daddy made it all right with the bank."

Her father, she said, was Elzie Jones. I had not known him, but she named two of his brothers, and I remembered both of them.

A book-signing is a bad social occasion, for me always uncomfortable and distracting. I have quoted, to my regret, just about all of that conversation.

And then in Dayton, Ohio, in 2013 I met that woman's brother, Elzie Jones's son, Charles Jones, who remembered the story of my father's help to his father, and who liked his memories of going with his father to my father's office. This was at a public literary event, no better for actual conversation than a book-signing. But he gave me his card: "Charles A. Jones, The Dayton Foundation, Chair, Corporate Boards Subcommittee for the Greater Dayton Commission on Minority Inclusion." I told him where I live and asked him to come to see me if ever he was passing by.

That probably was another conversation not to be resumed. Probably Charles Jones and I both thought it unlikely that we would see each other again. All of us nowadays know, like Robert Frost, "how way leads on to way," and we feel the sorrow of it. But I had and still have, nevertheless, some questions I wish I could have asked Charles Jones. I would like to know if he knew Helen and Henry Brown and other members of Helen's family after they arrived in Dayton. I would like to know how they fared, and if they looked homeward from up there with relief or affection or regret. I believe a good many black people moved from here to Dayton during the 1940s in search of something better, and I wonder what they found.

I have anyhow the testimony of Elzie Jones's children about my father's help to their father. In light of other things I know about my father, their story does not surprise me, but it does solidly confirm the possibility, perhaps the likelihood, that a white man could look through his history to recognize a black man as worthy of the help he needed. And surely in one version of the human conversation I am keeping in mind, two neighbors who know each other meet, one asks for help, and the other gives it.

10. Degrees

My title for this chapter is "Degrees of Prejudice," which I believe is a real subject but one extremely difficult to talk about. We are dealing, it seems, with amounts verifiable by experience but impossible to quantify. I am sure that anybody with some breadth of experience and a modicum of consciousness will know that prejudice necessarily manifests itself in degrees. In the course of these pages I have not often used that term, but I have spoken of many particular events, interactions, and relationships, many of which displayed a degree or intensity of prejudice probably different from any of the others. In no instance, I think, is the prejudice absolute. Even the anonymous threatening "notice" to my great-grandfather is not absolute, for it has the character of a particular person in a particular place and time, raising possibly mitigating issues and questions. The stereotype of racial prejudice, by contrast, is racism, an absolute. The only telling thing my several instances have in common may be that by their differences of degree they dissolve the stereotype, showing how little it explains.

Or we could say, maybe more usefully, that all prejudices, negative and positive, are generalizations, stereotypes of one kind or another. I suppose we should acknowledge that a stereotype can be dissolved, to a degree, even by personal animosity. But I think that only neighborliness entirely dissolves stereotypes by setting them entirely aside. The "good Samaritan" of Luke 10:30–37 may well have been prejudiced against Jews, but the Jew he saw by the wayside was a man fallen among thieves, who had robbed and beaten him and left him half dead. The Samaritan saw in that man not a Jew but a neighbor. Your "neighbor," literally, is "somebody who lives near you," but the word is defined in Luke as "somebody who needs your help." The Samaritan, then, "had compassion" on this neighbor, "went to him, and bound his wounds . . . and took care of him."

That prejudice exists in degrees identifies it as a human affliction, and suggests moreover that all humans, to some degree, are afflicted by it. Prejudice, carefully induced, motivates soldiers to kill one another in wars. It also causes some well-meaning people to assume that all who are in some way oppressed would be virtuous, sensible, and responsible if only they were not oppressed. In either case prejudice precludes authentic knowledge, therefore authentic judgment, therefore any appreciable degree of justice. It distorts or counterfeits reality. One enacts the only remedy when, as a neighbor, one looks through one's prejudice or brushes it aside, to see the face of a neighbor, an actual neighbor, worthy or unworthy, who in any event will have to be dealt with as a person, not as a representative of some category.

Of race relations here in my home country in a time now gone, though I know a good deal from experience and hearsay, all I am willing to attest without qualification is that we knew one another. My father and Elzie Jones knew each other and had apparently with some care judged each other. In this place, in that former time when neighborliness to a considerable degree mattered, they were neighbors. My father's help to Elzie Jones and the gratitude of Elzie Jones and his children to my father were and remain manifestations of neighborliness.

I think we can say with certainty that their story confirms the real value, the practical and economic value, of our knowledge of one another and of our place. Elzie Jones knew that he could ask my father for help. My father would have known, he would have needed to know, not only the worthiness of Elzie Jones but also, like Elzie Jones, the worth and worthiness of the farm he wanted to buy. That common knowledge, the product of many years of common history and experience here in our mutual home country, was a precious resource. So was the old and until then long-continued wish to possess one's own small farm or shop or store, and to be to that extent the master of one's fate, able to be of use both to oneself and to others.

Those resources, all depending on our already somewhat developed willingness even across the racial difference to live as neighbors, could have been more consciously cherished and nourished and improved. That, however, was an opportunity soon lost—if temporarily, as I hope, at least until a time yet to come—because after World War II the farm economy, even with the tobacco program, could not compete with the industrial economy. Floating upon the great incoming wave of industrial values—mechanical efficiency, economies of scale, speed, volume, labor-saving, technological change ("progress"), the desirability of something else—the law of neighborly love could not retain the limited power it had.

In the decline of neighborhood and neighborliness—accompanied necessarily by the decline of social, ecological, and economic health—we may finally recognize a starting place, such as we came to and did not recognize in the ruins after the Civil War, but having now, as then, less to start with than before.

CHAPTER IV

⁓

Sin

The Senate hearing on the nomination of Brett Kavanaugh to the Supreme Court, like that on the nomination of Clarence Thomas nearly thirty years before, revealed starkly how little of the means of concern and care our society now interposes between individual persons and what we know as "the public." On both occasions a committee of senators was expected, or they expected themselves, to deal competently with a woman's allegation of sexual aggression by the nominee. So far as the public was able or enabled to see, no such competence was available. The only witnesses on view were the accuser and the accused.

Neither of these proceedings could be, properly speaking, a trial. Because of its incompleteness, neither could be, properly speaking, a "hearing." They could be only "public exposures," inviting only "belief" in either the accusation or the denial. There was no effort in good faith, perhaps no possibility of such an effort, to discover any verifiable truth. As public procedures, they were only public embarrassments, degrading to everybody involved, including all of us who consumed the news. I am happy to have forgotten much that I once remembered of the Clarence Thomas hearing. But the confirmation of Brett Kavanaugh was followed by a clamor of public side-taking, according to sympathy or partisanship. This again was "news," but it served no public good. Sympathy either way is as understandable as it is unpreventable in such cases, but sympathy per se, like belief per se, is of no public or evidentiary value. Justice, as our court system rightly holds, must wait upon truth, which is to say verifiable evidence.

It can reasonably be concluded from either of these episodes that no satisfactory public opinion or judgment can be made of private behavior of which there is no reliable evidence or available witness. I suppose that, strictly speaking, there is no effective way for anybody to deal with anybody else's private behavior. It is plain enough that we cannot prevent misdeeds by outlawing them. They cannot be very surely prevented by fear or corrected by punishment after the fact. The most effective correction and prevention happens in the formation of a person's character by parents and neighbors. If sexual responsibility is not taught in childhood by parents and other elders, then recourse is only to the law: to public punishment for iniquities that the public by its nature fails to prevent.

By contrast, customary ways and prohibitions once governed private behavior, not perfectly but for better or worse. And these customs have been the business not of the public, which in some times and places has not existed, but of families and communities. And so now, when the predominant and often the only authority is public, we come repeatedly to a difficult and painful question: What has happened to the families and communities whose expectations and restraints, never public, grew directly from the circumstances and the needs of people living together? We need to ask, not because families and communities were ever perfect by their own standards, but because the public and the government are incomplete and in some ways useless when families and communities have disintegrated. When individual people no longer have access to, and are unreachable from, those older forms of local authority, it seems inevitable that a personal wrong or wound may fester for years in some solitary heart until it bursts out at last nakedly in public, in yet another "news show."

In more settled times and places, most people lived their private lives, only intermittently public, within and under the influence of the families and communities that formed their characters when they were children. Such a possibility has come more and more into disfavor since World War II, as our more and more public economy has depended increasingly upon extravagant consumption and what we call "mobility."

People's membership in their families and home communities has diminished and their membership in the public has increased as they have become consumers, answering to the influence of the electronic media and advertising, fashions and fads. The influence of local elders and rememberers, "home-folks," necessarily has decreased as the schools, indifferent to the value of local knowledge, teach the assumptions of the public economy and deference to expert opinion.

Also, according to our dominant legend, the route of success or career advancement or the realization of one's "potential as an individual" has led away from one's origins in family and community and into the "public sphere." By now the rural community, the small town, even the small city, are conventionally thought to be "backward" and drastically limiting of the powers, ambitions, dreams, and salaries of the "college educated" who, according to the same legend, are a sort of new class predestined to "success."

The public or the public sphere, centered in and ruled from the larger cities, is perceived as the sphere of self-realization and success. It is perceived also as the sphere of freedom, where one shakes off the burdens and constraints of local loyalties and the traditional or conventional forbiddings of religion and responsibility. This is surely exciting, and one can imagine how it quickens the breath of the careerist in a corporation or a university or a government.

But the public is not, except in the most remote and theoretical sense, a membership. It is nobody's home, and its gatekeepers are not filled with the spirit of welcome and hospitality. The freedom it offers is in fact the freedom of the richest and most powerful to reign and the freedom of the less rich and powerful to succeed as "human resources," perhaps highly paid, perhaps not—and, like all "resources" under industrial rule, to be used, used up, and discarded.

The public sphere at present is the realm of extremely powerful, wealthy, childish, and badly spoiled adult humans typified by Mr. Trump, his allies, and his rivals. These people conceive our country (most of it downgraded as "rural America") not as a republic, a land and people under God and the Constitution, but rather as an open range, a wide-open space, an unclaimed territory, where "anything goes" and the fittest survive (for a while, as warned by Shakespeare et al.). "Anything goes" was once the motto of the sexually liberated, who learned it from the captains of industry, who, since the start of the Me Too movement, seem to have owned it exclusively. They are liberals of sex and conservatives of money.

Within our wide-open public spaces, successful or not, we have become a public people, upwardly or downwardly or laterally mobile, within a vast national and economic public as unsettled as the inside of a corn popper. In more settled times, as here and there even now, members of families and communities have had at minimum the protections of subsistence, companionship, and mutual help, as long as they have had recourse to land and the cultural means. Members merely of the public have protections, still, as individual citizens: The government, the law, the police, the courts do protect them—impersonally, selectively, and intermittently. But the ability of citizens to protect one another by their companionship and help is narrowly limited. Mostly they seem to be alone, always in need, if not of food, clothing, shelter, or a drug, then of some readily available electronic connection or diversion. Or they shift from solitary distractions to solitary miseries requiring, typically, some form of professional help.

In the making of a community, a nation, or a civilization, the paramount issue has got to be protection. People gather together because they see that they can be too much alone or too few to be reasonably safe. It is not good that the man should be alone, says the second chapter of Genesis, and this seems to be the reason for the creation of other living creatures, culminating with Eve and marriage. It went on from there in the world east of Eden. The first protection is against loneliness. The next most immediately needed protection would be against bodily harm: against being killed or hurt by the violence of nature (storms, big carnivores, etc.), but also by the aggression of other people. Finally the protections, recognized first as needed and then as required, form the basis of civilization.

The biblical strand of Western civilization was founded upon the Ten Commandments, which Moses brought down from his meeting with God on Mount Sinai to the migrant children of Israel. Here are the ten, stated briefly:

I. Worship one god (the author of the commandments).
II. Don't worship idols.
III. Don't misuse God's name.
IV. Don't work on the sabbath day.
V. Honor your parents.
VI. Don't kill other people.
VII. Don't commit adultery.
VIII. Don't steal.
IX. Don't lie.
X. Don't covet.

These often are published alone (their divine origin and authority merely assumed or implied), like slogans at a political demonstration, and are similarly meant: to divide some from others. Displayed in this way, they become a sort of idol, a *thing* invested with political significance.

To be received in their real stature and significance, they require us to think about them, to understand their context and purpose and practicality. They were a gift given to a people to accompany the further gift to them of a good land. To occupy that land in the right way and so to keep it, they would need these instructions. I regret the Israelites' mistreatment of their Canaanite predecessors, which had too much the pattern of our own Manifest Destiny, but I still regard the Ten Commandments as a good set of instructions for people who wish to inhabit a land, to keep it, and to live in it as neighbors to one another. The ten, taken together, make a pattern of sense with the purpose of making something, namely a community, beloved and lasting.

I have known the Ten Commandments nearly all my life, have thought a good deal about them, and am grateful that there are only ten. I should recuse myself from discussing the third commandment if it means, as it is often thought to mean, Don't cuss. But I suspect that cussing may be a higher form of punctuation, and that taking God's name in vain may be to speak it with ostentatious piety or blabbingly or too often. The fourth commandment used to worry me when I thought (as instructed) that it meant Go to church. In fact it says, Rest from your work on the seventh day, as God rested on that day from His work of making heaven and earth. This, I think, is both good sense and one of the richest and dearest of thoughts. In general, I take the Ten Commandments, as perhaps Buddhists may take the Ten Grave Precepts, as good practical instruction for living a shared life.

The practicality of at least the first four commandments I know I will have to defend. In our scientific materialist and (as it thinks) altogether practical age, the first four commandments will appear to apply only to religion and to have no practical import at all. Their practicality becomes plain and even insistent, however, to caring and observant inhabitants of rural America—to those of us, that is to say, who live at the business end of an economy and way of life to which nothing is sacred, and by which therefore everything is eligible to be destroyed. There is, of course, no scientific support for the proposition that God made the world, infused it with life, and caused it to be richly productive and reproductive. But then materialist scientists cannot scientifically support their own proposition (thus equally "superstitious") that God did not do those things. And there is no end of evidence, plenty scientific, that humankind did not and cannot do those things. If our scientific materialist economy and way of life treats everything in the natural world, including its ability to reproduce and renew its life, as finite and therefore exhaustible "resources," which it does, and is therefore exhausting them, which it is, all of this can be computed to a scientific fare-thee-well. There are scientists and scientific economists who can demonstrate that it is more profitable to destroy these "natural resources" than to save them, and we therefore should not worry. Others of the same fellowship say that we should worry, and that our leaders should stop us from being so wasteful. These are apt to join the evangelists who preach that the end of the world is at hand. We still are left with the question of what to call our destruction of precious things that we did not and cannot make. Almost nobody, so far as I hear and read, calls it "sin." And "sin," like "love," is a word we have nearly ruined by misuse and overuse. To name rightly and exactly this terminal destructiveness of ours, I think we will have to go further in debt to the language of religion and call it "desecration" and "blasphemy"—which, of course, are sins. And so I approve the first four commandments for reasons practical enough.

Now, with us, the fourth commandment calls for an extra moment of attention. I suppose it has always been somewhat practical in the sense that resting from your work one day out of seven is good for your health. But in this nation, in the very advanced twenty-first century, work (except as "exercise") is in such disfavor, and rest is so highly esteemed, that our days of rest now include Saturdays and the several Mondays of national holidays. Our sin now is both breaking the sabbath and inflating it. The intended instruction of the sabbath day is that, while we rest, God's six days of Creation continue. All that we primarily depend upon, the world and its plentitude of good things, does not depend upon us—although, because of our ability to desecrate and destroy it, its good care and preservation does depend upon us.

It is above all clear that the Ten Commandments are not random or arbitrary, dangled off the mountaintop to be reverenced and obeyed for their own sake or in order to get to Heaven. Their first business is to advise the people in their wandering migration to a promised land, as I wish they had advised a later people migrating to the "new Canaan" of Kentucky, that they live within a set of circumstances not of their own making, the practical concern being *how* to live within those circumstances. The first circumstance, most dangerous to ignore, is that of sanctity and mystery, and for this we have the first four commandments.

The second circumstance is that of the land, the part of the created or natural world, that the people are to be given. This is the concern of the fifth commandment. Here it is, in the King James Version: "Honor thy father and thy mother: that thy days may be long upon the land which the Lord thy God giveth thee." Among biblical people, it is almost certain that an exasperated parent will use this to admonish a disobedient child, and it is almost certain that the child, if biblical enough and young enough, will take this "honor" to be a sort of elixir guaranteeing a long life. But this commandment, though applicable to individual parents and children, is addressed to all the people, and it sets forth one of the conditions upon which they may inhabit the given land for a long time. For that to happen the land's history must survive as a vital force within it. To the land given to them "for a heritage" the people must give their memories of it, handed down from parents to children, generation after generation. The children are to honor their parents no doubt by obeying them, but also by listening and remembering. Those of us who live now in rural America and are at all observant are compelled to see this commandment as strictly and fearfully practical. It is as important as life and death that we should remember what destroys the land and what saves it. Every farm and every field, every patch of every woodland in human use, must have attached to it, as a part of it, native memories of what works well and what does not. This kind of memory has become nearly extinct in rural America as the old have died and the young have departed.

The remaining six commandments, as is made plain by the tenth, tell us more particularly how to live as neighbors to our neighbors. The remaining circumstance in which the people must live is that of neighborhood.

The sixth commandment is "Thou shalt not kill" in the King James Version. The word "kill" in other translations and in commentaries is rendered as "murder." The comment in *The New Oxford Annotated Bible* gives what I suppose is the obvious reason: "This commandment forbids *murder*, not the forms of killing authorized for Israel, such as war and capital punishment." Construed this way, the sixth commandment forbids murder as a private enterprise, and makes it a monopoly of government, whether of ancient Israel or of any other nation that may subscribe to the commandments. It clearly would not do to allow a religious scruple to stand in the way of war and capital punishment, which after all are necessities of life.

But, since we are obliged to see the whole Bible, along with the classical inheritance, as fundamental to our civilization, and since the wholeness of heart that is peace is the subject of this laborious meditation of mine, it is necessary to quote Jesus's comment in the Sermon on the Mount upon such interpretations of the sixth commandment:

> Ye have heard that it hath been said, Thou shalt love thy neighbor, and hate thine enemy.
>
> But I say unto you, Love your enemies, bless them that curse you, do good to them that hate you, and pray for them which despitefully use you, and persecute you;

That ye may be the children of your Father which is in heaven; for he maketh his sun to rise on the evil and on the good, and sendeth rain on the just and on the unjust.

For if ye love them which love you, what reward have ye? do not even the publicans the same?

That no doubt is the most unknown widely published statement and the best-kept state secret in the history of the world. The Israelites themselves construed "kill" as "murder," and at Jericho, Joshua and his invaders established a terrible precedent: Having received from God, as they believed, permission to do pretty much what they wanted to do, they "consecrated unto the Lord" that city's precious metals and the metal pots and pans, and "utterly destroyed all that was in the city, both man and woman, young and old, and ox, and sheep, and ass, with the edge of the sword." This granted in effect a powerful permission to humanity to follow its lowest instincts, and the "Christian nations" since Constantine have followed Joshua rather than Jesus—Joshua and Jesus being opposite biblical persons with oddly (in Hebrew) the same name.

The advent of the nuclear bomb, one might reasonably have supposed, would have caused the great leaders of the Judeo-Christian nations to rethink the permission and policy inherited from Joshua, on the basis merely of practicality and common sense if not of the common sense of fear—but, as we know, even so low a light has never dawned. It is anyhow true that Jesus's command to love our enemies, for those who can bear to read it, retains its great power and beauty. It is a hard test for evolutionists, my friend Wes Jackson once said to me, to consider that the only sure antidote to nuclear holocaust became available two thousand years before it was most urgently needed.

In one way or another, all of the commandments have to do with neighborhood, which is to be made and held together by consent and obedience to all of them. But the importance of neighborhood becomes explicit in the tenth commandment, which places a conclusive emphasis upon the word "neighbor." It says, "Thou shalt not covet . . . any thing that is thy neighbor's." My Old Order Amish friends, I believe, would understand this to mean that your neighbors as themselves, your companions and workmates, are worth far more than anything they may possess.

By contrast, the industrial farmers of our time are economically constrained, and by the industrial orthodoxy are encouraged, to regard their neighbors as competitors, and to overcome them (and possess their farms) by means of newer technologies and bigger machines. Thus a fundamental relationship and obligation is broken by the now generally accepted "realism" and "necessity" of economic competition, which necessarily brings us to our present condition: a public consisting of dismembered families and communities and the virtually deserted economic landscapes of our country, where, as the parents grow old and die without successors, the children are distributed from sea to sea.

Remote as we now are from the life and practice once implied by the word "neighbor," it will help to remember the importance that Jesus gave to it and how seriously we are asked to take it:

Thou shalt love the Lord thy God with all thy heart, and with all thy soul, and with all thy mind.

This is the first and great commandment.

And the second is like unto it, Thou shalt love thy neighbor as thyself.

On these two commandments hang all the law and the prophets.

As he said, Jesus did not speak and teach these things in order to overturn the old law. He seems only to have been laying out to the fullest extent the implications of having and being a neighbor. The commandment to love your neighbor is "like" the commandment to love God. These two and their likeness to each other are effectively the sum of the old commandments. And he seems also to have been completing the sense of his second commandment when he said, "Love your enemies." What if your neighbor is your enemy? This is another refusal of the doctrine of "all except some." He didn't say to love your neighbor unless your neighbor is your enemy.

And now I must say again that the prescribed love is not the mere sentiment or the mere instinct to which we have reduced it. As I think the Amish, almost alone among us, have understood, love must be a practice, an economic practice, the basis of what some have called "the beloved community."

I do not intend at all the provincialism of saying that only the biblical tradition can teach us the importance of loving our neighbors. I do intend to say that if we Westerners want to understand ourselves, our inheritance, and our present disorder, we need to know the biblical commandments and why they were given.

Assuming that we can read and still are willing to do so, it is easy enough to discover or rediscover what the commandments are, as given in the passages I have quoted and in others. And with only a little thought we can see that they rest upon the perception that, for people wishing to live well together in a given place, some acts and attitudes of mind are divisive and destructive, and these the laws forbid. By reading somewhat further in the Bible, and in the literary tradition descending from the Bible, we will find examples enough of the happiness of people who take the commandments to heart and obey them, and the unhappiness of people who do not. The happiness of which I am speaking here is not that of "success" as we now use that term, but rather the truer and truly consoling happiness of knowing that one has done the right thing—the happiness of the "good and faithful servant." If the tables of the law recorded in Exodus are effectively replaced by Jesus's two laws requiring us to love God and our neighbors, we have still the same perceived difference between a kind of life that divides us and a kind of life that keeps us together. This difference, which imposes upon us humans a set of choices that we cannot escape and must make, is the basis of an outline of responsibility, of moral law, that seems not to vary much among societies that expect a significant measure of self-control or self-government from their members. We see the same difference in the opposed lists of the seven deadly sins and the four cardinal and three theological virtues.

I find this confirmed, for example, in an essay by Joseph Milne, "The Call of Justice," on Plato's *Laws*:

> It is a convention of our modern liberal conception of
> society that laws are not meant to make citizens virtu-
> ous, but rather to preserve individual freedom . . . And
> we know that Plato's view that the virtues serve as the
> basis for civil life was rejected in the seventeenth century

to be replaced by a "contractual" view of human obligations. And perhaps most people now think of the law as
obligations to be enforced, or even as restraints on freedom. . . . From Plato's viewpoint, however, when law-
making aims at the virtuous life and honors the highest
things first, and the things of necessity last, then the laws
will be loved by the citizens. They will be seen as drawing all members of the community into cooperation and
friendship.

This appears to explain the biblical understanding that the law of
God bestows blessing and delight and is a reason for rejoicing.

It is plain enough, I think, that the ancient laws were not
directed toward a society such as ours now is: a public, which the
journalist Paul Tenny in "Seeing Through the Mirage of Localism"
has described as "a collection of unrelated individuals whose interactions are mediated through various shallow and transactional
mechanisms, where common ground with a neighbor can only,
at best, be found in the most banal of trivialities." I want to offer
the small protest that in the remnant community where I live, and
in some others elsewhere, some family and neighborly working
relationships continue yet. But Mr. Tenny has accurately described
the condition that all of us everywhere are tending toward, and he
has confirmed my own estimate of the present condition of most
Americans. It is hardly an exaggeration to say that our present economy and way of life have about entirely inverted the order of heavenly and neighborly love prescribed by the Ten Commandments
and the Gospels. This can be fairly tested by asking what would
happen to our economy if the marketers and advertisers shifted
their appeal from anger, covetousness, envy, gluttony, lust, pride,
and sloth to justice, prudence, fortitude, temperance, faith, hope,

and love. Or suppose that our economy should attempt to found itself upon peace and thrift instead of war and waste. Such changes, perhaps necessary to our mere survival, cannot be possible until the good of families and communities can outweigh the malleable and spongy claims of public interest and individual freedom.

From our present point of view, the Ten Commandments are divided between what we call "sins" or "superstitions" and what we still see as crimes. As a public, we still somewhat effectively legislate against and prosecute crimes. It appears that we do this too selectively, for our prison industry is notoriously thriving, and is doing so disproportionately upon the crimes of disfavored minorities and the poor. Anyhow, we continue to be actively opposed to crimes, including murder, theft, and lying (in court, under oath).

What seems remarkable to me is that the old opposition to sin remains popular with us, though the sins we now popularly and fervently oppose are fewer than ever before. I am under constraint here to use "sin" as a necessary term, but I am not using it in its traditional sense as an act or thought that divides us from God or our neighbors. I am using it now to denote a wrong or a perceived wrong that is opposed with the zeal and the personal and public vindictiveness with which religious heresies once were opposed. For one accused of these offenses the accuser manifests no recognition of a common humanity, no sympathy, no mercy, no readiness to forgive. The accusation is meant to adhere to the accused forever, to be itself a punishment never to be lightened or redeemed by any repentance or reform. We seem to have retained the meaner passions of Christendom while losing the scripture, the cultural and artistic tradition, and the virtues. The worst temptation of religious people has always been to publish and punish the sins of (other) sinners in this world, with no patience or deference for the judgment of God.

By my count there are only four of these sins presently recognized and vituperated by our public: two by the conservatives, two by the liberals. The sins most hated by conservatives are abortion and any governmental interference with the accumulation of wealth; we can call it the sin of "regulation-and-taxation." Those most hated by liberals are sexual aggressions (short of actionable crimes), mostly against women, and manifestations of racial prejudice (short of actionable crimes), mostly verbal or symbolic and mostly against black people.

Abortion seems now to be the only sin publicly and passionately opposed by Christian conservatives. They have dabbled in opposition to homosexual marriage, but that may have been too complex an issue to generate enough heat. Abortion may be the ideal sin for public censure because it so neatly divides the innocent from the guilty: some women absolutely have committed abortion, whereas other women absolutely have not. Also abortion is committed only by women (and some male doctors, who anyhow are not Christian conservatives), leaving the men uninvolved and therefore innocent. We might be justified in supposing that all aborted babies are the products of immaculate conception. The whole drama of abortion, including the public exposure and opprobrium, ought to be construed as a sexual aggression against women. For this the only remedy would be to remove it from the capitals, courts, and other public places, and thus remand it to private life where it belongs, along with other sexual matters that by nature and by right are personal and private, none of the government's business.

In return for their opposition to the public sin of abortion, the political conservatives receive the Christian conservatives' opposition to the public sin of regulation-and-taxation. Having acquiesced in the Trumpian synthesis of sexual and economic laissez-faire, excepting only abortion, the Christian conservatives have sold their souls at immense profit to their friends the Mammonites, and a penny's worth of righteousness to themselves.

Sexual offenses against women are nearly all committed by men, which, like abortion, cleanly and simply divides the innocent from the guilty. This sin, strictly construed, places all women above suspicion, and it renders all heterosexual men suspect. Suspicion becomes extremely volatile in a highly mobile public such as ours, where relationships of all kinds tend to be brief and superficial, and it may be impossible to acquire an *established* good reputation. We walk on busy streets or gather in crowds as strangers among strangers. A man may appear to be kind, may kindly offer his help to a woman in a crowd or at work, but who knows what he may be thinking? What sexual wrongs may he already have committed? Thus the splendid world-enriching good fortune that women and men often are attractive to one another is brought under a general indictment, and is made a blight.

The dumbfoundment of the language of race relations seems to be concentrated upon avoidance of what we coyly refer to as "the n-word." A prominent white person who speaks that word aloud, apparently for any reason, within public hearing will now be as certainly ruined as any prominent man who is accused of behaving "inappropriately" toward a woman. Such a person will receive no chance for repentance or reform, let alone forgiveness, but will be forever condemned for the one offense by the great Many who share the felicity of moral perfection. Nowhere near so much power to shock and offend is now invested in any other word. We regard it as people once regarded biblical or Homeric signs and omens, as if the use of it may bring years of misfortune, the death of a family member, or defeat in war.

As an example of the extremity to which this anxiety can be carried I have saved a review by Thomas Powers of a book about the novels of William Faulkner. This was in *The New York Review of Books* of April 20, 2017. Mr. Powers begins with a testimony to Faulkner's importance:

> It would be a grave mistake for anyone trying to under-stand race in American history to overlook the novels of William Faulkner. Beneath their literary complexity can be found the clearest statement by anyone of the core abuse that has driven black–white conflict since slavery times, but first you have to pass a test.

Mr. Powers says a number of things in his review that are questionable, but my interest here is only in this "test," which comes from an evening in 1958 at Princeton when Faulkner met J. Robert Oppenheimer. Both men, for different reasons, were famous, Oppenheimer as leader of the effort that produced the atomic bomb, Faulkner for winning the Nobel Prize in Literature. Mr. Powers proceeds to their conversation:

> Oppenheimer said he had recently seen a television play based on a Faulkner story and asked what Faulkner thought of television as a medium for the artist.
> "Television is for niggers," said Faulkner. This is the test: Are you prepared to believe that the Faulkner who

said that might also have something important to say about black–white conflict in American history?

Mr. Powers sees this as a story, simple and obvious, revealing and condemning Faulkner unconditionally as a ready user of a forbidden word, and therefore "indelibly" a white southern racist. Although I willingly concede that this is a bad word, and the badness of Faulkner's manners on that occasion is as plain to me as to Mr. Powers, I see this story nevertheless as extraordinarily complicated, a tangle of threads requiring some trouble to pick apart.

To begin with, Oppenheimer asked the kind of question that people typically ask a writer whom they have not read, and especially if the unread writer comes from a part of the country known to be "backward." For all I know, Oppenheimer had read every one of Faulkner's books, but I assume, and I assume that Faulkner assumed, that if Oppenheimer had read any of them he would have recognized the obvious incompatibility between the character and style of Faulkner's work and the capacities of television "as a medium for the artist." I assume further that Faulkner, having as he thought fairly weighed the question, gave the sort of answer that he thought Oppenheimer would have expected from a crude white southern racist, his answer implying, "To hell with you." And so in only four words he insulted Oppenheimer, television, black people, and perhaps also the Institute for Advanced Studies at Princeton. It is not enough appreciated that Faulkner was a fine writer of comedy, with a delighted sense of the ridiculous. If he had wished to respond to a ridiculous question with a ridiculous answer, he would have known how.

Furthermore, I have no idea if Faulkner ever recorded his judgment either of Oppenheimer himself or of the atomic bomb or the use thereof. But Mr. Powers says only that the physicist was "celebrated . . . for building the first atomic bomb"—to be used, let us remember, against the "Japs." And so this story, this "test," as offered by Mr. Powers, balances Oppenheimer against Faulkner, the first atomic bomb against the forbidden word, and finds Oppenheimer apparently only "celebrated" and Faulkner immitigably guilty of a grave offense against humanity. And so Mr. Powers's "test" immediately raises another question that he does not ask: Are you prepared to confront the moral issues related to Faulkner's use of the "n-word" while ignoring those related to Oppenheimer's willing responsibility for the first atomic bomb?

I believe I am pretty fully aware of the magnitude and urgency of the problem that Oppenheimer and his colleagues worked to solve. I know the anguishing questions, once the bomb was made, about when, where, and how to use it—questions anguishing enough to have remained so, but that in fact were quickly answered; according to the historian David M. Kennedy's *Freedom from Fear*, the matter was decided "briefly and informally, during a lunch break." I have read and pondered the equations between the number of lives theoretically or possibly or probably saved by the bomb and the number of lives it certainly destroyed. And I know about Oppenheimer's tragic and preposterous wish to control the results of his great achievement. I give him limited respect and sympathy along with less limited dismay and fear. And I am grateful for Kennedy's reminder that

some scientists chose to work elsewhere for moral reasons. The physicist I. I. Rabi . . . turned down Oppenheimer's invitation . . . because he could not stomach the idea that making a weapon of mass destruction represented "the culmination of three centuries of physics."

To me Oppenheimer represents the romantic, starstruck kind of science that believes it must do whatever it can do, expecting to be celebrated for that. I cannot see that by being compared to him Faulkner is at any disadvantage.

Toward the end of his review Mr. Powers weights his verdict against Faulkner with a prophecy:

> The day is probably coming when younger readers, bumping into "the N-word" repeatedly, can no longer pass the test I earlier mentioned. But the word was an ineradicable part of Faulkner's world.

I would like to be at one with everybody who regrets this particular bad word and all of its relatives that misname disfavored groups of people. I regret its whole history and all it stands for, but Mr. Powers's prediction stumps me. I can't tell whether or not he is welcoming, or how much he may be welcoming, those younger readers who will no longer read Faulkner because his work will require them fairly often to read that word—even though if they do not read him they will never know why they should not.

But is Mr. Powers another of the good many who hopes never again to be reminded of the badness in our history? His foretelling of the coming of the Faulkner-avoiders baffles me, but his next sentence is clear and true. The word—after all, it is a *word*—belongs ineradicably to Faulkner's world. But it belongs also to *our* world, which was and is also the world of northern racists. It belongs ineradicably to our world, our history, our language, and our literature. Mere honesty, if not the need for understanding, requires us to confront it. To confront it, we have got to regard and quote it as a *word*, used at different times, with different purposes and intensities, by many different people, including black people. How possibly might we avoid it in studying and teaching our history? How could we learn or teach honestly the history of our literature and avoid *Huckleberry Finn*, and how could we speak honestly of that book without speaking, with the author and with Huck, of Nigger Jim? How could a teacher do justice to that book without reading aloud some of the great passages containing that word? To be afraid to do this in a public classroom is to make of political correctness a form of public censorship, denying the protection of the First Amendment to Mark Twain, and of course to other writers. Governments, as we know, can violate the First Amendment by ignoring it, but citizens can violate it by silence. There is no honorable way to dodge this issue.

But Mr. Powers's test in fact reaches far beyond questions about William Faulkner's or anybody's vocabulary. It reaches all the way to questions that are among the oldest, never satisfactorily answered. How are good people like Mr. Powers, and of course me, going to keep ourselves uncontaminated by the forces of badness in the world? Can we be sure that good books are written only by good people? How can we assure ourselves of the good behavior of the prolific and sometimes great author Anonymous? What are we to conclude if we catch a good person doing something bad? Or a bad person doing something good? Why does God permit the sun to shine and the rain to fall on the unjust as well as the just? If the unjust are nice-looking and mimic the language of the just, how can we tell the difference without knowing them, at the risk of contamination? Oh my!

Nothing more reveals our incompleteness and brokenness as a public people than our self-comforting small selection of public sins. They are startlingly few in number, perhaps for the reason that the news and the minds of journalists can supply room and public notice only to four at a time. And perhaps only a few sins have the requisite exclusiveness, sufficiently flattering the virtue or vanity, thus sufficiently inflaming the passionate righteousness, of those who oppose them, thus magnifying the evil of those who commit them. We could call them media-friendly sins. But their paucity also implies that their present status is arbitrary and tentative, as if these sins have been elected by popular choice and are replaceable sooner or later by the election of more newsworthy offenses.

I have dealt with sin so far by defining it backwards: by the way people respond to it. A public sin, I am assuming, is identifiable as such by its ability to evoke a large, vehement public antipathy. Witchcraft was once a sin of this kind. So was heresy. So was adultery. The scarlet *A* in Hawthorne's novel of righteous old New England would now stand for abortion, or perhaps it would be a scarlet *R* for racist.

Most sins—unlike racist slurs and symbols, sexual harassment, abortion, and regulation-and-taxation—do not divide the innocent from the guilty, ourselves from our enemies. So far as I have been able to understand from my reading, the old authors and authorities have understood sin to be any act or thought that divides us from God or our neighbors. In both the biblical and the classical traditions the prototypical sin is hubris or the attempt to "be as gods," not just arrogance but supreme arrogance: the determination to be responsible and answerable only to oneself. The consequence, always, is loneliness. Who could be lonelier than Macbeth after his murders? And Macbeth, though no doubt more evil than most, was no lonelier than anybody else whom nobody can trust. Maybe it would be somewhat clarifying to say that sin is destructive, or that it is destructive of necessary and irreplaceable things: sustaining relationships with one another, for example, or the good health of nature. Things of value can be temporarily destroyed, which may be temporarily divisive. But some things of value can be permanently destroyed, and that is far more serious. To destroy something of value that we could not have made and cannot restore—a human life, a mountain, an ecosystem—divides us from Creation and puts us into an immeasurable depth of trouble. The badness that comes with separation from our human neighbors must be obvious to everybody. The loneliness that comes with division from our nonhuman neighbors—our home watershed and its native plants, birds, and animals—is not so obvious to people of industrial nations but is nonetheless a badness. To those who don't believe in God, division from God will be no problem. However, there is a caveat here that applies to everybody: If you make your peace, your reconciliation, or even your quarrel, with your life in this world in terms only of what you yourself presently know or can understand, you almost certainly are going to be surprised. "Life," said Erwin Chargaff, "is the continual intervention of the inexplicable." (Chargaff was an eminent scientist, also a man of humility and great wisdom. I turn to his book *Heraclitean Fire* for consolation, assured that I will find it.)

By contrast with the little handful of public or newsworthy sins, the traditional lists of commandments, sins, and virtues have a human and a humanizing amplitude. They serve as a working definition of our species: Here is what is expected of us and what we are to expect of ourselves as human beings, and here are the ways we succeed or fail. The public sins, by proposing one or two things that good people don't do, make goodness easy. But the traditional lists, by their amplitude, stand resolutely in our way. They have seen us coming. To know them, to take them seriously, measuring ourselves by them and remembering the commandment against lying, is to take a real test that lasts a lifetime. Honest answers may not come either easily or finally. For example, you yourself may not have killed anybody, you may have nobody's actual blood on your hands, but to whom may you have given your proxy to do your killing for you? Or if you think you have no prejudice, can you remember that other people's memories of you may be truer than your own? And which is most important: innocence of prejudice by the standard of political correctness or the ability to do the right thing even if you are prejudiced?

Taking that test is likely to reveal to us that we may recognize sinners less by their sins than by our own. If this doesn't make us more virtuous or more humble, it ought at least to improve our sense of humor. A sense of humor and what Alexander Pope and Jane Austen called "sense" are in fact ways of knowing and taking seriously our inescapable involvement and complicity in the good and the bad that human beings do.

Among the discontented, particularly the liberal academics, conservationists, and reformers, it has come to be fashionable to blame Western civilization for whatever they have found wrong. Their indictment characteristically is supported by their agreement with people who agree with them. Their complaint characteristically is centered upon the Bible, of which the first and often the only verse cited is Genesis 1:28 in which the original couple are told to "replenish the earth, and subdue it," and are granted "dominion" over all living things. The settled understanding of that verse among the dropouts from Western civilization is that God made the world exclusively for us humans and gave it to us to do with it just as we please. It is true that some very bad inheritors of that verse have done and still are doing to the world according only to their own wishes. But this only means that the modern defectors from Western civilization are not alone. The wasters of the world do not derive their abuses from any "text," but rather from their instinctive greed and the capacities of their technology.

The modern infamy of Genesis 1:28 began, so far as I know, with an essay published in 1967, "The Historical Roots of Our Ecological Crisis," by Lynn White Jr. Because of the prominence he gave to it in his essay, that verse has been taken by his followers as a fair synopsis of the Bible, and thus has spared them the effort of actually reading it. It is not difficult to find verses in the Bible that fairly explicitly contradict the fashionable misunderstanding of Genesis 1:28 and its alleged "anthropocentrism." I have previously cited several of them several times. Here because neighborliness is so much a concern of this book, I should need to say only that the word "neighbor" is especially important and prominent in the Bible. The import of that word always tends toward Jesus's second law, that we should love our neighbors as we love ourselves. How can we love our neighbors by abusing or destroying the watershed or the ecosystem or the ecosphere on which we and they mutually depend? But for those who require a verse exactly contrary to the Lynn White interpretation of Genesis 1:28, I will offer Psalm 24:1: "The earth is the Lord's, and the fulness thereof; the world and they that dwell therein." So far as the records show, God still holds the deed to the whole property.

Another traditional means of recognizing ourselves and our perilous involvement in the world is the grand order of life-forms known as the "Chain of Being." This order is made of a descending series of connections—it is a *chain*—from God down through the orders of angels to humankind, and thence through the orders of animals down to the very least. I have turned to the Chain of Being several times in writing and often in my thoughts, for I have found it to be necessary. I am now turning to it again, partly because I need it again, and partly because I want to help to bring it back to mind. To my repeated surprise and dismay, I have read a number of disparagements of Western civilization by writers who assert that it is based upon a hierarchy of which humans are at the top, with the world and all of its creatures underneath. This seems to please the anti-Westerners, who believe that by exposing and condemning the heritage of the West they somehow raise the standing of another "worldview"—that of Science maybe, or of an Eastern or American Indian religion. I can respond only by saying that in my limited reading of the literature of "competing" traditions I have found much that supplemented or confirmed or clarified my own.

As I have been writing this, I have been reading Andrew Schelling's *Tracks Along the Left Coast: Jaime de Angulo & Pacific Coast Culture*, in which Schelling comments as follows on an Eastern Pomo creation myth, Marumda and the Kuksu being the world-makers:

> Once decided on a course of action Marumda and the Kuksu need to create the world five times. Four times they find it flawed. The people lack respect, harmony, duty. They talk too much, they eat badly. They sleep with their brothers and sisters. Marumda and the Kuksu have to destroy the world four times and make it again.

I cannot see this as contradictory to the world-making of Genesis. The common assumption is that, as creatures, humans are not autonomous. They are not made and turned loose to do as they please. Some things are expected.

The Chain of Being has fallen so far from memory, I suppose, because it is not scientific. But then it never claimed or pretended to be scientific in our sense of that term. Probably no scientist has ever seen an angel, let alone caught and dissected one. Angels are known to be extremely shy and given to flight at the approach of objective observers. They fear cameras and recording machines of every kind. That I have never seen one myself is no doubt owing to the notebook and pencil that I always have in my pocket.

Anyhow, there is no human-topped hierarchy in the basis of Western civilization. The industrial economy certainly is a hierarchy with a few people at the top, which certainly was invented in the West. But to argue that the industrial economy is a product of Western civilization is made impossible by the significance of the Chain of Being. It is perfectly true that the order represented by the Chain of Being is hierarchical. This offends an intellectual fashion that fails to distinguish between political and economic hierarchies and hierarchy in Creation or the natural world. I feel strongly in my upbringing and in myself a resentment against political or economic hierarchy, a resentment that is old in Western tradition. I am pleased beyond expression to know that the success of Odysseus's homecoming depended on his friendship with the swineherd Eumaios, and that the announcement of Jesus's birth was made first to the nearby shepherds. But though we of the West have longed for ages to see the lamb and the lion lie down together, for the time being and at suppertime the lion outvotes the lamb.

But what is indispensable about the Chain of Being is the human position in the hierarchy. It is in the midst, between the lowest angels and the highest animals. In that place we are delicately balanced and in great danger, because we are never free of the temptation to be either more or less than human. Both of those "possibilities," before we have tried them, can be extremely attractive. The problem is that neither is actually possible. We humans cannot be super-human or subhuman, angels or animals. Instead, we become inhu-man: If we cast off the human limits and the human controls, we become monsters of one kind or another, to one degree or another, and so may bring dire penalties upon ourselves and other people. King Lear decides to be superhuman: to retain control over his life while handing all the power of his kingship to his daughters. Mac-beth, by contrast, decides to be as freely instinctive as an animal, free of "all that may become a man," so as to take simply and directly what he desires. Being modern, scientific, limitlessly "informed," technologically powerful, and global in our reach and influence does not enlarge our place in the hierarchy of beings or change the game in our favor by an inch or an ounce. It is monstrous to produce an atomic bomb or any other of our limitless technologies with the assumption that humans are intelligent enough to control even the unforeseeable consequences. It is monstrous to attempt to be "free," to liberate ourselves, by classifying ourselves and our kind as merely animals or higher animals or animals with "big brains," and adopting the individualist ethic that animals supposedly have.

To be human is harder, lovelier, and for us more possible than to be an angel or an animal. If God is at the top of the chain or hierar-chy of beings, then the order of the world cannot be "anthropocen-tric" (a pretentious, ugly word that means "man-centered"). Our place is in the middle, which only means that we have both powers and limits, are both subordinate and responsible, are expected to be both obedient and magnanimous. Our position, we may say, requires us to love God and our neighbors, and to be "good and faithful servants" to both. As we are obliged now to accept the implications of our knowledge of ecosystems and the ecosphere—

or of our recovery of the "primitive" knowledge of those things—then our word "neighbor" begins to refer not only to humans, but also to creatures that are not human: the plants and animals, the rocks, the light, the water, and the air. And so we must occupy our place with gratitude for its privileges, but also with care and some uneasiness. To think of the world as human-centered is both a blasphemy and an ecological absurdity.

People who condemn Western civilization on the basis of Genesis 1:28 should be warned that they endanger themselves by ruling against the Bible without troubling to know it, and that to know it requires some critical intelligence. It can, for example, be read as a "spiritual" book of rules for getting to Heaven, but only by ignoring, among much else, the great deal that it has to say about economics and kinds of economies. As a willing inheritor of the Bible and a frequent reader of it, who also is often troubled by it and by some lines of its influence, I am finding both clarification and relief in a recent book by Walter Brueggemann, *Tenacious Solidarity: Biblical Provocations on Race, Religion, Climate, and the Economy*. What I seem to have been waiting for is Prof. Brueggemann's detailed tracking of two kinds of economy from Genesis to the Letters of Paul. One of these kinds he sees variously as the totalizing or extractive economy, the economy of great and accumulating wealth, the urban economy of royalty or empire. This is the economy of the overlordships of the Pharaoh of Egypt, the Persian Empire, the Roman Empire, and of Israel's own kings such as Solomon. These economies extracted wealth from the people of the land, the peasants, by such means as monopoly, low wages, debt, monetization, dispossession, and slavery—slavery being the end result of the extraction from the people of everything by which they might secure for themselves a measure of independence and self-rule. Prof. Brueggemann's neatest demonstration of this process is the "success story" in Genesis of Pharaoh's agent, Joseph, the son of Israel. Pharaoh has gathered up a great surplus of food. When a famine comes and the people are starving, Joseph sells them food from Pharaoh's hoard. For this, in the first year, he takes all their money. In the next year of the famine, the people having no money, Joseph doles out food in exchange for their livestock, both their meat animals and their work animals. The next year Joseph feeds them in exchange for their plots of land. The next year they have only their bodies to offer, and so to eat and live they become slaves. (No wakeful rural American can read that story without remembering our own history of dispossession. For example, from 1961 to 2010 the number of farmers in the United States declined from about 13 million to about 2 million—which brings us to our present "economy," in which almost nobody, black or white, owns "forty acres and a mule" or any equivalent. I will have more to say of this.

Beneath, so to speak, the Bible's theme of the totalizing economies of the great rulers, more or less parallel to it, and counter to it, is what Prof. Brueggemann calls "the economy of God," which, unlike the extractive economy of the rulers, is a collection of "neighborly economies." These are by nature *local* economies, locally adapted, subsisting upon home landscapes and upon local knowledge, skills, tools, the means at hand and underfoot, but also upon forgiveness (of debts and sins) and healing. This counter-economy of neighborhoods and neighborliness, the economy of the land and the people, is served by the prophets and by Jesus and his followers, the students and teachers of the kingdom of God, which is an economy contrary to the economy of extraction. These servants are poor unpaid dealers in things that are free, who go about comforting sufferers, healing the sick, feeding the hungry, looking out for widows and orphans, telling the truth, and taking their punishment. They are the carriers and performers of the great theme of neighborly love. Their lineage has never been "successful," but it has never ceased.

In the absence of intact traditional or customary means, in the shared life of families and neighbors, of knowing right from wrong, the issues of our merely public morality clearly are incomplete, scattered, arbitrary, and discontinuous. The life prescribed by political correctness or by the political aversion to regulation-and-taxation and abortion is too simple and scattered to offer truth or justice or courtesy or kindness or affection or sympathy or help to anybody in particular. Those public political codes serve mainly to make divisions between the innocent and the guilty, offenders and victims, winners and losers.

What are we to make, for example, of political leaders who advocate casino gambling or other sorts of "gaming" as a substitute for taxation? The people who raised me thought gambling a sin, and I see no reason to disagree. I admit that I don't care if rich people lose money they don't need, but to be in need of money and attempt to get it by gambling is surely a bad thing. Gambling is akin to usury as a way (the gambler hopes) to get money without work, and so it is unnatural and dishonest. And surely it is a bad thing for a government to depend on—and encourage—people's degrading wish to get money without work. To encourage the wish for such "winning" among even the poorest people is clearly more corrupting than to *give* money as "welfare."

Or, for another example, consider Thomas L. Friedman's

announcement (*New York Times*, January 9, 2019): "I believe there is only one thing as big as Mother Nature, and that is Father Greed—a.k.a. the market. I am a green capitalist." As a green capitalist, Mr. Friedman would put in place "a free market competition to ensure that mankind can continue to thrive on Earth." He does not say by what political means he would do this. But by "shaping the market," he would cause "our industries and innovators" to compete in "an Earth Race" to bring forth the technological solutions to the threat of climate change. The competition would be baited by Father Greed. The world-savers would be rewarded, not just by a saved world, which ought to be enough, but also by vast jackpots of silver and gold, mansions, yachts, and trophy wives or husbands. The rest of us will agree to this, of course, because the end of the world, or the end of the world as we know it, is very likely to mean the end of us. Mr. Friedman's ultimate appeal is to fear, which outraces even the greed of industries and innovators: "This may well be our last chance to . . . manage the unavoidable aspects of climate change and avoid the unmanageable ones."

But the Devil is a clever fellow. The danger in getting him to help us a little is that we will end by helping him a lot—and for this I again invoke Shakespeare. Mr. Friedman is not the first modern capitalist to understand the usefulness of greed (and of all the other old-fashioned sins). If greed will help you to get rich, then (to balance the heavenly scales) you can set up a charitable foundation to help (a little) the poor and others less successful and deserving than you. Father Greed has been a prominent figure in our history for a long time. He will help you to get rid of the Cherokee or the Sioux, if you think you have a better use for their land. He helped to establish Negro slavery in our country, and he helps to establish wage slavery here and in the sweatshops of poor countries abroad, in both instances for the high purpose of improving people less fortunate. We have taken his advice when we overcrop a field or overgraze a pasture, or when we clear-cut a forest, or when we destroy a mountain and a forest and ruin a stream in extracting a fuel soon burned to pollute the air, or when to replace our "inefficient" and therefore justly "failed" farmers we poison whole agricultural landscapes and their streams and rivers. Father Greed's most subtle expertise is "creative destruction." Just a little more exploitation or displacement of labor, a little more disemployment, unemployment, and homelessness, a little more abuse or destruction or "development" of the land, a little more firing and foreclosure and selling out and leaving home, a little more suffering—and then, very soon now, we will emerge as far better, richer, smarter, kinder, prettier people than we were before.

I am much indebted to Mr. Friedman's column, which displays with rare concision at least six of what I take to be characteristic falsehoods or superstitions of our public culture. First is the assumption that all we need in order to solve a great problem is one great new idea such as "green capitalism." Second is the assumption that "green capitalism," like any capitalism and any possible solution, must depend upon competition. Third is the assumption that this competition, like any worthy endeavor, can be motivated only by greed. Fourth is the assumption that the proposed competition will be sufficiently subsidized if the public and public leaders can be sufficiently motivated by fear. Fifth is the assumption that the ultimate and entirely sufficient great solution to the great problem will be no more than technological and industrial.

Mr. Friedman's sixth falsehood—the supposed equality between "Father Greed—a.k.a. the market" and Mother Nature—needs to be addressed at more length. This is arguably the dominant theme of our country's history since "expansion" became a political doctrine. It has been supported here so far by the "freedom" of many

American minds from all that is precautionary or restraining in the traditional cultures of either Europe or America, and by the truly unimagined abundance originally bestowed upon this "new world" by Mother Nature. Faced with such expanses of rich land virtually unplowed, unlogged, and unmined, who could have doubted that Father Greed could have pillaged and rioted here for millennia, with centuries remaining for the leftovers? Who could have believed that in the span of half a dozen human lifetimes we would have plowed, logged, poisoned, mined, and marketed our way into clear view of the limits of everything that has so far supported our "lifestyle" and our "high standard of living"?

We who are so proudly materialistic and realistic should not be surprised to learn that Father Greed can be equal and more than equal to Mother Nature by consuming, which is to say using up, her goods and by breaking her laws. But this can last only for a while, and then she begins to impose her limits, as she now is doing. We begin to see her now in the ancient aspect of her real standing and power, becoming visible again, at last, through our toxic smokes and among our heaps and scatters of trash: "Great Dame Nature," our shockingly stern, demanding, and impartial true Mother, after all.

Though the evidence of the dead end of Father Greed is found everywhere in history books and is all around us now, greed with us at present is not a sin. With us, it cannot rise, like abortion and racial insensitivity, to the boiling point of public disfavor because it is the old-fashioned kind of sin that gathers us together. Though it clearly is destroying both our land and our people, we don't notice it because all of us are guilty of it, whether directly or by proxies given to other people to be greedy on our behalf, and our guilt looks merely normal. To most people of religious faith, as to the materialists, greed is normal, altogether acceptable as an economic motive. We don't at present grant much standing to sins so unsparingly democratic.

Global warming seems a possible candidate to become a public sin, and no doubt the climate change movement would like to make it so. But its case, I think, is weakened and obscured by the question of the ownership of the sin. The movement of climate change "believers" is fastening its scarlet letters mainly to the fossil fuel industries and some politicians. It is remarkable how exclusively this movement concentrates upon global warming, virtually ignoring the waste and pollution of which global warming is only one of several bad results. If we connect climate change to its causes, as honesty requires us to do, then it becomes a sin like greed, of which we all are guilty. But the climate movement seems more or less to drift upon the assumption that, whereas all of us waste and pollute, very few of us are affecting the climate. Perhaps because so many of us are let off without even a scolding, the emphasis is always upon policy and technology: If the politicians would just agree to crack down on the fossil fuel industries, then, as Mr. Friedman wishes, the "green" innovators and industries would install the technologies of cooler energy and "the planet" would be saved. The deal we are being offered appears to be that we can change the world without changing ourselves. We will go right on running our cars and otherwise easing ourselves by the use of too much energy (of whatever color) while the saved world will be more and more desecrated by our established abuses, and also newly abused and made ugly by fields of solar panels and ranks of gigantic wind machines. We will, in short, abjure pollution and forge ever onward with waste.

The problem, as usual, is specialization in the movements of correction and reform, just about the same as we always have had it in the industries and in the conservation clubs: Do one thing and ignore everything else. Dig out the coal and ignore the real needs of the land and the people of the "coalfields." Save the "wilderness areas" and ignore the condition and the real needs of "rural America." The problem, generally ignored by the would-be saviors of this and that, is the likelihood that we cannot save one worthy thing without saving other worthy things, maybe all of them, along with our understanding of what is worthy. It does not seem possible that we can save the newly precious climate while we ruin the land and poison the water, or that we can save the Constitution and the rule of law while we ruin the people. This is not, with us, a new folly. We need to remember that we solved the one great problem of slavery while ignoring every issue raised by our manner of doing so, and that when the slaves were "freed," we resorted to an industrial system that exploits and enslaves people in other ways for other purposes, leaving them stranded and hopeless.

The problem is that we are a people who easily resort to violence, and we have an economy of "Father Greed—a.k.a. the market" that is violent throughout. It is too seldom recognized that we enable racial and sexual violence by our violence toward everything else. Our economy applies everywhere the principle of maximum force. We have after all been authoritatively informed that organisms, including ourselves, are machines replaceable by machines. This is why our piecemealing movements to save this or that so soon decline from any possibility of reasonable discourse to slogans, shouts, and a merely hateful contention in the capitols and streets.

I believe, and so far at some cost to friendships, that those of us who want to save worthy things need to be working together on the broadest economic front to re-form the relationships between our people and our land, which is to say our actual country. Nothing is more representative of our colonial approach to land use than our "cheap food policy," which has rated the entire farm population as dispensable and by now has dispensed with nearly all of it. "Cheap energy," the twin of "cheap food," destroys without recompense whole mountains and regions.

But of course a general movement to improve the connection between ourselves and our country cannot be merely some sort of back-to-the-land movement. We obviously can't improve our care for the land without improving our care also for the water, for the unbounded air, and for the communities of nonhuman creatures that are our neighbors in our ecosystems and watersheds. What we are talking about here is the making of a thoughtful, attentive, respectful, and *saving* economy, which, though it ought to be countrywide, would need also to be local, enabling, in the millions of small places in human use, the order of loving care that they deserve, and now desperately need. So far we mainly have asked of our country how it can produce the most money for the wealthiest people in the shortest time at the least cost. Now we must ask how we can make ourselves responsibly at home in it.

To begin, it is necessary to argue for the good health of the ecosphere, the whole living shebang, even though we can know it only partially and can serve it only in the places where we live. Only if the argument is fully made and made repeatedly can it be kept from declining into publicity, public relations, clichés, and slogans. The full argument will draw people and causes together, whereas special pleading divides them.

I don't, however, believe that we can see what must be done and what our duties are without recovering a firmer, more comprehensive understanding of right and wrong. That Thomas Friedman can write so affirmatively of greed in a major newspaper is hardly unique as evidence that perhaps most of us can no longer attribute an absolute wrongness to wrong—to what we used to call "sin" before the actual old-fashioned sins were understood (by the worst people) as indispensable to "the market," and before the very idea of sin was perceived as restrictive of the "freedom" (the wants and the wishes) of "autonomous" individual persons.

We define ourselves as human only in the weakest sense of that term by our inclination to call wrongs wrong only when we can attach them to other people. The consequent little handful of public or media-friendly sins work as breeders of division and hate, self-righteousness and reprisal. This seems to force the replacement of our old need and respect and love for human goodness or "virtue" by obsession with mere reputation or "public image" or public relations or publicity, or by fear of being caught in violation of some ad hoc code of behavior, or of being publicly accused or suspected of such a violation. There is, needless to say, a critical difference between love of right-dealing between neighbors and fear of public embarrassment. It may prove simply and obstinately true that the sins, rightly named and defined, and the countervailing virtues give to human life a moral structure that is indispensable. It is indispensable because, complicated and conflicted creatures as we know ourselves to be, it defines us complexly enough.

To return necessarily now to the problem of Genesis 1:28, that old bone-in-the-throat: It is precisely our dominion over the rest of Creation, which we have always had and would have had with no help from Genesis, that calls for, in fact demands, the virtues that constitute our truest human nature. It is our recognition of sin, of the real and absolute wrongs made possible by our dominance, that brings us to recognize the need for self-denial, temperance, prudence, mercy, neighborly love, repentance, and (we had better hope) forgiveness. The virtues, I think, are not limited or confined to Western tradition. They amount, in sum, to the condition of love. The real virtues, in their opposition to real sins, work against self-righteousness, division, and exclusion and in favor of the real happiness we may find in life responsibly shared—in conviviality.

That is to say that much more is expected of us, and needed from us, than what may satisfy the wishes and perceived needs of individuals and of groups divided by racial, political, sexual, or other differences. I will end this chapter by quoting from *Walking with the Wind*, John Lewis's necessary book, which says in a few sentences what I have just finished saying at length:

> I've always believed that the only way we will ever move beyond the barriers of race is to stop seeing everything through that filter. We have to be fair, consistent and accountable to standards higher and more universal than what particular race, age, gender, community, culture or country each of us belongs to. There are standards of honesty, decency and humanity that arch above all the differences that keep us apart. To appeal to those differences only continues to polarize us.

CHAPTER V

—————— ⁓ ——————

Forgiveness

1. Polarization

We remain polarized, and the longer we remain so, the greater the distance between the poles. This, I think, is because at the poles some people recognize themselves as accusers and condemners, and the others as sinners. So long as these categorical differences are maintained, the polarization, at any time and under whatever circumstances, can only be as extreme as possible.

By the old standards—the Ten Commandments, let us say, or the seven deadly sins—sin is understood as real, serious, *and common*. Sin is understood as common because the old standards are too comprehensive and unspecialized to permit any honest person to plead innocence. We recognize the sins of other people, at least somewhat, by knowing them in ourselves. So long as the old standards were generally recognized and taught, we humans, before we were very old, had become personally familiar with several sins from our own experience and self-consciousness. As we grew into knowledge of our own wrongs and failures, we became capable of being sorry or ashamed, and of wishing to be forgiven. And so we came to know that it was good both to be forgiven and to forgive. We learned too that forgiveness had, for the one who forgave, an excellent practical result: It put an end to hurts, angers, and grudges that, without its benefit, would accumulate and go on and on, perhaps forever. It made things new. It set us free. It preempted the logic that leads to violence.

Now, our advanced civilization having progressed beyond the guilt of all but a meager handful of highly specialized sins, simple arithmetic has given us an unprecedented multitude who are sinless. A properly educated conservative, who has neither approved of abortion nor supported a tax or a regulation, can destroy a mountain or poison a river and sleep like a baby. A well-instructed liberal, who has behaved with the prescribed delicacy toward women and people of color, can consent to the plunder of the land and people of rural America and sleep like a conservative.

However, a great many white liberals have surpassed their own sinlessness to take upon themselves the race prejudice, racism, and racial violence of their ancestors, or of other people's ancestors. Because there is thus no limit to the number of ancestors, and no limit to the number of supposable ancestral sins, the burden of guilt to be borne by these otherwise guiltless white people is exceedingly great and painful to bear. This suffering they offer to their black allies as expiation or amends for racist abuses going back to the beginning of slavery. Any attempt at score-settling, however possible it may be, can thus be no small thing, nothing so ordinarily human as friendship or neighborliness or help in solving a local problem. No. What is called for is something public, large, symbolic, and monumental. To this need a wicked but generous providence has supplied numerous statues, monuments, and other conspicuous honors given to officers, soldiers, and politicians of the Confederacy. Now all of these have become eligible for some sort of deletion. And not only these, but also any public work of art that reminds black people that their ancestors were enslaved, or that reminds white people that their ancestors (or other white people's ancestors) did the enslaving. To be rid of such reminders presumably is to be rid of the pain of remembrance, which is the pain of the knowledge of history. By this symbolic destruction of the sinful past, the way presumably is opened for the arrival of the sinless future.

But not even a peaceful future can be achieved by repeated contests, descended from the Civil War, that divide people into two militant sides, one entirely right, the other entirely wrong. From that comes the further division between winners and losers, which only leads to more polarization and a renewal of hostilities.

A categorical prejudice such as race prejudice seems to appeal irresistibly to people who can think well of themselves only by means of their supposed superiority to people they can believe are categorically inferior. As a trait of personal character, this is weak and thin, thoughtless and lazy. But the categorical anti-prejudice is the same thing in reverse, and is itself a categorical prejudice. Both prejudices are powerful, powerfully felt abstractions, by which people evade or sluff off the complexity of human nature and human lives. To these prejudices, individual persons become types or specimens, crowded together and anonymous. People can escape such anonymity only by talking, working, and neighboring together for a while, maybe for a long time.

As it now is, we have people identified by slogans and signs angrily accusing one another of anger, or hatefully accusing one another of hate. The cherishers and dependents of polarity have used the issue of Confederate monuments, and by now any monument or reminder objectionable to anybody, to renew and lengthen the Civil War. The national division is not seen by either side as a wound somehow to be healed, but is widened and deepened by both sides as evidence of their virtue and heroism. They turn their terrible swift swords against the dead.

2. A Statue of My Enemy

I once wrote an essay entitled "In Distrust of Movements," with which I still agree. It does not help that any movement is likely to call forth a countermovement, which makes two movements, which doubles my distrust. My misgivings about the anti-monument movement do not prompt me at all to join the anti-anti-monument movement. That is because I respect the likelihood that, like many troubling public issues, this one has more than two sides. And so I wish the discussion of it could be quieter and more careful than the movements and the news have made it.

But before I say any more on this subject, I would like to qualify myself a little by speaking of a monument that directly offends me. I have written before of the years in the first decade of the last century when the farmers in my part of the country, my family among them, consigned their tobacco crops to the only available market and received in return almost nothing, or nothing. This was the work of James B. Duke, whose American Tobacco Company was a monopoly. Limited neither by economic constraint nor by compassion, this man embodied and enacted the "right" of concentrated wealth to prey upon and destroy the people and the land communities of rural America, a "right" that members of my family have done all in their power to oppose for the last hundred years.

As he intended to do, James B. Duke became extremely rich. Like others of his kind, thinking of his "legacy" or of Judgment

Day, he eventually became extremely generous—"philanthropist" is the word, "lover of mankind." Out of James Duke's love for posterity, there emerged at length a great institution of higher learning named, modestly, Duke University.

In the fullness of time I was invited to take part in a meeting at Duke University. One evening during my visit, I came face-to-face with a statue of James B. Duke. I was surprised, because I had not wondered for whom the university was named, and I was shocked, because I knew very well who he was. About a century after his American Tobacco Company had so gravely damaged my home country and my people, he and I had met at last. I am in general suspicious of the philanthropies of the great industrialists and financiers, for I do not believe that their beneficence equals their damage to land and people, which of course it can never compensate or repair. And now I was facing one of them, with whom I felt an immediate personal connection. There stood my enemy in his imperturbable bronze, and there I stood thinking of my grandparents in their disappointment, grief, and fear. I will say that I was troubled, for I did not enjoy and I could not admire my feelings in that moment. But I was also clarified. That confrontation made plainer to me than before the actuality of that man, his life and fortune, our mutual history, and the difference between us. I became more able to imagine some stories that I know.

And so I do not have the least wish for that statue to be removed or for Duke University to change its name—not even if the mistreatment of farmers should ever become a subject of popular concern. That statue cannot signify to most people what it signifies to me. But I would like those who are capable of being reminded to be reminded. And I must go further. It may be that my encounter with my enemy's likeness forces a necessary question: Can I forgive

James B. Duke? Maybe so. When I imagine him coming to Judgment, I freely wish he may find mercy. And perhaps I am free of him; I rarely think of him, which may be proof of a kind.

It is worth noticing that some people at Duke University have become uneasy about its name because Washington Duke, James Duke's father, was a slave owner. This is of interest because the exploiters of black people have almost predictably exploited white people also. When both races are exploited, black people are likely to suffer disproportionately because of their color, but of course both races suffer. The rule appears to be that the sort of mind given to exploitation will not balk at the exploitation of anything exploitable, including people of any race or any other category. And the willingness to exploit people is never distinguishable from the willingness to destroy the land.

3. A Third Opinion

When I was invited some time ago to write a newspaper piece against the Confederate monuments, I refused. At the time I gave a number of reasons for my refusal. Since then my list has grown longer. I will state my reasons at length here, as an offering to the possibility of further conversation.

1. This seems to me another issue, in a long history of such issues, that is by nature divisive. In the beginning people are either for or against removing the monuments. In the end, insofar as this controversy, or such a controversy, can be ended, some will have won and some will have lost. Those who speak of compromise as a civilized way to heal political division have nothing to recommend here. This is one more confrontation, more or less a combat, that the winners will forget, again to be surprised to find that the losers have remembered.

2. The removal of the monuments may reduce pressure on city governments by temporarily quieting racial anger. But it will not make the two races less divided or less prejudiced. It will not improve the worldly lot of any black person or any other person. What we are up against is an extractive economy run by a tiny minority of the wealthiest people, and, from that, the impoverishment, pollution, and poisoning of the natural world, the disintegration of all human communities, and the ill health of individuals and families. Compared to these real and pressing problems that belong to us all, the removal of statues and other works of art is easy. The dead are ideal enemies. Opposing the dead is the most expedient route to virtue for public officials, as well as a perfect distraction from the problems that are present, urgent, and difficult.

3. The monuments speak or they spoke freely, as intended, for certain people of our past. To that speech we are, and we still should be, free in our own right to reply with the same judgment and care with which slavery and racism have at times been opposed. When the monuments are hidden, they are no longer telling us anything, and we are no longer answering. If we replace them with monuments in some manner opposed, they will not stand effectively in answer to the hidden ones. Many of us seem now to have agreed that history should be confined invisibly to libraries, schools, and graveyards.

4. The monument controversy has provided, and may provide again, a prominence to white supremacists or neo-Nazis that they want, know how to use, and would not otherwise have had. Those in favor of humane values thus give occasions and causes to their enemies and so perpetuate the organized racism that they oppose.

5. As treated, this issue is superficial, simple, and sensational, calling for responses so ready-made as to be automatic, unencumbered by study or thought. And so it easily has "made the news," and so

made itself subject to the "news cycle." It will become old news. Something then may happen to revive it as new news. But what are the advocates of equality and justice to do in the meantime? The actual work, which is to say the enactment, of equality and justice is unremitting, unspecialized, ordinary, and never finished, hard to keep in the news.

6. The argument over the monuments, such as it is, is not careful enough of history. Too many questions are left unanswered, largely because they have not been asked. The Confederate generals, for example, were not all alike. After the war, some of them acted in good faith to heal the wound that afflicted—and still afflicts—this nation. After the war, the Confederate general Jubal Early wrote to Robert E. Lee: "I hate a Yankee this day worse than I have ever done and my hatred is increasing every day." Lee replied: "We shall have to be patient, and suffer for a while at least; and all controversy, I think, will only serve to prolong angry and bitter feelings." What do we actually gain by packaging all these people together like so many identical buttons and calling them traitors? That only continues the Civil War, as evidently some people on both sides of our present division would like to do, but to no good purpose that this controversy has made evident.

In addition to its carelessness of history, or its rendering of history's complexities and enigmas into a simple formula, the anti-monument movement has proposed fairly often that people should not be reminded of any part of history that offends them. This seems to be ratified by the politicians and "educators" who hold that modern people don't need to know any history at all. But of course we cannot be freed from history even by ignorance of it. Our only power over it is to try to understand our old mistakes well enough to keep from making them again.

We seem to have come under obligation to deal repeatedly with the assumption that history is now irrelevant or obsolete, as if by our greater enlightenment we have killed the past and can depend on it to stay dead. But I can see clearly, now that I am old, that history has a way of being more recent and even more present than we may wish to think. Even as we measure human time, the Civil War happened not very long ago. The people who suffered it have not been dead for very long. We still have plenty of time to think again about it before we can safely conceal its evidence and forget it.

The public officials who have removed Confederate monuments, or who advocate removing those not yet removed, protest that they and their clients are not trying to revise or hide or forget history. But that is exactly what they are doing. If all the memorials and reminders of the past are removed from public view, then the past necessarily retreats into the pages of books. Local history is particularly vulnerable to this forgetfulness, for the books are too likely to overlook local history in favor of the great events of politics and war. This is particularly true of the history of Kentucky during the Civil War, which after 1862 was mostly local. Removal of the monuments ensures that there will be no more discussion of them at all ever again.

7. The most disturbing result, so far, of the movement to conceal the Confederate monuments and all other reminders of slavery has been to subject works of art, and so the arts, to a political "art criticism" that is both proscriptive and prescriptive, amounting to censorship. This is an arbitrary power of judgment, merely assumed, by which a city government or a university administration, at present and for a start, can condemn a statue or a painting for reasons merely political—and then, for reasons merely political, can commission a purportedly, and prescriptively, countervailing work of art. How can this power now be restrained so as to apply only to Confederate memorials or reminders of slavery? This is "criticism"

of the kind that has often banned books that contained "sex scenes" or "offensive language." And it is also of the kind that prevailed over Pasternak and Solzhenitsyn in the Soviet Union. I would not hesitate to defend the right of parents to determine or limit the works of art to which their children may be exposed by a teacher. But I do not acknowledge any right, let alone any right merely assumed, of any fraction of the public to restrict the rights of the public. The monument movement after all is an outgrowth of the civil rights movement, which held that no fraction of the public may restrict the rights of any other fraction.

We need to take more care to remember that all statues, even statues of Confederate soldiers, were made by artists and are works of art. As this controversy has continued, it has drawn not just Confederate memorials, but works of art of several kinds and times, including some that are explicitly critical of racism, into the force field of censorship. As an artist of sorts myself, I see the danger in this, and I am completely opposed to it. I want to remember that the architect and writer Graham Carey wrote in the 1930s that works of art are not "our slaves to be beaten and abused, worn out and thrown away." And I see no reason to trust censorship by a public movement more than censorship by church or state.

8. Underlying the phobia against monuments and reminders of slavery and the Civil War is the exceedingly perilous delusion of human perfectability: If we who are perfect, or nearly so, could demolish present evils or present reminders of past evils, then all of us would be perfect. This is the moral ferocity that sends out hunters after witches or heretics or deviants of any sort.

Much has been made of the fact that the monuments were erected in the early twentieth century, decades after Appomattox, their opponents suggesting that they were erected only in support of Jim Crow, to intimidate black people at that particular time. I would not rule out the involvement of such a motive on the part of some people at any time. It is true that the motives of human beings are often bad and often mixed. It is also true that sometimes their motives are more good than bad, and sometimes they are good. We know that some motives have been so bad as reasonably to be classified as inhuman. More often, I think, bad motives can, with care, be attributed to the human nature that belongs to us all. Fair-mindedness and good sense ought to advise us that the worst thing we can find out or conjecture is not necessarily the truest, also that all particulars are not necessarily explainable by generalizations.

We know that in the early years of the last century Confederate soldiers were still living who cherished their memories of friends killed in the war. Widows and children of fallen Confederate soldiers were still living, and they remembered their husbands and fathers with love. I think it is a mistake to discount out of hand the involvement with those monuments of friendship, love, personal loyalty, and lasting grief. It is simply wrong to withhold all sympathy from those feelings, no matter one's disagreement with those who felt them.

The Civil War now seems remote from us, a belonging of the other world before internal combustion and indoor plumbing; people now seem to know little about it, and so can have no informed judgment of it. Let us consider a more modern example. The Vietnam War, as a good many of us thought, was a bad one, as wasteful of life and health and the human commonwealth as the Civil War. In Vietnam the richest nation in the world used the most expensive and destructive weapons against the poor peasants of a poor country. It was shameful. But then many of the antiwar people attached the opprobrium of that war to the American soldiers who fought in it, which added a second great shame to that part of our history. I cannot think of any good reason why right-thinking and peace-loving people cannot oppose the bad policies of one side of a bad war and yet regard with compassion and respect the young soldiers of both sides whose only lives were expended in suffering and death. There is nothing admirable or reassuring in a photograph of comparatively well-fed college boys kicking the pulled-down statue of a Confederate soldier. Why should we not remember the compassion and generosity of General Grant toward just such soldiers at Appomattox?

The Vietnam War ended at last in 1975, almost half a century ago. In 1982, a Vietnam Veterans Memorial was dedicated in Washington, D.C. It listed the names of all of our young people who died in that war. Many veterans of that war are still living. So are many children, onetime spouses and sweethearts, surely some of the parents, of those dead. Even if we never heard about it, or learned about it from the news, can't we—can't any of us—imagine somebody going there, tracing with a finger the engraved name of a lost friend or loved one, one among so many thousands, and shedding tears? Having imagined those tears, would it not be possible for any of us now to imagine such tears shed at a Confederate memorial a hundred years ago? I know that whatever ideology those monuments were said then, or said now, to stand for, for many who saw them half a century after Appomattox they stood for the dead. I know that their grief can be imagined. But I know also that many of us now would refuse outright to imagine, and so far to grant, the humanity and suffering of an "enemy," and to me this is the most troubling revelation of the movement against monuments. It is also frightening, for such a principled numbness foretells only more killing.

One might think that to consider the involvement of human love in human history, and from that to make some offering of imagination and sympathy, would be almost second nature to modern Americans who have made "empathy" one of their commonest bywords. But love is an egregiously complicating variable. It is opposed to uniformity and hardheaded realism. It gums up mechanical thought. It plays the devil with objectivity. It disorders accounting.

If, as some of us still assume, we concern ourselves with our history, good and bad, in order to understand its goodness and its badness, and so to know as much as we can of the truth, good and bad, about ourselves, then our judgment of these monuments is not morally trivial or easy. We have put the truth at stake. We put ourselves in danger by ignoring anything, even love, that is actually involved. What seems most forgotten or ignored is the difference between a foreign war and a civil war. Unlike a foreign war, our Civil War belonged intimately to the consciousness of both sides. To the extent, always limited, to which we are a whole people, that war still belongs to us all, a common sorrow and a common trial.

Both sides of the monument controversy have shortcut the difficulty of history, and of thinking about history, by appropriating the monuments as symbols. To their most highly exercised opponents, the ones at the demonstrations, the monuments are merely symbols of slavery and racism. To their most aroused defenders, the ones at the demonstrations, the monuments likewise are merely symbols of slavery and racism. This obscures completely a passage of our history that in actuality is hard to understand and, for those with some understanding of it, hard to bear. And this simplifying and obscuring symbolism seems to have enabled, in some of the liberal writing about this issue, an implicit sequence of equations: Confederate soldier = only a defender of slavery = only a racist = only a white supremacist = purely a Nazi or neo-Nazi. And so the verdict of the monument controversy so far is the startling consensus that Robert E. Lee was no more than both sides agree that he was: a Nazi or a proto-Nazi, eligible to be hated by everybody except Nazis.

The problem, and it belongs to all of us, is that the story of Robert E. Lee, not the statue but the actual man, is a story inextricably involving love, love of several kinds, all inextricably involving grief. He is one of the great tragic figures of our history, who embodied and suffered in his personal life our national tragedy. As such, he deserves our study and thought. I don't think we can understand our Civil War and our history since without a competent understanding of the character and the life of Robert E. Lee. I will have more to say about him.

The threat to domestic tranquility is not that people take sides and disagree, but that the sides of a political division will assume the purity and passion of moral absolutism or moral allegory, in which the people on each side think of themselves as Good and of the people on the other side as Evil. The passions on both sides then are reduced to mere anger, fear, and hatred. A society with an absurdly attenuated sense of sin starts talking then of civil war or holy war, and trending toward the psychology of the battlefield. So absolute a division forbids actual thought or discourse about moral issues, as it forbids self-knowledge, humor, and forgiveness. It may be that such division is prepared by our convention of two political parties.

It may be that actual thought about a problem requires more than two opinions.

There has been a good deal of talk of the way political division has been intensified perhaps mainly by the social media, so that people need to deal little or not at all with the others who are politically unlike themselves. Such exclusiveness, it seems to me, is possible only in large towns and cities. In my own rural community, oriented to the very small town of Port Royal, it is not possible. This is not to Port Royal's credit, but is a matter only of the size and density of its population. This precinct voted for Mr. Obama in his first race, but in 2020 the majority of its voters supported the Republicans and Mr. Trump. My family and I are not Trumpists, but there is no chance that we could live here and have to do only with people who voted as we did. That impossibility in fact reduces our interest in who voted for whom. Often we have no idea. Almost never do we try to find out. When on our visits to town we meet our neighbors face-to-face, it does not occur to us to question if they may be our political opposites. We are asking how they are, and how are their families, and did they get enough rain. Somebody tells a joke, and we laugh. Our one store, which sells farm supplies, hardware, and some groceries, also serves breakfast and lunch. At the long table in the back, where mostly men sit and there is much talk and laughter, both political sides surely are represented, but there is almost no talk of politics. Perhaps this is because we live more in the wide world than city people do. All of us have had engine trouble or been stuck in mud or snow out on the roads somewhere, and who was there to help us but one of our neighbors? And we have all participated, on one side or both, in the ancient ceremony:

"Many thanks. What I owe you?"

"Aw, I may need help myself someday."

"Well. Much obliged."

In Port Royal, thanks mostly to its nature and circumstances, humanity remains a larger category than political allegiance.

If two neighbors know that they may seriously disagree, but that either of them, given even a small change of circumstances, may desperately need the other, should they not keep between them a sort of prepaid forgiveness? They ought to keep it ready to hand, like a fire extinguisher, in case it may prove useful.

4. General Morgan's Mare

John Hunt Morgan of Lexington, Kentucky, was one of "the young Bloods of the South" whom General Sherman described in his letter of September 1863 to Henry W. Halleck, general in chief of the Union armies. Those young bloods, Sherman said, were "brave, fine riders, bold to rashness, and dangerous subjects in every sense." Sherman named Morgan as one of "the types & leaders of this class," and he made plain that he regarded them with fear and a sort of respect: "They must all be killed or employed by us before we can hope for Peace."

Morgan lived up to Sherman's characterization by nature and on purpose. He seems to have been a soldier of recognized practical worth, but with a predilection for independent raiding and guerilla warfare. In July 1863, without informing his superiors, he led his division on an expedition into Indiana and Ohio, which resulted in his capture, which resulted several months later in his escape and resumption of command. That feat is known as the Great Raid. This no doubt was good for morale, and of course it made Morgan a hero. He was the Thunderbolt of the Confederacy, and was admirable in a way, but he seems to have cultivated the adjective "dashing," heroism for heroism's sake.

Of course, Lexington was proud of him. In 1911 it honored him and itself with an equestrian statue in front of the courthouse. This involved a historical problem, which led to an artistic problem. Morgan's heroism, so the legend goes, was somewhat compromised by the sex of his warhorse, his gallant charger, who was a mare known as Black Bess. This did not comport with the sculptor's ideal of chivalry. The upshot was commemorated by one of Kentucky's better poets—alas, anonymous—who, like all of our state's writers, had an unflinching eye for anatomical detail. Here are her or his lines on the unveiling:

> At last there comes the festal day
> > For which the Bluegrass waited.
>
> Now is unveiled the statue's face.
> > The throng's in joyous strife.
> "Praxiteles this sculptor is!
> > It's Morgan to the life!"
>
> The bunting parts now to display
> > The head of good Black Bess.
> The faithful likeness moves the crowd
> > To cries of happiness.
>
> At last the bunting falls away
> > And all now stands revealed.
> A gasp of horror sweeps the crowd
> > At what had been concealed.
>
> For down the corridors of Time
> > And up to Heaven's vestibules,
> Morgan fore'er will ride a mare
> > Equipped with a pair of testicules.

This is a monumental absurdity, a sort of cosmic detraction from the dignity of the occasion and "the sages of the Bluegrass" who were its sponsors, but is the absurdity only local and of a time? I don't think so. We are talking here about a passage of history terrible in its destruction and its suffering, which yet had a verge of absurdity, most serious perhaps in the incompleteness of its intended results: the "saving" of the Union and the "freeing" of the slaves. But there is an imperishable absurdity in the idea of war as a means of peace. There was absurdity also in the persistence of the imagery and language of chivalry particularly in the Confederate cavalry and its officers. And there was a good deal of absurdity in the contradiction between military discipline and Morgan's gaudy independence, as well as in the whole enterprise of military glory as it is celebrated by all equestrian statues.

But Lexington, home of John Hunt Morgan, is centered upon higher education and the life of the mind, home also to Transylvania University and the University of Kentucky. For many years some of the students, history majors no doubt, paid their own tribute to General Morgan and his gallant mare. And here again I must defer to our poetic ancestor:

> What saddens every Bluegrass heart
> Is a continuing tradition,
> For students in their annual pranks
> To alter Bess's condition.
>
> Now every year the faithful mare
> Must suffer violation.
> Her balls are painted every hue
> Known to imagination.

The most memorable color during my own passage through the history of Lexington was chartreuse.

Now, according to the sudden convention of the urban-academic liberal code, this monument has been stuck away to where it will no longer perpetuate the evil of the Confederacy. But surely the facts of the case leave us a little room to wonder: How much actually was left of this particular monument's power to serve the Confederacy? That piety seems to have been diverted and overthrown long ago by a historical accumulation of lore and laughter. I am pretty sure that I acquired my copy of "The Ballad of Black Bess" in the 1950s, and I am entirely sure that the academic program of testicular trans-figuration goes back much further. It is hard not to be amused and instructed by the way this statue, meant to honor a sectional hero, came to commemorate instead the common life merely of Lexing-ton. And so I am somewhat happy to record here my objection to this monument's removal. A truly enlightened city government would have illuminated Bess's testicles with an imperishable pink enamel, and affixed to the statue's base a bronze tablet bearing, deeply engraved, the full text of "The Ballad of Black Bess."

So time and human nature itself would have wrought a kind of forgiveness. This would be so if, as we seem to think, forgiveness leads to forgetting.

5. Forgiveness Overruled

Now I want to consider the recent removal of a statue in Louisville, Kentucky, an event that I think is truly ominous.

At a prominent site known as the Cherokee Triangle, this statue had been a landmark for 107 years: General John Breckenridge Castleman, wearing a "riding habit," hat in hand, sits astride an American Saddlebred (five-gaited) mare by the name of Caroline.

Horse and rider appear to be performing in a show ring, such as the one at the Chicago Columbian Exposition World's Fair in 1893, at which Castleman won the grand championship.

On June 8, 2020, this statue was "taken down" by the city government for the reason that Castleman, at the age of twenty, joined the Confederate cavalry under General John Hunt Morgan. Young as he was, Castleman was recognized as a capable soldier. He was at first made captain and, in 1864, major. Clearly a reckless young man, he was heroic enough to get captured as a spy in 1864 and sentenced to death, to be spared by the intervention of President Lincoln.

After the war, he became a responsible citizen of Louisville and the United States. In 1878, says his entry in *The Kentucky Encyclopedia*,

> Castleman revived the Louisville Legion of the Kentucky militia and in 1883 was appointed adjutant general of Kentucky.
>
> In 1898, his militia unit volunteered for service in the Spanish-American War. . . . Castleman was commissioned a Colonel in the U. S. Army. [His unit] participated in the bloodless invasion of Puerto Rico. Castleman was promoted to brigadier general . . . and served as military governor of the island. . . . After the assassination of Gov. William Goebel in 1900, General Castleman was again appointed Kentucky adjutant general and was instrumental in averting civil war in Kentucky.

In 1891, the entry continues, Castleman "founded the Louisville Park Department and was made park commissioner." Articles in the Louisville *Courier-Journal* have recalled a number of times that, as an advocate for the city's parks, Castleman fought efforts to segregate them. In an article for that paper on the day after the statue's removal, Andrew Wolfson wrote that Castleman had saved "black people from lynching as commander of the forerunner of the Kentucky National Guard," and that "During World War I, when three white soldiers refused to salute a black captain, Castleman condemned them."

The removal of the Castleman statue was preceded by a drawn-out controversy in the city. Unlike some other such disputes, this one in Louisville was not between an anti-monument crowd and a crowd of white supremacists. It was between city officials, who were under pressure to find something they could easily do to appease the city's liberal activists who had truly substantive complaints, and some citizens who valued the statue for its artistry and as a landmark.

According to an article by Ben Tobin in the same issue of the *Courier-Journal*, "Mayor Greg Fischer, who has wanted the statue gone for several years pointed to the wave of protests over [the killing of an innocent black woman, Breonna Taylor, by a Louisville policeman] as more evidence that Castleman's effigy had to go." This is plainly an abuse of the word "evidence." I do not believe, because there is no reason to believe, that this statue, which bears no Confederate insignia or any symbol or sign of racism, could have prompted a policeman to shoot an innocent black person.

It can be no service to truth or honesty that the forces of anti-prejudice allow only extreme opinions about the Civil War and the people who fought in it, which only makes it fightable again, and so forever. But a person who sees something of worth in Robert E. Lee or finds a fault in William Tecumseh Sherman is not thereby necessarily a white supremacist. Between the extremes there is room to accommodate much division of mind and judgment, much wondering and questioning, agreeing and disagreeing, forgiving and letting be—the sort of conversation that prevents violence and leads to peace and goodwill.

What most disturbs and frightens me about the now-settled fate of the Castleman statue is this: After writing of one of the exemplary acts of Castleman's long life of public service after the Civil War, Andrew Wolfson wrote, "But modern-day critics said Castleman shouldn't be forgiven for fighting for the Confederacy just because he may have done good things later." What, then, may be the point or purpose of opposing race prejudice and its consequences—what are the protestors asking for—if there is to be no forgiveness, no grant of kindness, to people like Castleman who change their minds? Without such forgiveness, the movement against the monuments is reduced to an enactment merely of hatred and revenge. But this principled withholding of forgiveness also is an appropriation of the judgment of God.

The problem here is with the availability of evidence. The famous rule in Exodus and Leviticus of "eye for eye, tooth for tooth" is intended to forestall the possibility of escalating acts of revenge without limit. The rule is *one* eye for *one* eye, or justice as perfect symmetry: If I kill your dog and then you kill my dog, the score is tied, we are even, and hostility can cease. This obviously works only when the magnitude of the first offense is exactly known. When the living judge the dead, as when "modern-day critics" condemn an entire life because of a condemnable small portion of it, the case is radically altered by the impossibility of the required accounting. The biblical rule that vengeance belongs to God now becomes applicable. And we can see why Jesus replaced the complication of justice with a simpler, harder rule, which seems to work when tried: "Love your enemies." Without that rule, or such a rule, and its implied forgiveness, Castleman's prosecution and defense can go on uselessly forever, the trial itself a kind of punishment. Without forgiveness, including self-forgiveness, what can be the tendency of public protests except toward more of the same? Is forgiveness just? Does it come before or after justice? If we ask, it hasn't happened.

To issue a policy of perpetual, presumably eternal, unforgiveness against many thousands of dead people, the "modern-day critics" have got to be people who are morally perfect. They must, moreover, have attained this distinction by the age of twenty, which was the age of John Castleman when he committed his unforgivable mistake. My handicap in dealing with this matter is that I can remember myself at the age of twenty. In that year I had almost achieved moral perfection—to be duly honored by my elders and teachers—but not quite.

6. Lee

I said that in order to understand the Civil War we need to understand Robert E. Lee. That seems right enough as a sort of formula or rule of thumb. But the pressure of human limitation imposes quickly the need to qualify. And so I will say that we can't in good faith try to understand the Civil War without trying to understand Robert E. Lee. I am, after all, a fallible and struggling writer, intent upon pursuing the truth that finally only God can know. And Lee was not a statue or a symbol, let alone a demigod. He was an imperfect human being something like me and something like his enemies then and now.

He is of interest to me and my effort here not at all because of his generalship, which I am neither qualified nor inclined to talk about. And I have nothing of my own to say about his attitude toward slavery, which he rightly thought an evil, but he was a white supremacist like many of his contemporaries, North and South, and he remained so. It is merely the truth that slavery set a limit on kindness and removed any limit on unkindness, as Lee himself demonstrated when he served as executor of his father-in-law's estate. About that, Elizabeth Brown Pryor's book, *Reading the Man*, removes any doubt.

His significance for my purpose in this book is that he embodied and suffered, as did no other prominent person of his time, the division between nation and country, nationalism and patriotism, that some of us in rural America are feeling at present. We speak of it now as the difference between industrialism and agrarianism, but it is essentially the same. It is the difference suffered by small farmers, black and white, who have lost their farms because of the national bias in favor of industrial agriculture, which became doctrinal and total after World War II.

When the Civil War began, Robert E. Lee was already an eminent man. He had served with the highest distinction in the Mexican War. General Winfield Scott, his commanding officer in that war, called him "the very best soldier I ever saw in the field." Later he served as superintendent of West Point. He was opposed to secession, which he foresaw as a calamity. He was not a defender of slavery. And yet when General Scott offered him the command of the Union army, which would have been the summit of his career and probably its triumph, Lee refused.

That refusal, I think, will be difficult for modern Americans to understand, let alone to regard with sympathy. Lee refused on the grounds of familial and local loyalty. Though he had so far had a career, and a distinguished one, he was not what we now call a "careerist." He was a man of a distinct, now nearly vanished kind:

far less a nationalist than a patriot, which is to say he was above all a Virginian. Here he escapes the modern mind, or the modern mind escapes him. The grounds of his refusal do not imply any kind of "behavior," as we now use that word; they name, instead, the standards by which he conducted himself. The difference between "behavior" and "conduct" may be fairly exactly the difference between the kind of human he was and the kind we are. Behavior can be motivated, it is true, by high principles, but also by impulse or instinct, whereas conduct is answerable only to the moral standards of persons in charge of themselves. Lee said, "I cannot raise my hand against my birthplace, my home, my children." Here it is necessary to know that for him, the words "birthplace" and "home" and even "children" had a complexity and vibrance of meaning that at present most of us have lost. Allen Tate said that Lee "fought for the local community which he could not abstract into fragments." Or we could say that he was guided by loyalties that he selflessly respected and intimately felt rather than by general principles telling him what he ought to feel.

He had sworn his allegiance to the United States, to which he had so far given his loyalty and his service. His father had served with distinction in the Revolution. The Constitution and the federal union were dear to him. He was fifty-one years old. To decide between his two loyalties, to the United States and to Virginia, and finally to resign from the army of the United States, was an agony for him. But he had fought in a nationalist war of territorial expansion in Mexico. He wished that our cause in that war had been just, but then he had been merely a soldier, dutiful and obedient, with no perceived need for concern about national policy. Now national policy had come home to him and was a concern. He knew well what it would mean to Virginia to be invaded by the army of the United States. I do not believe that he thought then of slavery or of states' rights. The crisis of the Union was now intimately and exactingly his own. Perhaps he alone, then or ever, could have felt the whole burden of his choice. Elizabeth Brown Pryor expresses it as sympathetically as any of us now could: "Everything he had ever been, everything he had worked for, seemed to have culminated in that offer of command, and now he could not accept it."

He said to General Scott, "Save in defense of my native state, I never desire again to draw my sword."

And General Scott replied, "You have made the greatest mistake of your life, but I feared it would be so."

We must be careful to understand that Scott "feared it would be so" because he knew Lee. A Virginian himself, he knew that Lee would defend Virginia because he belonged to Virginia. Now it seems as if, having rejected the possibility that one human might belong as a legal property to another, we have proceeded, over the years intervening, to reject the possibility that humans might rightfully belong in any sense to anybody or anything. But personal loyalty and fidelity also are ways of belonging, and in the long run are necessary to any order definable as human.

The word "belong" and the idea of "belonging" have changed in sense and force since 1861, and that change gives us the measure of another significant difference. Lee thought, and no doubt felt more than thought, that he belonged to his family, home, and state, and that this belonging was absolute: Whatever the defense of these required of him, he was required in honor to give. Now that old idea of belonging has had to give way to individualism—or, as we lately have put it, to the "autonomy" (the independence, self-direction, self-determination) of the individual. This must be classified as historical comedy: We captives of the industrial economy—who, by the measure of what we actually can do for ourselves, are surely the most helpless people who ever lived—now pride ourselves on our achievement of "personal autonomy."

Because of the modern American—but I think not the modern American Indian—alienation from the possibility of belonging to a homeland, it is difficult now to reckon with Scott's assumption that Lee's crucial choice was a "mistake." In an uncommonly intelligent article in *The New York Review of Books*, July 2, 2020, Jessica Riskin wrote that "a consequence of intellectual seismic shifts is that, by shifting the language too, they impede one's efforts to think, write, and speak about a time before they had taken place." This states well enough the problem for anybody now who attempts to make sense, within the stress and breakage after Lincoln's election, of the choice made not only by Lee, but also by those, less illustrious, who fought in his Army of Northern Virginia. In terms of the professionalism of Winfield Scott in 1861, as of the prevalent professionalism of our own time, Lee's choice was clearly a "mistake." I do not believe that Lee could have thought so, for he apparently held his profession to be subordinate to his life, which he could not conceive as divisible from the life of his people and his place. "Mistake" implies the availability of a possible alternative. I think that for Lee there was no alternative, and he made what was for him the only possible choice, never mind the pain and grief of it, and ultimately the tragedy of it.

As they fought through the four years of the war, Lee and his soldiers surely knew that, as Shelby Foote says, they were "outnumbered and outgunned and outmachined." Though the statistics fall far short of telling the whole tale, Foote provides them early in his great history to describe a difference that for the Confederacy was insurmountable. Here are several of his sentences:

> "According to [the Census of 1860], the southern population was nine million, the northern twenty million."

> "White males between the ages of fifteen and forty numbered 1,140,000 in the South, compared to 4,070,000 in the North."

> "The North had 110,000 manufacturing establishments, the South 18,000—1,300,000 industrial workers, compared to 110,000."

> "The South had 9,000 miles [of railroad], the North 22,000."

Page Smith, in his history of the war, wrote that "more than 2,000,000 soldiers and sailors served in the Union forces and some 600,000 fought for the Confederacy."

From the perspective of the war's end, Charles Bracelen Flood, in his book about Lee, sees it this way:

> For four years [Lee's soldiers] had held the Confederacy's main northern battlefront against forces that were frequently two and three times as large. Their situation had mirrored the disparity between the North, an industrial society with a population in excess of twenty million, and the South, an agricultural society with a white population of eight million and four million black slaves.

To know that the South held out for four years, winning some major victories, against such odds is to begin a significant detraction from the idea that the war was about slavery only, or even that it was only about slavery and states' rights. There can be no doubt that the primary cause of the Civil War was slavery. We have the testimony of John Quincy Adams's *Diary* that forty years before the war the Union was already irreconcilably divided over the issue of slavery, so much so that Adams foresaw that the consequence would be tragic. But from the point of view of the Confederate soldiers, the great fact of the war, once it had begun, was that their country had been, and was going to be, invaded. They shared with Lee a settled determination to defend their homelands and their people.

Of this Robert Penn Warren's maternal grandfather may serve as an example. He had been a captain of Confederate cavalry, but he startled his young grandson, who spent much time listening to him, by revealing that he had been a Union man and against secession. Moreover: "The old man also said he had known that slavery couldn't last." He thought of the Civil War (much as Lee did) as "a politician's war," not necessary but "just worked up by fools—Southern fire-eaters and Yankee abolitionists." And yet he fought for the Confederacy because at such a time "you went with your people."

In order to go with your people it is necessary to *have* a people with whom you identify and to whom you feel that you belong. To have a people in this sense you must have a place in which you and they have lived together for generations, and to which you mutually feel that you belong. Donald Hall says somewhere that people truly settled in a place will know their great-grandmothers' maiden names. In such a circumstance, people's attention will have begun to shift from that which belongs to them to that to which they belong.

In further confirmation, I will call myself as a witness. Both sides of my family have lived in the small neighborhood of Port Royal, Kentucky, for more than two hundred years, and I have lived as a member of it. I was born among people well acquainted with my great-grandparents, and now I know a number of people whose great-grandparents I knew. I know my great-grandmothers' maiden names. I grew up hearing and speaking familiarly of "home" and "home place" and "home-folks." Every day I cross the tracks of people, now departed, whom I knew and loved; I remember them and am thankful. I am, I hope, devotedly enough a pacifist—and yet I know that if my home country were under threat of an invading army, no matter if it were the army of the United States, no matter how righteous its cause, I would be powerfully drawn to go with my people in defense. I have, after all, spent many years doing all I could to defend my region (and others) against invasion by industrialism, an economy and ideology more alien to the health of the land and the people than slavery to the North or abolition to the South. I feel against the agribusiness corporations, the chain stores, and the developers something like the resentment that people in the South felt against the northern invaders. For that reason I feel for Lee and his finally exhausted army something like the sympathy that I feel for Crazy Horse. It is an incongruity hard to bear that the South's patriotic defense of its land and people, unique as it was in the history of white Americans, had to be also a war in opposition to the freeing and the freedom of four million black people.

I would not argue that going with your people necessarily makes you right or virtuous. Going with your people can be a good thing only if your people are good, and about this there will always be questions. The obligation to love our neighbors and our enemies may oblige us at times to stand apart and to disagree. I am saying that the need to go with your people is a part of history because it is a part of human nature, and that, with care, it can be imagined and understood. We would do well at least to try to understand it. People fighting for their own land and people *on* their own land are hard to whip—something our government experienced again in, for example, Vietnam, and again did not learn.

For the reasons I have given, it is for me impossible to read of Lee's army's last terrible days before Appomattox and then to imagine that those starved, ragged, barefooted, cold, and exhausted men thought they were fighting for the right of richer men to own slaves. Most of them were small farmers, owners or tenants, poor people. Why in such circumstances had those men continued their fight? Not, surely, for any abstract principle. They fought, I imagine, because of the patriotism (not nationalism) that grew from love for their families and their little farms, because of personal pride, because of their tested and proved comradeship, and certainly because of devotion to their general. According to Page Smith, of a population of 7,750,000 white people in the prewar South, only 342,000 owned slaves. So few, so well connected and powerful as those were, could disproportionately have helped to divide the country and bring on the war. But so few, I think, could not have defined or prescribed the allegiance of Lee's army. "Mainly, though," says Shelby Foote, "Lee's veterans fought for Lee."

Robert E. Lee is important to us, and I mean to all of us, because more prominently than anybody else he affirmed, obeyed, and suffered the need to defend his homeland and his people. I said earlier that he is a tragic figure. I did not call him a tragic hero because, instead of a "tragic flaw" in the classical sense of that term, the source of his tragedy, his local loyalty, was not to him and his people a flaw.

But Lee's personal tragedy, instructive as it is and ought to be, is only a tiny part of the tragedy of the war itself. To me, looking back, the Civil War seems overshadowed by a limitless immensity of sorrow. Its history is a compilation of losses, subtractions from this world's life, never to be restored. Its victories, by whichever side, were outweighed by losses, the battlefields strewn with destroyed men and boys, the dead, the dying, the permanently injured, the abandoned ones crying out in the darkness—all of them of both sides, by the rule of war, expendable as they had stood in their ranks alive and well at the start of the battles. (Now in our dreams as we walk in those nights among the fallen, must we take care to pity only those with whom we agree?) In addition to human lives, the war, as wars do, destroyed whatever else required expending or was in the way. I am thinking of the horses and mules that bore the riders and drew the cannons and the freight wagons, the farm animals, the creatures native to the fields and the woods, the mangled woodlands, the devastated farms, the destroyed dwellings, farm buildings, towns, and cities.

The Civil War itself belongs to the larger tragedy of our abuse of our country. Thomas Jefferson, in his time, was worrying about soil erosion. In the years before the Civil War, enlightened observers farther south were dismayed by the squandering of the forests and by the planters who farmed their land to exhaustion and moved west. The Civil War, moreover, was a major chapter in the history of industrialism. Since then the craving of the great corporations for cheap raw materials mined from the land—food and timber, fuels and ores—has been virtually ungovernable until now. In opposition to it so far there has been mainly an ongoing effort to preserve wilderness areas, fairly successful, but puny in comparison to the continuing and worsening damage to the landscapes of agriculture, forestry, and mining—the foreign land known as "rural America."

The diminishing few—black and white, though disproportionately black, farmers—who have wanted to own a family-size portion of that land, settle permanently on it, live from it, love it, and care well for it—those people have been purposely overlooked, left free only to bottom out and move to town.

As all modern wars have done, the Civil War provided incentive and reward for industrial progress. The northern victory proved the practical efficacy of industrial means, and it established the industrial ethos as the ultimate recourse and rule of American life. If we are rightly troubled to find the salutary patriotism of the southern side of the war corrupted by slavery, then we must be equally troubled to find that the northern side, which freed the slaves from legal bondage, also established the industrial system, which attached the expendability of soldiers to all working people, of whichever race, regarding them all as eventually replaceable by machines.

It is too bad that our history is so discordant, so mixed and tangled. But every good possibility now depends upon our willingness to resist simplification and to know the complexity of our story as it was. Our understanding of our history depends furthermore upon our choice of a standard by which to judge it. If, as we nearly always have done, we judge our past by the standard of the national economy or economic growth, we will seem from the beginning to have proceeded or progressed mainly from one success to another. By that standard the Civil War was a success. It impoverished the South, but in the North it was profitable to those in positions to profit. If, on the contrary, we judge by the standard of the health and wholeness of our land, then we are obliged to see our history as the record preponderantly of violence and waste. If we judge by the related standard of the establishment of permanent human life upon the land—Native American or African American or Asian American or European American—the record mainly is of one devastation after another.

Against the record of so much failure, I see Robert E. Lee's choice of his native place and his people as commendable and in the long run indispensable. Just for a little while, and within too narrow limits, it was possible for an eminent white man to imagine and affirm as sacred the cultural inseparability of land and people. After the Civil War that vision disappeared from our public and political life. It persisted of course in the cultures of tribal people and in the agrarian heritage of farming people of the several races, carried forward in the talk of families and neighbors more than in print. But the economy and the economic ambition of the public came more and more to be defined by corporate industry and its great captains, who looked upon the land as expendable capital and upon the people as expendable labor, while vocational choice was more and more replaced by the brute determinism of technological and economic progress, offering "jobs." These changes have been made, over the last century and a half, at an enormous cost that has been social, ecological, and (in the right sense) economic.

Whatever we may think of Lee, his presence in our history and in our present consciousness raises a question that we cannot answer or avoid by sequestering monuments and memorials. Under our present curse of slogans, such a question cannot be heard. But if we are to cohere and survive as an American people, we will sooner or later have to decide in honesty how to think about our imperfect forebears. What, for the sake of our minds' lives, are we to say of Lee, who was not a simple man or easily judged, and whose part in our history is too prominent to be ignored? What, if we thought, should we think of Virginia's other great Civil War general, Stonewall Jackson, who thought slavery immoral, and who never owned a slave, a man ferocious and devout? And what of General P. G. T. Beauregard, who after the war led a biracial political movement in Louisiana? Perhaps eventually we will have a government commission to award monuments in quarters, halves, and other fractions to the great figures of history.

7. *Times to Remember*

Divided, fearful, and angry as the American public now is, it bears a troubling resemblance to the state of Kentucky after the Battle of Perryville when it was occupied by the Union army. When armies oppose armies, they are in uniform, and soldiers have at least the security of knowing their friends and enemies by sight. But when a large, widespread civilian population is politically divided and under the dominion of one army, then social structures dissolve and institutions become corrupted by ignorance, weakness, and unmodified instinct. In Kentucky then, any member of a onetime community, or even a family, might be an enemy of anybody else. Suspicion almost necessarily took precedence over truth. Suspicion and accusation could do the work of proof and lead to punishment. "Sympathy" for the Confederacy, however "proven," became an actionable offense.

As what I suppose we must call the legal basis of that profound disease and disorder in Kentucky, it grieves me to have to cite Lincoln's proclamation of September 24, 1862, by which "all persons discouraging volunteer enlistments . . . or guilty of any disloyal practice, affording aid and comfort to Rebels . . . shall be subject to martial law and liable to trial and punishment by Courts Martial or Military Commission"; and by which "the writ of Habeas Corpus is suspended in respect to all persons arrested, or who are now, or hereafter during the rebellion shall be, imprisoned in any fort, camp, arsenal, military prison, or other place of confinement by any military authority or by the sentence of any Court Martial or Military Commission." From there the line of mere logic leads directly to the federal military prison in Louisville during the Civil War, and on to the military prison at Guantánamo Bay during our present perpetual war of national defense.

This, it seems to me, is exactly the possibility that calls for "eternal vigilance," or at least permanent nervousness, on the part of people determined to be free. I suppose we must concede the possibility of a national emergency calling for extraordinary measures. But if the president alone can proclaim an emergency, entailing drastic exceptions to the Bill of Rights, thus making our freedom secure only in ordinary or normal or unthreatening circumstances, what recourse do we have and how assured actually is our freedom?

What is also remarkable, and also threatening, is this: Even as public estrangement and division harden to the point of hatred unto death, the public language softens beyond any possibility of exact meaning. The only "persons discouraging volunteer enlistments" whom I can readily imagine would be frightened mothers and wives and sweethearts. And who, then or now, could restrict "discouraging" or "disloyal practice" or "aid and comfort" to the safe side of ambiguity, obscurity, doubt, and confusion? Thus is official sanction given to a set of named offenses, difficult or impossible to define, difficult or impossible to prove, but attachable to particular citizens on suspicion. This is virtually an invitation to official persons of a certain kind and proclivity to mistreat unofficial persons.

For the similar power it gave to suspicion and accusation, some of us will remember the Cold War and McCarthyism, so named for Senator Joseph McCarthy, who led from his Senate committee an anti-Communist movement. This was directed against public officials and other highly placed or highly visible people rather than the generality of citizens. For persons picked out, merely to be suspected or accused was damaging. Worse was to be "investigated." And again "sympathy" was an offense. A distinct and damaged category of persons was "Communist sympathizers." As now, a perfect coincidence or identification was made between offense and offender, sin and sinner: A Communist was nothing more and nothing less than a Communist, and thus to be hated entirely. At that time, the First Amendment was under assault and censorship vividly at hand. Books, including established classics, were banned and burned. Our present spasm of violent righteousness has also extended into the libraries, even though we are now less literate than we were in the 1950s.

Once a large public division is established over some single perfectly divisive issue, such as abortion or Confederate monuments, and once the difference begins to be expressed in name-calling and slogans, then reconciliation becomes impossible. Conversation between persons and public discourse among leaders have been replaced by weaponized language emblazoned on placards and T-shirts. There is no point or value in any political side's protest that *its* labels and slogans are harmless because of their truth. Once the labels and slogans are in the air, both sides are speaking the language of perfect division, which is to say the language of mob action or warfare. They are using language as a weapon, or set of weapons, by which opponents are made enemies. The people designated by this language are no longer actual or individual persons. They are becoming, or they are, targets. This puts us back into our too familiar, too deadly old dilemma. The only way for a division between enemies to be resolved is for one of the enemies to beat the other, resulting in the division between winners and losers, the only other perfect division, which requires that sooner or later the war or some version of it must be fought again. And we Americans are a warlike people. With us every effort must be a "battle" or a "war." Cancer victims die after their "battle with cancer." We fight "wars" against poverty and disease, and of course for peace.

This at least initially is a problem of language. The remedy or the beginning of the remedy, also obvious, is better, more distinguishing, and personally responsible language: conversation between and among people, public discourse among spokespeople, officials, and leaders. This means the use of language to describe in accurate detail, or in detail as accurate as possible, particular persons, places, and things—and also problems, opinions, judgments, thoughts, feelings. To make this effort is to urge one's language toward as much sense as possible, and it is to submit one's thought or perception to the test of language: Can this be put into words? Can this be plainly said and meant? Is this supportably true? We must bear in mind that the language of division is more perfectible than the language of agreement—for the reason that, for humans, evil is simpler, hence more perfectible, than goodness and truth. And we had better bear in mind also something that I am not the first or the smartest writer to notice: that for the making and sustenance of movements hatred is more effective than love.

Another problem for us now is that in order to speak fully, particularly, and plainly, we must be willing to be known. By that I do not mean that we should relinquish all decency and privacy. I mean merely the willingness to speak as and for ourselves, to account for ourselves, to bear witness. This seems to have become unusually difficult, perhaps because we have become so estranged from one another in our mobility and interchangeability, and therefore so vulnerable to suspicion. For fear of being suspected of some wrong allegiance, people now are likely to identify themselves by category. They speak as representative persons, hewing to the doctrinal line and the generalized and prefabricated speech of their movement.

It is clearly possible to embody pure greed in a corporation so that it invariably decides in its own interest. In the same way, pure anger or pure fear or pure hatred can be incarnated in a crowd or a movement. Individual people are more likely to have "mixed emotions" or to be "of two minds." If they retain a measure of self-knowledge and self-possession, their speech therefore will be pushed toward definition, distinction, and precision. If one's anger is qualified by love or respect or kindness, or only by the wish to make sense, then it cannot disgrace itself by being pure. If one has considered that it may be good or even necessary to treat one's enemy as a neighbor, or that an enemy may become a friend, then the purity of one's hatred is at least complicated by the question of what must or might be done.

If it is hatred that lends itself most readily to organization, and is prompt to make itself at home in organizations, then those especially who wish to speak of love, and of the works of love such as forgiveness, have got to speak for themselves. They will be found always to be standing somewhat aside, listening inwardly to instruction coming from their own hearts.

To the best of my memory, the most perfected of the public angers or hatreds in this country since our hatred of the Japanese during World War II is the present politically correct or leftist hatred of the Confederacy and the Confederate soldiers. This is a moral hatred, complete to the extent of incorporating the modern-day

critical principle of no forgiveness. And it is a hatred uncomplicated by fear, because these hated enemies all are dead. And so this
is a hatred of unusual purity, hatred true and whole and nothing
else, and it has a familiar eagerness to search out and punish dissenters and sympathizers. It is in fact a harder, purer, more vindictive
hatred by far than most of the veterans of the two sides displayed
toward one another after the Civil War had ended. At Appomattox,
Grant and his soldiers treated Lee and his soldiers with a wholehearted charity, amity, and respect. The war ended, in the presence
of soldiers who had fought it, in what was described as a stillness.

Such a stillness, precious as it is, is clearly a fragile and a passing
thing. In conversations with friends peripheral to the making of
this book over several years, I have received a number of warnings
of the retribution that will surely follow any interest that I may
show in understanding the Confederate soldiers, or any revelation
of any sympathy that I may feel for any of them, for any reason.
Above all, I could not speak of Robert E. Lee with any interest in
understanding him or with any sympathy.

My friends, I think, were afraid, now that I am old, that I am at
risk of some dire breach of political etiquette by feebleness of mind
or some fit of ill-advised candor, and they would like me not to stir
up trouble for myself. But I wonder if they have considered well
enough what they have asked of me, which amounts to a radical
revision of my calling. They are not asking me for my most careful
thoughts about what I have learned or experienced. They are asking
me to lay aside my old effort to tell the truth, as it is given to me
by my own knowledge and judgment, in order to take up another
art, which is that of public relations. By the rule of that art, I would
exert myself to discover what would be most pleasing to the public
or some parcel thereof, and then I would conform my work to the
pleasure of any group by whose displeasure I may be threatened.

I am not going to do that. It is plain to me that I am being asked—kindly, mind you—to take the path leading to censorship and falsehood. If censorship begins, and I fear it is beginning, it surely will be accepted first by the speakers and writers who already have learned to censor themselves. I am taking the side of the First Amendment, which I am no longer willing to entrust either to the so-called liberals or to the so-called conservatives. I want to be on the side of freedom.

I want also to be an honest old man. I want to take the risks of my effort to be honest, just as if I were a young man trying to be honest. In my own judgment, I would be less honest, less human, and would have less hope of being useful, if I agreed to or bowed to the strange principle of total hatred or total anger, or to its even stranger implication that we should condemn Lee absolutely, deny him any consideration or understanding as a figure of significance in our history, and yet keep him present and alive in our minds in order to hate him.

The language of pure hatred or pure anger is already the language of warfare, for those are killing emotions. An invariable program in war, and it was the same in the Cold War, is to direct toward the enemy a rhetoric of moral absolutism, which excludes imagination and sympathy. This is a betrayal of what in times of sanity we have called our "humanity" and the truth, goodness, and beauty that properly belong to it. My calling is to write the truth as I am able to know it, but it is also to serve and continue our long tradition of fidelity to the humanity of humans. In obedience to this calling, long lineages of writers and teachers have kept their imaginations whole, so as to offer understanding and sympathy to enemies, sinners, and outcasts: sometimes to people who happen to be on the other side or the wrong side, sometimes to people who have done really terrible things, sometimes to people judged to be low-down or beneath notice.

At the very headwaters of one of the two great streams of the Western tradition, Homer made an enemy soldier the brightest hero of *The Iliad*. Of all the great warriors of that Greek epic, Hector, a Trojan, is the one most fully imagined and most loved by the poet. Of all the deaths recounted in that poem of many deaths, it is Hector's that we most feel, because Homer so fully imagines, and so requires us to imagine, the grief of Priam, the king of Troy, who is Hector's father.

The enveloping story of *The Iliad* is that of Achilles' anger. But the last of the twenty-four books is moved by the grief of Priam. The final act of Achilles' terrible wrath is his killing of Hector, who in an earlier battle has killed Patroklos, Achilles' beloved friend. Achilles' hatred of Hector is like the fury of a lion, and it is almost limitless. Every day for twelve days after he has killed him, Achilles drags Hector's body by the heels behind his chariot. Unable to bear more of this desecration, Priam humbles himself utterly by going to Achilles, kneeling before him, kissing his hands, and offering a ransom of many precious things. "He has come," Guy Davenport says in his commentary, "without any reason except love, to beg for his son's body." He asks Achilles to think of his own old father, and the two of them grieve together, weeping for what is lost and to be lost. And so Achilles' anger at last is ended, not by his "settling of the score" with Hector, but by old Priam's sacrificial love for his dead son.

I am not always sure of the distinction between anger and hatred. It seems certain that they can operate together in an emotional violence with little power to do good but perhaps with limitless power, while it lasts, to do harm. And Homer seems clearly to have understood that this is a two-way harm. It afflicts both the one who is hated and the one who hates. It is the greatness of Achilles' anger, unappeasable by the death of his enemy, that measures for us the countervailing power of the helpless old king's love and grief. Guy Davenport's comment is illuminating both of the culminating sense of *The Iliad* and of my concerns in this chapter: "It is Priam who ends the anger; it is Priam who makes a human being of Achilles again, taking him from the abstract realm of pure action and absolute emotion, states of mind that are akin to madness and delusion." By his sympathy for Priam's grief and love, Achilles is made, at least for a time, "wholly human."

At the end of his long story of subhumans in the fury of war, Homer gives us the figure of a whole human, one of the greatest and most glorious of heroes, a half-god who can be made whole only by human love. I am sure that not everybody will come as close as I do to reading *The Iliad* as an antiwar poem. It seems certain nevertheless that Priam's humblement by his love and grief for his dead son, if we can see the truth of it, must remove forever some of the shine from Achilles' glory.

It is Priam who makes Achilles, his enemy, whole. And it is the story of Hector, living and dead, that makes *The Iliad* whole. If *The Iliad* were only a story of Greeks at war, told from the Greek point of view, we would have only half a story. But by way of Homer's imagination, by that only, our imaginations are required to realize the whole war, a war of two sides, not a Greek story but, terrible as it is, a human story. Without imagination, the Trojan War would have been reduced to its facts and numbers, and we might never have heard of it. Or perhaps it would have been reduced to a kind of propaganda: Oh, how magnificent we Greeks were, even then! And surely we could have got along without that. But blind Homer saw it with the eye of imagination, and thus he saw it whole, and thus we see it yet. Imagination showed him the rage of violent men at war, but it showed also that rage, not overpowered for we know it went on to its logical end in fire, but more than equaled by the love of a brokenhearted old man.

When Shakespeare wrote *King Lear* two and a half thousand years later, he showed us much the same imagination at work and much the same convergence of absolute hatred and anger with a totally dedicated and sacrificial love. The aged King Lear greatly deludes himself by his selfish, and extremely silly, notion that he can free himself of the cares of kingship by dividing his kingdom between the two of his three daughters who are most adept at flattery, and who prove to be far more selfish than their father. They prove, that is, to be perfectly selfish, and therefore to hate lethally anybody between their ravenous selves and what they want. The evil to which they entirely submit themselves is completed at last by their own destruction, but not before much else has been destroyed. The third sister, Cordelia, loves and serves her father unreservedly—even though, mistaking her candor for indifference, he has disinherited her. At the end of the play, Cordelia is destroyed by the evil in her sisters that has been released into the world by her father's foolishness. But the remarkable effect of the play is that the more it is darkened by the cruelty of her "self-covered" sisters, the more brightly her goodness shines. Lear's redemption comes, though too late to save Cordelia's life, with his recognition at once of the immensity in implication and result of his selfishness and of the selflessness, the heavenliness, of Cordelia's love for him, as undeserving of it as he has been.

Let us never be afraid to intrude upon the greatest treasures of our inheritance with a practical question. What do we get that we need from the stories of the suffering of these two old kings? We get to witness the work of love in its highest dimension of sacrifice and redemption, its making whole sometimes of the most partial and culpable humans. We get to sense the forgiveness that is always at work in the work of love. How, except in the presence of Achilles' most self-lowering and desecrating fury, might we see Priam as the bearer of that love? Only as the tragedy of King Lear darkens with a limitless evil do we see Cordelia lighted with the love, also limitless, that renews the world. These writers are not telling us that this love corrects the completed wrongs of the past or that it makes life easy. They are telling us that it exists and is necessary.

Most people would say almost reflexively that this theme of sacrificial love is Christian, assuming that it has its source and archetype in the Crucifixion. But as I have shown, we might with as much justice call it Homeric. In *The Odyssey* Homer gives this theme a prominence more crucial than in *The Illiad*. While Odysseus's home island of Ithaka and his own royal household are being plundered, fairly literally eaten up, by his would-be successors, Odysseus himself is in exile, the captive and lover of the beautiful sea goddess Kalypso. Seven years have passed since the hero started homeward after the war at Troy. Finally Athena has persuaded Zeus to allow the voyage to Ithaka to be completed.

But before Odysseus can depart, he must make, finally and forever, a choice that causes him no hesitation but is nonetheless momentous: He must choose between Kalypso, with whom he would "not die / nor grow old, ever, in all the days to come," and his mortal wife, Penelope, with whom to live as a mortal husband, grow old, and die. Kalypso argues strongly against Penelope and for herself:

Can I be less desirable than she is?
Less interesting? Less beautiful? can mortals
compare with goddesses in grace and form?

And Odysseus answers plainly:

My quiet Penelope—how well I know—
would seem a shade before your majesty,
death and old age being unknown to you,
while she must die. Yet, it is true, each day
I long for home, long for the sight of home.
If any god has marked me out again
For shipwreck . . .
                    Let the trial come.

John Milton of course knew *The Odyssey*, and in *Paradise Lost*
Adam's choice, after Eve has eaten the forbidden fruit, rhymes
exactly with that of Odysseus. Eve, still under the tempter's spell,
tells Adam what she has done, and Adam sees immediately that
they are doomed:

O fairest of creation, last and best
Of all God's works, creature in whom excelled
Whatever can to sight or thought be formed,
Holy, divine, good, amiable, or sweet!
How art thou lost! how on a sudden lost . . .
                    Some cursed fraud
Of enemy hath beguiled thee, yet unknown,
And me with thee hath ruined; for with thee
Certain my resolution is to die.
. . . .

Bone of my bone thou art, and from thy state
Mine never shall be parted, bliss or woe.

I don't think that I am capable of saying how odd, rich, and essential these matching crises are. These two great figures of our tradition have been forced, not by circumstances, but by their hearts' loyalty and love, into a paradox, apparently fundamental to human experience, but in my own reading most tidily stated in Luke 17:33: "Whomsoever shall seek to save his life shall lose it; and whomsoever shall lose his life shall save it." Both Odysseus and Adam must make themselves whole, or wholly human, as by their lights they conceive of wholeness, by choosing to become *only* human, forswearing for the sake of their merely human love any attribute of divinity.

The need to make such a choice may be the supreme test that humanity must face in this world. We face something of a test even in the effort to speak of it. Here is Thomas Merton's attempt in his prose poem "Hagia Sophia":

Who is more little, who is more poor than the helpless man who lies asleep in his bed without awareness and without defense? Who is more trusting than he who must entrust himself each night to sleep? What is the reward of his trust? Gentleness comes to him when he is most helpless and awakens him, refreshed, beginning to be made whole. Love takes him by the hand, and opens to him the doors of another life, another day.

(But he who has defended himself, fought for himself in sickness, planned for himself, guarded himself, loved himself alone and watched over his own life all night, is killed at last by exhaustion.)

As I needed to do, I have laid out here the terms and a part of the lineage of a tradition of the imagination that I have inherited and chosen. I have recalled four stories of sacrificial love, in three of which some manner of forgiveness is at least implied. Of the instances of forgiveness, the most exemplary, the most Christ-like, is Cordelia's, for hers is complete. Her forgiveness of her father does not excuse his offense or consent to disregard it, but instead wipes it away, casts it into nonexistence. Lear says to her: "I know you do not love me . . . You have some cause." And Cordelia replies, "No cause, no cause." I think that these stories are necessary to us, and perhaps more so now than ever before, because they stand directly in opposition to the determinism that, with us, has become so habitual and contagious. They signify a power in us, not to be morally or in any other way perfect, but to recognize wrong and to do what is right: to become in the finest, fullest sense human, even when it is "too late."

But in remembering these stories, I also have established a direction that leads into the heart of Huckleberry Finn, both the boy and his book, and into the heart of this book of mine. It is obvious that Huck is the narrator of his book, and that his therefore is its central consciousness. It may be somewhat harder at present, when he would be dismissed as "non-college," to notice that Huck's companion, the runaway slave known as "Nigger Jim," is the book's superior character: the adult who, unlike most of the grown men in the book, has actually grown up. Jim is the good father Huck needs. And he is the teacher who, purposefully or just by his presence, puts Huck strictly to his lessons.

In chapter XV, Jim on the raft and Huck in their canoe become lost to each other, riding the swift currents of the risen river through a blinding fog. For a while Huck has a rough time keeping the canoe afloat through "a nest of tow-heads" and brushy banks, and he imagines that Jim is having a rougher time on the raft. Finally the fog clears, the river is under bright starlight, and Huck makes it back to the raft. Jim is sitting asleep, exhausted by his labors, "and the raft was littered up with leaves and branches and dirt." When he wakes up and finds Huck alive, Jim is overjoyed: "Lemme look at you, chile, lemme feel o' you."

But Huck persuades Jim that they were never separated, that he had only dreamed the fog and the night's travail. Though it may come of a boy's ignorance, it is thoroughly a mean trick. To prolong his joke, Huck asks Jim what he makes of the trash that litters the raft. Jim looks at him "steady, without ever smiling," and gives him exactly the talking-to he needs, ending with a rhetorical whip stroke: "Dat truck dah is *trash*; en trash is what people is dat puts dirt on de head er dey fren's makes 'em ashamed."

Huck clearly has a lot of growing up still ahead of him, but he also is remarkable for his honesty and he submits to Jim's verdict: "It was fifteen minutes before I could work myself up to go and humble myself to a nigger—but I done it, and I warn't ever sorry for it afterwards, neither. I didn't do him no more mean tricks." Yes, it comes hard. It is a kind of test. He is an honest boy with a good heart, but with nothing in his culture that has spoken to his heart. Mark Twain is in possession of cultural resources superior to Huck's, and so far he seems to be observing Huck's education with a knowing eye, amused goodwill, and perhaps a kind of hope.

It is an education in friendship, which in this instance entails a curriculum unusually extensive and demanding. Huck has had friends before, but those were other boys. This friendship is with a grownup, a black man, a slave, with whom he does not expect to become friends, with whom he is slow to realize that he *has* become friends. This is his first experience of a demanding, a testing, friendship. It is certainly not the first or the last friendship between a white boy and a black man, but the education and the testing given by this friendship have to do with its utter isolation. The world they are carried through by the flowing river is pretty fully populated, but among all the people they meet there is not one whom they have known before, with whom they have shared a history or been at home. If there is to be a growth of the friendship that comes from shared experience, interdependence, and mutual trust, it can happen only between Huck and Jim. But they are from Missouri, a slave state, and they are a black man who is an escaped slave and a white boy who has helped him to run away. Huck's great test clearly is in the offing.

It comes when Jim is identified as a runaway, captured, and confined. Suddenly Huck is set upon by an unstoppable enlightenment. Now he must consider everything that demands to be considered. He begins with the thought that if Jim has got to be a slave for the rest of his life, it would be better for him to be a slave back at home where his family is. And therefore, Huck thinks, he should get word to Miss Watson, Jim's owner, so that she can reclaim her property. But then he thinks that Miss Watson would either sell Jim back down the river to punish him for running away or keep him at home to be always despised as "an ungrateful nigger." And this reminds Huck that if he himself should return home, "It would get all around that Huck Finn helped a nigger to get his freedom." This awakens his conscience and starts it "grinding." His conscience preachers him a fair sermon on the wickedness of his help to Jim and its proper punishment in "everlasting fire." To quiet his conscience, he writes to Miss Watson, telling her where Jim is and how to get him back. This makes him feel "all washed clean of sin" and finally able to pray.

The account of Huck's struggle with his "conscience" is of course satire, perfectly gleeful, savage, and just, even though for a boy so misled, with so sharp an understanding of his misleading culture, it is authentically a dreadful hardship. But Huck's ordeal is not just with his conscience; it is a struggle to the death between his conscience and his heart.

His letter to Miss Watson frees his mind, but instead of praying he begins to think. His thoughts recall the history of his and Jim's voyage on the raft. He remembers Jim's goodness to him. His memories, beyond his intention, bestow upon Jim a rightful distinction: "I see Jim before me." It is Jim, Jim himself, that Huck sees, not an escaped slave, not a specimen, not a representative of a category. He recognizes Jim as his friend and himself as Jim's friend. In the present circumstances each of them is the other's only friend. He looks then at his letter to Miss Watson:

> It was a close place. I took it up, and held it in my hand.
> I was a trembling, because I'd got to decide, forever,
> between two things, and I knowed it. I studied a minute,
> sort of holding my breath, and then says to myself:
> "All right, then I'll *go* to hell"—and tore it up.

The boy thus has put away childish things, or he appears to have done so, for this is as clear and true, and as traditional, an instance of sacrificial love as any of the four that I previously described. But so to identify it is to take it more seriously than Mark Twain was able to do, and it brings us to a question that he was unable to ask.

What, we nevertheless must ask, will be the effect of Huck's resolution to lay down his life, his eternal life, for his friend? How will the rich and finally drastic experience of his river voyage with Jim work upon him in his life as a grownup?

We will never know, because Mark Twain promptly brings Tom Sawyer into the story, into the tried and settled friendship between Jim and Huck, and the forever boyish Tom makes of the book's final chapters a farce that degrades Huck and makes Jim the victim of a prolonged mean trick.

By the book's end, Huck is no longer thinking of himself as Jim's friend, or as anybody's friend. Thinking of himself now as a separate and individualist individual, he resolves to "light out for the Territory" to escape civilization, of which he says he has seen more than he can stand.

As it has happened in the story he has just finished telling, he has encountered several people who might, with justice, be considered civilized: chiefly Jim, in the fatherly care and kindness he gives to Huck, but also a few selfless women. Within narrow limits, Mark Twain could imagine human goodness. He could imagine Huck's painful submission to his heart's turning toward Jim and away from slavery. But he could not imagine how Huck might continue to live and to grow up under the influence of his experience and of his verified heart. Huck might, imaginably, have grown from the story he has told us of his boyhood into a responsible man. To say "a responsible man" is the same as to say a responsible member of a community. To imagine such a person probably requires at least an attempt to imagine, if not a beloved community, at least a community somewhat settled and inclusive and coherent. Mark Twain could not imagine that, and his failure was of a piece with the failure of his time. The American economy and society of Mark Twain's time was not hospitable to community life or community economy. That is not a lofty judgment, for our time has inherited the failure of Mark Twain's time and has made it progressively far worse.

In Mark Twain's time the great public enterprises were the westward movement and territorial wars under the doctrine of Manifest Destiny, sectional division and civil war, the establishment and growth of industrialism, industrial corporations, and industrial fortunes.

Mark Twain died in 1910. In the following eleven decades, that we can with reason think of as "our time," the great public enterprises have been, above all, a succession of foreign wars demanding and justifying a permanent industry of national defense (so called), which, in addition to their immeasurable toll in human lives and dwellings, has been limitlessly expensive to some and limitlessly profitable to some others, and which in turn has urged and justified the invention, manufacture, and accumulation of weapons able to destroy entirely everything they supposedly are meant to defend.

But also the industrialization of agriculture and forestry—virtually the whole countryside—which has completed the industrialization and commercialization of virtually all of human life.

Also the cheapening of food, always at the expense of land and people, leading to the ruin of both.

Also the cheapening of energy, always involving the assumed dispensability of land and people and the ruin of both.

Also the construction of the interstate highways for the sake, as advertised, of national defense, but at an extreme cost to local life, local communities, and local economies.

Also the introduction and normalization of television as the solution, as advertised, to a number of problems.

Also the introduction and normalization of computer technology as the solution perhaps of all problems.

Also the opening, by extravagant public spending, of the new frontier of "space" as the solution of the problem of public boredom.

All of these and other such projects, when not directly opposed to the possibility of settled communities, nevertheless distract from and obscure that possibility. People who have tried to defend their communities against such "developments," now and again succeeding, have been dismissed as "sentimental" defenders of small old-fashioned things against great new things. How could such people be taken seriously?

Well, let us see. At present two large public problems have attained the distinction of public notice: the impoverishment and oppression of many black people in the cities, and the emergence of pandemic as a possibly normal inconvenience. If the forces of public improvement deal with these things as they habitually do and are doing, they will identify and hate some enemies, protest with signs and slogans, enact some laws, and spend a great deal of money.

But suppose they should see what is plainly visible: that people could deal better with such problems if they were living in communities that were reasonably self-sufficient and economically intact. Are there things that could be done to foster such a possibility? I believe so, and I will suggest the following:

1. Build regional food economies around the larger cities to remove from food as much as possible of the cost and the risk of long-distance transportation, to reduce the consumption and waste of energy, to reduce air pollution and the threat of climate change, to encourage local food production, to improve the quality of food, to diversify and stabilize local employment, to conserve local farmland and farm communities.

2. Sharply curb the use of volume discounts by the likes of chain stores and restaurants. This could be accomplished by requiring fair, or parity, prices, to be paid to primary producers such as farm-

ers, and this obviously would depend upon production controls. The discounts then would have to be given by manufacturers and others in "the middle," who would not find them much to their taste.

3. Ration the use of energy, including energy that is "clean" or "green," to conserve resources, to promote the good health of what Aldo Leopold called the "land-communities," and to foster local economies.

4. After those measures were in place, then it would make good sense for government to sponsor cheap loans and other incentives to small businesses and small farmers.

5. So that the land can be owned by the people who use it and depend upon it, and who therefore are most qualified and motivated to use it well, every possible step should be taken to keep speculators, investors, and rich hobbyists out of the land market.

That is what I think it would take to place a proper value upon communities both human and natural, and so to make us at last a society of responsible grown people.

Perhaps all that I have been saying is pointless or useless or unrealistic or even outrageous to the modern-day haters and withholders of forgiveness. But I have been describing in the terms of my faith the line of work I want to continue and defend. Given my vocation and commitment, my mind and imagination (my heart!) would be falsified if I did not sympathize with Lee in his fidelity to the bond between land and people, so rare in the history of white Americans, so great an agony for him, so great a difficulty for us because it was joined, in him, with the history of race prejudice, which is, sad to say, the history of the North as well as the South. I respect Lee's fidelity to the bond between land and people because that bond is real. It is real physiologically, but also as part of the culture or the religion of the settled communities of all races. It is not made less real by our choice to ignore it, and so to dishonor and greatly damage our land and ourselves.

8. Peacemaking

When Lee wrote to Beauregard after the war "that true patriotism sometimes requires of men to act exactly contrary, at one period, to that which it does at another," he was speaking from experience. His choice at the beginning of the war to resign from the Union army in loyalty to Virginia was in a sense balanced by a choice, perhaps equally significant and painful, on the day of his surrender at Appomattox.

That morning, one of his generals suggested, as probably was expectable, that instead of surrendering, Lee should release his men, still armed, to escape on their own through the Union lines and continue the war as guerillas. This was a possibility real enough, as Lee recognized, and he foresaw the further suffering of the land and the people that would result: "We would bring on a state of affairs it would take the country years to recover from." Defeat had not taken from him his responsibility either to his men, to his country, by which undoubtedly he still meant Virginia or the South, or to himself as the man of influence he knew he was. Now the right thing for everybody was surrender. And so he made his way, impeccably dressed, to his meeting with General Grant.

After his own arrival, Grant, perhaps as a gesture of hospitality, made some conversation about his and Lee's service in the Mexican War. But he talked almost alone. It was Lee who called the meeting to order: "I suppose, General Grant, that the object of our present meeting is fully understood. I asked to see you to ascertain upon what terms you would receive the surrender of my army."

Grant's terms were generous. Lee's men would not become prisoners of war, but would be free to go home, subject to certain small legalities; the officers were to keep their sidearms, horses, and baggage. And then, at Lee's prompting, Grant added the provision that Lee's men who had furnished their own horses or mules would be allowed to take them home to work their small farms. "This will have the best possible effect upon the men," Lee said. "It will be very gratifying and will do much toward conciliating our people."

Lee eventually spoke of his wish to hand over to Grant the several hundred Union soldiers who were his prisoners, and who, like his own men, were starving. Grant, understanding, said, "I will take steps at once to have your army supplied with rations." And then, Lee being unable to say how many rations would be required, Grant said, "Suppose I send over twenty-five thousand rations, do you think that will be a sufficient supply?" At this revelation of the material wealth of Grant's army, Lee said, "Plenty, plenty. An abundance. And it will be a great relief, I can assure you." From that day, Lee did not permit anybody in his hearing to speak unkindly of Grant.

To Grant surely an enormous relief, as to Lee a most grievous ordeal, their meeting had been remarkably cordial. As Lee rode away, Grant and the other federal officers respectfully raised their hats, and Lee in response lifted his own.

In Richmond, some days after the surrender, he said to a young Confederate soldier who was wondering whether or not to fight on: "Go home, all you boys who fought with me, and help build up the shattered fortunes of our old state."

Rather than join some of the other former Confederate officers in defiance or exile, Lee maintained his old loyalty to Virginia: "I cannot desert my native state in the hour of her adversity. I must abide her fortunes, and share her fate." This sharing of fate is the act and the essence of the devotion to one's land and people that is properly called "patriotism."

I have told so much of Lee's story at that critical time in order to give some sense of the quietness and dignity with which he accepted the defeat of his people and his own failure, all the while continuing to do what he saw as his duty. There was never from him, so far as I have read, the least hint or tone of bravado or defiance. After his surrender, he seems to have been ruled by the wish that the divided country might be reconciled and healed.

Though I am sure that in many ways the minds of Grant and Lee were not alike, I am greatly impressed and moved by the decisiveness and completeness with which both of their minds changed from war to peace on that day—April 9, 1865—at Appomattox. At the start of that day their mutual problem had been war. By the time they sat together to talk of terms, the war was finished. For Lee the change from war to peace was simply the meaning of surrender, but his acceptance of the necessity of it, and of the consequent need for peace, made him gracious. Grant, whose terrible headache of that morning had ended with the war, recognized the same need, and it made him generous. They were accustomed to responsibility. They had lived a long time without illusions. Graciousness and generosity carried them immediately beyond any impulse of defiance on one side or vengeance on the other. We must submit probably to some bafflement in order to see this as the wonder it was: that these men went almost at once from leadership in a war of all-out brutality, as brutal as technological progress so far could make it, to highly civilized decorum and courtesy. What the two of them made together, and with astonishing dispatch, seems to me to have been a kind of forgiveness.

Maybe we can begin to understand forgiveness by considering it first as a matter of practicality. If you have a problem to solve—such as ending a war and starting a peace—surely you have got to decide what you want. Do you want to solve the problem, which is the work at hand, or do you want to submit the past to justice or revenge, or reprise your victory? Grant wanted to end the war and begin the peace. Lee clearly understood this. But he still was his army's leader, and he represented his soldiers to the extent that he reasonably could: They would need to take their horses and mules with them when they went home. Grant saw the reasonableness of this request, and he granted it. They were reasonable men, speaking in good faith. They were also men limited and flawed, merely human, but when they parted at the end of their momentous meeting, they had put no obstruction into the way of peace between their sides.

The sides they represented, as we know, also were limited and flawed, and there would be plenty of obstructions. Even so, the meeting at Appomattox that produced an authentic, if limited, attempt at peacemaking is a good story, worth telling and hearing again and again. It seems now to have no place in public consciousness. But anybody who knows the story must be dismayed to see that the Civil War has become the standard trope of both sides of our current political strife, in which the Right flourishes the Confederate flag (along with the American flag!) as a symbol of its disaffection, and the Left can speak of rural America as "the new Confederacy."

Who were the Confederate soldiers? Mostly they were country people who, if they were not poor whites before the war, were likely to have become poor whites by the time it was over, and they would remain so for generations. They are the missing persons of the now fashionable urban-academic-liberal history of the Civil War and of the South before and after. Mostly the Civil War was not fought by the sons of planters, the dangerous young men on horseback that so attracted the notice of General Sherman. Mostly they were not people who, and whose children ever after, were made rich by the labor of slaves.

People who hate all Confederates, it seems to me, are oversimplifying themselves in order to do so. They seem to be war propagandists looking for a war, relishing the division of people into abstract or stereotypic categories of Good and Evil, placing themselves among the Good—the Good, as ever in such divisions, being divested of imagination, sympathy, compassion, mercy, forgiveness, and thus another version of evil. For a sound idea of what actual goodness is and how it works, there are traditions that will serve us. We don't need a tradition to teach political hatred.

The problem with hate, especially when it becomes doctrinal or political—a prejudice, in short—is its need for other faults, such as pride and self-righteousness, and the need for victory. And so, to be practical again, forgiveness enables us to use our minds for something besides hate—for, let us say, the work of living and caretaking that is most our own to do.

I am unsure how much I have felt of the settled and sustained hatred of the feuding families of old, or of the haters of "the deep state" or "the new Confederacy," but when I was young and could spare the energy I felt plenty of personal dislike and anger, which I enjoyed very much. I learned eventually that such emotions use up a lot of energy and so are weakening. They also are powerfully distracting. They distort one's sense of what is real and necessary and valuable.

And so I believe I know with enough authority that hate and anger, and the fear that often is involved with them, are the worst of all the motives for work, except maybe for greed.

The right motive for work, as I believe I know also from experience, is love. Love, to begin with, clears the mind of the oversimplifying, mind-destroying emotions that prepare us to make war. When our minds are clear, our eyes are free to look around and see where we are, and who all and what all are there with us. We then can see both the damage we have done to our country and its remaining great beauty. We can see that we are not on "the planet" but in one of its places that, with care, can be intimately known. Love for that place shows us the work that it asks us to do in order to live in it while seeing to its need, and ours, to be whole.

I was a boy during World War II. Along with the worry, the grief, the gold stars in parents' windows, I remember the perfection with which I and my fellow boys sucked up the war propaganda and spouted it as a part of our play and daily talk—an utterly alien, officially sanctioned and sanctified, language of hating enough to kill. But as the war and its "labor shortage" wore on—late in the war, I believe, or soon after—German prisoners of war were brought into our neighborhoods to help in the tobacco harvest. One thing that penetrated the numbed war language for me was the hearsay I got of the farmwives who cooked for the prisoners as they always cooked for harvest hands—and who, with their unobstructed hearts, saw them as the sons of mothers. "Why, some of them were just children!" I heard. And: "One of them, I just could tell, could not have been a day over fourteen!"

In that language I hear, as I must have heard, the unprescribed, unorganized, unorganizable, unrecruitable tenderness that recognizes the vulnerability of the persons, places, and things of this world. It is this tenderness and nothing else by which we make for ourselves home places and make ourselves at home in them. I have retained a sort of ache from those farmwives of Henry County who fed and yearned over those young mothers' sons of Germany, so cruelly fated and far from home. It is that ache, I think, that tells of all that is precious and suffering in the lives of the living world when they have been incorporated into the structures of hatred and death. It asks us, I think, for a language able to speak of those things. It tells us, I think, that thoughtful people, before speaking, have got to look and listen through the veils of general purpose until individual faces appear and individual voices are heard. Before speaking, they have got to look past the distorting mirror of property value until they can see the life itself of at least their own among the world's innumerable, unaccountable, unique places.

I may have understood well enough the practical usefulness of forgiveness, but about the way it actually takes place in the hearts of individual persons I am not so sure. I think it may be one of the great mysteries, easier to write around than to write about. The need for it is easily shown, but I don't think there is a recipe for it. Its examples, however, can be powerfully instructive.

It surely must come in part from one's realization that all humans, including oneself, are painfully flawed and incomplete. And I think it must have some relation or resemblance to the mental faculty we call "a sense of humor." I don't mean the laughter that comes of other people's embarrassment, or necessarily the laughter at jokes. I have in mind the laughter that is qualified by our acquaintance with our private autobiographies. (If yours is as spotless as the virgin snow, I beg your pardon.) This is the humor of "Thou shalt love thy neighbor as thyself" or the almost funniness of "Forgive us our

trespasses as we forgive those who trespass against us." Those sayings, it seems to me, rest upon a wise and generous laughter that is
meant to wedge or wear a breath of space between our selves and
our opinions, and so to keep us from becoming a mere gadgetry of
politics and war.

This makes obvious what is wrong with "The Battle Hymn of the
Republic," which I so much dislike. Its author, I am sure, was more
or less a normal human, but her song implies that she never had a
minute of fun in her life. Her words are uttered through a mask of
terrific seriousness. When God has come gloriously to your side in
war, any touch of humor might admit some hint of doubt or confusion or uncertainty. Humor must be excluded, and to do that it is
necessary to exclude humanity.

9. Freedom

To invite God's participation in your war is at best an embarrassment. Again from World War II, I remember a Sunday morning
when, in response no doubt to something we had heard from the
pulpit, my mother quietly asked me to remember that in Germany that day people like ourselves were praying for victory and
the safe return of *their* loved ones. I have remembered that, I am
sure, because of its difficulty. I must have had in mind the good-
versus-evil allegory of war propaganda, which my mother had now
undone with a single sentence spoken as casually almost as a comment on the weather. She had opened my imagination to the actual
two-sidedness of the war, to an unsolvable contradiction: If you can
approve of a war and yet imagine your enemy in likeness to yourself,
there is no resting in peace.

It seems to me that President Lincoln in his Second Inaugural
Address described the same contradiction:

Both sides read the same Bible, and pray to the same God; and each invokes his aid against the other. It may seem strange that any men should dare to ask a just God's assistance in wringing their bread from the sweat of other men's faces; but let us judge not, that we be not judged.

But he had already judged and had assumed God's approval of his judgment. According to my own belief, Lincoln was right about slavery and right about God's disapproval of it. But in attempting to align the politics of the Union and the war with the Bible, he seems, as if against his will, to be drawing the outline of his own anguish. Having judged, and having held firmly to his judgment through four years of war, he can now only revert to the old ideal of "eye for eye, tooth for tooth":

> Yet, if God wills that [the war] continue . . . until every drop of blood drawn with the lash shall be paid by another drawn with the sword . . . so still it must be said, "The judgments of the Lord are true and righteous altogether."

And then comes the great, reverberant closing in which he sets forth the pattern of a hope taken from elsewhere in the Bible: "With malice toward none, with charity for all . . ." It is magnificent and very beautiful. But we can say of it only what Lincoln himself must have known: It was both too late and too soon.

In so public a statement, with its crisscrossing references to the Bible, I feel the presence of the mere man who was, because of his high placement and fate, one of the eminent sufferers of the war, wielder of great power who reckoned daily with its effects and its limits, counting the costs. And I felt both sympathy and a kind of relief in coming upon so confiding a sentence as this, from a letter written by Lincoln in April 1864: "I claim not to have controlled events, but confess plainly that events have controlled me." I was reminded that, during the Mexican War, Emerson had written, "Things are in the saddle, / And ride mankind." And so we have another complication in our complicated history. How much, after all, have our nominal leaders been in charge or in control of what has happened to us? How much have they been led by events, and events by things? How much has our destiny been slanted or bent by the prophets of science and industry, who have held that we *must* do whatever we *can* do?

Or, to try for more sanity, let us ask what is the limit of human responsibility. After we have set in motion a great violence—started a war, set fire to the fossil fuels, dropped a nuclear bomb—what is then the human power to control the results? And then to try again for sanity: On what scale is it possible for humans to think and work without being eventually surprised by large-scale bad results? These are questions delayed, now, for how much too long? And can we, after all, realize that justice attempted simply as the evening of a score—justice without imagination or sympathy or mercy or forgiveness—can destroy everything?

Such is the dusk or darkness in which we stand to judge one another. If God has measured the drops of blood drawn by the sword against the drops drawn by the lash, no living human ever will know. And I am sure that all the politicians, priests, preachers, judges, and journalists in Louisville cannot weigh John Castleman's service to the Confederacy against the good deeds he did later. Such talk only returns us to the unendable effort to equate vengeance with vengeance.

The ferocity of the anti-monument movement comes from the absoluteness of its judgment, which implies the unmitigated evil of the accused and the moral perfection of the accusers. If *they* had been born white in central Kentucky in 1841, *they* would have mounted no horse to ride with Morgan's calvary. If *they* had been born to Thomas Jefferson's parents in Virginia in 1743, *they* would have owned no slaves. But people who have self-knowledge will be brought sooner or later to some compassion for their enemies. We ask for justice for other people. For ourselves, if we know ourselves, we plead for mercy. And so—with imagination, with sympathy—we may offer forgiveness.

But what, really, is the likelihood that honest Americans of any color or kind in the present age can find themselves even approximately innocent? The "original sin" of race prejudice is not the only inclusive sin we have got to deal with, and our racial sin is not readily or neatly dividable from several others. All of us, though most of us don't know it, are complicit fairly directly in the land ruin that is far advanced over virtually our whole country. We all are addicted to the fossil fuels—and we seem ready to continue that addiction by an unlimited exploitation of the "green" energy of sun and wind. We all contribute to the pollution of the water and the air. We all are "benefitting" from our wars, our war economy, and the threat of nuclear doom. We all are guilty of the concatenation of wrongs now customarily oversimplified and reduced to "climate change." To those and other collective sins we must add the ones we commit singly on our own initiative. And so, at least: Let him who is without sin cast the first stone.

But it is not possible to think this far without realizing again that we are now defining our society as a public composed of individual persons with virtually no intervening structure. Between our separate selves and the public, we now have only remnant and disintegrating communities or none at all. And here I am grateful to have still available, from Martin Luther King Jr. and his followers, the probably indispensable goal of the Blessed or Beloved Community.

It has become easy for us to construe the terms "community" and "land" and "country" as ideas only or as figures of speech. But I need to take those terms literally. In my own efforts to think about a beloved community, I have had to understand it as inevitably a *placed* or *landed* community. The people inhabiting a place, a homeland, would be a community, first of all, because they all belong in common to that place and in common share its fate. The commonality of the community would imply, but also would require, inclusiveness. All the resident humans of whatever kinds would be included, along with the place, the land itself, and its nonhuman natives. A further requirement is that the entire membership of the community would be bound together by an economy adapted to the place and able to use, cherish, and preserve it in its native wholeness and health, as signified by its continuing beauty. It is *thus* blessed and beloved.

I come to this thought of community necessarily, I think, in order to escape the dead end represented by the "modern-day critics" who have decided against forgiveness of the Confederate dead. When individual persons gather in protest, they become a public or a faction thereof. Though they have a common grievance, and the common motives no doubt of fear and anger, perhaps of hatred, they need have nothing else in common. What is remarkable about this public event is that by its fear it is focused upon the future, which it extrapolates from the past. It is most curiously stuck, absent from its present.

The principle most opposite to fear and anger is forgiveness, which has its being and force only in the present. Forgiveness can happen only in the presently living souls of persons and in their communal memberships. There can be no doubt of the existence of public fear, public anger, and public hate, but there is no public love or public forgiveness. There can only be the public unwillingness to forgive that is implied by public fear, anger, and hate.

Forgiveness, as understood and required by the Lord's Prayer and other parts of scripture, is clearly a principle of religion. But an enforceable secular or legal version seems to be necessary also to political freedom. Without forgiveness of at least this kind, we could have no justice. We could have no thought of fitting the punishment to the crime. Any transgression of any law would make the offender an enemy of the state and punishable as a traitor. This is the official ideology of "the Party" in George Orwell's *1984*. Orwell could imagine it because he had seen it foreshadowed in the totalitarian states of his time, and no doubt also in the tendency of technological and industrial progress toward an anti-democratic centralization of wealth and power. Given the political will and a deludable public, all that would be wanting would be a total technology of surveillance.

We approach this, it seems to me, in the allegorizing of the Civil War as a contest of pure good against pure evil. In understanding such a contest, or in writing its history, there can be no imagination, no sympathy, and no forgiveness. The division over the Civil War monuments immediately came to this absolute extremity of judgment. We may thus be freed of the study of history, troubling and unending as that must be, by the "modern-day critics" who would like to bring our questionable history to an end by means of a doctrinal solution that forbids questions.

What I fear most are political and cultural orthodoxies that condemn dissension with no need to consider or answer it. In thinking of my own often marginal writings, I am glad I can turn for encouragement to bell hooks's essay "Censorship from Left and Right" and to Thomas Merton's meditations on the Soviet suppression of *Dr. Zhivago* in "The Pasternak Affair."

If the danger of thought control was not immediately obvious, it ought to be becoming obvious by now, when the taking down of monuments explicitly Confederate has progressed to taking down, for example, the Castleman statue, and to efforts to conceal or destroy any public work of art that recalls slavery or the white people's atrocities against the American tribes or perhaps anything at all that might be offensive or embarrassing to any faction with the power to take it down. Thus a tendency or a progression has been established that may, by its own logic and momentum, be extended to the statuary of graveyards, to the contents of museums, to works of art and artists, to the books in libraries, to publishers and writers, to history itself. Without forgiveness there can be no limit to accusation and retaliation. And "forgiveness" is a word now unused in our public language.

It is fearful to think that without the reconciliation that comes with forgiveness, and with no public inclination to forgiveness, we can have no freedom. The Trump conservatives have pretty thoroughly signaled their indifference to the honor traditionally given to truth-telling and the pursuit of truth, without which freedom of speech means nothing, thought cannot take place, and politics is reduced to the calculations of power alone. The liberals were pleased to censure Mr. Trump's free-flowing prevarications and fantasies, and to deplore his designation of the media as "the enemy of the people." But as if helplessly bound to the reciprocation of polar politics, they too impede and encumber truth and the pursuit of

truth by standardizing a too simple version of history; by the practice of a totalizing justice, according to which a person partly wrong
is declared to be entirely wrong; and by a dangerous inclination
toward official censorship in university administrations and city
governments, in the media and museums.

Thus we submit to the determination of instinct and the primor-
dial symmetry of striking and striking back. If the conservatives
strike at freedom in quest of power, then so, in their way, must the
liberals. But forgiveness—the real forgiveness of which the secular
version is a shadow—puts an end to anger and hatred because it
is radically unsymmetrical. It is not caused by the fear and strife
that make its occasions. It comes from the opposite direction. If
it cannot, in the moment it is most needed, come from love, then
it comes by submission to the rule and the possibility of love. It is
the most difficult and necessary and practical of all the virtues. It
unsticks us from the past. It frees us to have our being in the present
world. And no human can set its limit.

I think that the most exemplary forgiveness of our time occurred
when a gunman entered an Old Order Amish school and shot ten
children, five of whom died. The heartbreak of it is signified by
the supreme charity of the oldest of the students, a thirteen-year-
old girl, who said to the killer, "Shoot me first," hoping that her
death might be enough, and the younger ones would be spared.
And so, though her hope failed, she grew suddenly from girlhood
to sainthood. The Old Order Amish, unlike most Christians, take
literally and practice in their congregations Jesus's teaching of
neighborly love and forgiveness, even though your neighbor may
be your enemy. After the killing of their children, the stricken par-

ents went to the killer's mother, bearing to her their forgiveness and consolation.

They remember that Jesus forgave from the cross those who had crucified him.

CHAPTER VI

Kinds of Prejudice

The real subject of any writing on problems of race is racial prejudice. As with any subject, the closer you get to this one the less
simple it becomes. In order to think about it, we need to remember
that race prejudice divides into three kinds:

1. Prejudice as established or sanctioned by law seems to be the kind
that is simplest. The notable examples are slavery as originally legalized in the Constitution, and the laws providing for segregation.
Removing such laws does not remove the prejudice.

2. Legalized prejudice necessarily originates in social prejudice that
is conventional or customary, dependent upon established expectations and forms of behavior.

3. Personal prejudice seems to me to relate to legal and social prejudice as both cause and effect. It varies in degree from the creeds of
racist groups to biases that are semiconscious or unconscious. Of
the three kinds, personal prejudice, so various and dispersed, may
be the hardest to deal with, but of course it is the fundamental issue.

If the problem of personal prejudice seems the hardest to deal with, the problem of legalized prejudice seems the most deceiving. This is because the problem, so large and apparently so simple, seems amenable to a large, simple solution. Bad law logically would be remediable by good law, and that would be that. If slavery was a great evil, and if the Civil War put an end to slavery, replacing bad law with good law, then the Civil War was a good war, all right-thinking people should agree that it was, and they should be forever entirely approving of the North and forever entirely disapproving of the South.

If I could see it that way, I suppose I should be grateful, for then a good many of my latter days would be spared the burden of this difficult writing. But I am not able to see it that way. I am, to start with, unwilling to come to rest with the idea of war as a solver of problems. I am happy to agree that slavery in the South was a great evil that should have been stopped. And since it was stopped by war, it is easy to argue that war was the right way to stop it. But I would argue that war was a poor way to stop it, even if war had been provably the only way to stop it. And if war had been provably the only way of reuniting the nation, I would argue that it was, and plainly enough, a poor way also to do that. In fact, it failed to do that. If it had succeeded in doing that, then Reconstruction would have succeeded.

If, having said that the war was a bad solution, I should be asked to propose an alternative that would have been better, I would laugh. Given the sectional division as it had been for a long time and as it was when Lincoln was elected, there was no alternative. The two sides could only leap into the dark with all the power and money they could command and all the optimism they could work up. My only responsible reply is that our history might have been less tragic if either side could have adhered to its professed faith—

"Love one another," "Love your neighbor," "Love your enemies"—instead of its actual faith in solutions violently forced.

I would venture further to notice that the Civil War, in keeping perhaps with the nature of war, though it had a formal or official end, has continued in its consequences until now. Perhaps I am looking backward (and forward) so skeptically because I am a Kentuckian. Kentucky was a slave state that did not secede, which already hints at the intimacy and bitterness of the divisions that the war made here. It divided families and set neighbors against neighbors. After the Battle of Perryville on October 2, 1862, the state was occupied by federal troops. Under the command especially of the Union general Stephen Burbridge, from August 1864 to February 1865, the occupation was tyrannical, involving retaliatory killing and arbitrary imprisonment, and it was deeply resented. The official violence of the war caused or excused acts of unofficial violence among neighbors that continued for decades after Appomattox, and that we may never have gotten over. We had here a civil war in every sense.

The social and familial division and the related violence that we suffered so intensely in Kentucky were felt varyingly all over the South, for its people were not ideologically uniform. The people of the North were divided too, but I think less so. And they seem to have been undismayed by their part in the war's destructiveness, which was perpetrated almost entirely in the South. This may help to explain the naiveté of their expectations following the war.

I have made plain enough the sympathy I feel for the Confederate soldiers insofar as they conceived themselves to be defending their families and their people, their homes and their homelands.

The Civil War seems to me to have been, to an extent sufficiently noticeable, a conflict of patriotism, which is to say love for one's actual country or the land under one's feet, against nationalism, which is to say allegiance just short of worship to a political idea or ideal and to a government. This difference is well illustrated by the anthems of the two sides: the jaunty "Dixie," which celebrates the "land where I was born," versus "The Battle Hymn of the Republic," a hymn sure enough of a sanctified nationalism, in which the ever misfortunate Jesus once again shows up in uniform.

But I also take seriously Charles Bracelen Flood's notice that the war opposed an agricultural society to an industrial society. This is complicated by the facts that there were of course many small farmers in the North, and that the slave-powered plantation agriculture of the "cotton South" was obviously a prototype of the machine-powered big-farm industrial agriculture that now dominates and degrades our whole country. Nevertheless, at the time of the war there were in the South many of the small and often poor farmers of whom Grant was so charitably mindful at Appomattox, and in the North the machinery and the values of industrialism were already well established. The North made of the war a profitable enterprise. It is certainly arguable that the true beneficiaries of the war were not the southern ex-slaves for whose freedom (as far as it went; not far) so great a cost in human life and suffering had been paid, but rather the soon to be "gilded" capitalists and corporations of the North, who after the war were capitalizing on the land and resources of the South, the West, and soon enough all of rural America. John Ruskin, observing from across the Atlantic and owing nothing to American public relations, declared that what the dividedly restored Union chiefly gained from the deaths of so many of its best young men was "putrefaction and the morality of New York." The morality of New York, wherever located, has given us, as we know, an ever-accelerating exploitation of the natural and human commonwealth, plus a number of charitable foundations, art museums, and the like, which will never repay or expiate their originating costs to land and people. We should not settle upon the goodness of the Civil War without considering that the North may have won because it was further advanced than the South into our present age of general violence, industrial weapons, and a few persons unimaginably rich. The Confederacy was destroyed and the slaves emancipated in only four years, but in the 160 years from Lincoln to Biden, nothing has effectively limited the power of too much money.

From the standpoint of the North, the Civil War was fought to restore the Union and to free the slaves. Using what David Ehrenfeld has called "end product analysis," which names one of the sadder human limits, we can say that the war did free the slaves, after a fashion, and restore the Union, after a fashion. In order to do that, as we see by the same form of analysis, the Union generals Grant and Sherman invented "total war," which means maximum force relentlessly applied to whoever or whatever is in the way of victory. "There is a straight line of logic," Robert Penn Warren wrote, "leading from Sherman's theory [of total war] to Coventry, buzz bombs on London, the Dresden fire raid, the Tokyo fire raid, and Hiroshima."

I think Warren's sentence is right, and it gives a terrible exactitude to that "straight line of logic." I am much indebted to his elegant little book, *The Legacy of the Civil War*, which was meant to be, and is, a correction to the powerful tendency to oversimplify the war and its results. His treatment is complex, and he has the courage to say that the war was a tragedy and a crime. Because I so value his book, I wish I could stay with him all the way to the final page. But he brings the book to rest, after all, upon rhetorical terms such as "glory" and "grandeur" and "nobility gleaming . . . redeemingly," and there I part with him.

I distrust and dislike those words and such words. If there is hope for us humans, it is in the possibility that we can come down not only from our irreconcilable "positions" that live upon hate and anger, but also from glory and grandeur, all the way down to the unsensational, daily, lowly work and sacrifice of peaceable life. The language of such a life is not rhetorical. It does not tend toward glory and grandeur. It speaks in exacting detail of land and people, lives and places, work, good work, neighborhood and neighborliness, love, grief, and joy. As opposed to the rhetoric of triumph, the rightly guiding words are "humble" (*humus*, ground) and "ordinary" (*ōrdō*, order) and "familiar" (*familiāris*, domestic). Only the humblest, quietest, most beautiful and durable work of the workaday world can effectively oppose and answer the overbearing work of human power and glory.

Our quest for power and glory, demonstrations of our cleverness so spectacular and "revolutionary" as victory in war, has given us the vainglory of technological progress, which we have followed in blind faith nearly to the destruction of the world. Now we need to reduce the scale and the technical means of work in order to consider its quality and to stop its destruction of irreplaceable and necessary things.

The resort to total war calls seriously into question the North's attachment to the Union and its preservation. I find plenty to disagree with in Plato's *Republic*, but Socrates' remarks there about civil war are sound, and comparatively civilized. In a war of Greeks against Greeks, he says,

> if either party devastates the land and burns the houses
> of the other such factional strife is thought to be an
> accursed thing and neither party to be true patriots. . . .
> But the moderate and reasonable thing is thought to be
> that . . . their temper shall be that of men who expect to
> be reconciled and not always to wage war.

In contrast to the discretion and foresight of Socrates' (hypothetical?) Greeks, we have the perfect enmity and moral autonomy of an invading army in Sherman's conception of civil war: "[W]e will remove and destroy every obstacle, if need be, take every life, every acre of land, every particle of property, everything that to us seems proper" and "we will not account to them for our acts." Or here is Shelby Foote's comment on Sheridan's devastation of the Shenandoah Valley: "To hurt the people, the land itself was hurt . . . A full year later, an English traveler found the Valley standing empty as a moor." Whether by intention or simply by implication of the means employed, the generals of the North and their armies looked upon the South as a foreign country. They did not, and probably could not, wage war in the temper of men who expect to be reconciled.

There is also a straight line of logic from Sherman's March to the Sea, and other northern aggressions against the land of the South, to the industrial destruction of the natural world and the land economies as it continues today. The Civil War was a war of industry against agriculture, not only because of the triumph of industry then and now, but also because of its immediate devastation of the land and destruction of the means of farming as a part of the strategy of total war. And here end product analysis shows the results, from the standpoint of the "good war," to have been somewhat remarkable.

According to C. Vann Woodward, one of the several impediments in the South to the postwar reconciliation of the sections

> was the enduring effect of devastation and pillage by invading armies. The loss of every third horse or mule and almost half the agricultural machinery in the South meant reduction in productivity and in some states reduction in the acreage cultivated. Two mules and one plow could not do the work of three mules and two plows.

The land was devastated and pillaged, not only to deny sustenance to Confederate armies, but also to punish the people of the South. It seems to have been forgotten then, and often until now, that among the thus punished southern people were the four million freed slaves, who were of course farming people, and who would have to compete against poor white farmers for bare survival in a drastically depleted agricultural commonwealth. The lot of them, both black and white, would serve in effect as a captive workforce in servitude to an agricultural economy ruinous of both land and people. "Between 1865 and 1925," Thomas D. Clark wrote, "Both white and black farmers rapidly sank into the economic peonage of the staplecrop system of rising debts and falling prices." Sherman's idea of punishing the land in order to punish the people is not different in intelligence from the agri-industrial idea of punishing the land in order to feed the people—or to "feed the world," as the propagandists put it. Both are instances of a radical ideological disconnection between the fate of the land and the fate of the people that continues to plague us and to grow worse.

If there is any further question about the totality of total war in service to human freedom and the coming of the Lord, it would surely be answered by the further career of the victorious and morally assured federal army, which proceeded from triumphal victory parades at the end of the Civil War to a war of extermination against the tribespeople of the West.

But it seems not only reasonable but necessary to ask how successfully the ideology of total war—continuing in mass killings of old people, women, and children all over the world, and for us solemnized by our own participation and our "stockpiles" of nuclear weapons—can be confined to military uses and ends. Once we have officially depreciated human life to justify the indiscriminate or massive killing of any people officially designated as "enemies," how can we keep that same depreciation from being applied unofficially in our streets and workplaces and schools?

It is clear anyhow that war as we have known it for a century and a half has done more in the line of family destruction, the final separation of husbands and wives and of parents and children, than southern chattel slavery ever did. And yet while we have raised a fervent and much noticed public passion against one variety of slavery, bad as it was and as its aftermath has been, we seem to look upon war as a normal way to make a profit and to settle a dispute. Some of us will remember antiwar protests that happened here, but that was long ago.

Slavery, anyhow, was once a legal institution in several states of the Union. Insofar as the Civil War was a war over slavery, and insofar as it removed entirely the legal basis of slavery, the Civil War was a success for the forces opposed to slavery. The war ended legal slavery, which was all it could do. It did not end racial or human injustice. As the winners invariably do, the antislavery side pronounced it a good war and, with the tacit consent of its thousands of dead young soldiers, declared that it was worth all that had been sacrificed. Emerson said in 1862, and perhaps many people would still say, that the Emancipation Proclamation was "an event worth the dreadful war."

The war, however, had been comparatively a simple matter. Two governments had consented to war as a legitimate and acceptable way to settle their dispute. Two great armed powers had fought until one was finally defeated and destroyed by the other. Militarily, there was nothing more that needed doing. There were no leftovers. When the war ended, the most prominent legal structure of racial prejudice also was ended.

But what of the social presence and manifestation of that prejudice that existed in the made minds and settled customs of most of the white population of the South, and that thrived just about everywhere in that wide region? Militarily it is possible that an enemy can be beaten with fair efficiency, because in war the enemy is bunched together by military discipline and purpose, and so is massively available to be punished to the point of defeat. But the end of the war in victory for one side and defeat for the other can hardly be guaranteed to destroy the identities or allegiances of the two sides. Defeated, the losers of the Civil War went home and thus were dispersed throughout their region. There was no longer any way to keep them bunched up to be overpowered and controlled. Many of them went home under advice from some of their own leaders—Robert E. Lee, for one—to live in the spirit of peace and reconciliation. But that advice was not enforceable, and not everybody took it. Once the defeated are scattered, there is no way to keep them subdued. The history of my state of Kentucky testifies abundantly and tragically to this. The bequest of war to "peace" was continued division and more violence.

Considering the cost in wounds and deaths to both sides, as well as the fact and portent of the devastation of the land and economy of the South, the war's end brought to the North an exultation that now seems childish. Walt Whitman, who had seen some of the worst of the war—the hospitals filled with hurt and dying boys, the heaps of their sawed-off hands and feet, arms and legs—wrote several heartbreaking poems about the personal suffering and grief of it. His poem of 1865, "Come Up from the Fields Father," ends with a mother's absolute, unresolvable grief:

> She with thin form presently drest in black,
> By day her meals untouched, then at night fitfully sleeping, awaking,
> In the midnight waking, weeping, longing with one deep longing,
> O that she might withdraw unnoticed, silent from life escape and withdraw,
> To follow, to seek, to be with her dear dead son.

It is hard to see how he could have got past that and the other poems of grief, and all that he had actually seen, without some permanent scar, doubting or distrusting from then on the great abstract slogans and partisan causes.

But at the war's end, instead, he was jubilantly foretelling a new age of reconciliation, love, brotherhood, and industrial progress. In the same year he could write:

Turn O Libertad, for the war is over,
From it and all henceforth expanding, doubting no more,
    resolute,
sweeping the world . . .
Turn to the world, the triumphs reserv'd and to come . . .

By 1876, his "recitative" directed now "To a Locomotive in Winter,"
he has swallowed, hook and all, the bait of the technological future:

Fierce-throated beauty!
Roll through my chant with all thy lawless music, thy
    swinging lamps at night,
Thy madly-whistled laughter, echoing, rumbling like an
    earthquake, rousing all,
Law of thyself complete, thine own track firmly holding . . .

This is at the same time outlandish poppycock and a most dire
capitulation. By 1876 the railroads had triumphed and industry's
law unto itself was securely in place. Whitman could not have fore-
seen how firmly his "emblem of motion and power" would hold to
its own track, disregarding all else, but his blusterous optimism still
is hard to forgive.

Writing about a century later, Page Smith was appropriately less
elated:

In the initial euphoria of peace it was widely assumed
that the problem of black Americans had been settled
by emancipation. . . . One thing is abundantly clear—*no*

Americans, black or white, politicians, reformers, theorists, or seers, had any idea of the difficulties inherent in the notion of "reconstructing" the South.

That seems simply to have been the truth: Nobody had any idea of the enormously complicated problems that lay ahead. The oblivion of the North may have been caused partly by the simplicity, for the North, of the problem of the war: If your eyes have seen the glory of the coming of the Lord, all you have to do is beat the hell out of the people who have failed to see it. Partly also the North may have been beguiled by the sometimes too sanguine parental assumption that there is nothing like a good whipping to ensure moral reform and a righteous life.

For reasons obvious enough, none of the northern leaders had answered or could have answered the overwhelming question: What next? Negro slavery, as a legal possibility, had been neatly and finally ended by the war. Among the leftovers, beyond any military solution, were more than four million ex-slaves, legally free, but merely set loose and widely scattered. For a long time, as human history is measured, the two races had been living together in the South on established terms, however objectionable those terms had been. Within the limits of their differences, they had come to know one another. The black people had known as well as the white people where they were geographically. Whether or not they could have been said to be in any meaningful sense "at home" in the places they nonetheless thought of as "home," they at least knew familiarly where and how they so far had lived.

Now the old establishment was overthrown. The black people now belonged to themselves, but they belonged nowhere. They were responsible to nobody but themselves, and only they were responsible, so far as they could be responsible, for themselves. The slaves once belonging to a plantation now might sass their former master to his face and leave him with no help, but he could console himself with the thought that he now was as free of them as they of him, and he now owed them no care. They no longer had a value as property or the sustenance that had naturally followed from that value. They needed to live, therefore to work. They could offer themselves to their former master or to another landowner as sharecroppers, but they had no bargaining power. And sharecropper and landlord were likely to be about equally captive to an exploitive agricultural economy. Being free, so far as they were free, and encumbered by their racial disadvantage, poor black people were in competition with poor white people in the god-awful predicament of one-crop farming, sharecropping, and the predatory lien system that put farmers in bondage to local merchants, all within an economy in which farmers bought high and sold low.

It may now be impossible to imagine how disordered and desperate the economic plight of the newly freed black people must have been. They also suffered, I believe, from a sort of symbolism that has been attached to them by their history. From what I have observed and heard and read, I think that for poor white people, during the time of slavery, the slaves symbolized the wealth, the social standing, and the disproportionate power of their owners. To struggling poor whites, slaves were something else that the rich people *had*. This is a subjective matter and I am guessing a little, but I will offer in corroboration William Faulkner's story "Barn Burning." Though the main character in that story is racist, the subject is not race. It is the outlawry and rage that can come from long poverty combined with the sense of both an imposed inferiority and a superiority merely inherited and assumed. Faulkner understood exactly, it seems to me, the way such rage attaches itself to symbols.

The grudge against slaves, and later against black servants, as symbolic of wealth and arrogance lasted, I think, a long time. But then, after the Civil War, it seems to me pretty certain that for many southerners the black people, the onetime slaves, came to symbolize defeat, grief, and humiliation. And so their misfortunes accumulated.

It is hard not to think that the war that ended the legal problem of slavery made the problem of racial prejudice worse among white southerners than before. If there was no economic or social equality among the white people of the South, how could there have been any hope for equality between them and the black people? There was more or less an economic equality between poor white people and poor black people, but that equality put the two races into competition against each other. It could not, for example, have been encouraging to racial equality or good feeling that, according to C. Vann Woodward, "there was an almost universal preference among Black-Belt landlords for Negro tenants and workers."

The antislavery people of the North could not have wished to free the slaves into no more than sharecropping and wage work in subservience to white landlords. But who was going to assume responsibility for so many people newly set free in circumstances so unkind and so unsettled? Here it is necessary to remember that the black people of the South were not entirely destitute and helpless. They knew the country. They knew how to work, how to make do and get by. They knew how to hunt and fish and to use the wild provender of the woods and fields. And they had other great cultural resources that they had laid up for themselves. But as they themselves thought, like the landless poor white farmers they needed a way to acquire small farms for themselves. With or without farms of their own, they needed (like their white counterparts) to learn reading, writing, and arithmetic. They needed economic power, such as an asking price for their work or their crops. They needed to be helped into viable economic, social, and political citizenship.

So much help obviously was not forthcoming from the white people of the South, and so it was attempted for a while by the people of the North. This was Reconstruction. There is no need here to go into the details of that project, which would require a better historian than I am. For my purposes here, I need only to notice that Reconstruction was carried out mainly by people of goodwill, that it had the proper (and legal) purpose of giving substance and meaning to emancipation, that it lasted about a dozen years, and that it failed.

It failed because it was another project of the North to be enacted in the South. The two sections were still divided and at cross-purposes, as they had been in the war and long before it. The people of the North and the people of the South were still strangers to each other, and they did not like each other. People who think of the Civil War as a conflict purely of good against evil seem much inclined to think that after the war the South should have recognized the justice of its defeat, repented of the sins of racism and slavery, accepted correction, and done the right thing by the free black people. This certainly is reasonable, but it is psychologically uncouth. It probably shows a deficiency of self-knowledge, for it overlooks some fundamentals of human nature: People who are at home in their own country do not like to be invaded; people do not like to be beaten, especially when their defeat involves the deaths of kin and friends; people do not like to be visited by outsiders who have come to improve their politics and correct their morals. If my neighbor became my sworn enemy because of my sinful behavior, wounded me severely, burnt my house and barns, drove off my livestock, stole my horses and my crops, and then visited me on my sickbed with his Bible to make me as good as himself, I would not wish to give him the satisfaction. This we know as cussedness, a trait deplorable but common.

For such deplorable reasons, Reconstruction failed. Having lost the war, we might say, the South won Reconstruction. It was a low, dishonorable victory, for by it the black people of the South were condemned to powerlessness, exploitation, and sometimes most cruel and shameful abuse, for the next hundred years. By winning the Civil War, the North had stopped racial prejudice so far, but only so far, as it was legally instituted in slavery. Reconstruction, by contrast, was opposed by the social version of racial prejudice, which now was merely customary, widely dispersed and ingrained in the hearts of white people. This was an enemy more formidable than the Confederacy, partly because the customary prejudice was also ingrained in the North. As we know, it could and can be opposed, but it cannot be, in the usual sense, defeated. The only victory over it is in all that is implied by "a change of heart." To put it another way: Reconstruction failed because, as probably most southern white people saw it, it could be offered only as retribution and accepted only as a second defeat. The problem may have been public, but it could be solved only by persons and communities.

The solid goods produced by the Civil War and Reconstruction were the Emancipation Proclamation and the Thirteenth, Fourteenth, and Fifteenth Amendments to the Constitution. These great statements grow directly from the declaration "that all men are created equal; that they are endowed by their Creator with certain unalienable rights; that among these are life, liberty, and the pursuit of happiness." After the ratification of the Fifteenth Amendment in 1870, Jefferson's statement meant more definitely what it said than it had before. But like the Ten Commandments,

the fifteenth Psalm, and Christ's two laws of heavenly and neighborly love, these fundamental American laws are ideals that judge
us as sternly as they instruct us. We have confirmed them by our
failures as much as by our obedience. They stand above and beyond
us with a sort of majesty. Beyond those great accomplishments, the
one incontestable result of the Civil War and Reconstruction is the
proof (again) that human beings cannot be made virtuous by force.
A sinner, merely beaten or merely killed, is a sinner still.

Or—to try again—to say that the South won Reconstruction is
to put it too crudely. Before the war, for many years, the issue that
divided the sections was slavery. During the war, the immediate
issue for both sides was the war itself: the invasion of the South by
the North, not freedom versus slavery, but a nationalist offensive
versus the defense of a homeland by people who, with some justice,
thought of themselves as patriots. After the war the salient political
issue was that of racial equality. That was the aim of Reconstruction, but the conflict then was between occupation and resistance
or subversion.

Reconstruction's project of racial equality rested upon moral
ground that was exceedingly quaky. In the first place, the power
even to attempt to impose racial equality upon the unwilling white
population is itself a sort of inequality, but also an impossibility:
great power derived from victory in war employed to enforce a submission that among the defeated did not exist. In the second place,
the North was itself divided on the issue of racial equality, which
effectively cancelled the possibility that racial equality could be
established by the will of the people anywhere in the country. In the
third place, the hostility formalized and solidified by the war had
become immediately a long-term moral obstruction that ensured
the continuation of race prejudice, and delayed further national
consideration of racial equality for a hundred years. However we

may line it out in story or analysis, our history from the start of the Civil War to the end of Reconstruction was profoundly a disorder, a disaster, a darkened tumult, a bloody mess. This is why Shelby Foote said (in conversation) that this country has two great sins against it: slavery and emancipation. He meant emancipation as it was achieved.

The end of the Civil War fell upon the country, particularly the North, much as the coronavirus pandemic fell upon it a century and a half later. The Union victory, fully intentional from the start and foreseeable for some time, seems to have been almost a surprise, as if nobody had been able actually to expect it. There apparently was no plan either for the defeated and devastated white people of the South or for the freed slaves. There was no Marshall Plan, or any plan. The black ministers who spoke with Sherman in January 1865 knew in clear, practical terms what the freed people needed—land of their own and the means to work it—and Sherman evidently concurred. But how possible, actually, would that have been for the whole South and all the freed black people? The black minis-ters wished that their people might be settled in "colonies" of their own. They did not want to be "scattered among the whites," because they foresaw the troubles implied by the racial and sectional divi-sions. But to have confiscated the necessary acreage and deeded it securely to new black owners would have committed the North to a permanent military occupation of the South. Instead, the incom-plete and perhaps uncompletable project of Reconstruction was attempted for a few years and then perhaps inevitably abandoned.

What seems to have been necessary was a plan to help the freed slaves to make a stable, sufficient life and living for themselves—but also, and just as urgently, a plan to do the same for poor white people of the South, so that they would not be competing for scraps and pennies with black people. And this only bespeaks a disheartening difference between necessity and possibility. It is finally not possible to imagine how, once the war had begun, a victory by either side could have reconciled either the races or the sections. We can only acknowledge that freedom counts for very little if the free, black and white, have no viable economic choices. It seems furthermore that, faced with the settled bad fact of legal slavery, abolitionism proved to be a hollow virtue. Though empowered by an overwhelming military victory, the antislavery forces could not conceivably have imposed, from afar and outside, a just economy upon the hurt and angry South. Their case was not helped by the rich industrialists of the North who had no wish for a just economy anywhere.

To understand the limits of the public means of opposing prejudice is to understand as well how limited must be the effectiveness of public protest. I have taken part in quite a few public protests myself, as I have said. But these events seem now to be too much regarded as "all we can do." Too many of us appear to have decided that all our problems can or should be solved by the government. And so the protesters, like nests of baby birds, look upward and cry out for sustenance from on high. But the government as it now stands is an unlikely mother bird, for it is mainly a flock of caged layers. We certainly do need to protest, but not to the neglect of the small local tasks and projects that, with the help only of ourselves, can make things a little better. John Ruskin said that "all effectual advancement towards . . . true felicity of the human race must be by individual, not public effort." And before Ruskin, William Blake had written: "He who would do good to another must do it in minute particulars; 'General Good' is the plea of the scoundrel, hypocrite & flatterer."

———————— ❧ ————————

CHAPTER VII

Prejudice, Victory, Freedom

Ever since opposition to Negro slavery became a political movement, race prejudice has been a prominent public issue. Its focus, necessarily, has been upon law and law enforcement. Of a legal wrong how do you make a legal right? And once you have made a legal right, at perhaps an incalculable cost, never repayable, what have you got?

We know that prejudice can defy the law without bothering to know it. But our Constitution forbids laws against prejudices and prejudiced speech. With us, so far, states of mind cannot be outlawed. But we need to pay some attention to unprominent prejudices that are merely habits of ordinary life: prejudices, I mean, against farmers, country people, people of small towns, white southerners, white people, white men, men, Kentuckians, Kansans, manual workers, poor people, people who have not attended college. Some intellectuals are prejudiced against anybody of any religion, and this they see as honesty and courage.

Lately among leftish politicians, intellectuals, and journalists, another prejudice has been revealed: a half-hysterical fear and hatred of a country called Rural America, which they have not seen except distantly and swiftly from the interstate highways or from thousands of feet in the air. Seen thus "objectively," Rural America is filled only with Trump voters, disbelievers in science, climate change deniers, racists, sexists, homophobes, backward "non-college" country people, manually working white people with dirty hands and blue collars. The further revelation is that when urban Americans speak of "our country" they are using a metaphor; they mean the government, the economy, the military, the transportation system, and the more spectacular parks and wilderness areas; they don't mean the actual country from which they mine their food, clothing, shelter, fuels, and ores. Their own actual country is to them a foreign and an alien land.

Whereas we have opposed to the more prominent prejudices both social opprobrium and some legal recourse, we still freely insult farmers with all the means of categorical prejudice, and (partly as a result) farmers may now be the most threatened minority among us.

It is wrong to rank prejudices as good or bad. All prejudices are of a kind and are allied. They thrive on ignorance, and they belong to human nature. When we make a judgment against people we don't know, that is prejudice. When we make a judgment in favor of people we don't know, that also is prejudice. A favorable prejudice is as disguising and blinding, as unjust, and may become as damaging, as an unfavorable prejudice. Negative and positive prejudices, in fact, often work in tandem. Farmers, for example, are both idealized as "children of the soil" in close communion with Nature and God and are held in contempt as dispensable yokels who do "mind-numbing work."

I doubt that there is any identifiable group that is not the object of an antipathetic prejudice. As an old white southern rural man, always a farmer, I am aware that my own eligibility is obvious and manifold. Though my suffering has not been great—I have seldom been personally affronted and have never received an amorous pinch—I know that the several prejudices for which I am eligible are varyingly harmful and have done damage. I can testify that it is no pleasure to feel a stranger's ready-made contempt working under your skin. When I have felt it, it has made me mad. This leads me to think that one of the harms of prejudice must be the negative, wasteful, and wasting emotion that it causes.

People who suffer unprominent prejudices have no prominent remedies. No farmers are going to sue or publicly embarrass anybody for denigrating them by caricature or "hate speech." And thus we are instructed. The only real remedies for unprominent prejudices, as for prominent ones, are particular knowledge, common decency, and good manners. And here I can say (with some authority) that if an administrator at one of the land grant colleges of agriculture should decide that each of her faculty members should get to know one farmer, she would fall conspicuously short of success. It happens that professors and researchers in a great agricultural college are educated, sophisticated, and of course remunerated several steps above the ability to converse with a farmer. What on earth would they talk about? I am reminded that I may be speaking here from a prejudice of my own. Maybe so.

It is love that leads us toward particular knowledge, and it helps us to learn what we need to know. It leads us toward vocation, the work we truly want to do, are born to do, and therefore must learn to do well. I am talking about the hardworking familial and neighborly love that commits itself and hangs on like a hair in a biscuit. This is love that can be enacted, whether or not it is felt. The solutions that this love advocates come from knowing what is right, not for the future, but now and always. Its solutions propose everybody's good, not spoils to the victors, not victory. Love, opposing the waste and pollution of a beloved place, does so because it understands health as wholeness, good for everybody, even for those who defend waste and pollution as "freedom." In the absence of love, the dominant motives almost certainly will be fear, anger, and hate, from which nothing good can come. Fear, anger, and hate beget two sides, each the enemy of the other. Love is given up as a motive, health and wholeness as the standard or purpose of work. Each side works only for the defeat of the others, telling itself that its victory will bring righteousness and peace "in the future."

Anger and the other negative emotions, understandable as they may be, are now the preferred motives of politics, including the politics of race. Anger raises the volume of outcries for justice, but it also corrupts the idea of justice with impulses of punishment or revenge. The ruling principle is that the scales of Justice should be balanced. In the highly ordered procedures of our courts of law, the principle of balance is effective and it does tend toward justice. But we know that in the currents of public or political life, justice is apt to become merely a slogan, and instead of balance there comes a sort of rhythm of retributions passing back and forth between two hostile sides. The wrong in this is the establishment of a war-like logic that calls for the final, but never actually final, defeat of one side by the other. The bad result, immediately and in the long term, is the exclusion of love as a motive. This seems to me to be the risk attached to the call for "reparations," as that term currently is understood.

The underlying or justifying assumption of the movement for

reparations seems to be that the slaves by their labor during the time of slavery produced a cumulative great fund of wealth, from which they of course did not benefit, but from which all white people more or less uniformly have benefitted to this day. Contemporary white people's standard response to the reparations project, I imagine, is always going to be that *they* did not enslave any black people or own any slaves. This, obviously, is true. The iniquity of fathers may be passed to their children, as the Bible says, but the children at least did not *commit* their fathers' iniquities.

But do they now, or did they or their families ever, own any wealth earned by slaves and handed down to them by slaveholding ancestors? There is a pretty fair likelihood that the answer, for any particular now-living white American, is no. People living in the southern Appalachians or other topographically rough lands in the South were unlikely to own slaves. Many Appalachian families were Unionists and opponents of slavery. They were subsistence farmers at the time of the Civil War. Many of them later became coal miners, and still later became jobless and extremely poor, or they moved to industrial jobs that did not make them wealthy. The people who took grants of land under the Homestead Act of 1862 most likely had no slave-earned wealth; people in need of 160 acres were not rich. I have no statistics, but to me it seems expectable that hereditarily poor white people are much more numerous than hereditarily rich white people. And we know of the long existence of "poor whites" in the South: people you will find, along with poor blacks, in the books of William Faulkner and Erskine Caldwell.

Because of my preoccupation for many years with the history and fate of rural America, I have been preoccupied also with questions about money, chiefly, Where does it come from? And, Where does it go? I bear in mind that money is an exceedingly poor measure of real wealth, but it seems to me that even our presently questionable supply of money must originate in the natural world, for there is no other source. From the land, the wealth rises first into what I would call "the land economy"—the work and earning of farmers, forest workers, and miners. Those people make the world's goods available to the corporate sector, which takes them at the lowest possible price, and then profits at the highest possible rate from their resale, manufacture, packaging, and marketing. This we call "the economy." By means of it, there are now a lot of people who have too much money—far more money, I believe, than could be responsibly earned. In addition, there are the large sums of money that are gathered up by various forms of usury. It seems to me that in this enormous, complicated, obscure so-called economy, any wealth derived specifically from the exploitation of black people would be extremely difficult to locate. That does not invalidate the case for reparations, but there is a great complication that we can't escape and so we need to remember: This unstable money-measured economy has flourished for a long time—however temporarily—upon the exploitation and steady depletion of both the land and the people. I mean nearly all of the land and nearly all of the people.

In this economy it is true that black people and other people of color have suffered in general more than white people, but a lot of white people also have suffered. Some of the suffering is distinctly that of black people, for it includes the history of chattel slavery in the South and the racial oppressions that followed. But sometimes both races have suffered the same oppression. In his essay on reparations, Ta-Nehisi Coates speaks of the "second slavery" that ruled over the freed slaves in the South after the Civil War, but, as is now the custom, he ignores the poor whites who at the same time lived under the same rule. This was the lien system, which was in every sense a form of slavery, except that the sharecroppers and poor farmers were not owned as chattels by the merchants they were obliged to borrow from. The merchants owned only the livelihoods that they in effect loaned annually to the borrowers at usurious interest. White and black farmers of course were thrown into competition for the scant livelihoods afforded by this system. And this of course could not have been conducive to easy relations between the races.

It is certainly true that the prejudice against black people has been a burden to be borne, with some variation of fate and fortune, by all black people. That all white people have benefitted from the forced labor and impoverishment of black people is not true. In *Dixie's Forgotten People: The South's Poor Whites*, Wayne Flynt makes the contrary point that southern poor whites too were impoverished by slavery:

> Historians, Northern abolitionists, and even some antebellum Southerners . . . blamed slavery for the presence of so many dispossessed whites. In the slave economy, Negroes monopolized agricultural and nonagricultural jobs. Planters rented out their skilled slaves who competed with whites. . . . The presence of slave labor, together with the poor white sense of racial superiority, also placed a stigma on certain types of labor; some students of poor whites argued that slavery stigmatized *all* forms of physical labor in the South.

I will return in Chapter VIII to the stigma on physical labor to argue that, originating with slavery, that stigma was a contagion that spread eventually over the whole country, North as well as South.

Though they have experienced their own large share of prejudice, poor white people have had few advocates, and they have not figured at all, so far as I have read or heard, in current discussions of the problems of poor black people. Their fairest advocate, within my own reading, was Martin Luther King Jr., who stood up for them in a chapter, "The Days to Come," of his book *Why We Can't Wait*, published in 1964. In that chapter he proposes a Bill of Rights for the Disadvantaged, which would provide, in accordance with a principle in common law, "a remedy for the appropriation of the labor of one human being by another." He has in mind, expectably and properly, the black Americans descended from slaves, and he is arguing first of all for them. But he goes on to these remarkable sentences:

> The moral justification for special measures for Negroes is rooted in the robberies inherent in the institution of slavery. Many poor whites, however, were the derivative victims of slavery. As long as labor was cheapened by the involuntary servitude of the black man, the freedom of white labor, especially in the South, was little more than a myth. It was free only to bargain from the depressed base imposed by slavery upon the whole labor market. Nor did this derivative bondage end when formal slavery gave way to the de facto slavery of discrimination. To this day the white poor also suffer deprivation and the humiliation of poverty if not of color . . . In one sense it is more evil for them, because it has confused so many by prejudice that they have supported their own oppressors.
>
> It is a simple matter of justice that America, in dealing creatively with the task of raising the Negro from backwardness, should also be rescuing a large stratum of the forgotten white poor.

King's Bill of Rights for the Disadvantaged is an early version of reparations, but here King acknowledges the need for a remedy that is not exclusive. What is especially moving to me in this passage is his understanding of the likely racism of the people he is including in his hope. Maybe it is not sufficiently appreciated that King was a Christian, who steadfastly included everybody, even his enemies, within his advocacy and his good will. He seems to have understood and accepted fearlessly that his faith above all should not be limited in its reach and embrace. Late in his life he was extending his charity and care to the battered fields and villages of Vietnam, and I will need to think again of that.

It appears to me to be wrong, and always potentially misleading, to think with concern of black Americans without eventually thinking also of white Americans, with whom the black Americans share somewhat the same identity, as for example consumers in a consumptive economy, and more than somewhat the same fate—just as it would certainly be wrong to think at any length about white Americans without thinking also of black Americans.

If, after the Civil War, the forty acres and a mule, which the freed black people knew they needed and which they asked for, had been granted only to them, excluding the poor whites, that would have established a bottom class of landless poor whites. It would have guaranteed a continuing racial animosity more bitter and extreme than Jim Crow. Just as a matter of practical politics, the landless poor whites would have had to be included in that so far illusory bounty.

I regard such supposing as that with suspicion, but as a sort of parable it may have validity. It suggests to me that it may be impractical, even dangerous, to make too special a thing of black poverty. That there also are many impoverished white people ought to suggest that race prejudice is not the only cause of poverty, and that it may not be the major cause. For that reason I see real promise in the thinking of the Louisville politician Charles Booker, whose anti-poverty project is called "From the Hood to the Holler," by which he means that, in our generally poor state, a sufficiently radical concern for poverty would extend from the poor, mostly black neighborhoods of western Louisville to the poor, mostly white counties in eastern Kentucky. We cannot be sure what may come of this, but I think we can be sure that something *could* come of it, because it comes from actual thought. As a rural Kentuckian, I hope that a project so expansive and unifying can include also our other rural counties, which are not notoriously poor but are poor enough and are eligible, I fear, to become much poorer.

My contention, which by now should be plain, is that the sins of the past are real; that they have done real damages that afflict us now and will afflict us in the future; and that reparations therefore are called for, but not exclusively to one category of people. Maybe it is for the sake of coherence and economy that arguments for reparations are sometimes so focused upon black people. This most surprisingly and obviously leaves out the reparations that are owed to the American Indian tribes. But people of other races and origins also have been seen as distinctly inferior, and also have been used for the fundamental work that some white people have thought themselves too good to do. For example, the dependence of our food supply upon the "stoop labor" of Mexican migrants has been notorious for a long time.

But I need to argue also that reparations are not owed exclusively to humans. We are using our land, our country, increasingly with the same condescension and cruelty with which we have used the racial minorities whom we have subjugated to our use and convenience. Slavery, in one form or another, has arguably been a constant of American history from the beginning until now.

If we want to get to the root of that problem, I think we have to consider first of all the dominance, among those who have been dominant, of the willingness to separate things that belong together and, above all, to separate land and people. This may derive from the circumstance that, except for the Indians, all of us came here, and even in human time not so long ago, as immigrants separated from our homelands. That it is dangerous to separate land and people we could have learned—and so far have failed to learn—from the Indians, or from the freed slaves and other agrarian Americans.

The freed slaves asked for land to go with their freedom, because they knew that to have a piece of land of their own under their feet would be the means of having and preserving such actual freedom as they might derive from the formality of emancipation. Their thought in this matter clearly agrees with that of Thomas Jefferson, and so it confirms and encourages surviving agrarians.

As we know, the freed slaves got no land that they did not buy for themselves—which a remarkable number of them did in the half century following the Civil War. But they knew what nearly all of us have now forgotten: that the most fundamental freedom, more fundamental even than the freedom of workers to choose their work, is freedom from hunger. They knew that as long as they could not produce food for themselves from their own land, as long as their only economic resource was their labor, they could not be securely free—unless to work or beg or starve is a free choice. They were true prophets in their time, and they are true prophets still.

Their truth was verified by the numerous farmers and tenant farmers, black and white, who would remember that in the depressed years of the 1920s and '30s, "We were poor, but we were never hungry" or "We were poor, but we didn't know it." If the freed slaves' wish to own land could have been granted, then *they* might have led us into an agrarian economy in which democracy would have rested upon the widespread possession and use of small economic properties.

Our founding documents said nothing of freedom from hunger because there was at that time no apparent need to do so, for the agrarian assumptions then prevailed. It was probably not conceivable then that the Declaration of Independence should have named the right to eat. It is, however, of the greatest importance to remember that the rights it does name were understood as God-given, not granted or conceded to us by the government of Great Britain, or by any government ever. They were ours by a divine deed of gift, defendable by war, as proposed, but not procurable by war. We have conceived of them since then as defendable mainly or only by war. It seems not to have occurred to our teachers and leaders that our rights to "life, liberty, and the pursuit of happiness" might most effectively be defended by the reasonable and attainable economic self-sufficiency of persons, households, and local communities.

What we chose instead is our present domination by industrialism, in which working people gave up their vocations and useful properties in exchange for "good jobs" or jobs of any kind or no jobs. The corporate industrialists promote technology and strive for job elimination, while the politicians praise technology and promise "job creation." And now that "jobs" and "job growth" and "job creation" prevail over us, self-employment is not a possibility even spoken of, though many people must suffer for want of it. Maybe it is now too difficult or too painful for us to think that the primary, and one of the worst, oppressions of chattel slavery was to be deprived of the freedom, independence, and joy of self-employment—yet such exactly was the longing and the vision of the freed slaves.

In the generation before mine, farmers here in my home country commonly spoke of their esteem for their freedom in working for themselves according to their own ways and standards. Sometimes they spoke explicitly of the continuing pleasure of being unbossed. Now most of the few remaining full-time farmers are in bondage: captive clients of the agribusiness corporations and the banks. (I am unsure what to make of their supposed dependence on subsidies and handouts from the federal government, in place of an authentic policy of fair prices and production controls. Perhaps this is a sort of addiction.) These also are results of the breaking of the ancient bond, both practical and sacred, between the land and the people. Now we have been weakened and sickened by the belief that the work, skill, conscience, and care of many small farmers can be adequately replaced by technologies, and by the further belief that landownership can be adequately replaced by weekly or monthly infusions of money. Money is inflatable, and is continuously inflating—another normality of our time—whereas the real value of the land, however we may price it, is never more or less than our absolute dependence on it.

Another reason that forms of slavery persist among us is our inclination to measure all things, even time, by their worth in money. By this measure, the world contains many things, some essential things, that are unpriced or priceless, and therefore are worthless. By this measure, my talk of a sacred bond or of love as a necessary motive becomes nonsense. Things that bring or earn money have a clear and certain kind of worth and are granted certain protections. When they lose their connection to money, their worth falls immediately into doubt or into worthlessness. They have no intrinsic value that extends securely beyond or above market value. A worker whose work is unneeded, or who has no work, has no computable worth and is economically worthless. The land overlying a seam of coal is worthless. It is called "overburden" and is cast over the mountainside, to overburden then an equally worthless forest or stream.

This also is attributable to our willingness to separate things that belong together. The land, the coal, the forest, and the watershed originally belonged together in a certain relationship, the worth of which was originally measurable, we may say, by its endurance for millions of years as part of an enduring world. Such is our economy that the money-worth of coal becomes an explosive force that tears apart the members of the original membership that we once called "Creation," the individuated parts of which become not only worthless by decree of the market but assume a negative worth as pollutants or other troubles debited to the future. This is the real and continuing horror of a strictly materialist economy and way of life.

According to the requirements and the influence of this economy, my home river, the Kentucky, is understood and treated as an individual—a ditch, a drain, a gutter, a sewer—separate from everything that belongs to it: from its watershed on the one hand, and from the human communities that drink from it (and pollute it) on the other. Its money-worth, its only protection, is momentary and occasional, often interrupted by stretches and intervals of worthlessness. As a result, its original sustaining membership is broken up. The black willows and wild grapevines that once (beau-

tifully) lined its banks are gone. So are the muskrats. Ad infinitum?
Who knows?

There is a great bitterness surely in realizing that black people, as
long as they were enslaved, were granted a limited personal protection by their dollar value. In the absence of all human and humane
considerations, it was bad business to maim or kill them as long
as they could be sold. This may be the closest our economy—*our*
economy, not the South's or the North's—has come to granting a
value to our fellow humans apart from their labor or their professional services. A further bitterness must be to realize that, as soon
as they were free, black people became dispensable—worthless—
just like the poor white people, valuable only for the work they
could be got to do cheaply, and with the added disadvantage of
being black.

Worthlessness is the industrial common denominator of all
workers apart from their work, of all the unpriced native plants and
animals, and of the land and the streams apart from their market
value. Our economy obstructs, actively and purposefully, our still-
surviving wishes to grant intrinsic and transcendent worth to all
the members of the living world as our neighbors, fellow creatures,
"the least of these my brethren."

This economy rests upon our faith—apparently unshaken
by much failure—in the "success" of our self-abandonment to a
technological and economic determinism that is self-destructive
because it is heartlessly and measurably destructive of the world
and of life itself. Such an economy, now far gone along its predestined way, cannot, on its own terms, be adjusted or reformed so
as to preserve equality or freedom or any other of our professed
"values."

The thought of reparations paid in money to the descendants
of enslaved black people, if they are to be paid within the accepted

framework of the present economy, has got to raise the question of what would be repaired. No doubt it would increase the "buying power" of the recipients, increasing their spending and consumption. And so this project would be advertised as a "stimulus to the economy" and a boost to "job creation." Thus by increasing the monetary wealth of black people, the general economy would be improved—which is to say that it would be made worse in its damage to the natural commonwealth that supports us all. And all of us, all the races, would remain as depressed and diseased, and as economically vulnerable and helpless, as we were before.

The freed slaves, whose feet, unlike ours, were solidly on the ground, wanted forty acres and a mule. The fulfillment of that wish, had it happened, would have approached as nearly as possible to an actual repair of their condition: It would have afforded them the means to replace the mastery of their white proprietors by their own mastery over themselves. The conceptual distance from a grant of land to a grant of money brings us into a different world, a different understanding of economy, and a different kind of people. The land is substantial, it is a fundamental good, and its real value is something like infinite. Money, with us, is something like an idea. As things now stand, the value of reparations paid in money would necessarily be paid in inflated money continuously inflating. We are considering the difference between earth and air.

Ta-Nehisi Coates's essay on reparations refers to Charles Ogletree, a Harvard law professor, who "argues for . . . a program of job training and public works that takes racial justice as its mission but includes the poor of all races." That seems far more promising. The knowledge of how to work—if that is what is meant by "job training"—cannot be inflated. And by its expansiveness, such a program might finally reach to improvement of the legendary "forty acres," which probably were badly farmed under slavery and almost certainly are badly farmed now.

Because I am a rural American, a member of a rural community and a farming family, my point of view is different from that of most urban liberals and urban conservatives. I am unlikely to forget that, from the earliest beginnings of civilization until now, the people who have done the actual work and borne the actual risks of food production have often been ruthlessly exploited, and without concern or objection from the mere consumers of food. They have often been, virtually or actually, a captive labor force, which is to say slaves, and they have been people of all available races. Today, if you advocated production controls and fair prices for farmers—as I have, as I do—you would find no ally in the media, the universities, or among the people's representatives. I don't need to say that no publicly visible person is now suggesting reparations to farmers. And if such reparations were to be suggested and undertaken, the eligible farmers would be hard or impossible to find. That is because all who have been destroyed as farmers by the "free market" have become varieties of city people, dispersed and indistinct among the crowds of other city people.

The farmland, anyhow, is suffering for want of those absent farmers and the caretaking once at least potential in them. Repair most certainly is owed, by all of us, to that land. It might be that Prof. Ogletree's program could be turned to repair of both land and people by means of reconnecting one with the other by the good and satisfying work once known as "husbandry." Such an effort, it seems to me, would be almost unthinkably complicated and difficult. But, sooner or later, it seems to me also that it will have to be attempted.

As merely a political matter, I think that a program of monetary reparations exclusively to black people would be ruinous. It could be done only as another contest, like the Civil War, that would divide us again into winners and losers, and along a line of difference that would be racial and racist—a disaster. The winners, as before, would gloat over their victory. The losers, to the surprise of the winners, would remain enemies of the winners. And there would be nothing then to keep white people from declaring the problem solved. "Now we have paid them off, as they asked. Now at last we are free of each other. Let us go our separate ways."

One of the most troubling problems with slavery is that, in a number of versions, it continues. The legal enslavement of black people in the American South was stopped by the Civil War, and at the end of the Civil War we stopped calling slavery "slavery." After the Civil War the large landowners of the South continued to depend upon cheap labor. And the cheap laborers, black and white, were captive and enslaved to the degree that, wherever they were, they had no choice but to be cheap laborers. (The need in agriculture for cheap labor is inseparable from the frequently depressed prices for agricultural commodities—a problem of which I will need to say more.) What are we to call people who have no choice but to do the work they do, whether they like it or not? I think that they are slaves, and that we do them and the truth a disservice by not calling their servitude by its right name. We might apply the same name to highly paid professionals who cannot escape work they consider demeaning or destructive. The common denominator of slavery, wage slavery, and salary slavery is choicelessness.

The public mind, which we recognize by its public language, is wonderfully adept at shirking any of its responsibilities that are difficult. If the Civil War ended slavery, then the word "slavery" now designates only slavery as it existed in the South before the Civil War. And so the women and children who are captured and forced into prostitution are not being enslaved. They are being "trafficked."

If you belong to the "labor pool" or the "job market," and you and your family are dependent upon the only job available to you, though you are now not owned in fee simple as a marketable property, you are what rightly has been called a "wage slave." You are free of your present employer only if another employer offers a higher bid for your work, or if you are willing to live on the street. Meanwhile, your connection to a place or a community, perhaps your "home," is counted as worthless—when, like the land, it ought to be accounted as priceless or beyond price. Here is what Hilaire Belloc wrote on this subject in the 1930s:

> The pursuit of wealth as an end, and as almost the only end, has resulted in the destruction of all those safe-guards whereby the individual wealth of the many was guaranteed. As a consequence there has arisen, through the action of unlimited competition, a polity in which a few control the means of production and the many have become wage-slaves under those few.

This is more extensively true now than it was eighty-some years ago. By "the individual wealth of the many," Belloc meant small farms, small shops, and small stores, owned and worked by individuals or families. He was describing the lot of the many then, the many more now, who can help themselves, or attempt to do so, only by some sort of protest. He said further: "The modern man demands, and is at peace in, the regular enjoyment of payments doled out to him by his economic masters at regular intervals." As a condition of peace, this is fragile, apt to be temporary, dangerous for both the wage slaves and their masters.

But if slavery in the prewar South is the only slavery, and is no more, it follows that all of us now are free. We are so sure of this that we proudly tell our children, "You can be anything you want to be"—which, even for the richest and most fortunate of us, is manifestly not true. We believe also that every young person is possessed of a "full potential" that may freely be realized in one or another of available "jobs"—or in a succession of available "jobs." College students are said to be surrounded by "alternatives," as numerous as TV channels, among which they may freely choose.

The real extent of our freedom now may be pretty well tested by asking how many of our young people might reasonably aspire to self-employment. How many could reasonably, or within a reasonable margin of safety, wish to be small farmers, or small independent merchants in their small hometowns?

If you were a young person here in Henry County, Kentucky, and you wanted to continue the life and work of a small dairy farm handed down to you from your grandparents and your parents, here is what you would have to think about. In the year 2018, Dean Foods "terminated" one hundred of its contracts with small dairies in this region, two of them hereditary farms owned by two of the last families to live from farming in this county. The problem for those small dairies was that they had come into competition with Walmart, which had built its own bottling plant in Indiana. For Walmart it is "good business" to deal with a few large dairies rather than many small ones. There is *nobody* in the commercial, political, scientific, academic, journalistic structure of the present food economy who can speak effectively or offer any practical help for the small dairies. If you now were a young person in Henry County who grew up on a small dairy farm, who loved it as a family heritage, who loved its work and wanted to do it for the rest of your life, what would you think of your prospects and your freedom?

But the problem is more serious—and, if you please, more democratic—than that. Suppose you wish to be free to breathe uncontaminated air, to drink water assuredly uncontaminated by toxic chemicals, to swim or fish in an unpoisoned creek or river, where in our country would you choose to live? You certainly could find no such freedom in my part of the country. From what I hear and read, it appears that the streams are polluted with toxic runoff wherever there is farming or mining. And of course there is no place in the world where you can be free of air pollution.

In a civilization such as ours, in which a major aspiration and mark of success is sedentary or "white-collar" work, or freedom from work of any kind, some form of slavery appears to be necessary, a constant. Because "the better people" invariably think themselves "too good" for it, physical work was at first assigned to slaves or peasants or the "working class," who have been replaced so far as possible by mechanical, chemical, and other technologies. But these technologies have depended on energy from the fossil fuels. Unlike the energy (mainly solar) from the bodies of human workers and work animals, the fossil fuels fume and smoke. And so we enslaved the atmosphere (the air we breathe) to carry away, as we thought, the smokes of our furnaces and factories and vehicles. We enslaved the waterways and the rain to carry away, as we thought, the liquid wastes from our factories, refineries, and sewers. Thus most of us, as we thought, took a step above the slaves and other menials who once emptied the chamberpots, cleaned the privies, and planted, cultivated, and harvested the crops.

Our solutions, so far, to the problem of slavish or menial work, and our wish to do none of it, are themselves forms of enslavement more damaging and more permanent in their effects than the problems we started with. The enslaved rivers and winds that carry away our waste don't carry it far enough. The dirty work, which most of us now are free of doing, is dirtier than before, and we live with it more intimately and dangerously than before.

We have enslaved the earth also by requiring the economic landscapes of farming, forestry, and mining to feed, clothe, and shelter us, warm and cool us, and keep us shopping, without maintenance or recompense or any of the affectionate kindness and care which it requires of us and which, at our best, we often gave to it. Meanwhile, for want of the bodily work that most of us once devoted to our bodily lives, we have such further problems as physical weakness and ineptitude, sickness, obesity, and male impotence—all of which have become resources of our "economy."

And so for the sake of freedom from certain kinds of work, we have seriously degraded the creaturely commonwealth of earth, water, and air, and ourselves along with it. It is true that if you are black or poor or rural you are likely to live closer than some others to the sources of pollutants, but in general our degradation of the natural world and all of its goods and services afflicts us all. It is the summit and summary oppression, the master problem, that in one way or another includes all the others. Unlike many of our smaller problems, this great one does not divide us. All of us help to cause and continue it, and all of us suffer from it. Even those of us who do most to cause it, and those who most strenuously excuse and defend it, are just as much hurt by it as the rest of us. The difference is illusory. It is not possible for this problem of the enslavement of all Creation to divide us into the two sides of oppressors and oppressed. And the solution, or its many solutions, which will be good for us all, cannot classify some of us as winners and others as losers.

This problem, which now confronts us everywhere and all day every day, can be corrected only by correcting our understanding of work and most of our ways of working.

CHAPTER VIII

~

Work

1. Land Greed and Land Need

Robert E. Lee said before the Civil War that he thought slavery "a greater evil to the white than to the black race." His reasons for this judgment are not clear to me, and I don't think there is a measurement by which such a "greater" can be determined. But I too think that the white race in America—as well as the black race, as well as American society in general, as well as the American land itself—has been grievously damaged by slavery and the prejudices that preceded and followed it. For my first authority on this I need to turn to another historical figure, comparable to Lee perhaps in his costly integrity and sense of duty, but a man of a different kind, from a different place, and forty years older.

To anybody looking for a truly moral and upright American politician, I think I can name no better candidate than John Quincy Adams. Son of John Adams, one of the most prominent of the Founding Fathers and our second president, John Quincy Adams was, for a single term (1825–1829), our sixth president. More remarkable than his presidency, and his years of distinguished public service before that, was his representation of his Massachusetts district in the United States House of Representatives from

December 5, 1831, until his fatal cerebral hemorrhage, during a session of the House, on February 21, 1848. Through those years, as an elderly and then an aged man, he stood and spoke virtually alone against both slavery and the persecution of the Indians.

He was a man of bewildering complexity. He surely was one of the best-taught, best-read, most learned and articulate people ever in American politics. And yet he was humble, absolutely opposed to self-promotion even as a candidate for office, and yet he was proud. He believed "that moral principle should be the alpha and omega . . . of every discourse." His soul, as Yeats observed of Swift's, could be lacerated by indignation. He was a worrier, anxious for himself and his reputation, and yet, on his feet, outspoken to the point of ferocity and utterly fearless. He was not a perfect man by the measure of his time or ours. But in confronting the faults of his time and his own faults, he held himself to the highest standards of human goodness, and to his unrelenting wish to be a better man than he knew he was.

He toiled amid an almost laughable collection of long-held resentments and grudges. But his intelligence was direct and sharp, and he told the wrong of slavery with no hesitation or waste of words:

> The Declaration of Independence not only asserts the natural equality of all men, and their unalienable rights to liberty; but that the only *just* powers of government are derived from the consent of the governed. A power for one part of the people to make slaves of the other can never be derived from consent, and is therefore not a just power.

That was written in his diary in March 1820, when he was James Monroe's secretary of state. The logic of his argument then could not be dented, and he remained faithful to it for the rest of his life. He also knew and said often that slavery was as directly opposed to the Christian Gospel as to the Declaration.

For nearly all his life he observed the country from the vantage of its capital. He saw too clearly, was too intelligent and honest, ever to disguise from himself the disease at the root of the union of states. The disease was racism. He had already begun to suspect that the union would at last be broken by slavery: "I take it for granted that the present question [the Missouri Compromise] is a mere preamble; a title page to a great tragic volume." And he also saw through the shams of the nation's treatment of the Indians; this is from his diary of August 1839:

> There is nothing left of the most powerful tribe of the Cherokees in Georgia. Such is the inexorable Law of the white man, and the administration of the Government of the United States is moulded upon it . . . An inflexible determination to extirpate the race of Indian Savages [is] the white man's law on this continent.

I know that the gavel or the sword of political correctness will fall upon that word "Savages," sentencing Adams to the imperfect and therefore dispensable and forgettable past. But that is only because political correctness has no historical imagination. He did in fact believe that the European people were destined to spread over and dominate the continent, and he was to that extent a Manifest Destinarian. But he believed in decency too, and in the sanctity of treaties. He knew it was wrong to give one's word and then, at one's convenience, take it back. And he knew that there was nothing of democracy or Christianity in regarding our predecessors as a sort of varmints to be driven or hunted out of our way.

He is worthy of our remembrance and respect because, unlike most of us in his time and ours, he saw steadfastly by the light that was available to him. Marginal as he was to the exercise of power in his time, limited by his time as he necessarily was, he is yet an invaluable participant in our history, for he was trying always to follow, at considerable risk and cost to himself, the line that his heritage and his conscience prescribed as right. This was difficult and it was lonely. Here, for example, is his description in his diary of the politics of Washington in 1837:

> In the South the slavery question is a perpetual agony of conscious guilt and terror, attempting to disguise itself under sophistical argumentation and braggart menaces. In the North, the People favor the whites and fear the blacks of the South—The Politicians court the South because they want their votes—The abolitionists are gathering themselves into Societies increasing their numbers and thriving upon persecution—But in proportion as they increase in numbers and in zeal they kindle the opposition against themselves into a flame; and the Passions of the Populace, are all against them.

Through this thicket of forces and passions he made his way with unresting care to preserve his integrity while protecting the limited political effectiveness that he actually had. He was sympathetic to the antislavery groups in the North, who regarded him as an ally, and yet he kept aloof from them. The schemes to colonize freed slaves in Africa he thought were "impracticable." He doubted the possibility that slavery could be ended gradually. And yet he saw in the abolitionists a turbulence of spirit and an emotional logic leading to the bloodshed that he foresaw but could not consent to. He chose his fights with some care, taking a stand most willingly when his principles were clear and his feelings undivided.

The two politically dominant subjects during Adams's tenure in the House of Representatives were slavery, as established and militantly defended in the South, and westward expansion, which was a project of both the North and the South. It was the coincidence of those two interests and their coalition, for instance in the buildup to the Mexican War, that so isolated Adams in his opposition to slavery and to violence against the Indians. Though of no practical effect in his time and his own reckoning, his advocacy casts a clarifying light on our history that we would not otherwise have had, and that we would be poorer without. By his witness and the measure of his example we see clearly, as we greatly need to do, that so shortly before the Civil War the North was not the citadel of virtue that, afterward, it believed it was.

The Civil War ended slavery by replacing it with a conventional racism that the whole country kept mostly quiet about for the next century, while it completed westward expansion and the subjugation of the Indians, and began imposing upon the land the extractive economy that has flourished until now.

In our uprooting and displacement of the Indians and in slavery and its aftermath, we practiced two different kinds of racism against two different races, and with bad motives of two different kinds. Manifest Destiny, as we named the nationalist lust for land or "territory" that impelled us into the Mexican War and on into California and the Northwest, implied to us in the freedom of our superior strength a "right" to the land, no matter to whom it had belonged or who had belonged to it before we wanted it. Our motive in this was greed—although, as we know, any one of the sins is invariably reinforced by others.

Here our history obliges us to make a distinction between land greed, which pertains to nations or governments or people with too much money, and land need, which pertains to people pretty much in general. Land greed is performed by force, often military but also economic, or by the right of eminent domain, to remove people from their land for a use designated by the remover as "better." Land need is a feeling felt by people who perceive their weakness when they have no land that is rightly their own, that they rightly belong to.

Land need has been felt and often suffered by people of good sense who have been at all aware of their condition as humans. It was land need that made the American tribespeople at home in their original homelands. It prompted the freed slaves' plea for "forty acres and a mule." It was partly or entirely the motive that brought immigrants from many "old" countries to this "new world." It was Thomas Jefferson's understanding of land need that supported his recognition of the small landholders as essential to democratic government—a principle that we have overturned and forgotten but not disproved.

I will tell again a story that I have told before. A good many years ago at Iowa State University there was a conference in which a highly credentialed agricultural economist presented his theory that there is no significant difference between renting a farm and owning one—thereby discounting entirely the security, independence, satisfaction, and happiness of owning and belonging to one's own farm. There was in attendance, thank God, a farmer unintimidated by "advanced degrees," who stood and answered: "Professor, I don't think our ancestors came to America to *rent* a farm."

In considering our westward movement and our taking and

occupation of the land, we may never be able to say exactly when and how the government's greed in the conquest of territory became dispersed and private in the efforts of incoming families to satisfy their need for land. This theme of settlement and home-making, authentic as it has been, has proved to be a minor one in our history, and also a fragile and a tragic one. For the dominant theme has been domination, and we must ask also when the settled small landholders came to be regarded as another breed of obstruc-tive and backward "natives"—to be superseded in their turn by the operators and technologies of industrial agriculture, which would reinstate on the land the taking-by-force, this time economic, of our wars against the Indians.

2. *The Calhounian Division of Work*

Greed and land greed were no doubt involved in slavery, but sec-ondarily. The primary or originating sins of slavery were pride and sloth. If you willingly degrade necessary work by assuming that you are too good to do it, and if your "superiority" determines that the work so degraded will be the hard work that is done by hand, then you have opened an economic vacancy most conveniently and appropriately fillable by slaves. And here I need again the testimony of John Quincy Adams. This is from his diary entry for March 3, 1820:

> I walked home with [John C.] Calhoun, who said that the principles, which I had avowed were just and noble; but that in the Southern Country . . . they were always understood as applying only to white men. Domestic labor was confined to the blacks; and such was the preju-dice, that if he, who was the most popular man in his

district, were to keep a white servant in his house, his
character and reputation would be irretrievably ruined.
I said that this confounding of the ideas of servitude
and labor, was one of the bad effects of Slavery—but he
thought it attended with many excellent consequences—
It did not apply to all kinds of labor—not for example
to farming—He himself had often held the plough—So
had his father—Manufacturing and mechanical labor
was not degrading—It was only manual labor [that
was] the proper work of Slaves—No white person could
descend to that—And [slavery] was the best guarantee to
equality among the whites. . . . I told Calhoun I could not
see things in the same light—It is in truth all perverted
sentiment—mistaking labor for slavery, and dominion
for Freedom.

Reading this at a remove of two centuries, I don't know how Calhoun (or Adams) distinguished "manual labor" from farming
or manufacturing or "mechanical labor." "Holding the plow," I
assume, refers to guiding a breaking plow drawn by a team probably
of mules, and I would describe that as handwork. Any of the physical or material work done in those days would have required the use
of somebody's hands. Whatever status was assigned to "holding" a
plow, we may be sure that no aristocratic hands would have "held"
a hoe or an axe or a spade. But Calhoun's significant distinction
is between work that is not degrading, and therefore suitable for
white people, and degrading work fit only for slaves. Adams defines
the trouble exactly—"mistaking labor for slavery, and dominion for
Freedom"—and he clearly thought that the trouble affected both
races. It is certain that a mistake damages first—and, in the long
run, perhaps most—those who make the mistake. And it is merely

obvious that people who become "too good" to do the fundamental work, requiring the use of the hands, make themselves fundamentally ignorant and helpless—as was demonstrated in many of the big houses of the South when they were deprived of their slaves. And surely, in general, it would be a bad mistake to become immediately and entirely dependent upon people to whom you have given no reason to regard you as a neighbor.

As for Calhoun's belief that slavery was a guarantee of equality among the whites, I think that is false both circumstantially and logically. The problem was that most southern white people could not afford to have their degrading manual work done for them by slaves. Most of them were country people, farming people, living from their own work done with their own hands, with their own hands correcting their own mistakes and cleaning up after themselves. But in their circumstances they could not avoid remembering—the work itself reminded them—that their "betters" saw such work as degrading. By assigning specifically to slaves the manual work considered degrading, the slave-owning aristocrats degraded that work for everybody, black or white, who did it. By degrading the work, they degraded the workers. It became possible, and even irresistible, for white small farmers or sharecroppers to feel themselves degraded and insulted by the work they did and had to do, even as they were doing it. I remember hearing of a tenant farmer in my own neighborhood who felt that the cicadas were laughing at him for his degradation by the hard, hot work he was doing in his tobacco patch. It became possible for people who could not escape hard manual work to despise themselves for doing it, and, from that, possible to despise the land that required it of them. Thus the set of values and attitudes by which the Old South aristocrats placed themselves above the fundamental work of the world in their time, values and attitudes meant to define the superiority of a class, instituted a (so far) illimitable cycle of degradations. It degraded the fundamental work itself, in both status and quality. It degraded everybody, black and white, who did that work. And inevitably—provided that the workers consented to the aristocratic values and attitudes—it degraded the land on which the work was done. (The conversation between Adams and Calhoun is essential to the sense of this book. But my disapproval of Calhoun's view of slavery should not be taken to mean that I join in the currently fashionable demonization of all southern apologists for slavery. Like many humans who have been eminently in the wrong, Calhoun had some qualities that were admirable.)

In the slave states before and after the Civil War—and also, if less vividly, in the other states—we see at work two conflicting and more or less parallel attitudes toward the land and its work. All the time that individuals, families, and farming neighborhoods were moved by land need and the traditional set of motives related to landownership—to home-seeking, homemaking, and home-keeping—there was a top stratum of landowners who were wealthy enough to suppose that they were superior to the need for land in small parcels and to the handwork of the land. For whatever bad reason, there seems always to be a number of people, sometimes a large number, who willingly judge and condemn themselves by the standards of their self-denominated superiors. The freed slave who pled for "forty acres and a mule," like the needy white farmer who eagerly homesteaded 160 acres, manifested a commitment to a life of sometimes difficult bodily work. This commitment, moreover, implied both familiarity with such work and belief in the worthiness of it. But the nation's dominant ambition, increasingly from the Civil War until now, was set by the slaveowner, not by the freed slave or the white small landowner.

In his argument with Calhoun, Adams was speaking in affirmation of the value to the country and to democracy of "the plain freemen who labor for subsistence," presumably on their own farms or in their own shops. Calhoun, speaking self-consciously as an aristocrat and in defense of his class and its values, divides human life and work into the permanent grades of higher and lower. (He clearly could have granted no standing to Jefferson's "aristocracy of talent and virtue," with which Adams might have concurred, though he did not like Jefferson.) Perhaps the greatest irony of our history so far is that in our public life we have favored and democratized Calhoun's values and pointedly disfavored Adams's. The ideal or dream that sent the railroads west was not the flourishing homestead of the small farmer; it was the money pile of the captain of industry. According to the settled formula of our present age, "success" is to become college educated and then by "mobility" to be lifted above the "mind-numbing" bodily work of (let us say) farming, to (let us say) a well-paying rung on some "corporate ladder." How democratic may be the results in actual achievement or satisfaction or happiness or "fulfilled potential" or even pay, we do not ask. The only respected question is how to rise "up" above the work of the body and the hands, the degraded and degrading work, no matter whose "lower" life and livelihood may be sacrificed to one's climb. In this ambition, if in nothing else, we are close to being one people. We all, black and white together, want to be John C. Calhoun. Never mind that there was a time when many people of both races shared the one wish to own a piece, even just a small piece, of their country.

But in fact the public ideal now is a life less strenuous, less burdened by work and responsibility, more carefree and careless, than

Calhoun's. The superiority of Calhoun's social class rested upon Negro slavery—which, if we understand slavery as the lack or the want of freedom, was only one kind of slavery. For perspective, we may need to remember Allen Tate's comment on slavery in his biography of Stonewall Jackson. Mindful, as he had to be, that commerce and industry had in effect won the Civil War, Tate said: "Commerce and industry required a different kind of slave. He would be a better slave; he would have the illusion of freedom." If machines answer the human wish for perfect slaves, which it seems they do, does this not confirm us in our adoption of the role of slave masters, who in their dependence, were slaves of their slaves?

Consumers of industrial products participate in the industrial economy virtually as captives, because of their total dependence on the products, and because of their lack of responsibility for the quality of what they buy. The condition of industrial consumers is of a piece with the condition of industrial workers, who are captives of the "labor market" and their need for jobs, and who have no responsibility for the kind and quality of their products. The English artist, philosopher, and "Christian revolutionary" Eric Gill was one of a lineage of writers who have recognized the slavishness inherent in industrial work, which constricts the role of workers from that of persons fully human to that of "animals or automatons." "The test of a man's freedom," Gill said,

> is his responsibility as a workman. Freedom is not incompatible with discipline, it is only incompatible with irresponsibility. He who is free is responsible for his work. He who is not responsible for his work is not free.

Gill published this definition of freedom in 1929. In 1936, lecturing at Harvard, Graham Carey said substantially the same thing:

Art, according to the old idea, is not the making of a
particular kind of thing, but is the making of any kind
of thing at all, when that making is conducted with full
humanity, that is, by Men as Men. Men are most Men
when they exercise their human intelligence, for the possession of this intelligence distinguishes them from the
lower animals and machines, and from men working as
the lower animals and machines work. Men are also most
Men when they exercise their human will.

In their remarks on work, on the making of things, both Gill and
Carey are arguing from what I take to have been the fundamental
condemnation of slavery as it was in the American slave states: It
treated human beings as, by definition, less than fully human. And
this obviously implies the same reduction of the humanity of the
owners of slaves.

Both Gill and Carey are saying also that the industrial system
has no use for the full humanity of its workers, whether they are
in offices or in factories—unlike, I will add, the culture, the non-
system, of agrarian farming. And this raises immediately the question of the meaning and worth of equality in an economy that
equalizes people by reducing their humanity to a common low
level.

And so we are obliged to see that slavery, since we got rid of it
in its Old South variety, has remained too much with us in other
versions. As I said earlier, we have also enslaved the very substance
of the world to empower our machines, often for frivolous uses. We
have enslaved the waters and the winds to carry away our "waste."
And we have enslaved the land by subjecting it to the industrial
system of large single crops or "monocultures" of annual plants
grown year after year on the same ground without rest or winter

cover, fertilized only by chemicals, and protected from weeds and insects only by poisons—subjecting it, that is to say, to forced labor in defiance of compassion, natural law, and human responsibility.

But we must ask also how much our people may have enslaved themselves by the now customary wish to be "free" of work. To deal with that question, we will need to ask more particularly about the character of various kinds of work and the various conditions in which work has been done.

3. Work in Slavery, Work in Freedom

The history of the races in this country is now obscured by the intervention of a large ignorance or forgetting. Most antebellum slaves were country people who did farmwork, but now almost everybody, black or white, either lives in the city or in an economy determined by urban life and urban values. Very few people of either race have done any farmwork of the pre-industrial kind, and many of us, especially those who have been to college, have done no hard physical work of any other kind. Moreover, physical or "menial" work has always been despised by people who thought themselves above it, and abhorrence of it is now general and conventional in our society. This prejudice accounts for slavery, for low pay for manual work and "the working class," for the general depreciation of bodily life, for the replacement of vocation by "job," for labor-saving, labor-replacement, and so forth.

The field crops of the Deep South have never been grown where I live, and I know little about them. But I know at least that they are seasonal like all other crops, and that the work in them varied from one season to another. From preparation of the ground for planting in the spring until the crops were laid by, and again during harvest, the work would have been fairly constant and fairly urgent.

But even for slaves there would have been rainy days when there was less to do. In most places the work would have been minimal on Sundays and some holidays, or there would have been "days off." In winter, before electric lights, the nights grew long and there was more time free of work. Like the resident hired hands after slavery and before the hourly wage, slaves were employed "straight time"— every day, the year round. This means that they worked when there was work to do, and were still employed—on hand, available if needed, and maintained—when there was little or no work. (By contrast, workers who are paid by the hour are employed only when there is work to do, and are then expected to work all the time they are being paid. This obviously diminishes both the security of the worker and the quality of the work. The hourly wage mitigates against pausing to think and taking time to work well.) And so however rigid the system of slavery might be made, there was some slack in it just because of the nature of things. And often slaves "took up the slack," for example, by hunting and gathering in the woods and swamps that adjoined the croplands. Human nature, in other words, took advantage of the opportunities afforded by nature. According to the historian Mart Stewart,

> Hunting and fishing in the surrounding woods and water-
> ways were an important source of food for slaves. Not all
> slaves hunted—some plantation surroundings were not
> rich enough in game to yield much to hunters, and going
> off the plantation without a pass was too risky in some
> neighborhoods. But many did, if not with the rare guns
> they were able to use as hunters for their masters or that
> they owned themselves, [then] with an ingenious array of
> snares, set traps, and turkey pens. Or whatever else was at
> their disposal. . . . Hunting put meat in the pot: on the

Georgia and South Carolina coasts . . . slaves may have procured nearly half the meat in their diets from wild sources . . . Most slaves devised ways to carve out some of their "own" time to expand their exploitation of local resources beyond the fields or apply specialized skills off task to cultivate, hunt, or gather after their work in the fields was done.

Stewart says also that "masters often encouraged some property-ownership by slaves—they believed it would make them less likely to run away." Apparently, then, the ownership of the slave-owner, which might be strict and all but total within the boundary of the field during the hours of fieldwork, was significantly and suggestively limited outside that boundary and at other times. The dark of night and the provinces of nature offered a limited freedom that slaves could take just by knowing how to take it. By taking it and making the most of it, they kept themselves humanly intact. In this they set an example, it seems to me, that ought to be instructive to us all.

We know also that as they worked they often sang, and their work songs were a powerful cultural resource. Singing together and talking to one another while they worked were other ways of keeping themselves heartened and intact, individually and as a community.

As a matter of course the slaves learned well both the cultivated and the uncultivated land they lived in and likely were native to. They learned to live in it both from their compulsory work in the fields and from their relatively free venturing "beyond the fields." And so their wish, after emancipation, for land of their own was informed by a placed intelligence that was particular and practical. That wish signifies their competent understanding of work in relation at once to their known need and to their known country. They knew, as I believe some people always have known, that to be truly free they had to have underfoot, as Faulkner put it, "a little earth for their own sweat to fall on among [their] own green shoots and plants."

And so in addition to our understanding of slavery as bondage and subservience, it seems necessary to understand it also as education by experience. The primary thing that slaves learned from their experience surely was the whole catalogue of objections to slavery. But in addition to the knowledge of land and land use that they may have brought with them from Africa, they learned the white people's ways of farming, bad as some of those were. And they would have learned most about the country itself and the nature of it, in the places where they lived and worked, from their hunting and gathering in the uncultivated margins of the farms: the woodlands and the streams. I think we should be careful to appreciate the persistence of hunting and gathering among farming people of both races, especially where the land was somewhat hilly and partly wooded. And we probably should suppose that much of that hunting and gathering was learned from the native tribespeople whose really sophisticated inhabitation and use of the land-communities preceded what we call "settlement." This knowledge, or these knowledges, amount to local cultures of inestimable value, which now are lost as a result of any of the several kinds of "mobility."

But there is something in the nature of work itself that requires respectful thought. It has always seemed remarkable to me that hired hands, who would be paid as long as the work lasted, would be eager nevertheless to get it done, and often also to do it well. This investment of pride in work, which in return gives satisfaction, is fundamental, I believe, to the human nature that unites us all. I don't want to rely on my own observation and experience to show this common quality—especially since I am attributing it to slaves. And so for corroboration I will reach far outside the history that interests me here.

In writing his novel *One Day in the Life of Ivan Denisovich*, Alexander Solzhenitsyn drew upon his own experience as a prisoner in one of Stalin's Siberian work camps. If there is anything more a trial than slave work in the hot sun of the Deep South, I suppose it might be the slave work of prisoners in Siberia at twenty degrees below zero. Ivan Denisovich is not a stand-in for the author. He seems to be an ordinary Russian laborer, a proletarian, who became a common soldier and then, on suspicion, a prisoner with a sentence of ten years in the work camp. His imprisonment is made worse by his knowledge that he lives under the absolute rule of men who wield power without law or principle, who might double his sentence on a whim. He and his fellow prisoners form a broken sort of community. There is little they can do to help each other, but they do what they can.

At the beginning of his day, Ivan Denisovich feels unwell, and he thinks of going to the sick bay. Instead, he allows himself to be marched off to work with his fellows. Their work is to lay blocks into the walls of a building. In the extreme cold the mortar has to be heated. Ivan works as a mason, performing the exacting task of laying the blocks level and keeping the wall straight and plumb. The great power of this book comes partly from its repeated overturning of our preconceptions about the experience of such work in such circumstances. As he begins his work, Ivan passes from the peculiarity and strangeness of his own predicament into experience common to all workers. I think that everybody who has taken up difficult work will recognize this: "It was hard starting a day's work in such cold, but that was all you had to do: make a start, and the rest was easy." And once he is working he forgets all about feeling sick that morning. This too, I am sure, will be familiar to a lot of people who have worked in better conditions. In the story of his day's work, moreover, Ivan is revealed as a conscientious workman, even though he has no reason to be. He does not dawdle or shirk. He works well and takes pride and satisfaction in his work. At the moment the workday officially ends, Ivan's foreman tells him to dump his unused mortar over the wall, but he keeps working until he has used it up. He does not have it in him to waste anything. And so he ends his workday on his own terms:

> If the guards had set their dogs on him it wouldn't have stopped [him]. He moved quickly back from the wall to take a good look. All right. Then quickly up to the wall to look over the top from left to right. Outside straight as could be. Hands weren't past it yet. Eye as good as any spirit level.

Solzhenitsyn never forgets that from an "objective" point of view this is a day in the life of a downfallen man living near the limit of human endurance. But the story, as told, leads us step by step toward an entirely different realization: From the point of view of Ivan Denisovich, of his *soul*, it is the story of a triumph. Through the day he accumulates small pleasures—his work, the fragment of a blade that he successfully hides in one of his mittens, a little extra food, his acquisition of some tobacco, several acts of kindness— that are made large and significant by the harshness of his predica- ment. As I write, I am remembering one of my granddaughters,

309

farm raised, who as a small girl was pleased to discover how much her hard work in the heat of the day could improve a drink of water. And Ivan Denisovich at the end of his day, when he has climbed at last into his bunk, is wakeful, "in such high spirits after such a good day he didn't really feel much like sleeping."

Solzhenitsyn requires us to consider that there may be something redemptive, some power to keep us whole and sane, in work itself. That is because Ivan's work, insofar as he is self-motivated, is so set apart from its circumstances, from the forces that supposedly compel it, as to be work for its own sake. If such an achievement was possible for Ivan Denisovich in his circumstances, which Solzhenitsyn knew from his own experience, then it seems supposable that it would have been possible in the circumstance of slavery in the American South.

John Lewis, the civil rights leader and U.S. congressman whose book I quoted earlier, was raised in a farming family, but he did not like to farm—for which he is not more blameable than he would have been if he had not liked to run for office. In spite of his antipathy to the work she did, his tribute to his mother is wholehearted:

> First, last and in between, life on this earth—at least life as she has always known it—is about work. She doesn't say this in a sorrowful or complaining way, not at all. When she speaks of working, it is as if she is describing a sacrament, a holy act. Yes, work is hard, she'll say. And yes, it can seem thankless at times. But it is a pure thing, an honest thing.

So far, she seems to be speaking, like Solzhenitsyn's novel, of the redemptive power of work for its own sake, but her son continues:

> All my mother remembers is working, she says with pride. She also says she does not remember ever feeling poor. "We never saw too much money," she says, "but we always had what we needed. Meat, vegetables, everything, we raised that for ourselves. All we ever had to buy were things like flour and sugar, that's all."

Thus John Lewis's mother, Willie Mae Carter Lewis, testified to the virtue as well as the pride and satisfaction of a certain limited and reasonable independence that she and her family received from the land, which they earned and deserved the use of by their hard work. This independence relieved them of the embarrassment of depending on others for what they could supply to themselves. It also relieved them of too much dependence on money and the money economy, in which farming people have almost never had an advantage.

Most of the people of both races who prized this independence, and who worked to secure it for themselves, are now long gone from this and other "developed" countries, but in my early years I heard, and I have read, much testimony to the worth of it. This testimony, along with confirming examples, has come from agrarian people both black and white. But I am thinking now about black people and what their connection to the land meant to them, and so I have begun to string together from books by and about black people a set of passages that belong indispensably to their history and to the life of my own mind.

Lemon Swamp and Other Places: A Carolina Memoir preserves the recollections of Mamie Garvin Fields as they were spoken in conversation with her granddaughter, Karen Fields, professor of sociology at Brandeis. The grandmother remembers a day when she and another girl, her cousin, received a pointed racial insult from a storekeeper in a small town. This is her comment:

> That didn't worry me for long, though, because it wasn't necessary to associate much with the poor buckrah, and Grandpapa was what we thought of as wealthy back in those days.
>
> Grandpapa's farm was large, and I thought he had all there was to have. He was a great cotton farmer, and he had a garden of everything. Then, too, he grew practically every fruit we have in South Carolina—peaches, strawberries, pears, plums, apples, pecans. My grandfather never bought food, except maybe some flour.

She goes on to speak of the hominy and grits he had from his own corn, and of his "hams and chickens." She says that he held his cotton off the market until he could get his price; he was "known for that independence." He was "well off enough to be able to wait."

I am pretty sure that her grandfather's ability to wait for his price was more limited than she implies, for a single farmer's power against the market has always been small at best, but I don't doubt that he could wait a while. And his granddaughter is right in seeing his ability to wait as a measure of his independence. In an economy over which they have little or no control, the ability of farmers to feed themselves from their own land is a means of keeping their land and therefore their independence. But we must consider also what it must have meant to the grandmother as a young girl to be able to weigh the white storekeeper's insult against her grandfather's bountiful farm and his independence.

4. *Nate Shaw, a Free Man*

A book that has belonged both to my consciousness of racial history and to my understanding of work, since shortly after its publication nearly fifty years ago, is *All God's Dangers: The Life of Nate Shaw*. The man renamed "Nate Shaw" for the sake of privacy was a black man born in Alabama in 1885, a farmer all his life. Determined to free himself of the thoughts and ways of slavery that had limited his father, he worked hard and capably, and he became, for his race and place and time, extraordinarily prosperous. He was near to buying a farm of his own when, in the early 1930s, he joined the Alabama Sharecroppers Union. In December 1932 he got into a "shootin frolic" with some sheriff's deputies who had come to attach a neighbor's livestock. He went to prison for this, and was fifty-nine years old when he got out in 1945. Seriously set back by his long absence, he continued his life as a farmer, still a "mule farmin man" though the time of tractors had come.

In 1971 he told his story to Theodore Rosengarten, who recorded it in thirty-one sessions amounting to 120 hours, edited and ordered the transcript, and published the book in 1974. Prof. Rosengarten's accomplishment in this enterprise is a monumental service both to Nate Shaw and to the history of the people and the land of his place in his time. If our debt to Nate Shaw is larger, we owe it only by way of our indebtedness to Prof. Rosengarten, his devoted amanuensis.

Nate Shaw could not read or write. Partly because of that, I suspect, his memory is prodigious and exact. By any standard, his language is remarkable. It is distinctly a local language, but also distinctly his own, made so by its particularity and eloquence, and by the ever-awakened feeling that propels it and shapes its syntax. Unlike the public language that is dominant among us now, Shaw's language never lapses into platitude or resorts to "as they say," but is quickened constantly by reference to actualities and tangible details immediately known and judged: "what I have touched with my hands and what have touched me." He never remembers a mule, of the many he has known, except by name and character. He recites the tritest version of racial enmity only to refuse it in the same breath: "The niggers hates the white folks, the white folks hates the niggers—and they're brothers and sisters." He says, "I feel my best sympathy and hold my best judgment for the poor Negro of my kind and the poor white man." He remembers the kindnesses he has received from white people and enters them into his record: "brave man, good man, white man with sympathy."

But he knows, from the abounding evidence of his own experience and of all he has heard and seen, what the burden of his people has been. He resents it with entire understanding and in bitter detail. But he never repeats or utters on his own anything resembling a slogan. He speaks, from the center of his being, his carefully realized need to be whole and free. He says:

> Anything tries to master me I wish to remove it. And I'm willin to slap my shoulder to the wheel if it's ary a pound I can push.

He says:

> My color, the colored race of people on earth, goin to shed theirselves of these slavery ways. But it takes many a trip to the river to get clean. . . . If the Lord see fit to able me to stay here and see it, I'd love to know that the black race had fully shed the veil from their eyes and the

shackles from their feet. And I hope to God that I won't be one of the slackers that would set down and refuse to labor to that end.

Like Mamie Garvin Fields and her grandfather, Nate Shaw understood the primary importance of independence, which to him meant dependence on himself to provide for himself and his family to the limit of his ability to do so: "I was dependin on the twist of my own wrist." And with him the need for independence seems largely to have been in reaction to the example of his father, who had been a slave until he was fifteen years old: "My daddy was a free man but in his acts he was a slave. Didn't look ahead to profit hisself in nothin that he done." For a born farmer such as Nate Shaw, independence is one of a set of traits or virtues belonging to agrarianism, as it appears, always much the same, in oral traditions and in writing. Thus if your father has been too submissive to fate, too accepting of circumstances, too willing to be what he has been or is expected, by others, to be, then you must learn from your experience, exert yourself against "old slavery thoughts," and require of yourself the skills and the work of independence. You must make yourself as much a producer and provider and as little a mere consumer as you can be. You must learn to farm, to garden, to grow fruit trees, to be a teamster and a blacksmith.

To make the most of your good sense and your ability to work, you need your own land, and this was the need that governed Shaw's life. His effort toward ownership of a farm, continuous from his early life, was broken by his term in prison, but he was clearly a farmer by vocation, and also by choice. Though he knew well the obstacles he faced in Alabama, he had no wish to move north, and he refused a parole bargain that required him to leave his home

THE NEED TO BE WHOLE

country and live in Birmingham. He knew also that land is of little avail to a farmer who does not love it and the work that it requires, and who does not take responsibility for it. Such love and such responsibility make a good farmer, and a good farmer is by definition a land-saver, a conservationist. Unlike too many farmers of his time and since, Shaw was aware of the harms of one-crop farming:

> [Y]ou take the average farmer, when the price of cotton fell, why, he just quit foolin with wheat and oats altogether for cotton, cotton and corn. Now, by God, they're leavin the corn off.

And he understood as well the wrong of owning more land than one needs and can properly use and care for.

Because he was called to it and loved it, Shaw went eagerly into the work, and this set him apart from his father. When his father admonished him that he was working too hard, he replied:

> I got to work. I'm born to work. I can't sit around and jaw and talk and kill my time with you or nobody else. My hour has come to get in the field.

From work, from diligence and competence at work, come independence and self-respect, the pride of self-accountability, a necessary dignity. Counter to this, for both races, was the depreciation of work that came from slavery:

> [S]ome work, like pickin cotton in the fields, white folks didn't fill a basket—most of em. That was niggers' work. And if a poor white man got out there and picked cotton, he was pickin cotton like a nigger.

And from an entirely different direction, also applying to both races, was the depreciation of work by dependence on the government:

> I know people who used to would work ... but since the government been givin em a hand-down they wouldn't mind the flies off their faces.

A part of Shaw's effort was working for a lumber company, using his own wagon and team of mules to haul logs or sawed lumber. He took to this work as he took to farming, and for the good reasons that in it he was self-employed—he had no boss—and he found pleasure in it:

> I loved that work. I always was a man that liked workin in the free air. If the sun got too hot I'd set down if I wanted to. Nobody to tell me not to. . . . And if that lumber was good lumber, it was a pleasure to load—it'd load smooth and it had a nice scent. It waked you up to haul that lumber.

It is of the greatest importance to understand that when the work is right for the worker, when it is rightly done under the right conditions, the smallest pleasures give happiness and support life.

As with many farmers of his time, much of his love and his pride was invested in his work teams and his proficiency as a teamster:

> Twice a day if I'm plowin, mornin and night, I'd brush and curry my mules. Keep my mules in thrifty condition, keep em lookin like they belonged to somebody and somebody was carin for em. Mule love for you to curry him; he'll stand there just as pretty and enjoy it so good.

317

And when he was hauling lumber:

> [I] wouldn't put on a foot over a thousand [board feet] if
> I was under any reasonable hill at all; buck it down, pick
> up my lines, call up there, "All right, babies, let's get it."
> You'd see them big heifers fall out then. O, my mules just
> granted me all the pleasure I needed, to see what I had
> and how they moved.

The depreciation of work, and of the very idea of *good* work, has involved as a matter of course the depreciation of pleasure. It has in fact involved the elimination of pleasure from work, and its assignment exclusively to not-working or to so-called recreation. Most people seem to have no idea how this has impoverished us.

Work, pride and competence in work, a proper measure of independence, love for land and creatures, careful husbandry of things in use, the faith that came to him when he needed it most, pleasure in what he had: Over the years, despite the deprivations imposed by racism, despite the disfigurement of his twelve-year imprisonment, Nate Shaw gathered to himself the virtues and rewards of his calling and made himself, as he would have allowed, almost whole.

All God's Dangers is a book of 561 pages. In the course of those pages, every one of which is readable and interesting, Nate Shaw delivers a remarkably detailed autobiography. The details are given for their intrinsic interest, because he likes or needs to remember them. And so we don't ask what he was "like" or what he represented. He was not "like" anybody else, and he does not speak as one of a category, but exactly as and for himself.

Having thought carefully again of his book, I have to say that nothing I have experienced or heard or read better exposes the limits of political correctness. It is at once obvious that to this code, as to the doctrinaire urban liberalism that brought it forth, Nate Shaw is entirely unexpected: a black farmer, born in Alabama twenty years after the Civil War, who is not only "non-college" but illiterate, who is nevertheless fully competent and independent in his use of his mind and whose language is fully, sometimes elegantly, expressive of his thought, and who loved and praised the work of his hands. As always, political generalizations and stereotypes just vaporize and blow away in the presence of an actual person's actual story. Nate Shaw was what Henry Thoreau would have called "a standard man," and we can know this by knowing him somewhat as he knew himself.

5. Ernest J. Gaines: The Freeing of Imagination

Another book that has belonged intimately to my thoughts and my heart, since its publication in 1983, is the novel *A Gathering of Old Men*, by Ernest J. Gaines. The story told in this book takes place in the "quarters" of a sugarcane plantation in Louisiana. The quarters, once, was a sort of village, consisting of small houses with galleries (porches, as we call them here), a church, a graveyard. Generations, first of slaves and then of fieldhands, passed their lives there. Once it was populated by families, people kept subordinated and assigned to the "degrading" hard work of the fields, who yet as a measure of self-respect kept their homes neat and orderly, the dooryards planted with flowers. Now it is a remnant of what it was, some of the houses empty or vanished, the dooryards grown up in weeds, the remaining houses occupied, so far, by a few survivors, once useful and busy, now grown old. They are a superseded people, cast aside and left behind when the tractors came into the fields and the young people, suddenly obsolete, moved away to urban jobs or urban joblessness, often sending their children back home to be brought up by grandparents. The old are stranded, living out their days as leftovers in leftover houses. They are the last. When they are gone there will be no more like them, and the quarters will be taken by the weeds, and eventually by the tractors.

At about noon on a day in cane-harvesting time Beau Boutan, a Cajun farmer, is killed in the quarters, in the yard of an elderly man, Mathu, who by nature and in the way of things is foremost among the black people. The case, as at first perceived by Sheriff Mapes, appears to be simple and clear: The Cajun farmer, a racist bully, was killed in Mathu's yard by Mathu's twelve-gauge shotgun, and of all the black people, the sheriff thinks, only Mathu has the courage to shoot a white man. But by the time the sheriff arrives, the case has become astonishingly complicated. It is, astonishingly, love that has complicated it. Candy, a young white woman, the youngest member of the family to whom the plantation belongs, was orphaned as a child; she received much of her upbringing from Mathu, and she is devoted to him. When the sheriff comes into Mathu's yard, he is confronted by Candy, who is there as protectress of "her people," and who confesses to the murder. But she has sent word around, and also present is a sort of miscellaneous platoon of elderly black men, each carrying a twelve gauge shotgun recently fired, and each also confessing to the murder.

While the stumped sheriff can only stand and listen, one by one, the old men tell their reasons supposedly for killing Beau Boutan, which in fact are their reasons, had they been courageous enough, to kill other abusive white men. They have reasons enough, heartbreaking enough. But the testimony that interests me now is that of the man known as Johnny Paul. To preface what he says, I need to say that the dead man, Beau Boutan, and his family are the ones who have rented the fields and brought in the machines to replace the black people who once worked there and belonged there.

Speaking to the assembly of the confessed killers and the several spectators, some of them elderly women from the quarters, Johnny Paul asks if they can see there what they saw once but don't see now. The sheriff, Mapes, is mystified and impatient.

"Yes, sir," Johnny Paul tells him, "what you see is the weeds, but you don't see what we don't see."

"Do you see it, Johnny Paul?" Mapes asked him.

"No, I don't see it," Johnny Paul said. "That's why I kilt him."

"I see," Mapes said.

"No, you don't," Johnny Paul said. "No, you don't. You had to be here to don't see it now. You just can't come down here every now and then. You had to live here seventy-seven years to don't see it now. No, Sheriff, you don't see. You don't even know what I don't see."

Johnny Paul proceeds—in defiance of the sheriff's modern impulses of haste, officialism, and impatience—to recall into the minds of the other old people the vision of what they don't see:

"Y'all remember how it used to be?" Johnny Paul said. . . .

"Remember?" he said. "When they wasn't no weeds— remember? Remember how they used to sit out there on the garry—Mama, Papa, Aunt Clara, Aunt Sarah, Unc Moon, Aunt Spoodle, Aunt Thread. Remember?

Everybody had flowers in the yard. But nobody had four-
o'clocks like Jack Toussaint. Every day at four o'clock,
they opened up just as pretty. Remember?" . . .

"That's why I kilt him, that's why," Johnny Paul said.
"To protect them little flowers. But they ain't here no
more. And how come? Cause Jack ain't here no more.
He's back there under them trees with all the rest."

Johnny Paul, facing the remains of the quarters, the trees of the
graveyard, the field beyond, is asking himself and the others still
living to remember when they were an established, a settled, people. Constrained as they were by the bounds and usages of racism,
they were a living community with the dignity of being useful, to
their employers of course but also to themselves, and, within their
constraints, ruled by the councils of the elders seated on the galleries. Their self-respect, inseparable from their long and continuing
dwelling upon the land, was announced by the dooryard flowers
blooming faithfully year after year. (It is moving to remember here
that one of Ernest Gaines's teachers, Wallace Stegner, wrote that his
mother, married to a waster, yearned for just such a permanence of
perennial flowers for herself.)

The flowers assert an old claim, an old belonging of the people
to the place, of the place to them. Johnny Paul knows very well the
statement of the flowers, but so do the other old ones, and he only
asks for the flowers to be remembered. But his own statement is
not yet complete. To complete it, he must call upon the elders, the
people most his own, to remember their work, to see it as it was,
and to honor it:

"Lord, Lord, Lord. Don't tell me you can't remember
them early mornings when that sun was just coming up

over there behind them trees? Y'all can't tell me y'all can't
remember how Jack and Red Rider used to race out into
that field on them old single slides? Jack with Diamond,
Red Rider with Job—touching the ground, just touching
the ground to keep them slides steady. Hah. Tell me who
could beat them two men plowing a row, hanh? Who?
I'm asking y'all who?"

"Nobody," Beulah said. "That's for sure. Not them two
men. Them was men—them."

Johnny Paul nodded his head. Not to Beulah. He
wasn't looking at her. He was looking way off again,
down the quarters toward the field.

"Thirty, forty of us going out in the field with cane
knives, hoes, plows—name it. Sunup to sundown, hard,
miserable work, but we managed to get it done. We
stuck together, shared what little we had, and loved and
respected each other.

"But just look at things today. Where the people?
Where the roses? Where the four-o'clocks? The palm-
of-Christians? Where the people used to sing and pray
in the church? I'll tell you. Under them trees back there,
that's where. And where they used to stay, the weeds got
it now, just waiting for the tractor to come plow it up."

Johnny Paul had been looking down the quarters. He
looked at Mapes again. The people had been nodding
their heads, going along with him all the time.

"That's something you can't see, Sheriff, cause you
never could see it," he said. "You can't see Red Rider with
Job, Jack with Diamond. You can't see the church with
the people, and you can't hear the singing and the praying. You had to be here then to be able to don't see it

and don't hear it now. But I was here then, and I don't see it now, and that's why I did it. I did it for them back there under them trees. I did it cause that tractor is getting closer and closer to that graveyard, and I was scared if I didn't do it, one day that tractor was go'n come in there and plow up them graves, getting rid of all proof that we ever was. Like now they trying to get rid of all proof that black people ever farmed this land with plows and mules—like if they had nothing from the starten but motor machines. Sure, one day they will get rid of the proof that we ever was, but they ain't go'n do it while I'm still here. Mama and Papa worked too hard in these fields. They mama and they papa worked too hard in these same fields. They mama and they papa people worked too hard, too hard to have that tractor just come in that graveyard and destroy all proof that they ever was. I'm the last one left. I had to see that the graves stayed for a little while longer. But I just didn't do it for my own people. I did it for every last one back there under them trees. And I did it for every four-o'clock, every rosebush, every palm-of-Christian ever growed on this place."

We might say, rightly, that Johnny Paul is preaching the funeral of a community, in farewell recalling and praising it as it was. He also is including himself among the mourners, and his speech is a lamentation, biblical in its finality and sorrow: "How doth the city sit solitary, that was full of people!" More significantly, I think, he is recording a deed, not the notice or formalization of the ownership of real estate to be found in courthouses, but an entitlement more authentic and far older. He is reciting the history of life and work, works and days, suffering and pleasure, love and loss, by which a land and a people belong not only together, but to one another.

What the now-fashionable liberal version of our history has failed to prepare our people to expect, let alone to honor, is Johnny Paul's pride in the work his people did, his testimony to the pride they took in doing it with skill. Bodily work, daylong, in planting or cultivating or harvesting a crop can be hard, hot, and miserable, as Johnny Paul and others have testified, as I know myself from my own experience. But as Johnny Paul suggests, it can also be exuberantly competitive and companionable. If two good hands, good mule men, raced to the field in the morning, that denotes elation, probably hilarity, and most certainly a workmanly pride in their mules and in themselves. Johnny Paul's people did not work like devices or machines, or puppets whose strings were pulled from above. Like Ivan Denisovich, like Nate Shaw, they gave themselves to their work. "Them was men—them," Beulah says, reminding us, in our pressing need to be reminded, of the possibility that men might derive a sense of their manhood from their proficiency and swiftness at work, rather than some sort of violence or dominance over other people.

But in order to understand how forlorn is this small gathering, this ceremony that Johnny Paul and the other speakers improvise out of the history of their souls, and how distinguished these elders are as the last of their kind, you need to recognize that Johnny Paul's speech is not political. If you were traveling in another country, and you came upon such a gathering in such a place and heard such a speech, you would suppose that the occasion was political, and that the speaker was appealing for justice against some great violence, some purge or pogrom, some driving into exile. But Johnny Paul is speaking in modern America. He is identifying a wrong that in fact belongs to us all, that should have become a political issue, but it never did, because there has never been a constituency to make it an issue.

Legal slavery in its day in America raised a crucial question that gained public standing and demanded an answer: Given our professed religious and political values, how far are some people justified in treating other people as properties and as work animals? Much that Ernest Gaines has written raises a question directly descended from that earlier one: Given our professed religious and political values, how far are we, or is our economy, justified in regarding working people, of any race, as inferior machines properly to be replaced and displaced by superior machines? Or to put it a little differently: How far are we justified in regarding a "job," even a "good job," as appropriate compensation for the loss of a homeland, a home community, and for the loss of a communal speech that evoked a local geography, a local history, and the patterns of local loyalty and responsibility? Or to put the question in its rawest form, as I know it occurred to Ernest Gaines: How could we ever have been justified in merely forgetting a suddenly obsolete young black man raised on a Louisiana plantation, and leaving him merely free to migrate to some distant large city where he will have a good chance of dying, still young, by violence or a drug?

A Gathering of Old Men has come to exemplify for me the right way, at least one of the right ways, for a person to contribute to the good-faith conversation about our racial history and present race relations that is so urgently needed. It is the right way, I think, not because it speaks for a political side, but because it is supremely a work of imagination and therefore supremely a work of understanding and therefore of sympathy.

This book is one of the results of Ernest Gaines's long effort to imagine what he knew better than he knew anything else: the life history, the lifework, the life and the lives of his own people in his own place, the land and community that he never ceased to think of as home. He had his upbringing in the quarters of a Louisiana sugarcane plantation such as he has repeatedly written about. He lived there until he was fifteen years old, when his parents, who were living and working in Vallejo, California, sent him a train ticket. He had never lived anywhere else, had never traveled, but he left home, carrying a worn-out suitcase containing a change or two of clothes and a lot of food prepared for him by "the old people" to sustain him on his journey. Worried and afraid, because he was alone and entering a life he could not foresee, he rode the bus to New Orleans and the train from there to California. In Vallejo he lived and went to school in a mixed neighborhood of blacks, whites, Asians, and Latinos. He became a reader of books. He attended San Francisco State, and in the school year of 1958–59 he was a Stegner Fellow at Stanford. I too was a Fellow in that year. We got to know each other then, and there was kindness and care between us until he died in November 2019—sixty-one years. The kindness and care, I think, will survive us both.

(Not long before he died, I sent him a copy of these pages, in which, following convention, I had called him, as a living man, "Mr. Gaines." Before long he telephoned and said to Tanya, my wife, "It's all right. Tell him not to call me Mr. Gaines." I had resisted my impulse to call him "Ernie." After he was gone, I couldn't call him "Gaines.")

California obviously was a great gift to him, a godsend and a deliverance. It gave him the teachers, the reading, the friends, and the time he needed to become a writer. But he did not become a California writer. By the time he walked out to the highway to catch the bus to New Orleans in August 1948, his subject had been given to him beyond any giving back. When he left the quarters he was full of knowledge of the place and the people he belonged to, and he was still speaking the language that had been in his ears and on his tongue all his life. This was the heavy oak block, as he has put it, that he had to learn to carve.

To know a place and a people is not by some distance the same as to imagine them. Imagination does not produce reporting, though it may help. Imagination produces art, which for Ernest Gaines needed to be the art of fiction. "Fiction," as I am always happy to remember, comes from a Latin word *fingere*, meaning "to form." The art of fiction enables a writer to imagine what he knows in the form of a story. Imagination involves knowledge, understanding, perception, and insight, but it also enables you to see, hear, taste, smell, and feel what you know, to know absolutely and forever what you know. I think Ernest Gaines was eminently a man of imagination, but in 1948 when he left Louisiana for California, imagination was only a power within him that he could not reach or use. I don't think he had it in any available way when he first began to know that he needed it. In order to have it he had to find and learn a language that could tell first to himself and then to others what he knew and what he felt about the small place that he was native to not by his choice, but that he chose to belong to. Or did he merely choose to submit to its choice of him? That choice would have been by way of the old people of the quarters who saw that he was exceptional, and who sent him on his way to California with enough food to signify their love for him and to help him along.

It must have seemed to him that the needed language more or less composed itself, and I would guess that this seemed to him to take too long. He clearly learned much of his language and of the ways of using language, along with much else, from the writers he eagerly read, in and out of school: Faulkner, Hemingway, and Welty, Tolstoy, Chekhov, and Turgenev, Shakespeare's tragedies, the Greek tragedies. The influence of the Greek tragedies is unmistakable in *A Gathering of Old Men*.

But this language that he acquired by study, the language of books, could not entirely fill his mind. It could not become usable by him until it met and made room for, somehow mated with, the home language that most intimately belonged to him. I am not capable of saying how the book language was influenced by his native language, but I feel sure that such an influence occurred. I think he would always have been conscious of how a language too obviously literary would have embarrassed his native language or other speakers of it. This is suggested by his conversation in his published interviews, which is as literary as it needs to be but also has the fine plainness that belongs to honesty and to good manners. His speech has the modesty that is permitted by self-confidence, and it is readily humorous. The quality of humor seems to belong both to his character and to the character of his work. He is not a comic writer but, like a lot of country people I have known, people of both races, he seems always alert to the possibility of something comical or funny or ridiculous, something you can have the pleasure or the relief of laughing at—just because he can't get along without it. He could have been confirmed in this by Faulkner or by Shakespeare, but I think his sense of humor is a gift that he brought with him to California. The qualities of his conversation carry over to the omniscient voice of, for instance, *In My Father's House*, the language of which is entirely capable and entirely free of literary pretension. And yet, in that book you can feel what he acknowledges in interviews: his relief when he can shift to dialogue and dialect.

If his book language and conversation are under the influence of his native speech, there is also a current of influence running in the opposite direction. When the rural black people in his fiction speak for themselves, as they often do, they don't speak the dialect of "local color," which identifies itself by phonetic spelling, and they don't speak, either, in imitation of actual speech, which, as he has acknowledged, would be unreadable: "[I]f you stuck to the way people talk along where I come from I don't know who could read it. I couldn't read it." He renders the dialect, instead, mostly by conventional spelling, somewhat by grammar and diction, but mainly, I think, by the shape, inflection, and energy of the syntax. In this way he makes dialect remarkably articulate and, when it needs to be, remarkably eloquent. His fine ear for the spoken speech of his people becomes a fine ear for their speech as he represents it in writing. This transformation of spoken speech to written speech cannot be made without an acuteness of hearing that is both natural and conscientiously learned. When, for example, he uses the phonetic spelling "garry," he does so because the three syllables of "gallery," if pronounced, would violate the character and the rhythm of the language being spoken. It would sound pretentious.

I know that I risk presumption in examining so closely the language of a fellow writer, but I want ever so much to try to understand the biographical origins of such precisely powerful language as this:

> "But you still don't see. Yes, sir, what you see is the weeds, but you don't see what we don't see.... You had to be here to don't see it now. You just can't come down here every

now and then. You had to live here seventy-seven years
to don't see it now."

Language probably cannot be made more particular than this. It
is both completely clear and completely personal. It is particular
in the sense that it could be spoken only by this man in this place
at this time. Ernest Gaines knew well several old men something
like Johnny Paul, and he also thoroughly imagined Johnny Paul.
He knew, I am pretty sure, that when Johnny Paul invents the verb
"to don't see," he acquired a needed and compelling exactitude,
and also, with some conscious pleasure, made a joke on the English language. It is not an illiteracy. I know from my experience,
and I believe that Ernest Gaines knew from his, that the amount
of formal schooling is of no importance here. The conventional
assumption that limited schooling limits intelligence is as false
as the assumption, also conventional now, that physical work is
"mind-numbing." (Both assumptions apparently are derived from
the propaganda of the education industry, which holds that education can happen only in a school, that all schooling is good and
leads only to good results, and that a college degree is as necessary
as food.) Johnny Paul's mind is not numb, and he clearly has the
author's respect. Here, in fact, he speaks for the author, for what he
is saying here follows closely the outline of a lament (and a rebuke
of technological determinism) that the author spoke a number of
times in interviews and in other works of fiction.

What is important is that Johnny Paul is an accomplished talker
because he is a member of a talking and storytelling community,
a community that knows itself and understands itself by listening
to its old people tell its stories, and so, by this constant reminding, remembering its history. By this telling and listening, it also
incorporates into its history the passing events of the present. *A*

Gathering of Old Men, in one of its aspects, is a performance by the community of this traditional reminding and remembering. These are people, moreover, who for centuries have been talking and listening for pleasure. People who know one another well, who work together and rest together, also talk together. They talk together necessarily for practical reasons—for what we now call "communication" and "information"—but also, and even more, for companionship, for sympathy and encouragement, above all for pleasure. This means that they make an effort to talk well. They notice and remember when something is spoken in the right way. When they are at work alone, they entertain themselves by putting their thoughts into words. They tell and hear over and over again the same stories, and so that art is practiced and improved. They remember and invent "sayings." That is the school in which all his life Johnny Paul has been thoroughly a student. And so, when he feels urgently the need to speak, he is prepared. Because he speaks so fully and particularly for himself, he speaks also for the others— even for the sheriff, Mapes, who takes a while to know it.

The wonder of Johnny Paul's speech is that it belongs entirely to the place. That exactly is the point he is making to Mapes. The wonder of Ernest Gaines's art is its ability to make that speech belong just as entirely to his book. In such a way, in a better time, local life might be brought into a sort of balance against public life, and so become able to protect itself.

What is the use, in a book about race relations, of paying so much attention to language? I think it is more than useful. I think it is necessary, because the usefulness of our conversation about this subject, if ever we are to have an authentic one, will depend on the kind and quality of the language we use. And I don't know a writer whose language offers a better example for people trying, as I am trying, to learn to talk than that of Ernest Gaines. His language locates him particularly and exactly in his native place and its history, but this does not limit him. In his books, like Johnny Paul in his speech, Ernest Gaines speaks so fully and responsibly of what he knows that in speaking for himself he speaks also for others. His language, moreover, is so attentive to the details and qualities of lived lives, and so mindful of itself, that it displaces us from the loaded abstractions and slogans of public confrontation and returns us to the lovely possibility that people can talk *with* one another. No language could be less available, or more determinedly unavailable, to the purposes of hatred and violence than that of this book or this writer. Because he speaks of and from his own small place, which, as he knows, is only one in a mosaic of thousands of small places, the South cannot be for him an abstract idea as it is for many less settled and located people. Having so particularly placed himself, he cannot speak as a representative southerner any more than he can speak as a representative black person.

Because he has the language to do so, he can tell a story about a community of people who know one another, a story that is able at its extremities to include in its knowledge even the villains, whom it understands along with the others. It is in his dealing with the book's villains that we see in full the generosity of Ernest Gaines's imagination, which he does not withhold from anybody, so aloof is it from mere side-taking. Where imagination goes, sympathy goes, even compassion. At the end of the book its villain, Luke Will, has come with several racist friends, in order, as he has supposed, to lynch the black man who killed Beau Boutan. Luke Will is a racist, a roughneck, an overbearing oaf, who is stupid enough and brave enough to be dangerous. If Ernest Gaines were the sort of writer who likes shortcuts or who thinks the purpose of a story is to deliver a moral message, he would need only to withhold his imagination and Luke Will would be stereotyped as the White Racist whom all the politically correct people love to hate.

Luke Will has come, as he supposes, to force his "superiority" upon maybe a few cowed black people, only to be confronted by a dozen and a half old black men, all of them armed with loaded shotguns. It becomes plain to him that his own deadly purpose has trapped him in a predicament that may be deadly to him. When finally the danger has come clear to him, he says to the man next to him, his friend Sharp, "If you make it and I don't, look after Verna and the kids."

Surely, many a reader has been stopped by this. It stopped me. It has stopped me every time I have read it, and by now I have read it many times. It is one of the most moving sentences I have ever read. One is moved of course by the man's thought, in his mortal danger, of his family. But just as moving is one's recognition at the same time of the writer's perfect generosity. He looks through the stereotype with which Luke Will himself has cornered himself, and he sees the distorted, self-diminished poor creature that Luke Will actually is. As bad a human as he is, he is human and a fellow human. If this moment has beauty, and I think it does, it is the beauty of a thing completely imagined. When I wonder if I have read anything similar to this—a writer's natural allegiance overpowered by compassion—I remember several lines from Yeats's "Easter 1916," his elegy for those who were killed in the Easter Rebellion in Dublin in 1916:

> This other man I had dreamed
> A drunken, vainglorious lout.
> He had done most bitter wrong

To some who are near my heart,
Yet I number him in the song;
He, too, has resigned his part
In the casual comedy;
He, too, has been changed in his turn,
Transformed utterly:
A terrible beauty is born.

As the drunken, vainglorious lout of Yeats's poem is at last "transformed," so Luke Will, in the terribly bright moment of his own transformation, understands the real danger to himself, as to others, of the presumed superiority of his whiteness. In another of its aspects, *A Gathering of Old Men* is a book of transformations. The murder of Beau Boutan and then the resistance of Candy and the old men are transformative events. The old men recover self-respect and solidarity relinquished long ago. Mathu and Candy stand free of a dependence on each other that had become wrong for them both. Even Mapes is moved from his officious pride, condescension, and impatience to sympathy and respect. To these and others come moments of realization or illumination or, to use a word favored by Ernest Gaines, "elevation." The right work of stories, as they operate in books and then in the world, is to change the mind by elevating it to the dignity or rectitude proper to humans— or as he put it in speaking of his novel *A Lesson Before Dying*, "to salvation, to the uplifting of the soul." Ernest Gaines's preoccupation with this change that other writers have called "epiphany" or "metanoia" joins him to the great tradition of Western literature, and it has to do with his interest in wholeness, in the sense of the coherence of an individual life within itself, and in the sense of the completeness that an individual life receives only from a shared membership in a community or in understanding, in sympathy. To him, a person is not an "autonomous" or "liberated" individual or a "human resource" or an animal with an opposable thumb and a "big" brain, let alone a machine, but rather an incarnate soul. And if we are able to consider that a writer's obligation or privilege is to invest his work with the power to uplift the soul, then we begin to see with how great a seriousness this writer accepted his vocation. He spoke more directly about this in his 1994 conversation with John Lowe:

> A writer doesn't choose a profession—he *has* to do it, but not because of community, but because of something even bigger than that. The Old Man upstairs has to get someone to help him carry the load; he gets writers and artists to help him do the work.

This is direct enough, but uneasily so. The man speaking is a writer exceptionally traditional in the present age of the world, and in consciousness of this he speaks of God as "the Old Man upstairs." If I am rightly understanding him, he uses this almost joke partly because of his uneasiness in speaking so. You don't have to be black (though it surely helps) to be painfully aware of the discrepancy between the behavior of much of organized Christianity and the teachings of Jesus. But partly also, by speaking so lightly, Ernest Gaines seems to be offering to those who will not take him seriously a courteous permission to take him lightly.

I take him seriously, for he is not the first in Western tradition to think of imagination as the means, in any of the arts, whether writing or painting or carpentry or farming, of joining human work rightly to the work of God. To take him seriously is to see in his work an effort to understand and to bring within reach of imagination the meaning of human wholeness, which certainly would involve and even require that joining of the low and the high: earth and heaven, the human neighborhood and the kingdom of God, health and holiness. The realization of this wholeness has been the supreme task, always verging on failure, of the lineage of traditional artists. Often it has been best known by failure to reach it or to be able to speak of it, as Dante can express only by his speechlessness his vision of the Light Supreme. Many a story has told of the effort, or the failure, to be whole. In Faulkner's *Light in August*, Lena Grove's unrelenting pursuit of the father of her child is an effort to be whole. She feels herself to be a fragment, and she is driven by her vision of the rightness of the wholeness of a family.

Wholeness as an idea or a possibility clearly is not easy to limit. The ecologists of our time also reach toward a vision of an earthly wholeness: of an ecosystem, let us say, in possession of all its parts or members—a wholeness, as this effort of mine bids me to notice, within which we humans can fit only by humility, generosity, and goodwill. The best of the ecologists reach further by conceding the mysteriousness of this wholeness, knowing that what they know of it reveals their ignorance of it. And then we may remember Jesus saying to the woman who was healed by touching his garment, "Daughter, thy faith hath made thee whole."

Taking Ernest Gaines so seriously, and so perceiving his wholeness as a writer and the imaginative reach and power of it, I am led back to Johnny Paul's speech, which I am understanding now as coming from a recovered wholeness in himself. From that wholeness, enabling him to speak for the living and the dead as he speaks also for the author, he recovers the memory of his and his people's wholeness in their work.

6. Crystal Wilkinson: The Tragedy of the American Home Place

The several passages I have gathered here speak for the persistence, among black people of the rural South, of the traditional agrarianism that I learned from people of both races, beginning in my earliest childhood, and that I have sustained in my thoughts ever since, partly with the help of the books I have been quoting. Thinking again about these passages has given me pleasure and a needed comfort. This agrarianism, this high regard for all that is implied by a person's and a people's belonging to their homeland, survived principally by word of mouth from ancient times, appearing only intermittently in the written record. Though it remains important and necessary, as shown by the bad effects of the modern forgetfulness of it, it is scarce in the writing of both races in our time, though it has continued. If it had continued among us with, say, half the force of technological determinism, then many of our newsworthy problems, including climate change, would now be significantly smaller and slower, and some would have been prevented. But that it has survived and continued at all is a wonder deserving our thanks.

And so I am grateful and also happy that the last of the passages I want to think about here is from a novel published in 2016: *The Birds of Opulence* by my fellow Kentuckian Crystal Wilkinson. This novel deals mainly with a household consisting of a lineage of women, headed by the widowed great-grandmother, Minnie Mae Goode. There is also a faithful, useful man, Joe Brown, Minnie Mae's grandson-in-law, and his son, Kee Kee. The Goodes, who are farm people, have moved into a nearby small town in rural Kentucky.

The central event of this book is an epic church picnic, "Dinner on the Grounds." This is a gathering of the local black people—and by now, 1976, their far-scattered kin—that goes back, Minnie Mae declares, to slave times. Dinner on the Grounds draws home the community's "wayward children, even those who live as far off as Texas or California," and so begins a heartaching comedy of misfitting relatives, which Crystal Wilkinson understands as one more chapter in the misfitting of country people and city people, a comedy always revealing itself as tragic and destructive. The returnees

> show up talking city talk and driving long, shiny black Cadillacs and red sports cars. They bring exotic gifts for their relatives—silver trays for chitterlings and fried potatoes and crystal goblets for Kool-aid and sweet iced tea. The mothers and grandmothers say, "Thank you, baby," and will wait for the out-of-towners to leave before placing the items in the attic with the other strange things their kin have brought home.

On the day before Dinner on the Grounds, Minnie Mae's sons arrive in a "shiny white Oldsmobile." They are awkwardly conscious of their difference, now, from their country relatives. Their greetings are too hearty, "they laugh too much," they "look uncomfortable and out of place in their clothes." There is some congeniality, some telling of funny stories from when they were young and living at home. But, Minnie Mae having gone to bed, the brothers get to the business they have on their minds. Their mother is getting old. The time is coming when she may need expensive care. "We'll be a whole lot better off if we start making some plans." And so they have turned their minds to the one family property of any value that can be sold: the small ancestral farm that lies not far from town. "We was thinking that we ought to sell the homeplace." This completes the revelation of the brothers' estrangement from the rest of the family. A coldness falls upon them, and they part for the night mostly in silence.

It remains for the two brothers to present their concerns to their mother, Minnie Mae herself, who, while she lasts, will have the final say. In the time that they have lived in cities, she has always expected her sons to return twice a year and go with her to their home place, in the spring to plant the early garden, in the fall to set the place to rights before winter. Though she and her family have lived in the nearby town, they have continued to cherish the home place and to take a part of their living from it. Minnie Mae has imposed these seasonal duties on her sons as a way of keeping them mindful of their home place and responsible to it, or as a way of trying to do so. And so here we arrive at the very heart both of Crystal Wilkinson's book and, I think, of our country's history: the progressive homelessness of all its races.

In late August 1976, the three of them have again come to the home place on their autumnal visit. And then occurs a scene realized in the particularity of the time and place, which yet the author requires us to perceive as ancient. Some might see it as a biblical archetype, but surely it is older than the Bible, older than farming. It has happened countless times in countless generations. The aging parent, near to death and full of knowledge, offers the land to its inheritors, its inheritors to the land:

> "This is y'all's what-for," Minnie Mae says, placing one
> hand on her hip and the other one spreading far and wide
> from one edge of the knob across the creek to the other
> side. The moon is out and the farm is glowing behind her.
> "All this," she says, "been up under your people's feet since

slave times. My mamma and daddy worked this land, and
their momma and daddy before them. . . . All y'all was
raised up on money the tobacco brought in and the garden food we put on the table. Over that ridge there is a
graveyard, a whole village of our folks over there. . . . You
boys played over there in them fields when you was little."

But the older son replies, and the younger agrees:

"Mama, I don't see why you don't sell this old place. None
of us set to be farmers. We all got our own lives. Good
lives. It's just setting here growing weeds. . . . You know
you're getting too old to keep putting in a garden, and
look at the house ain't nothing much left but firewood."

This, may God help us, is the voice of sound economic sense, of
realism, of reason, in our time. In her reply, Minnie Mae speaks
pretty faithfully for many of the elderly farm people I have known.
Her rage is old, coming from way back, and so is her heartbreak:

"Hush your bad mouth. Can't even see yourself when you
feasting your eyes right in the looking glass. Hush your
ignorant mouth. This ain't about no grade a wood on no
house. . . . Not one, but two full-grown fools. . . . You are
a shame before God, your daddy, and all your people."

Crystal Wilkinson's summation of the tragedy of Minnie Mae,
which I will quote to conclude my consideration of this book, is
more modern than ancient, but by now it is one of millions. Many
of us no doubt believe that the dominant story of modern America
is that of the "success" of the transfigured executive or politician

who has levitated from "a little farm at the end of nowhere" to wealth and power. But the tragedy of Minnie Mae has been suffered on such little farms millions of times, all over the industrial world.

> But when it comes to [her sons], once the initial hugs are made, the general "How are yous?" delivered; once dinner has been served and eaten; then foreigners step into the bodies of Minnie Mae's babies.

And I am remembering now that somebody, I believe it was C. S. Lewis, wrote of the falsehood of the belief that one's life belongs to oneself.

I know that in my response to the obsolescence of Minnie Mae, as in my response to Nate Shaw and Johnny Paul and the others I have quoted here, I am speaking for a tiny minority of all races. And yet if we are interested, as we claim, in the "quality of life," which must include quality of mind, the truth remains that Minnie Mae's mind is stratified, like the soil, down to the bedrock of ageless human experience. She knows and feels as immediately as touch the history that appraises her family's land as priceless: It is the practical means of life and independence, an actual foothold in the actual world, the source of an indispensable confidence and pride. She identifies with the land. She sees her people reflected in it. Her sons' minds, on the contrary, penetrate no farther down than the pavement that supports their shiny cars and their "good jobs."

This, I repeat, is not a racial matter. The sons have realized the dominant ambition of modern America: a good-paying city job and the freest of freedoms, freedom from any obligation to the past, and from any need the present may have for anything or any reminder of the past. And so Minnie Mae and her sons enact their version of a drama in which Minnie Mae's past is ancient and the sons' past belongs mainly to the brief era of industrialism. Once again, and for the millionth time, a heritage and a homeland are at first offered, and are then refused in the delusion of individualist autonomy, independence, and disconnection.

7. Debt Slavery

In putting together my small agrarian sampler, I have meant to pay tribute to a tradition and to several of its voices that have been confirming and sustaining to my own life and work. For the five samples I have taken from the testimony of black people, I could have supplied five from white people saying substantially the same things. But I have needed the testimony specifically of black people, and not only because this book is about race relations. The special worth of black agrarianism is that it seems to have been understood as directly opposed to slavery and to what Nate Shaw called "slavery ways" and "old slavery thoughts." Though such knowledge by now has evidently been worn away by migration, modernization, and mortality, many old or old-time black people seem to have held passionately to what slavery had so recently taught them of the value of landownership, a home place, as the support of freedom and independence.

In her book *African American Environmental Thought*, Kimberly K. Smith describes a reasonably expectable division of black people's attitudes toward the land. She quotes Eldridge Cleaver who said that during slavery "black people learned to hate the land." And then she states the opposite thesis, again referring to Cleaver: "as Cleaver himself recognized, there has long been among blacks 'a deep land hunger.'" The problem here is the difficulty of keeping those two statements in a firm historical relationship. By Cleaver's time, something like land hate had come to prevail among people of both races who had been frustrated in, or indoctrinated against, their old land hunger. And the proposition that slavery taught black people to hate the land, though it seems logical enough, is overturned by the preponderance of evidence that the freed slaves, like a lot of white people at the same time, longed for farms of their own. (Here, as often, to understand the history of one race it is necessary to remember the history of the other.)

On January 12, 1865, twenty "colored ministers and church officers" met in Savannah to be interviewed by Secretary of War Stanton and General Sherman. Asked what they understood "by Slavery and the freedom that was to be given by the President's [Emancipation Proclamation]," Garrison Frazier, spokesman for the group, replied:

> Slavery is, receiving by *irresistible power* the work of another man, and not by his *consent*. The freedom . . . promised by the proclamation, is taking us from under the yoke of bondage, and placing us where we could reap the fruit of our own labor, take care of ourselves and assist the Government in maintaining our freedom. . . . The way we can best take care of ourselves is to have land, and turn it and till it by our own labor. . . . We want to be placed on land until we are able to buy it and make it our own.

Of the twenty black churchmen, nineteen said they would prefer to live in "colonies" by themselves (because of the prejudice against them) rather than "scattered among the whites."

The wish to "assist the Government in maintaining our freedom"—Frazier meant as soldiers—is touching both as an indication of gratitude and as a forlorn hope. As for the wish to live in colonies separated from whites, that seems to me perfectly understandable, even reasonable, except that it probably would have required a prolonged, massive military occupation of the South by the North. But in his definition of freedom, Frazier was exactly right, and in so saying, moreover, he defined the land need not only of his own people, but particularly also of the poor white farm people of the South, and of people in general. The "progress" from subservience under a master to subservience under a boss was not what the freed slaves had in mind.

As maintainers of freedom, we know that governments are variable. They do not always make the laws and regulations that freedom requires, they do not always enforce the laws and regulations that they make, and over the longer reaches of time they come and go. An established and settled bond between land and people is another matter, for we know that peasantries have outlasted governments and empires. The problem in this age of the world, as we also know, is that both communism and capitalism are antipathetic to the existence or the formation of such a bond, and that both are destructive of it by violence either military or economic. And so it seems to me to be necessary, now maybe more than ever, to keep in mind the contradiction between agrarianism and slavery. That is because the destruction of the bond between people and land leads to a number of evils, of which slavery is only one.

The slavery that was formally ended by the Emancipation Proclamation and the Thirteenth Amendment was succeeded by a new form of slavery that swallowed up the poor people of both races. The instrument of their enslavement was "the lien system," which bound a farmer inextricably to a single merchant. C. Vann Woodward defined it this way:

> The seeker of credit usually pledged an unplanted crop to
> pay for a loan of unstipulated amount at a rate of interest

to be determined by the creditor. Credit was advanced in the form of supplies . . . to the extent that the merchant considered safely covered by the probable crop. The "interest rate" was greatly augmented by the price charged on the goods, and the universal practice was a two-price system, the cash price and the credit price. The latter price was always higher, "never less than thirty per cent., and frequently runs up to seventy per cent.," said [Henry W.] Grady.

A farmer so bound to a merchant, whether the farmer was black or white, was obviously in a condition of abject choicelessness—in short, of slavery.

To understand race relations we must consider, obviously, differences of history and experience between black people and white people. In considering these differences, partly I think because we no longer know one another as well as once we did, we don't very well resist the temptation to reduce ourselves, our history, and our experience to categories and abstractions. And so we introduce into our thoughts another oppression, mostly unacknowledged, by which people of both races find themselves, as the unique persons they know themselves to be, enshrouded by the expectations, the stereotypes, and the prejudices of other people. Resistance to this, as my sampler shows, comes from personal knowledge and testimony, from imagination leading to sympathy, from storytelling—the subject matter of reading and conversation.

From the same sources we can consider the points at which the history and experience of the two races converge and what, beyond our fundamental humanity, we have in common. Our present restriction of the word "slavery" to designate only the enslavement of black people in the antebellum American South tends somewhat harmfully to exaggerate the difference between the races. If we know something of the history of race relations, we know how certain passages of the Bible were used to defend slavery. But in fact, as American slaves well knew, the Bible recalls with entire disfavor the enslavement of the Israelites in Egypt. And that disfavor is hardly confined to Exodus. *The New Oxford Annotated Bible* gives us Proverbs 22:7 translated this way:

> The rich rule over the poor,
> and the borrower is the slave of the lender.

If we remember that verse, and with it the Bible's condemnation of usury, then we know that the poor of both races were enslaved by the lien system in the postwar South. The association of luxury (supported by debt) and slavery goes back in English literature at least as far as *Piers Plowman*, Book V, which quotes from an unidentified Latin source: "Thou art the slave of another, when thou seekest after dainty dishes; feed rather upon bread of thine own, and thou shalt be free." That sentence resonates with agrarian tradition wherever that tradition appears. It speaks the fear of enslavement-by-debt, coming to us from the experience of both races. And it touches us as we are today.

The convergence of the experience of poor white and poor black is acknowledged, along with the ever-present racial divide, in this remarkable passage from *All God's Dangers*:

> O, it's plain as your hand. The poor white man and the
> poor black man is sittin in the same saddle today . . . The

control of a man, the controlling power, is in the hands
of the rich man. . . . That class is standin together and the
poor white man is out there on the colored list.

The reasonable question at this point is inescapable: Why, in their
shared oppression and great need, did the poor white people and
the poor black people not make peace and cooperate in some sort
of neighborly help to one another? The answer, as I suggested earlier, must be that people who are scrambling for coins and crumbs
in order to survive, as poor farmers were doing then, as credit-
dependent industrial farmers are doing now, are likely to think
of neighbors as competitors or enemies rather than friends. And
here we must think also of the advantage to "the rich man"—to the
cheapener of "labor" at any time—of any division that preserves
the vulnerability of the working poor. However, as presently I will
show, there is evidence that after the Civil War poor farmers of
both races sometimes did cooperate.

As I write of the history that both divides and unites us, I am
often tempted to wish it had been simpler and easier to understand. But the more I work to make it clear, the more complicated
and obscure—and interesting—I find it to be. The racist argument
has always been so simple as to need no comprehending. It simply
divides the two categories, white people and black people, by a line
theoretically straight, and opposes one category to the other. The
actual history of the races, as their stories divide and converge—
as they both, for instance, move from farm to city, suffering the
same uprooting, burdened by their old division—is complicated
enough, questionable enough, and interesting enough to keep us
reading and writing, asking and answering, talking to one another,
and thus enlarging the possibility of friendships among us. That is
why it is distressing to see the antiracists resort to the same catego-

ries and draw essentially the same straight line as the racists. These simplicities are dissolved by any unpresuming, earnest conversation between a black person and a white person. Or they are dissolved by friendship or affection between a white person and a black person, as they were for me in my childhood and have remained.

8. Official Prejudices

Another difficulty of our history, also involving likeness and unlikeness, is the role of institutional racism in the decline of the population of black farmers in the South in the twentieth century. My guide here is the historian Pete Daniel, whose book, *Dispossession: Discrimination Against African American Farmers in the Age of Civil Rights* was published in 2013. This is a mighty work of research and writing because of the light it sheds and the disgrace it exposes. In his book's early pages, Prof. Daniel sets two landmark ironies side by side: The first is the remarkable success of black farmers in acquiring land for themselves, despite racism and violence, in the half century following the Civil War. The second is the steep decline of landownership by black farmers at the time of the great achievements of the civil rights movement in the 1960s.

The contrast, partly, is that between the lives and the work of actual persons in the actual world and the work of institutions in the world of policy and politics. Here is Prof. Daniel's account of what actual persons achieved after the war:

> Slaves emerged into freedom with a keen understanding
> of farming that allowed many to navigate the boundary
> between exploitation and sufficiency. In rural areas, blacks
> and whites necessarily worked side by side, and despite
> white supremacy, friendly relationships developed across

the color line. Industrious African American farmers deferred when necessary and earned the respect of their white neighbors, learning . . . how to cultivate white support. A combination of husbandry, diplomacy, and ambition allowed black farmers to secure land and the fact that so many succeeded during some of the darkest years of racist violence testifies to their character and determination.

This seems to me to be promising. It shows us the expectable and natural land need of the black farmers poised against the customary prejudice of their white neighbors. Customary prejudice, as we know, can harden into hatred and violence, but it does not have the rigidity of legalized or institutional prejudice. It has a certain flexibility. It does not necessarily prohibit "friendly relationships." The historian Thomas D. Clark, in an interview given late in his long life, confirms the coexistence of race prejudice and friendly relations in the Mississippi farming neighborhood he knew as a boy in the early twentieth century, and I believe that it prevailed here in my part of Kentucky into my own time.

But we can't appreciate fully the meaning of Prof. Daniel's sentences until we have considered that the "friendly relationships" between the races came from their working "side by side." These black and white small farmers, neighbors divided by a notorious difference, necessarily *worked together*. I know from my own long experience of handwork, of fieldwork, with neighbors that this requires, in addition of course to knowledge and skill, a sympathetic cooperation not unlike that of dance partners or even of lovers. This is a necessary intimacy without which the collaboration of two workers or a crew is impossible. No merely customary difference or prejudice could prevail against it or in any way modify it.

Prof. Daniel's account of postwar cooperation between poor

black people and poor white people seems promising to me because that cooperation was a practice of neighborhood, occurring freely and naturally. The neighborliness was incomplete, as we know from that word "deferred." But we speak of something as incomplete only when we recognize the possibility of its completeness. How we know about completeness is not always clear to me, as a mere human who perceives many things as parts without knowing how they fit together. But in his last novel, *The Tragedy of Brady Sims*, Ernest Gaines evidently sees the long acquaintance of the sheriff, Mapes, a white man, and a black man, Brady Sims, as completed in friendship, respect, love, and finally grief.

It is imaginable then that, left alone in conditions of reasonable social and economic stability, friendly relations might have yielded a customary and then a legal equality. But here is Prof. Daniel's account of the countermovement:

> The decline of black farmers after World War II contrasted starkly with their gains in the half century after Emancipation. By 1910, African Americans held title to some 16 million acres of farmland, and by 1920, there were 925,000 black farms . . . After peaking in these decades . . . the trajectory of black farmers plunged downward. In a larger sense, there was an enormous decline among all farmers at mid-century. Between 1940 and 1969, the rural transformation, fueled largely by machines and chemicals and directed by the USDA, pushed some 3.4 million farmers and their families off the land, including nearly 600,000 African Americans. From 1959 to 1969 alone, 185,000 black farmers left the land, and only 87,000 remained [by 1974]. Farm failures were endemic, and in the 1950s, about 169,000 farms [of all races] failed

annually; between 1960 and 1965, some 124,000 failed each year; and 94,000 per year failed between 1966 and 1968.

"Directed by the USDA." Prof. Daniel means that the U.S. Department of Agriculture—along with the colleges of agriculture, the agricultural scientists, and of course the corporate suppliers of agricultural machines and chemicals—had subscribed unconditionally to the idea that progress required the replacement of farmers by machines and other technologies. Among the nonfarmers of academic, official, and corporate "agribusiness," this version of progress had become a religion, from which there were no dissenters. The statistics that Prof. Daniel reproduces might have changed some minds, if any minds among these agri-progressives had been available to be changed. But Prof. Daniel's subject, in part, is the intellectual paralysis that had seized the entire academic, scientific, bureaucratic, corporate establishment that had turned to promoting the industrialization of agriculture at any cost.

Much has been made of the corporate falsehoods having to do with tobacco and cancer and with the fossil fuels and climate change, but no public notice at all has been given to another such falsehood that is equally shameless and is, though unrecognized, a part of the falsehood about the fossil fuels: the "scientific" doctrine that human farmers and local cultures of husbandry can be replaced by machinery and toxic chemicals without harm either to the land or to the people. This obviously is false. The falsehood is the subtraction from agriculture of the human presence, attention, love, and artistry that are necessary both to the health of the land and to human health. The result, if not the purpose, of this doctrine has been the gathering of many small, democratic livelihoods on the land into a few plutocratic fortunes in the cities. Lately some critics have noticed the large hypoxic (which is to say dead) zone in the Gulf of Mexico, an illness of the water caused by runoff from grain fields in the watershed of the Mississippi River. The critics suggest that the guilty farmers should be charged for this damage and thus forced to stop it. What the critics fail to see is that the remedy—better farming, less grain, more perennial cover, more farmers—is no longer available as things now stand. The choice now is between toxic farming and no farming.

The reigning program of industrialism, fully sanctified by corporate wealth and political power, and extended fully to agriculture after World War II, has been the substitution of technology for all that is and has ever been involved in human work. This is the top-down enforcement of mechanical abstraction upon the inherent particularity and intimacy of the work previously done by human hands. The power was removed from individual life and initiative and given to indifferent mechanical processes.

That substitution has been accompanied, perhaps inevitably, by the substitution of money, and related measures or symbols of monetary wealth, for the real wealth of land and the real goods produced by the land, starting with food, clothing, and shelter. Once these substitutions have been accepted as valid or normal by the attending experts, thinking may proceed logically enough, but with the logic of fantasy.

In 1977, I heard Earl Butz, formerly secretary of agriculture, say with perfect confidence that, as personal property, a life insurance policy was as good as a farm. In *The New York Review of Books*, December 5, 2019, Benjamin Nathans declared just as confidently of "the world's wealth" that "the majority of that wealth is currently held in the form of financial assets (stocks, bonds, mutual funds, derivatives, bank deposits, etc.)." This statement comes with no hint of a connection between financial wealth and the natu-

ral world, natural resources, or the land use economies. This ignorance or willful ignoring of the real sources of financial wealth is
not limited to the science of economics. For want of a steadying
consciousness of the economic importance of nature and natural
law and the responsibilities of land users, the modern enterprise of
conservation also becomes superficial and false, shifting from cause
to cause as "environmental" emergencies enter and depart from
the news.

This disconnection, which is fundamental to public consciousness in the present world, appears to be a deliberate achievement
of the financial sector itself. Reviewing Sarah Dry's *Waters of the
World* in *The New York Review of Books* of December 19, 2019, Jenny
Uglow wrote that in India when "the summer monsoon had failed
in three of . . . seven years . . . an article in *The Lancet* estimated in
1901, around 19 million people had died of hunger—though as
Dry points out, the famine was due less to lack of rain than to the
British imposition of a cash economy, which deterred farmers from
the traditional practice of storing grain for hard times." Though our
present food economy, which destroys all the means of food production, cannot continue indefinitely, we may still hope to avoid
hunger on such a scale in the United States. Even so, "the British
imposition of a cash economy" on the farmers of India is exactly
analogous to the determination by the United States Department
of Agriculture—along with the rest of the agri-industrial faithful—
that the traditional subsistence economies of farm households had
become uneconomic: Farmers could no longer afford to feed themselves from their own land by their own skills and their own work.
With the money they would earn in the time they rescued from the
trifling work of subsistence, they could buy their food.

One does not need to be an expert to see that if people can
be stopped from supplying their own needs, then an enormous

advantage accrues to the sellers who will supply the people's needs for money. Thus, at a single waving of the agri-industrial wand, so much of people's working lives was transferred from production to consumption. Thus "the economy" was improved by way of social and cultural damage. And so we see in proof the progressive genius of industrial agriculture, to which the corresponding geniuses of the universities, the government, and the press voiced their unanimous consent and unrelenting praise.

We need not think that this orthodoxy of agricultural industrialism could make itself so watertight because its members were uniformly doctrinaire, or because they every one were passionately evangelistic. The passionate fidelity of these nonfarmer or antifarmer experts more expectably went to their lucrative good jobs, professorships, and research grants. Once their technological revolution was set upon its rails, huge monetary investments became dependent upon it, whereas very little profit could be mined from the old disciplines, loyalties, affections, and virtues that constituted "husbandry." Here are two passages from Prof. Daniel's book that verify one of the miracles of the high-modernist faith in science-technology-and-industry. This:

> When [Secretary of Agriculture Orville] Freeman arrived at the USDA in 1961, there were over 96,000 employees ... and roughly 13 million farmers. In 2010 ... there were 113,000 employees and only some 2 million farmers.

And this:

> The increase in programs and the USDA's swelling bureaucracy had an inverse relationship to the number of farmers: the larger the department, the more programs it

generated, and the more money it spent, the fewer farmers that survived.

The fortunate thousands in the USDA, like their fellow thousands in the classrooms and laboratories and corporations, were careerist professionals, never obliged to look outdoors at what the farmland and the farm people actually required of them, or at the effects of their industrial purposes upon the actual land and the actual people. It is not conceivable that officials so positioned might see or suspect a correlation between the decline of the farming population and the wasting, the ecological degradation, and the increasing toxicity of the farmland and the rivers. But contrary to the popular assumption, it was these people—highly credentialed urban professionals, not, or certainly not only, "the racist rednecks of rural America"—whose prejudice so drastically reduced the population of black farmers.

Another popular assumption is that there has always been a perfect symmetry in race relations by which any loss by black people is equaled by a gain for white people. This extends to the allegory of Good versus Evil popularly applied to the Civil War, and supportable only by a popular ignorance of history. Prof. Daniel's testimony leads to a different and more useful conclusion: Under the influence of a general prejudice against farmers, farmers of both races will fail, but black farmers, because of their vulnerability also to race prejudice, will fail in larger fractions:

> In the 1960s, the number of southern white farm owners decreased from 515,283 to 410,646, and the number of white tenants dropped from 144,773 to 55,650. Farms owned by blacks fell from 74,132 to 45,428, and black tenants declined from 132,011 to 16,113.

To a member of a farm community who has been watching and aware for a long time, numbers such as these are hardly surprising, but a heartbreak adheres to them that does not wear away.

Prof. Daniel's statistics establish beyond doubt the operation of three prejudices within the Agricultural Stabilization and Conservation Service, the Federal Extension Service, and the Farmers Home Administration—the bureaucratic structures meant to assist farmers. During the period in question, no category of farmers increased or remained stable. All declined, though some declined more than others. The three prejudices, obviously, were these: (1) the prejudice against farmers; (2) the prejudice against small farmers; (3) the prejudice against black farmers, most of whom were small farmers, and who therefore suffered three prejudices.

The prejudice against farmers seems to be about as old as farming. According to James C. Scott's necessary book, *Against the Grain*, the earliest states were founded upon dependable surpluses of cereal grains, which depended upon a population of captive farmers. One of the reasons for war in those times was to capture slaves for farming. The working people of that time who had "good jobs" that spared them from degrading physical work, kept their hands clean, and earned respect, were the scribes who kept the accounts of the stores of grain—clearly the predecessors of the USDA's antifarmer bureaucrats. The modern prejudice against farmers and farming was abetted, and consciences quieted, by a cosmetic philanthropy. Just as slaveholders had assured themselves that they were uplifting their slaves from savagery to civilization, so the agri-industrial orthodoxy could praise itself for "freeing" farmers from the "backbreaking" and "mind-numbing" work of farming.

The prejudice against small farmers came only with the industrialization of agriculture, which began to dominate the landscapes of rural America after World War II. The official disesteem for small

farmers was announced by Eisenhower's secretary of agriculture
Ezra Taft Benson who told his constituents to "get big or get out."
The doctrinal rule by that time was that there were "too many
farmers."

That black farmers were likely also to be small farmers, and thus
were subjected to a triple dose of prejudice, raises a question that I
cannot conclusively answer. It nonetheless needs to be asked, and I
will suggest an answer that seems likely. Prof. Daniel's thesis is that
"black farmers suffered the most debilitating discrimination during
the civil rights era." This, as he makes clear, was both an established
fact and much noticed. Secretary Freeman was informed by the
U.S. Commission on Civil Rights that racism infected every office
in his department, and much pressure was brought to bear. Here
is Prof. Daniel's summary of the result: "The civil rights and equal
opportunity laws of the mid-1960s prompted USDA bureaucrats
to embrace equal rights rhetorically even as they intensified discrimination." My question, simply, is Why?

The conventional, therefore expectable, answer also is simple:
race prejudice and hypocrisy. The real answer, I suggest, is more
complicated and more disheartening: If the United States Department of Agriculture had given the required help to black small
farmers, the same help would have been required for white small
farmers. This would have amounted to a fundamental change in
the nation's agricultural policy. By 1965, when Secretary Freeman
directed his staff to put an end to racial discrimination, the application of the technology of industrial war to agriculture had been
aggressively in progress for twenty years. Secretary Benson had
come to power in 1952. In 1967, President Johnson's "special commission of federal food and fiber policies" would advise him that
the country's biggest farm problem was a surplus of farmers. To have
installed a policy to benefit small black farmers, and therefore small

farmers, in 1965 or at any time from then until now, would have required virtually a diametric redirection—against a perfect consensus of experts and an incalculable institutional and economic momentum—of all the federal and state agricultural bureaucracies, the land grant colleges of agriculture, and the immense, industry-supported apparatus of agricultural science. I don't believe that such a change could have been intended, let alone accomplished, in the 1960s. Though the destructiveness of industrial agriculture is now obvious and undeniable, I don't believe that such a change of direction can be intended or accomplished yet.

The virtual eradication of the farm population and the concurrent waste and degradation of the farmland are direct and inevitable results of the industrial revolution in agriculture. That revolution rests upon two fundamental errors: the assumptions, first, that humans and other creatures are limitlessly replaceable by machines and chemicals, and, second, that the destruction of land and people is a limitlessly payable cost of agricultural production.

The fraud and the damage, which in fact were always evident enough, were disguised or camouflaged by a line of official poppycock that, with much "scientific" help from the universities, acquired the status of holy writ, and it has not changed. In 1967, the president's "special commission on federal food and fiber policies" proclaimed that "the technological advances in agriculture have so greatly reduced the need for manpower that too many people are trying to live on a farm income wholly inadequate for them." For the discarded "too many," the commission proposed "better opportunities for the farm people," "a more comprehensive national employment policy," "retraining programs," and "improved general educational facilities." This clumsy bit of propaganda was offered as the official solution to the problem of inadequate farm income. But farm income was inadequate then, as it is now, because of the famous "cheap food policy," by which the government (liberal and conservative) forthrightly has sacrificed the livelihoods of rural producers to the "higher standard of living" of urban consumers. Thus it was merely reasonable that the most modernized expertise and the most sophisticated sense of public responsibility could have supported a policy to reduce the farmers to fit the inadequate income rather than to increase the income to preserve the farmers.

Let us recall that, according to Prof. Daniel, between 1940 and 1969, 3.4 million farmers, including 600,000 black farmers, were "pushed" off the land. In 1967, the year when President Johnson's commission made its report, one of the greatest of human migrations was under way, and the president's experts saw no problem. But look at their language. The "manpower" that in 1967 had already been defined as replaceable by "technology" is now defined as replaceable by robots. Human work has been understood as machine work, the humans therefore as machines, or as outmodable and discardable machines. That is to say that humans—ourselves—once accounted as "living souls" no longer count as living, much less as souls. And then by what measures, and whose, do we calculate "too many" and "inadequate" and "better opportunities"? People speak in this way in order to avoid the trouble of knowing what they are talking about. And in my opinion, people who prescribe "education" as a solution are fairly dependably up to no good.

Here is Prof. Daniel's appraisal of that great leap forward from the perspective of about half a century:

> USDA personnel, many educated at land-grant institutions, often denigrated farmers who did not accept their gospel of science and technology . . . Knowledge handed down or gained by trial and error was devalued and for-

gotten while formulaic methodology and machines grew in importance. The staggering human cost that accompanied this transformation was eclipsed by the celebratory sheen of tractors and picking machines, insecticides and herbicides, and hybrids and genetically engineered seeds. . . . Science and technology, the tale went, ended backbreaking work, freeing sharecroppers and tenants to move to lucrative urban jobs.

There were undoubtedly some in the farm-to-city migration who were volunteers, who "needed to go where the lights are bright," as a merry rural sociologist at the University of Kentucky assured me circa 1965. But Prof. Daniel is right, and unusual, in speaking of that migration's "staggering human cost," for those thousands of country people of both races were suddenly uprooted and countryless, and the "lucrative urban jobs" too often were not available. This migration was not dependably a "success story" or "the fulfillment of the American dream." In speaking of it as "freeing" farm people from "backbreaking work," Prof. Daniel of course is quoting what he calls the "heroic fable of capital-intensive agriculture." When economic and literary and scientific intellectuals and other professionals and professors wish to free themselves of any actual thought of the country they actually live in, they speak with pleasure of all the unfortunate white and black farming people who have been "freed" from the degrading work of farming.

9. Land Need and Good Work

And so we must return to the subject of work. In speaking of the American races and their history, we are likely to be dealing also with the history of work. In thinking of that history's theme of the desire or the need of some "superior" people to be free of "degrading" bodily work, we are carried necessarily back to slavery and its apologists. I referred early in this chapter to John C. Calhoun's division of kinds of work, not-degrading and degrading, and his assignment of degrading work to slaves. The degrading work, as I said, though it was thought to be suited only to slaves, could not be restricted to slaves. White people who had no slaves also were relegated to such work and to the implied degradation. In an article written for *The Atlantic* in 2015, Ta-Nehisi Coates quotes what is apparently an editorial published in an Alabama newspaper, the *Muscogee Herald*, in 1856, that speaks with contempt amounting to hatred of "the Northern . . . and especially the New England . . . small farmers who do their own drudgery, and yet are hardly fit for association with a southern gentleman's [black] body servant." I don't suppose that southern small farmers who did their own drudgery would have been rated significantly higher than the northern version.

I am reminded here of a *New York Times* review (January 4, 2019) of a movie set "in the backwoods of Kentucky." Of a sylvan genre of horror movie, the reviewer observes that "at some point, an attractively trembling woman will be forced to run like the dickens from a yokel who butchers his own meat"—which cuts a shade too close to the easily routed self-esteem of the present author. I can only protest that after butchering our own meat we yokels are usually too tired for the pursuit of women who can run and tremble at the same time.

It is conceivable that a highly structured Old World society, with an established peasantry centuries old and endowed with sustaining traditions of good work, might survive for a long time this kind of snobbery in its upper class. But in a society so unsettled and volatile as our own was and is, it seems extremely dangerous to apply such terms as "degrading," "mind-numbing," "drudgery," "nigger work," and "shit work" to work employing the body and the hands, and almost invariably to the work of using and caring for the land. And so the infection of slavery, owing to our democratization of the values of Calhoun and the master class, has become an epidemic that afflicts us all, afflicts our land as well, and all of the natural world. This pattern of degradations is perfectly compatible with, and is of a piece with, industrialism and its economy of consumption and waste. That pattern and that economy are directly opposed by the principles of agrarianism, which contradict the principles of industrialism at every point.

One doesn't have to look far to see the term "agrarianism" misused or sentimentalized. Dictionaries that I have looked into define the word rather vaguely as relating to landed property, land cultivation, or programs for equitable land distribution. Such definitions are unobjectionable but also unhelpful. I have needed the words "agrarian" and "agrarianism" for many years, and I have heard, read, spoken, and written them fairly often. As I understand it, agrarianism, unlike industrialism, recognizes and accepts absolutely the dependence of the human economy—like human life, like all life— upon the natural world. A number of requirements—or laws, as we should call them—follow from that. The first of these laws holds that land in human use must be used well, must be well loved and cared for, not wasted or degraded in any way. It follows, logically and obviously, that agrarian people of any race do not scorn or hold in contempt the work of the body and the hands—the arts, the skills, the knowledge, the passion and patience and devotion— required by the best use and care of the land. We can converse about the nature, quality, comeliness, and desirability of that work only by using the terms and standards of agrarianism. Industrialism offers only some kind of "job," low-paying or high-paying, or no job. It does not propose that the job should be interesting or healthful or pleasing, or even useful or necessary.

The principles and ethics of agrarianism unwind from the impulse that I have called "land need." My father devoted much work and thought to the operation of our regional version of the New Deal tobacco program, which he saw as a practical fulfillment of land need as anciently recognized. He used to say, "If you want people to love their country, let them own a piece of it." He was not speaking of a "second home" or a "retirement home" or a "retreat," or of a farm of plantation scale, supportable only by gang labor or large machines. He had in mind a farm of reasonable size, where a young couple could plant their marriage, raise their children, and *make* a living that was not just a paycheck but a substantial, complex domestic economy, coming from their own soil by their own work and the work of family members and neighbors. Though this was "Jeffersonian," my father did not get it from the printed record, as I have done in confirmation of what I learned from him and my other teachers here at home. It had been handed directly to him through the generations back to the vanishing point: the need for an established, vital economic connection between people and the land under their feet. I can, and I do, believe in the possibility of a kinder, more loving and lasting American civilization, but I cannot imagine such a thing coming to be if it does not inherit and embody this agrarian vision of a people stably and conservingly settled upon the land. It must be taken from printed pages if oral tradition cannot carry it through the present convulsion.

Land need comes from the felt and sensible need for independence, both in the sense of a reasonable economic self-sufficiency and in the sense of being one's own boss. Those needs were often voiced by early settlers and freed slaves, and by agrarian people I have known, particularly in my young life. The idea in its basis and origin was a powerful wish to be free: to *not* be a starvling, a pauper, a scrounger, an underling, a peon, a *slave*. It seems to me virtually certain that the agrarianism of both races involves a reaction against slavery. Many Europeans who migrated here must have come remembering a subordination to landlords tantamount to slavery, and thus regarding landownership as tantamount to freedom. That supposition, in fact, is supported by a body of evidence that human slavery was widespread in human experience from very early or "primitive" times, but especially so after the emergence of the earliest city-states, with their ruling classes and bureaucratic governments. My acquaintance with this subject comes mainly from two books: Gary Snyder's *The Great Clod: Notes and Memoirs on Nature and History in East Asia* and James C. Scott's *Against the Grain: A Deep History of the Earliest States*. Both of these books take as a starting place the neolithic village, which incorporated the nonpolitical principle of the neighborhood or community and lived upon highly diverse, locally adapted economies of hunting, fishing, gathering, and perhaps some farming. Apparently they were, as we would say, free and democratic in comparison to the organized states that came after.

Of the change from the village economy to that of the state, Gary Snyder says, "How a free, untaxed, self-sustaining people can be made into a serf or slave populace whose hard-earned surplus is taken by force to support a large class of non-producers, is perhaps the major question of history." According to Prof. Scott, the crucial surplus was that of the cereal grains, grown on prime agricultural land. These crops were amenable to accounting and taxation by the state because—unlike, for instance, the root crops—they were "visible, divisible, assessable, storable, transportable, and 'rationable.'" Both writers agree that the means of converting crop surpluses to state power was writing, record-keeping, the "technological progress" of that time, and a new "educated" class of government clerks scouting the countryside, keeping track of the crops, reporting to the rulers.

The result was an entirely new order of human life. Here is Prof. Scott's description of it:

> On the one hand, groups of priests, strong men, and local chiefs were scaling up and institutionalizing structures of power that had previously used only the idioms of kinship. . . . On the other hand, thousands of cultivators, artisans, traders, and laborers were being, as it were, repurposed as subjects and, to this end, counted, taxed, conscripted, put to work, and subordinated to a new form of control.

Gary Snyder, I think, gives us the tightest summary of this change and its effects:

> The invention of writing . . . and a class of clerks provides the organizing pathways for re-channeling wealth away from its makers. In primitive society, surpluses are exchanged directly among groups or members of groups; peasants, however, are rural cultivators whose surpluses are transferred to a dominant group of rulers . . .
>
> The rulers become persons who are alienated from direct contact with the soil, growth, manure, sweat, craft —their own bodies' powers. The peasants become alienated from the very land they used to assume belonged to Mother Earth herself, and not to a Duke or a King. . . . The old religion of gratitude, trust, and exchange with

nature is eroded. The state seeks only to maximize its stance, and it begins to seem possible to get away with excessive exploitation of nature itself, as the scene of impact is moved over the hills, into the next watershed, out of sight.

And then this writer, who has been watching for a long time from the forest of the Sierra Nevada foothills and doesn't miss much, draws the inevitable parallel between that early slave-dependency and "our own fossil fuel era": "energy beyond imagining—'energy slaves' available—throws a whole society off keel into excess, confusion, and addiction."

Considering the obvious advantages to the people of wealth and power of some form of slavery, we need not be surprised that it has remained with us for so long. It is equally unsurprising that among European immigrants to America the memory of their previous landlessness and subservience would not have survived for long. Once people are free—and many of those immigrants, newly settled on their own farms, considered themselves free—there is no need to remember slavery or slavishness. But as often happens, if we look, we find the memory surviving in our language. And our language bears convincing evidence that we have behind us the experience of prevalent slavery. According to C. S. Lewis's *Studies in Words*, the English word "free," like its counterparts in Greek and Latin, originally meant "not a slave." And the Rev. Walter W. Skeat in *A Concise Etymological Dictionary of the English Language* gives us this: "Orig[inal] sense 'dear, beloved'; hence applied to those of the household who were children, not slaves." Our language also recalls the oppressive division between Anglo-Saxon peasants, the "churls," who tended the hogs, the sheep, and the cows, and their Norman conquerors who ate the pork, the mutton, and the beef. The word "slave" itself comes from "Slav," referring to the enslavement of Slavic people early in the Middle Ages. And we must think also of the word "freeman," meaning a person not enslaved, which survives still as a given name and a surname, as if to celebrate some old emancipation.

What survived in consciousness, I think, was not the sense of individual words, but related attitudes leading to things said. I have written before of the boast that was fairly commonplace among the agrarian farmers who were my elders as I was growing up, and who would state emphatically the fundamental tenet of their self-respect: "They may run me out"—or "sell me out" or "shoot me"—"but they'll never starve me out." They would be talking about their subsistence or household economy that they supplied aboundingly from the ground underfoot and their ability to live from it: their vegetable gardens, poultry flocks, milk cows, slaughter hogs, fruit trees and vines—plus the fruit, flesh, and fish that Nature provided at no cost. This was a freedom, understood as self-sufficiency and independence, that they could have only as landed people, tenants or owners. This is what Nate Shaw meant when he said he depended "on the twist of [his] own wrist." It is partly what one of my own teachers meant when he said, "Every tub needs to sit on its own bottom." By that he meant also that a proper self-sufficiency was owed as a courtesy to one's neighbors: You could not be independent of neighbors and neighborly help, but you should not depend on others to do for you what you should do for yourself. Or to put it another way: For neighbors you don't want slaves, or people dependent on slaves; you want people as self-sustaining and freestanding as yourself. The neighbors most able to come to you when you need help are those who are caught up on their work at home.

Who were, and are, the people most likely to remember such principles and sayings and to hand them down through the generations? They would be, I think, the agrarian farmers, who prized their foothold, their subsistence from the land they farmed, at least as highly as their ability to produce for the market, and who have always been more or less marginal to the concerted purposes of the civilization they happened to be in.

I am relying, now that I am in my eighties, on my sense of shortened time. Now the European phase of American history seems much shorter to me than it did when I was twenty or forty or sixty. My mother was born exactly three hundred years after the settlement at Jamestown. I was getting on into my seventies when we passed the four hundredth year. I have now lived about a fifth of the 415 years since 1607. I am far past any ability to suppose that we Kentuckians developed such culture as we have after we got here, or that we packed it in with us from Virginia. Now I feel in my bones that when my friend told me that every tub needs to sit on its own bottom, his mind was drawing from somewhere way back in the history of tubs.

And so, again maybe to understand the survival here of agrarian culture, I want to return to James C. Scott's book and trace briefly the second of its major themes, which has to do with the people he calls "barbarians." The city-states with their captive farmers depended upon expanses of highly arable land, flat and fertile, to support continuous crops of cereal grains—a way of food production that sounds as specialized and oversimplified, which is to say as bad, as the corn-and-bean agriculture of our own time. This left the steeper ground, like the hill-and-holler topography of my own country, to the barbarians, whose economy and diet seem to have been exuberantly diverse. They lived in the hills or in other landscapes marginal to the agriculture of the city states. "The barbarian zone," Prof. Scott says, "is a zone of hunting, slash-and-burn cultivation, shellfish collection, foraging, pastoralism, roots and tubers, and few if any standing grain crops." Their food production, he says, was "illegible," which is to say that it was not measurable or accountable by the state bureaucrats. And he says: "If the barbarian realm is one of diversity and complexity, the state realm is, agro-economically speaking, one of relative simplicity." He speaks of the barbarians as "uncaptured." And he makes this important clarification:

> I am using the term "barbarian" in an ironic, tongue-in-cheek sense. "Barbarian" and its many cousins—"savage," "wild," "raw," "forest people," "hill people"—are terms invented in state centers to describe and stigmatize those who had not yet become state subjects.

"Barbarian" thus is one of a set of pejoratives such as "rural" and "country" have come to be in the usage of the urban-industrial sophisticates of urban America. It seems then that the people of wealth and power in the earliest cities recognized just two classes of country people: slaves and barbarians. We should not forget this when we think of the present division between urban America and rural America.

~

I am, as often before, in water over my head, but it seems to me that a fairly direct line can be drawn from the barbarians of Prof. Scott's book to the agrarian farm families I have known here in my own country, and who since 1945 have been steadily dying out.

Although the occupation of Kentucky by people of Old World stocks has been more unsettled than settled, local cultures and ways, even so, have been remarkably influenced by topography. If you start northward from Shelbyville toward my own home country around Port Royal, you will pass at first through a broad, gently rolling, naturally bountiful landscape of excellent farmland, now tragically taken over by the "farming" of corn-and-beans. But as you come on northward the shaping of the land becomes more abrupt and, you might say, notional, for it is feeling more and more the influence of water. You are more apt to see water flowing in the hollows, more fields fenced and grassed, and more grazing livestock, now chiefly cattle. From somewhat south of New Castle and over the ten miles to Port Royal you will be crossing first the tributaries of Drennon Creek and then those of the lesser watershed of Cane Run. As you feel more and more the drawing power of the Kentucky River, still four hundred feet below the highest heights of the land, the ridges grow narrower, the slopes steeper, the creek valleys deeper. Here historically the farms were smaller, worked by the owners and their neighbors. There were fewer black people during slavery or employed as hired hands afterward. The narrower the uplands, the steeper and more wooded the slopes, the deeper the hollows, the more at home and diverse the subsistence economy would be, and the more would be the resort to hunting and gathering.

I knew well, as neighbors with whom I swapped work and talk for many years, several aging members of a family that had "always" lived on its fairly large farm of hills and hollows, as well as some ridgetops and creek bottoms that could be conservingly cropped. In the generation before mine, when their family was fully populated and functioning, my friends told me, the men always rabbit-hunted for two weeks after their corn was gathered and before tobacco-stripping began. They ate their game of course and sold the surplus, but this also was the pleasure that they had not learned to call "recreation." They were amusing themselves, as they often did anyhow at their work. Well on into my own time as their neighbor, the two brothers who remained at home always put their boat in the river and fished with trotlines during the weeks between the laying by of their crops and the start of the tobacco harvest. This again was a way of freely feeding and pleasing themselves. They always kept a good hound or two for hunting at night. One of them, when he was younger and still felt like it, hunted and trapped for furs. They gathered the wild provender of the woods and fields. When the time was right and backwater from the river covered the creek bottoms, they and other members of their family would be standing in the shallows with gigs and pitchforks, watching like so many herons for the big carp.

My point, of course, is that these people and such people, who once belonged to my home countryside, were to a significant degree uncaptured, like Prof. Scott's barbarians. They were not, I think, as free or culturally as coherent as the Neolithic villagers and the barbarians. They were more vulnerable to the demands and hard times imposed by an increasingly dominant urban-industrial economy, and they were reconciled to seasons of extremely hard work. But their subsistence economy remained intact. Whatever may have been the condition of the larger economy, they kept warm in the winter and they ate well.

In general, among the farmers of the more marginal land, my own family included, there were a number of principles or traits that appear to have come from experience that was old, perhaps ancient:

1. Devotion to the elaborate subsistence economy that I have described. I remember that the households of both sets of my grandparents, and well into my own lifetime, made their own soap for washing dishes and clothes.

2. Fear of soil loss from too much plowing of slopes, to which they often felt themselves to be driven by debt and hard times. This was always a mistake. My father would say, with a bitter emphasis, "You can't *plow* your way out of debt."

3. A concomitant fear of debt, which made the farmers more subject to economic forces they could not control. Farming seems always to have been enclosed by a larger economy in some way, or in some ways, alien to it. In Kentucky, the rural economy came early under the influence of urban markets. "Borrowing money is borrowing trouble."

4. A related conviction in favor of livestock, grass, and grazing. On many farms there would be cattle, sheep, and hogs, all pastured.

5. A related opposition to growing grain crops for cash. "The grain grown on this farm has got to walk off," meaning that the only grain exported from their farms would be in the flesh of their livestock going to market.

Within the scope of my own memory, then, we started with a culturally complex, diversified, small-scale agrarian agriculture, dependent primarily on sunlight and natural law, and oriented to the survival of the farm and its family. From that we have now progressed to the extremity of the agriculture of corn and soybeans, culturally simple, ever increasing in scale, totally dependent on cash and credit and on purchased technology, energy, and fertility: an economic trap that thousands of ex-farmers have borrowed money to enter, and then have grown "too big to get out" except by failure and bankruptcy. It may startle us to realize that of Prof. Scott's two contrasting land economies of several thousand years ago—the barbarian economy of complexity and freedom versus the city-state economy of "relative simplicity" and slavery—the second is fairly analogous to our present "scientific" agriculture. Slavery did not begin with the capture and sale of African black people, and it did not end with their legal emancipation.

I think that agrarian Americans in general reserved a certain doubt that slavery was forever ended by President Lincoln. And I think that white small farmers in the South, owners or renters, were aware long before the Civil War of the curious inversion by which mastery becomes slavery. People do become slaves by being forced to do "degrading" work, but people are degraded also by having that work done for them by slaves and thus becoming help-less to do it for themselves. The master class, insofar as it kept itself free (which is to say incapable) of work they thought degrading, became in practical effect subordinate to their slaves—the slaves of slaves. I think that white small farmers saw that this was so and saw that it was contemptible. My evidence for this is the survival of a boast, implying a judgment, among farmers of my father's generation and the one following: "I won't ask another man to do anything I won't do myself." By that rule, one becomes free, mor-ally and economically, by being one's own slave, cleaning up one's own messes. (This implies an ecological law, now for most of us impossible to obey, for one's own economic life: Don't make messes that you can't clean up by your own effort.) The modern version of enslavement to slaves is enslavement to machines and chemicals, which has become fairly notorious.

For a considerable number of people to possess the freedom implicit or possible in landownership, a certain scale or limit obviously is required. In the early years of my own life in the Burley tobacco region of Kentucky, the complex culture and labor-intensity of the staple crop, and the persistence of the use mainly of mules single and in teams for traction in fieldwork, tended to keep the farms to a size that was both democratic and suited to the topography. Industrialization, together with the loss of the tobacco economy and the importation of the totally industrial corn-and-bean agriculture of the Midwest, has by now enlarged the acreages of the annual crops, increased the farm acreages owned or rented, and forced the replacement of the homegrown work of families and neighbors by that of migrants. Industrialization is not the only cause of the decline of our communities and community economies, but it is a major cause.

For many years, my standards of reference and measure in thinking about the issue of scale have been my own community as I knew it in the 1940s and the Amish community centered in Holmes County, Ohio, as it has so far remained—and as, in fact, it confirms the value of my hereditary community of the 1940s. Topographically the two communities are similar; they both occupy landscapes varyingly hilly, best farmed in family-size parcels. But whereas my community is continuing to decline economically and in other ways, the Amish community remains coherent, economically and culturally. The size of the farms there, varying mostly according to topography, remains in the neighborhood of one hundred acres. I am acquainted, for example, with two good, very productive Holmes County Amish farms, one of 80 acres, one of about 120, each the sole support of its resident family. The reason for this economic good health, so far as I have discovered, is that the Amish, alone among the Christian denominations known to me, have understood Jesus's second commandment, "Love thy neighbor as thyself," as requiring a practical, economic commitment. Neighbors are to love one another by work as well as by kindness. If one takes that commandment seriously, one cannot replace one's neighbor and one's neighbor's help with a machine or a chemical. Thus the neighborhood becomes an economic asset, unaccounted and untaxed, belonging to each of its members. The practical limit required by the commandment is imposed by the use of horses for farmwork and local travel. The size of the farms and the radius of each family's daily economic and social life, both acreages and distances, are determined by the speed and endurance of living creatures. Small-scale shops and trades can flourish on this scale, and in Holmes County the small towns are thriving as they were thriving here in my county seventy years ago.

The fundamentalists of religion and the fundamentalists of science make themselves equally ridiculous by reading the first chapters of Genesis as a kind of science and a kind of history. Those chapters, of course, give us one among many "creation myths." The distinction, for us, of the myth in Genesis is that it is one of the sources of Western, our own, tradition. Our literary culture teems with remembrances of it, references to it, and retellings of it. The only part of the Genesis creation story that I resist is 3:17–19, where our need to live by work is construed as a curse—which, my friend and Bible scholar Paul House advises me, contradicts the importance assigned to work in earlier verses of Genesis and in other parts of the Bible. The favor given to the idea of work as a curse suggests to me that our modern disdain, now surely enlarged by ignorance, of physical work outdoors in the weather is an ancient thing under the sun, probably older than the Bible. Its origin, then, would be in the human trait (or deadly sin) known as sloth or laziness. If I were allowed a footnote to Genesis 3:17–19, I would like to describe the circumstances in which hard work in the hot sun might be considered a curse, as opposed to the circumstances in which it has been considered a privilege, even a blessing.

Work that is done on too large a scale and that goes on the same, day after day for too long a time, work in which the worker makes only a part and not the whole of a made thing, work that is poorly compensated and unthanked, work for the benefit only of strangers, work that does harm to the world and other creatures, work that is done too fast and is poorly done, work that is ugly in the doing and in the result, work that one does only because one is obliged or compelled to do it, or that one must do because it is the only work available—such work may properly be thought a curse, and may receive curses in response. Such work may cause people to think slave thoughts and adopt slave ways. "Thank God it's Friday" is a slave thought.

Good work, like the practice of neighborly love, depends upon a certain propriety or limitation of scale. For work to be pleasing and satisfying to do, good in performance and in result, the scale must not be so large as continuously to enforce haste or overwork. Rightness of scale prevents enough work from becoming too much. The scale is right, particularly in farming, when work can be done at the right time. As the scale of grain farming has increased here in my country, the idea of "the right time" is ignored or forgotten, and the huge machines, also out of scale, wallow through the rain-softened fields, leaving gouges that would break a true farmer's heart.

The issue of scale is fundamental and all-important. But good work is complex in its making. Once the scale is right, other indispensable qualities are combined with it to make the work right. When it is not solitary, work benefits in happiness and quality from good companionship among workers—from, obviously, the working-well-together of workers who know one another well. Good work employs the mind as well as the body of the worker. It embodies the difference between knowing how, using skill, improving with experience and working by rote as in effect a machine or a machine part.

It makes a great difference for the better if the work is the worker's vocation. People who are in no way "called" to the work they do, if it is only their "job," find little reason to work well, and they feel like slaves. The *Temenos Academy Review* recently published an address, "Education in Art," that Ananda Coomaraswamy presented at Harvard in 1947, and here is what he said about vocation:

> In a truly civilized society men should be able to earn their living by doing such work as they would rather be doing than anything else in the world. It is only where, as Plato says, a man's vocation is also his means of livelihood, that "more will be done, and better done, and more easily than in any other way." This I have seen with my own eyes in India where men are proud of their hereditary vocations, whatever these may be; under these conditions, hours of labor have no meaning, since one is naturally inclined to do as much as one can; the labourer is worthy of his hire, but he is not working *for* hire, and would often rather work than play or eat.

When I read to the end of that last sentence, I laughed because it reminded me of a story.

A good many years ago, to write an article for my friend Maury

Telleen, editor of *The Draft Horse Journal*, I went with my son to visit a good Amish community in Indiana. Will Schmucker and his nephew, Martin Schmucker, whose small farms adjoined, were among the finest breeders of Belgian horses. Toward evening on the day of our visit, our hosts began to show us their horses. At Martin's direction, his children, some of them very young, began leading horses from the barns and, one after another, trotting them up and down the lane in front of the farms. The horses were of all ages, and in conformation, motion, and style they met, with remarkable consistency, a high standard of excellence. We were watching what amounted to a horse show of rare quality, put on with considerable painstaking and effort, for an audience of two.

The two barns held a lot of horses, and the show went on at such length that I began to feel uneasy. My son and I had not come as buyers. Even considering the exhibitors' obvious pride and delight in them, the horses were being shown as a kindness that we had no way of repaying.

"Martin," I said. "It's late. You all need to be eating your supper."

It had not occurred to me that Martin was the third member of the audience. He said, "Around here, we eat when there's nothing better to do."

When the scale is right, and the work answers the calling of the workers, "such work as they would rather be doing than anything else in the world," then the work comes to be motivated by love, and that changes everything. When work is done for love—of the place where it is done, of the materials, the artistry, and the product of the work, of the people it is done with and for—then the sign or evidence of it will be beauty. Both the work and its result will be beautiful. Ugliness in work, or in its results, is a sign of something badly gone wrong. In my early years, when farming here was smaller in scale and far more a discipline of the eyes and hands than now, an adjective often applied to work was "pretty." Of mowing a field or cultivating a row crop with a walking or a riding plow, you would hear, "Oh, that's pretty work." That work can give pleasure is one of the happiest things we can know of our life in this world.

If, under the right conditions, work can be rewarding, something people can be glad to do, even reluctant to stop doing, then we were wrong to have decided, as we seem generally to have done, that sedentary work or light work or easy work or brief work or no work is better than good work. The idea that human workers can and should be replaced by machines, which has been the ruling dogma of the industrial revolution until now, is radically reductive and deterministic—I would say nihilistic. It reduces us and our work by subtracting artistry, love, beauty, workmanly pride, pleasure—all the qualities and powers that enable us effectively to love one another and our home places in this world. The idea that work is bad, long an axiom of so-called industrial civilization, forestalls as a matter of course any effective opposition to the replacement of human workers by industrial devices. Such replacement obviously is promoted also by the vast increase of degrading industrial jobs.

The reigning experts, politicians, columnists, and other announcers of public truths customarily do not ask why the "advance" of drastically reductive technology is called "progress." They do not propose that any mere person might or should have a choice for or against the adoption of such technology. They do not suggest that freedom may require, or depend upon, the willingness to deliberate upon and exercise such a choice, against as readily as for. They appear instead to believe that the choice has been made for us by some superhuman power or fate, and that the future of technology is as fixed and unchangeable as its past. Thus, so far as the public powers are concerned, human beings are now as reduced, as deprived of their traditional qualities, standards, and aspirations, as so many specimens, skinned and stuffed. But technological determinism is really no more than a fashion or a fad, and it can be chosen against, as the Amish have done. The rest of us can choose against it by refusing to buy anything we don't need. Speaking of course just for myself, I have gained far more happiness from my refusal to buy a television set and a computer than from anything I have ever bought. And I have experienced intense happiness from work done with old (cheap) technologies—a pocketknife, a hoe, a pencil—and my bare hands.

10. The Fate of an Agrarian Culture

All that I have to say about work was learned or powerfully influenced by my membership in an agrarian community focused upon excellence. The Burley tobacco economy, which was once the mainstay of my part of Kentucky, was the basis also of a distinctive culture. It was a culture shared by both races for as long as both races lived and worked together here. Burley tobacco was an exceedingly demanding crop. Its growth from seed, through transplanting, cultivation, harvest, and preparation for market, occupied virtually the whole year. Its production involved many steps, each of which required knowledge, skill, experience, both a settled methodology and routine, and the ability to make variations of work in response to variations of seasons and the weather. Though it was grown in comparatively small acreages, it required far more thought and bodily work than any other crop. By the time a crop of Burley tobacco reached the warehouse, every plant and finally every leaf would have been carefully handled and appraised. Until well after World War II, because of its need for such intimate care, this crop was resistant to technological shortcuts. To produce the crop at all, a farmer had to rise to a high threshold of ability and diligence. The growers were in fact artists, though that word was not used. The best were called "tobacco men," a term of distinction not easily earned or lightly given. Their art was the staple, the primary dependence, both of the farms and of the professions and small businesses of the towns.

Before I go further, I need to acknowledge the extreme difficulty of tobacco as a subject of this writing. I have put myself into the fairly absurd predicament of needing to speak in praise of a regional economy and culture founded upon a crop now known to cause cancer. I am in about the position of a teetotaler obliged in honesty to respect the artistry of viticulture and winemaking.

After the surgeon general's report on tobacco and cancer was published in 1965, it was impossible to defend tobacco as a farm crop, and I did not attempt to defend it. But insofar as many farm families remained dependent on the tobacco economy, it remained right to work with one's neighbors in their tobacco crops, as I most certainly did though I grew no crop of my own. And it remained right to defend the tobacco program because of the rightness of its principles, as I did and still do.

In its sustained emphasis upon *qualities* of soils, of husbandry, and of the product, the culture of tobacco seems fairly closely to resemble the culture of wine. Here, from a report written by Joseph Buckner Killebrew nearly a century and a half ago, is an observation of the interrelationship of nature and culture in the production of tobacco:

> While each distinct soil formation gave particular qualities to the plant as to texture, color, flavor, and general

structure, these may be modified by culture and curing into still greater variations of character. A knowledge of what quality or property is wanting may enable the grower so to apply his fertilizers or to manage the curing process, as greatly to enhance the value of the product; and a want of this knowledge may also cause the grower to destroy, by imperfect cultivation or curing, the very quality which gives the product its highest value.

That, I believe, gives a fair idea of the meticulous artistry, and its relation to market price, of the farming culture in which my father's father was then living, and into which my father and I were born.

Such refinement of perception, judgment, and skill continued well into my own lifetime. I grew into the ability to do the work from playing around it and at it as a child. And as I grew into the work of tobacco, I grew into the love for it that surrounded me everywhere, and also into appreciation of the beauty of it in almost all its stages from plant bed to market. I remember saying to my father when I was still only a big boy that I imagined our people might still grow the crop even if it brought no money. My father did not agree—he said he knew what I meant. I had begun, anyhow, to live into the agrarian passion for farming and for good farming that motivated my father and a number of others whose influence I grew up under. The ceaseless interest in quality that we invested in tobacco extended also to the other crops and the livestock of our then highly diversified way of farming. "Good" was the adjective conventionally applied—"a good un," the old men of the generations before mine would say with emphasis, or "a damn good un"— but we meant "beautiful" as often as we meant "sound" or "useful." Of our annual field crops, tobacco was by far the most beautiful. And much of our work in it, hard as it was, we called "pretty."

I am fortunate to have good evidence of the kind of crop and work that I am talking about. In 1973 the writer and photographer James Baker Hall made a set of photographs of the harvesting of Owen Flood's tobacco crop of that year. Jim Hall and I had been friends then for twenty years. Owen and I, in 1973, had been friends for twenty-nine years, since I was ten. Of that year's crew of fourteen, several of us were old friends and workmates. It was mainly a traditional crew of work-swapping neighbors.

Yeats wrote somewhere that "things reveal themselves passing away," and I remember that when I look at Jim's photographs now. For in 1973 a force of change had begun to work upon us that we had already experienced, but the extent of which we could not then have imagined. The horse and mule teams had been supplanted by tractors in our fields more than twenty years before. It may have been longer than that since any of us had worked in a tobacco harvest with black people. The surgeon general's report was eight years old in 1973. More chemicals, more poisons, were in use in tobacco production. That year's crop would be Owen Flood's last. He died in March of the next year. Several of us in that 1973 crew would continue to work together for decades. But the kind of workers we were, and the kind of work we were doing, were passing from the world, not to be replaced. If today a moviemaker should want to reproduce our 1973 tobacco harvest, no such crop could be found, nor any actors who could do our work as we did it.

Not long before Owen died, an unsuspecting young man informed him that, according to the experts, you no longer needed to use a hoe in your tobacco crop. Owen said, "I clean the weeds out of my crop for the same reason I wash my *face*." His workmanly pride demanded cleanness, a forthright clarity, as a part of the beauty he desired as one result of his work. What Jim Hall's photographs show, because *he* so clearly saw it, was a beautiful crop being harvested, entirely by handwork, in a beautiful way. The tobacco plants individually and standing together were beautiful. The long curving rows, following the contour of the sloping field, were beautiful—"*too* long," you might have heard from a man working the hard, hot way from one end to the other. The cut "stickrows" were beautiful. The tobacco was beautiful so carefully loaded on the wagons. The inverted stalks, carefully spaced and regulated, were beautiful hanging in the barn. And the ground, cleared of the crop, was virtually weedless.

We must not forget the harm of tobacco, or the difficulty of dealing with the harm of it. At the same time we should remember the crop as the support of an agrarian artistry that continued for generations and supported in turn a local culture that, apart from its harm, was exemplary.

What Jim's photographs couldn't show, of course, was the heat, sweatiness, scratchiness, difficulty, and weariness of the work. Or the conviviality of it—for especially when we were in the barn, working close together, we were talking on an endless variety of subjects, and we were laughing at somebody's joke or witty remark or some funny story remembered and retold, which would remind somebody of another. We talked to amuse ourselves and each other, and the talk eased our misery and was precious to us.

One of our 1973 crew was a small swift-witted man by the name of Eddie Sharp. Eddie was raised as an orphan by his grandparents and two unmarried uncles. He was crippled in one leg by a childhood disease—to avoid explaining the unusual ailment that had done the damage, Eddie always attributed it to "polio"—and he probably never weighed more than 125 pounds. But his uncles worked hard, setting an example, and Eddie came up behind them, working hard, expecting of himself what they expected of themselves and of him. He always did his full share of whatever work was going on, and I never heard him complain. He and my son Den, who at eleven was the youngest member of the 1973 crew, went on swapping work as neighbors and friends until 2011, when Eddie died at the age of sixty-five.

In 2002, Jim Hall selected and arranged his photographs as a book, *Tobacco Harvest: An Elegy*, to be published by The University Press of Kentucky, and the photographs were exhibited at our county seat in the late summer, about tobacco-cutting time, of that year. I wrote an introductory essay for the book, and here is my paragraph about Eddie:

> When the photographs were shown at New Castle, Eddie Sharp was there, looking at his young self at work, by then with twenty-nine more years of such work behind him. Standing in front of one of the pictures, explaining it to a listener who wanted to know, he said, "That was *hard* work. There wasn't any way you could do it to keep it from being hard. But you wouldn't believe the fun we had."

Eddie's affirmation was dear to me. When I heard him speak so of our work, I felt spoken for. We had done hard work together, had suffered it and enjoyed it, often both at once. Eddie never farmed land of his own. He and his uncles lived most of their lives as tenants on the same farm. It was anyhow land under their feet that was well-known to them, that they knew well how to use. One of the uncles killed himself, and nobody ever knew why. As I knew them in their work, all three were intelligent, observant, confident, humorous men. Eddie never went to college, but he was as far from stupid as any professor he might have had. The hard work he had done, and he had done plenty, had not numbed his mind or broken his back. He had made peace with his hardships, and was properly grateful for his pleasures.

Because of the migrations of the country people during and after World War II, I have had to complete my account of agrarian experience by speaking of what I learned as a white person working with white neighbors. The last black people who worked on my father's home place, for example, were gone before 1950. They were so familiar and established a part of the life of that place as I first knew it that their absence from it still seems to me to have marked a change of times.

A change of times was exactly what it was, for whether they stayed or went away, the younger people of both races had set out for the modern world, its monetary standards, and its entirely different understanding of work. When I think of myself as I was in 1950, when I was sixteen, I can see that without quite knowing it, in fact without knowing very consciously much of anything, I was caught up in that migration into the modern world. Farming itself was on its way into the modern world—and I was not sufficiently conscious of that. Insofar as I was conscious, I took internal combustion to be as normal as breathing. Though the knowledge cost me some grief, I knew that I was supposed to become educated, and that the drift of education was away from such a home as I had, and away moreover from the kind of person I had been made so far by my upbringing and experience. It took me, after 1950, fifteen years, many miles, a lot of looking around, before I could begin to sense the real worth and pertinence of my agrarian upbringing, and then consciously to turn around and reclaim it.

Now as I look back I can see that I owe much of my sense of farming and farmwork to the black hands, chiefly Nick Watkins, whom I accompanied at their work, and sometimes worked with, in my childhood, and whose agrarianism my reading has confirmed. They are part of what I don't see when I look at my small native country now. What I don't see also is the life, the liveliness, the self-assured vitality of the agrarian "world" I shared with them and took to be normal during my childhood, which had ended, or had at least been radically changed by the changing of times, by 1950.

However the histories of our two races have differed and diverged, I think they converge upon the theme of agrarianism. I think it has come to both races ultimately from the human experience of land need: the fear of enslavement, the desire for freedom and independence. That is why I have so often felt that Ernest Gaines has spoken for me. It is why I feel so touched, confirmed, and even encouraged by the passion of Crystal Wilkinson's Minnie Mae in *The Birds of Opulence*.

I must ask my readers to imagine the recognition and sympathy, the mutuality of grief, with which Johnny Paul's great speech about all that he "don't see" resounds in my mind when I look at my native town, not much larger than the "quarters" of a Louisiana plantation, and I see the empty lots and the vacant houses, some with wild bushes branching across the front doors, and I don't see the well-keeping and its pleasure in itself that once made even so small a place the vital center of its countryside and its consciousness, and I don't see the people necessary to its well-keeping who have died and not been replaced, whom I am among the last to remember alive. The racial differences, whatever they may be, are subsumed into the one grief, which declares itself to be indigenous to our country in our time.

And I must ask particularly my urban readers to imagine that the tragedy of Minnie Mae—whose sons can think only of selling her farm, their birthright, pricing her own life and meaning at nothing—is both a major and nearly an unknown theme of modern American history. It is a major theme because by now it has been repeated so many times. It is a theme so nearly unknown because it has been suffered almost exclusively by old-fashioned old people, old agrarians often enough, like Johnny Paul and Minnie Mae who are too passing, too nearly gone, to have a political or public force, and who anyhow have no place in the ever-displacing scientific and technological world-to-come of industrialism. Because they are old and long-memoried, Minnie Mae and Johnny Paul are entirely awakened to the possibility of a rightful, completing and completed, human dwelling upon the earth, a possibility that is comely and uplifting to know and to desire even if unrealized. The vision of that possibility and of the loss of it brings them to grief.

We have sufficient testimony that this grief exists and is real. Now we must ask if it reduces merely to nostalgia, as the apostles of the Technological Answer would insist—or if, instead, it is the felt appraisal of a real, really valuable, finally necessary human capacity that now, by our public culture, has been radically depreciated and given up.

11. The American Dream Progresses

My own answer to that question will have to begin by noticing what I take to be the radical mutation of "the American Dream" during my lifetime. I don't remember hearing the American Dream much mentioned in private conversation, but we still hear of it often in public pronouncements, usually with reference to the proposed right of every American to realize it. I am taking the phrase seriously enough to suppose that it must be truly democratic—the name of what a significant number of Americans want.

Here in my home country in the early part of my life, the local version of the American Dream was still, as it had long been, the ownership of an economic property in which a person, a couple, or a family could invest life and work to earn a decent living: a farm, say, of a hundred or two hundred acres, a small town grocery or hardware store, a barbershop, a medical or legal practice with an appropriate office, a repair shop of some kind, a drugstore, or just the equipment and know-how to set up as a carpenter or electrician or plumber (or all three). A kind of symbiosis operated among these small enterprises. The economy was based to a large extent upon the local countryside and so were people's amusements. It was largely a personal economy, in which parties to any transaction were likely to know one another. Knowledge served as a kind of currency. Credit would be extended or withheld on the basis of live knowledge. Sometimes goods or services might be rendered only on the basis of known need to customers or clients or patients known to be unable to pay. Doctors or lawyers might be paid in produce or work. The grocer from whom a farmwife bought her coffee, sugar, and flour would buy her cream, eggs, and old hens. Underlying this economy of small properties, trades, and professions was the desire for a measure of personal independence or self-sufficiency or self-determination, which was the desire to be unbossed—free. I know I will be accused of "romanticizing the past," of "nostalgia for a world that never existed." But I am only generalizing the working principles of a kind of life once lived here by people merely human. It was a life humanly possible and actual, unique to its time and place, instructive no doubt, but not perfect and not reproducible. I know that other communities something like it were widespread at the same time in other places.

That old, intimate economy was destroyed in the course of not many years by the industrialization of agriculture, the diminishment of the farming population, the coming of the chain stores and volume discounts, the disconnection of lives from places and properties, the normalization of "mobility," the livings made by commuting to work and to shop, the separation of life and work, the reduction of community to "bedroom community." I have tried several times to make an accurate description of this great change, only to end in uncertainty about the chronology of events and the real order of causes and effects. I feel confident only that I have rightly described the difference between what we were and what we have become.

A recent speech given by John Logan Brent, judge executive of my county, a man much younger than I, confirms my own sense of an established and continuing economic decline. If we consider stagnant commodity prices (for tobacco, milk, corn, beef cattle), the changing climate, and current trends in agriculture, he said, we "would have to go back to the 1930's to see an overall picture as bad as it is today." He spoke of the decline in the number of full-time family farms, and of the increased acreage given to large-scale grain-growing operations. "In 20 years," he said, "my hometown [of Campbellsburg, population of about 600] has lost 2 hardware stores, a lumberyard, a Southern States [farm supply dealership], a farm equipment dealership." He spoke of "farms rutted, soil compacted, washes where they have never been before." He said, "Fire departments struggle for volunteers. Volunteer EMTs are almost all gone. In general I am seeing us become more and more of a bedroom community, and seeing the population become less engaged as a whole in school, local politics, shopping at home, and even attending local churches."

Such economic and circumstantial changes have required the American Dream to shift from the ownership of a small economic property and self-employment to "a job" and the subordinate status of employee, whether in industry or an urban profession.

And, apparently for most of us of all races, work of any kind, or the need to do it, has become objectionable. For this we have as evidence the premium now placed upon weekends, vacations, and retirement, particularly "early retirement." For nearly all of us, any work requiring bodily effort, especially if it is outdoor work, bears the taint of degradation placed upon it by Calhoun and the master class he spoke for, who wished to displace degradation from themselves to others less worthy. That most of us now pretend or aspire to that class is revealed by our dependence, nationally, upon immigrant workers, and also by the convenience, ease, or effortlessness we willingly pay for in, for instance, automobiles and ways of eating. That a whole nation of people, including young people, need to be spared the effort to crank up a car window surely exceeds in luxuriousness the most slave-served aristocrats of the Old South. It is not hard to suppose that the American Dream eventually will be realized as early interment with a smart phone.

As a nation and a society, then, we have traversed the great difference between a populace of many property owners, most of them self-employed, and a populace mostly of jobholders or employees. This has changed the fate of our country radically and drastically. When people become jobholders, they no longer have an established relationship to our land, our country itself. In our economy, which is overwhelmingly industrial and urban, employees are now by definition mobile. The choice of permanence of residence is denied them as a condition of employment. They can be fired or "terminated" as collateral damage in the course of industry's unending effort to cheapen production, they can be replaced and displaced by new technology, they can be required to move in order to keep their jobs. If they "succeed," they will be more or less expected to move to a more expensive housing development or suburb. When they retire they likely will follow other retirees to a place warm in the winter.

And so we have seen, in about one lifetime, a massive migration of our people that has involved a commensurate change in what our people aspire to. This great change obviously cannot have come cheap. Prof. Daniel acknowledged its "staggering human cost." But Prof. Daniel is merely a citizen and a historian. He told an interviewer that the officials, authorities, and experts, to whose work and responsibility his book was directed, have said not a word in response. In fact the officials, authorities, and experts who have been obliged to notice this change have spoken of it as inevitable or as progress or as an improvement in the lives of the migrants. None of them, so far as I have heard, has attached a cost to it or admitted that it had a cost. Once a change has been attributed to progress, especially if the progress is understood as predestined or inevitable, there ceases to be any question of cost. Progress is accounted as a good or a gain at 100 percent net. The cosmeticians of progress do not subtract.

By their negligence or indifference, the officials, authorities, and experts have left the accounting to those of us who still are living in rural America and who care about the places where we live. But we know we cannot count in numbers or dollars the costs of the departure of so many from the economic landscapes of our country.

We know that the resultant damages to nature and culture are permanent, ongoing, and accumulating—therefore immeasurable.

From what I have seen, I believe that city-bred people who move into the country and undertake to farm for a living, or only to produce their subsistence, find the transition to be awkward and slow, to be completed not in weeks or months but in years. Partly this may be because the transition is likely to involve a movement from employment as a subordinate in an organization to self-employment and to relatively solitary responsibility. But this transition also confronts the newcomer immediately with the need for competent knowledge of a place, a part of both the natural world and human history, which cannot be known immediately and which can never be known fully. This transition is now customarily understood (by city people) as a simplification of life. There could hardly be a bigger mistake.

By contrast, when farm people move to the city, whether voluntarily or under economic constraint, they lose almost immediately their consciousness of land need and land responsibility. They are separated entirely, finally, and all at once from the culture and practical knowledge that sustained them on the farm. The most obvious reason for this is economic: Suddenly, and if they are so fortunate as to be employed, everything they need is available at the cost only of money and the effort it takes to shop.

We can suppose, maybe reasonably, that someday some of our people may return to our country, maybe enough of them eventually to use it and conserve it at the same time. But that can happen *only* eventually, slowly, and with much difficulty, for the people who would come back could not bring with them the culture that was almost immediately forgotten and forsaken by the people who left.

12. Culture, Work, Economy

But now, having spoken again and again of "culture," I can no longer avoid the curious doubleness to be found in that word. Here is the first definition of "culture" that is given by the *American Heritage Dictionary*: "the totality of socially transmitted behavior patterns, arts, beliefs, institutions, and all other products of human work and thought." I take that to be true and useful. But if it is the first definition according to the authorities of the dictionary, it is the last to be considered by the people of our society, if they consider it at all. Under that definition we must consider, for instance, our landfills and their contents as artifacts of our culture. And so culture, by definition, calls for a comprehensive work of cultural criticism that mostly we have not done or ever intended to do. Modern Americans might fairly be identified as a culture by their disinterest in the reasons for the waste of the persons, places, and things that they have wasted.

Within that large, comprehensive culture that consists of all that we are and do, there is the smaller, more exclusive culture customarily thought of as "culture" and as "high culture." This culture learns, studies, and variously enjoys a selection of records and relics preserved in museums, libraries, and concert halls. Civilization owes unquestionably an enormous debt to the artifacts and human lineages of high culture. But high culture, as maintained and propagated by the institutions named above and in some academic departments, has a bad way of ignoring or excluding and depreciating what I am now obliged to call "low culture," the on-the-ground culture that informs and supports the work of "working people."

Low culture certainly includes arts in the high-culture sense of the term, but also what we might call life arts or economic arts. It is low culture that keeps us fed, clothed, and sheltered. The aim of industrialism obviously has been to reduce these arts to rote process and routine, thus cheapening them, and making them finally imitable, thus replaceable, by machines—and so putting them beyond the reach of vocation, living artistry, love for places and neighbors, and any ability to respond to living needs. The estranging words are "growth," "efficiency," "speed," "ease," "better," "new," and "more." The result is an overbearing purposelessness of the human economy and so of human life, a workaday nihilism. When the low-culture arts become outmoded or old-fashioned or obsolete, matters of record only, they are classified, in the view of the institutions of high culture, as "folklore" or "folk arts," which pretty much are names for dead culture.

The agrarian cultures of husbandry and husbanding are by nature and the way of the world living cultures that can exist only so long as they are alive. They are ways of thinking and doing that continue in the world by being taught, not in schools but in the course of daily work and talk, by older people to younger people. And to deserve the name of "culture," this handing on of the arts of responsible work must happen often enough among enough people over a long time. Such a culture also preserves, keeps in place, and depends upon the history of the countryside, the stories, the knowledge of landmarks, the points at which the stories of people and land converge and become one story, the memories of what has worked or failed in the use of the land—all of which answer the never fully answered question of *how* to work. A living culture of work lived close to the ground, carried forward into time in the ordinary work and speech of every day, is as far as possible unlike any record that may be made of it. It may be documented as "oral history," its stories may be remembered and written into books, it may be pictured in old photographs, but no true likeness of it can ever be reenacted or reproduced. When such a culture dies, it is not only dead, it is *gone*.

And so the loss of the cultures of husbandry, incomplete or inadequate as they often were, is not a matter only of history or sentiment. Husbandry is the discipline of thrift and thriving, of fruitfulness and frugality, of care and caretaking and taking care. When husbandry departs from the land, human livelihood begins to pass away, and human life itself acquires a deadline. Only a great forgetting and a great ignorance could suppose that the loss of such cultures would not register as damage that is ecological, economic, and social.

When farming people migrate to the city, their forgetfulness of what they have been is completed in their loss or their giving up of their former language. As a part of a culture of country work, its language can survive only by living among its native subjects, its references. Divided from what it is *about*, the language dies like an uprooted plant. Also, once they have pretty thoroughly displaced themselves into a city, country people will not want to be caught "talking country." Removed from the country, country speech can be used only to make fun of country people.

We must remember that country people, mainly farmers, who do not commute to town jobs but continue their dependence upon the land and the adverse land economy, are now a tiny minority, whom the public has consigned to "degrading work," and whom it therefore holds in contempt. That contempt, as should be obvious by now, is a necessary subject of this chapter. I will need to speak of it again, for the forgetfulness of the country people who have moved to the city is immediately at one with urban America's forgetfulness of rural America, a forgetfulness that amounts to nearly perfect ignorance, which many urban Americans express as contempt: What they don't know is not worth knowing. This is why transplanted farmers, even knowledgeable ones, do not become an urban lobby for good farming or farmland conservation. They are likely to have experienced the dire economic predicament of farmers and its dire effects upon the land and people, but they are not farmers anymore and they have no need to remember. This is exactly as if black people should turn white as soon as they understand the effects of race prejudice.

Good long-term care of the land, anyhow, requires an established language just as it requires an established human community. An established language is adapted to its place, like the rest of its native organisms. It lives only in a set of relationships among people, places, and things, and among people, their personal memories, and their common history. In speaking of the tragedy of the extinction of California Indian languages, I think Andrew Schelling gets the complexity of language survival about right:

> You need more than grammar and vocabulary. You need stories, jokes, instructions, daily banter; people need to tease one another, to speak when they've fallen in love; to raise children, to teach children, to scold children.

I know from experience that the conversation of a crew of longtime neighbors at work together on one of their farms, referring to memories, places within places, untold stories, absent people and animals, would be mostly unintelligible to a stranger. (The barbershop conversation in Ernest Gaines's last novel, *The Tragedy of*

Brady Sims, is a perfect example.) Compared to so truly communal a language, so complexly and intimately referential, a language merely public or standard is a blunt instrument. To say this is not to imply a rejection of public language, in which I am now writing, but only to acknowledge one of its limits.

It is merely true that our national language now is entirely urban. A language so contained within city limits cannot, by its nature, speak of rural life or rural economy or rural problems. No doubt it is for want of competent language that economists, columnists, other public intellectuals, and of course the politicians rarely speak in any detail of the world of what they call "natural resources" and take to be infinite, or of the land economies of farming, ranching, forestry, and mining. Or perhaps they assume with the public at large that, since "they" have always "managed" such things, "they" will continue to do so. Or perhaps from the air or the interstate they look at the farmland, green with its pestilence of soybeans and corn, and see it as "open space," restful and beautiful. Or if they adhere to any organization or movement describable as "green," perhaps, having no need to eat, they see "all that land" as suitable for solar panels, wind machines, "development," and "job creation." It is anyhow economically and politically ominous for so many millions of people to inhabit, and live from, a country of which they know virtually nothing.

The problem is in the likelihood that people cannot see or think about anything of which they cannot speak, and in the further likelihood that they cannot know or know about anything that they do not in some measure love. But the so-called conservatives have spoken of the land and valued it as a fund of "natural resources," to be used or used up at will and at any cost, so long as the payment of the costs can be delayed until "the future" or shifted onto the country people and the land. This no doubt has been expedited and justified in conservative minds by the abstraction, almost the spiritualization, of value from the actual economy of tangible properties and goods to the economy of money or finance. Thus it becomes possible for economists and bureaucrats to speak of renting a farm as equivalent to owning one, or to rate a farm as equivalent to a life insurance policy of the same market value. If the countryside is emptied as the country people gather into the allegedly better life of the cities, and in consequence a great national fortune in livable houses and usable farm buildings is abandoned to rust and rot and fire and the developer's bulldozer, that is everybody's loss, which supposedly nobody pays. All that has been ruined and lost may once have been loved, worked for, and cared for by now-lost people, but how do you quantify love and subtract it from the gross? And why should you?

Among the so-called liberals—the green capitalists and socialists, the environmentalists, lovers of nature and the wilderness, the objectors to abuses, the political correctors—almost none have objected to the abandonment and ruin of rural America, or to the plunder and waste of natural resources. They do object to the burning of the fossil fuels, because of climate change, but they also wish to be air-conditioned and overheated, overfed and underworked, and above all they want to keep driving their cars—all of which reminds me of John Lukacs's observation in 1984 that environmentalists "failed to recognize that the pollution of 'the environment' was the result of the pollution of minds."

Our wish to live "above" the fundamental earth and the fundamental work by which we live is more complicated and consequential than we know or probably can ever know. The terrible irony of it is that this ambition to go upward and be above all supposedly low-down and degrading work has ended in subordination for nearly all of us. The good jobs in industry and the footholds on the corporate ladders are available only to employees, people willingly answerable to bosses. Whatever ability and ambition may be involved, so also is a certain passivity or submissiveness, an attitude that Nate Shaw would have condemned as "slavish."

And not only are nearly all of us employees, risen from the land and from its "degrading" work, submitting every day to authority, judgment, and standards not our own, but nearly all of us also are helpless in a way that our agrarian forebears, black and white, greatly feared to be and generally were not. That is, we have no personal or communal homeland to fall back on in case of emergency. At the time of the most recent government shutdown, 800,000 people, government employees, were said to be "living from paycheck to paycheck," with nothing in reserve. According to *The New York Times* of May 24, 2019,

> Four in 10 American adults wouldn't be able to cover an unexpected $400 expense with cash, savings or a credit-card charge that could be quickly paid off . . .
>
> About 27 percent of people surveyed would need to borrow or sell something to pay for such a bill, and 12 percent would not be able to cover it at all . . .

So many of us, then, are entirely dependent on money, of which, after "cost of living" and inflation, just about nothing is left. This uprisen multitude, in short, is supported only by the drifting sand of an economy sublimated into money. They are about as helpless as slaveholders dependent upon their slaves. To those thousands entirely dependent and tottering on the economy of money, we must add the rest of our population of shoppers and consumers who are dependent on our declining stocks of topsoil and other natural resources.

In contrast with the multitude of holders of corporate or government jobs, dependent upon the economy of money, who must live in fear of the want of money, let us remember John Lewis's family who drew their life supports from their own work on their own land, and were to that extent self-sufficient and independent. John Lewis wrote of his mother that she "does not remember ever feeling poor." My point, of course, is not that everybody should be farmers like the Lewises, but that, in our disdain for farming and farmers, we have discarded the example of Mrs. Lewis. Most of us now are living like the grasshopper in the fable, who did not work in the summer to provide for the winter.

The worst kind of decadence and snobbery played the devil with the slave states of the antebellum South: the forever false proposition that some people, by some distinction of race or class or wealth, are too good to work in their own behalf at anything describable as manual or degrading. The Civil War did not put an end to the snobbery any more than it put an end to racism but spread it to the North and began its democratization by the industrial ideal of "labor-saving."

To despise conventionally the working people of the countryside and the industrial "workforce" of the cities, at the same time replacing them with technology wherever possible, is a dead-certain way to build an immense popular fund of resentment and anger. The genius of modern conservatism has been to turn that resentment and anger not against the money-people and corporations who have controlled the economy in their own interest, but against labor unions, "welfare cheats," "environmentalists," and other harbingers of "socialism."

If you can sufficiently degrade the work that working people do, and then persuade them to despise themselves for doing it—easy to do when the aim of the whole culture is to escape it—then it requires only a sort of logic to enlist them as allies of their presumptive betters, who also despise them.

The racial issue could never have been resolved by the plantation system, which required few owners and many workers. By the same token, it could not—and cannot—be resolved by the industrial version of the plantation system, involving few owners, more "managers," and many workers—some of whom will be, virtually by the intent of the system, unemployed. Economic fairness, and therefore racial fairness, cannot be accomplished by a system that can think to free slaves only by making them hirelings. As some of Prof. Daniel's data suggest, the racial division might finally have been resolved, given enough social stability for enough time, by Jefferson's idea of a nation of small landholders. Does this mean that it might still be? We can be certain at least that it cannot be done by laws imposed upon a public made up of transients and strangers.

13. Two Americas

Some time ago a friend who keeps watch over the outcasts from his university's library sent me a valuable small book: *Seven Lean Years*, by T. J. Woofter and Ellen Winston, published in 1939. It is devoted to rural problems before and during the Depression, and to the hope for solutions to such problems. Early in the book I found the following list of the conditions that made American agriculture "vulnerable to the onslaught of the depression":

adverse farm prices, years of soil abuse, of allowing water to leach away the precious topsoil, of putting all the eggs into a one-crop basket, of cultivation of wide areas which should have been left in native grasses or forest, of accumulating debts, and of exhaustion of supplementary forest and mineral resources.

A good deal of attention and effort was applied to these rural problems during the presidency of Franklin Roosevelt. The New Deal's helps to farming and farmers were marred by racial discrimination and other imperfections, but they were the result at least of a public and political recognition that the American farmland was part of America, our country itself, and that farmers were in charge of it, to care for it well or poorly. Some of those helps, like the tobacco program, lasted a considerable while before they petered out in the face of "conservative" opposition and under the great weight of general indifference.

And now Woofter and Winston's list of the problems of agriculture in the 1930s is again perfectly current, as far as it goes. All we need to add now is the absence of several million farmers along with the precious topsoil they might have saved, and the presence of machines too wide for the roads, and the millions of tons of toxic chemicals with which the farmers have been replaced.

For about as long as I have been trying to learn about and write about the land economies, I have wondered at the extent to which economists and other highly credentialed intellectuals could write in articles and editorials and columns about the national economy or the global economy, the nation or the globe, without ever mentioning the state of the economies of the land and the state of the natural world on which all else depends. So oblivious were these people of the fundamental human economy that they seemed to me to be spirits, much concerned with the economies of cars and computers, information and service, but in no need at all of food, clothing, and shelter.

When Donald Trump was elected president in 2016 with the support of some "rural states," all of a sudden these intellectuals, or the liberal fraction of them, discovered rural America. As some of their intellectual forebears had known as late as 1952, this land had been discovered and inhabited by humans for some time. But like Columbus of old, these successors in the twenty-first century had never been here before. It rose before them like a bad dream abruptly and inexplicably real: an unvisited distant land full of people wearing blue shirts, with dirty hands and numbed minds, all so perfectly bigoted and backward that it did one's heart good to despise them. The columnist Paul Krugman had their number early:

> down-on-their-luck rural whites who are troubled to learn that all those liberals who warned them that they would be hurt by Trump policies were right, but still support Mr. Trump, because they believe that liberal elites look down on them and think they're stupid. Hmm.

He thought also that they voted for Mr. Trump because "probably" they are racists and sexists.

I don't believe that Mr. Krugman actually knew, or knows yet, any actual working-class rural white people. I am pretty sure that he does not live in rural America, where maybe he would need, if not to live, at least to come and stay a while in order to know why rural people might be troubled, and why their trouble may not be attributable to bad luck.

It happens that I live in rural Kentucky, one of the poorest and most Trumpish parts of rural America. I know from what I have read and experienced and from what I see every day that, especially since about the middle of the twentieth century, rural America has been treated by the conservatives and the liberals as a foreign country in which to sell high-priced machines, chemicals, fuel, and credit, and from which to purchase low-priced farm crops, farm animals, fibers, timber, fuels, ores, and other raw materials—low-priced partly because as little as possible has been paid for maintenance or restoration of the land. Rural America has been used also as a place to obtain cheap labor until even cheaper labor could be found in, for example, Mexico. Except for the people living in it, nobody has thought about our actual country unless they were looking for another way to exploit it.

As a result, rural America is depressed both ways, a place where farmers are going bankrupt, small businesses are failing, the young people are leaving or addicted or dying, where the land is overpriced and overworked, misused and abused, where we are never far from the sight of something once cared for but now mistreated or abandoned or going to waste. I have a friend thoroughly knowledgeable of farming and the farm economy. When he and I recently were driving around my neighborhood, I said, "As much as is being taken from it now, it would be far more productive with good care." He said, "It looks *poor*."

I did not vote for Donald Trump. He affronts and endangers much to which my heart belongs. And I can go with Mr. Krugman so far as to say that I am sure some rural people are racist, sexist, and otherwise, by my standards, wrong. And I think it is likely that many of these people voted for Donald Trump. But at this point I would like to stop and think. My life has been long enough to permit me to know some people, some of them belonging to rural America, who were guilty of thinking some bad thoughts and doing some bad things. But as strongly as I have disliked some of those people (not all of them), I do not think that any of them could be adequately or fairly characterized by listing their faults. The sorest of the growing pains of ignorance may be the discovery that most partly bad people are partly good, and that the best of us are no more than partly good.

I am sure that rural people are as complex, taken one by one, as city people. But rural America, though equally human, certainly is different from urban America, and much of the difference is that rural America still bears the opprobrium placed upon it by slaveholders and by other kinds of self-denominated aristocrats, who saw farmland as a place for degrading work, fit only for slaves and other menials. Also the drastic reduction of the farm population and the movement of country people into the cities have made rural America politically negligible, especially in presidential races. And so, from where I look, it is clear that rural America has no political party. The Republican Party opposes taxes and regulations, and recites its fabulous "trickle-down theory" and its unmeant wish for smaller government—a platform that is politically disreputable and that ignores the problems peculiar to rural America. The Democratic Party is equally ignorant and thoughtless of the problems of rural America and has none of the force or presence it might gain in rural America from authentic farm and conservation policies. I don't think either party could address competently the problem of soil erosion, or the problem of glyphosate, a carcinogen sold as Roundup, now present in breakfast cereals. Mr. Trump, who has, strictly speaking, no policies and no ideas, won by reaching over the heads of both parties to the economically troubled working people, learning to appeal to their worst instincts, and thus answering the question: Why not something different?

I quoted Paul Krugman's characterization of "rural whites" from his *New York Times* column of April 7, 2017. From his columns and the writings of other economists I have read, I make two assumptions: first, that he sees himself, and is seen by many others, as a spokesman for urban America, and second, that his view of our present economy is widely shared. He believes that the economy of material commodities is giving way to the economy of immaterial commodities—that manufacturing, for instance, will continue to be reduced in economic importance by "services" and "information"—and that this is good or if not good, then inevitable. This version of the human economy begins with exclusion of the economies of nature and of land use. The progress of Mr. Krugman's ignorance of rural America is therefore worth considering in some detail.

His column for November 9, 2018, after the election of that fall, is titled "Real America Versus Senate America." In it he dismisses, rightly, the sentimental claim that "real America" consists "of rural areas and small towns." But for this he substitutes, after the fashion of our current politics, the opposite and equally false proposition that "the real real [sic] America in which we live . . . is mostly metropolitan." Thereafter he uses the phrase "real America" to refer to urban America. "Real America," he says, "is racially and culturally diverse," which we are to understand as good, whereas rural America "is still very white," which, he implies, is bad. "Real America," moreover, "includes large numbers of highly educated adults," whereas rural America "has a higher proportion of non-college whites." And then, remembering perhaps his manners, Mr. Krugman assures us that "none of this is meant to denigrate rural, non-college, white voters"—for which, of course, all us rural white people wish to thank him.

I want to pause here to remember Pete Daniel's comment on "the staggering human cost" of official agriculture's bias against "non-college" education:

> USDA personnel, many educated at land-grant universi-
> ties, often denigrated farmers who did not accept their
> gospel of science and technology, echoing an enduring
> national tradition that pitted book learning against com-
> mon sense and prized technology at the expense of hus-
> bandry. Knowledge handed down or gained by trial and
> error was devalued and forgotten while formulaic meth-
> odology and machines grew in importance.

Mr. Krugman's formula, non-college = uneducated, comes from the same snobbery. As some would rate the worth of citizens by race or wealth, Mr. Krugman would do so by college degrees. He seems to have swallowed, without feeling the hook, the education industry's advertisement of the absolute necessity of a college degree for every-body. This is what we might call "college ignorance," for it ignores the non-college truth that a locally adapted culture of husbandry, which alone can protect both the land and the people, comes from the local history of trial and error, which survives by being remem-bered locally and handed down, just as Prof. Daniel says. It is true that a college education has often led to upward mobility, for what that is worth. But pro-college fashion and propaganda have also misled some young people or led them into too much debt, have depreciated the value of work that does not require a college degree, and have caused a shortage of people who do such work.

As the column's title warns—and we rural Americans *should*

take warning—Mr. Krugman's synonym for rural America is "Senate America." This alludes to Article I, section 3 of the Constitution of the United States, which provides that "the Senate of the United States shall be composed of two senators from each State" Mr. Krugman thinks this is extremely unfair because it "gives fewer than 600,000 people in Wyoming the same representation as almost 40 million in California." Mr. Krugman is not alone in thinking this thought. But one may suppose, as have a good many people, that the men who wrote the Constitution were as aware of this discrepancy as Mr. Krugman, and that their purpose was the protection of minorities against majorities, or the little against the big. But Mr. Krugman is pleading a special case, unable maybe to see that Article I, section 3 was written in anticipation of such special cases: The underpopulated states, he believes, are the home of Trumpian "white nationalism—hatred and fear of darker people, with a hefty dose of anti-intellectualism plus anti-Semitism." This is at least a verdict without a trial against a lot of people, which Article I, section 3 certainly anticipates. It is remarkable anyhow that Mr. Krugman, a liberal who rightly opposes the subjection of darker minorities to a white majority, coldly and in the same breath advocates the subjection of the citizens of Wyoming, merely because they are a minority, to the more numerous citizens of California. And so I say, Long live the dead white men who wrote Article I, section 3.

As a rural American, I willingly notice that Wyoming contains 97,000 square miles of land, all of it valuable and ever more valuable as more and more land is "developed," and also a considerable wealth of what the liberals and conservatives call "natural resources," implying always that since the resources are "natural" they are available to humans at no cost. I recognize furthermore that without its two senators, Wyoming would be far more vulnerable to corporate plunder than it now is. And so we might be obliged to consider its two senators as representing, in addition to its small number of people, the great land of Wyoming.

As a rural American, I know I have stepped onto a patch of soggy ground. For I know that Kentucky's politicians, its two Parties of Coal, have in general protected the people poorly enough, and the land not at all. If Kentucky's two senators had been stalwart in protecting their land and people against predation, that would have been a far better result of Article I, section 3. But that law, like any other, is justified by its protection of a good possibility. As long as we have it, it remains possible that Kentucky's two senators may eventually do their best to defend their state, and their ability to do so is ensured by the limitation of more populous and powerful states to two senators.

In his column for November 20, 2018, Mr. Krugman arrives at the (to him) new perception that America is divided "into two economies":

> Over the past generation, America's regions have experienced a profound economic divergence. Rich metropolitan areas have gotten even richer, attracting ever more of the nation's fastest growing industries. Meanwhile, small towns and rural areas have been bypassed, forming a sort of economic rump left behind by the knowledge economy.

To anybody acquainted at all with the history of the economy of rural America, the only thing remarkable about this insight is that it might have been made, just as accurately, three generations ago. Mr. Krugman has not made the completing perception—no doubt because from where he is looking he cannot see—that the purpose of industrialism almost always has been to gather rural wealth at the least possible cost into the cities. If that is not understood, then one cannot understand how the Appalachian coal counties, in their natural endowment among the richest in our country, came to be inhabited by some of the poorest people. Without understanding that industrial purpose, for another instance, one cannot see that the vaunted "cheap food policy" sacrifices farmland and farmers to the illusion, immensely profitable to the agribusiness corporations, that industrial technologies have solved, or soon will solve, *all* the problems of food production. But Mr. Krugman, being himself a spirit, does not notice urban America's dependence upon rural America for the cheapest possible food, clothing, shelter, heat, and light. And so, to him, the two economies appear to be divided merely by "a political chasm." And so he can write: "Can this chasm be bridged? Honestly, I doubt it." Well, an observant rural American might suggest that the chasm, which certainly does exist, might be bridged by economic fairness to rural America—by, for example, the now discarded principle of parity pricing for agricultural products. But because of his ignorance of rural America, and his eagerness, therefore, to condemn it, he cannot imagine that rural Americans can have suffered economic injustice, or that they might deserve justice. And he is far, far from the realization that all of us, even urban Americans, owe justice to our suffering land. He is also flirting dangerously here with the fundamentalist equation between wealth and virtue.

But Mr. Krugman has not finished thinking about rural America, and his point of view grows loftier. His column of March 19, 2019, begins with a dab at universal truth: "Things clump together; the periphery cannot hold"—which is to say that while rural America disintegrates, urban America gathers force—which, further, is Mr. Krugman's update of a famous line by William Butler Yeats,

"Things fall apart; the centre cannot hold," which has a fair chance of surviving even so brilliant a revision.

Mr. Krugman goes on to notice that some Democrats are talking of ways to get rural votes and to revise rural economies. And he is bighearted: "There's nothing wrong with discussing these issues. Rural lives matter." Even so, people should not become too forgetful of economic determinism, that great simplifier. It is fine to think of possible improvements:

> But it's also important to get real. There are powerful forces behind the relative and in some cases absolute economic decline of rural America—and the truth is that nobody knows how to reverse those forces.

Six million people were farming in 1950, he notes, and that number has now "fallen by two-thirds." He does not attempt to say why, because, I suppose, he cannot identify the "powerful forces." It does not occur to him even to ask how a population of farmers might be affected by being forced to buy on a "free market" controlled by the sellers, and to sell on a "free market" controlled by the buyers; or by being forced to produce under contracts written by the corporate purchasers, who set the purchasing price and require the producers to take all the risks; or by being forced to produce under the burden of out-of-control production surpluses, which benefit everybody in the farm economy except the farmers. All this of course amounts to legal theft by "powerful forces," and perhaps this should be of no concern to highly educated urban Americans because, after all, it is legal.

Mr. Krugman also mentions the reduction of jobs for coal miners, who are more helpless economically even than farmers. And he speaks of the rural tragedies: "the prevalence of jobless men in their prime working years" and the "surge" of deaths by drugs, alcohol, and suicide. Even though these are bad people with whom Donald Trump is still popular, their lives matter, and Mr. Krugman proposes ways to help them: good health care, good education, economic development, public investment, employment subsidies, "possibly job guarantees"—a list of easy answers to hard questions. But even such largess, he believes, cannot "realistically" be expected "to produce a political turnaround." Mr. Krugman is sure that some rural people will see this column "as typical big-city condescension," but:

> I'm simply trying to get real. We can't help rural America
> without understanding that the role it used to play in our
> nation is being undermined by powerful economic forces
> that nobody knows how to stop.

Thus "we," getting real, are very cheaply let off. "We," seeing "realistically" that nothing really can be done to change rural America politically, really can wash our hands of it, cede it to Mr. Trump, and get on with constructing an indomitable political majority in Real America.

The problem, as many rural Americans (I among them) know, is that rural America has little to gain by changing politically, if no other change is made. If "we" would be content only with political change in rural America, then pretty soon rural America would be much worse off than it now is. The problem, which Mr. Krugman believes is exclusively rural American, is that in rural America *both* the people and the land are suffering progressive diseases that, if no substantive healing is begun, will get worse. Urban America, moreover, has no immunity from these diseases.

Therefore, if Mr. Krugman really wanted to get real about rural

America, if he wanted to be intellectually responsible, he would give up his ready-made stereotypes and clichés. Wondering, for example, why some scholars who study the regions of rural America now speak of the "Appalachianization of America," he might go look for himself. He might put on his tall boots and set his feet upon the actual ground of rural America. Instead of interviewing people drinking coffee in small-town diners, he could find good guides to take him walking across the eroded and toxic croplands of Iowa. He would not need to leave Iowa to study, with capable guides, the rivers polluted with silt and toxic chemicals. He would have to decide whether or not to drink from the municipal tap-water drawn from those rivers. In Kentucky or Pennsylvania, he might find an honest forester or forest ecologist to show him the degradation of nearly all of the forests. He would find maybe a diversity of local people to show him around the coalfields of Kentucky and West Virginia: the gashed and gutted mountains and the drastically fragmented forest. He could talk with the people he met, not by asking about Donald Trump or the Green New Deal or sexual identity or immigration or climate change, but in order to know them a little. That would be a start, possibly directing his mind beyond "college" to actual learning.

But such a start seems not likely to be made. At *The New York Times*, Mr. Krugman's two Americas thesis has already become conventional. Here, from the *Times* of May 24, 2019, are some sentences by the columnist Farhad Manjoo:

> Creating dense, diverse urban environments ought to be a paramount goal of progressivism. Dense urban areas are quite literally the "real America"—the cities are where two-thirds of Americans live, and they account for almost all national economic output. They're good

for the environment—we can't address climate change without increasing urban density. Finally, metropolises are good for the psyche and the soul; density fosters diversity, creativity and progress.

City life, these writers appear to assume, is autonomous, isolatable, independent of other life in other places—although "the environment," as usual, is out there somewhere, and cities should be good to it, as of course they are. What the spokespersons for the "real America" apparently cannot know, though it is obvious to any patriotic rural American, is that America does not consist of two economies divided by a chasm, but rather of two unequal partners joined for life by one two-ended, one-way economy. Its digging and sucking end is in rural America, which thereby will become ever poorer until exhausted, and its disgorging end is in urban America, which thereby, for some people and for a while longer, will become ever richer. For people content with this state of things, and evidently there are a lot of them, Urban America = Real America = Prosperous America = Virtuous America, and Rural America = Mysteriously Poor America = Bad America = What? Perhaps Senate America? But what, actually, is it? With nature and the land economies discounted and ignored, that question cannot be answered.

Another way to describe this division as it now stands—not in my mind, but in what I suppose must be called the mind of urban America—is to say that urban America is a nation without a country: a government, an economy (of a sort), a military force, some national parks and "wilderness areas," but without an emotional or imaginative relationship, or even a recognized economic connection, with the merely rural landscapes that once were "our country." Evidently urban Americans see nothing wrong with this, or they see something wrong but only in rural America. But given the current promotion of the college degrees necessary for good city jobs, it is hard not to see in this division the full flowering of the Calhounian distinction between work that is not degrading and work that is.

14. A New Secession and an Invitation

In an article in *Harper's Magazine* of November 2018, Jonathan Taplin extends the Krugman two-economies thesis into a sort of political or ideological geography and a warmed-over rhetoric of sectional conflict. The occasion of his essay is a prophecy on Twitter by Norman Ornstein:

> By 2040 or so, 70 percent of Americans will live in 15 states. Meaning 30 percent [of the voters] will choose 70 senators. And the 30 percent will be older, whiter, more rural, more male than the 70 percent.

Mr. Taplin will not pause to ask how much power, if any, should be allotted to people who are old, white, rural, and male. Just that quartet of adjectives (describing, among others, me!) rises before him and says "Boo." To document his horror, he too utters the fearful name of Wyoming.

The threat of "minority rule" comes, Mr. Taplin says, from "design flaws in both our Constitution and our internet." And so, the approach of "an age of extreme minority rule" having become apparent with the election of Donald Trump, we are coming into a crisis that is both technological and constitutional. To Mr. Taplin's way of thinking, the only hope is in the Tenth Amendment: "An epic states'-rights battle looms, with governors like Jerry Brown and state attorneys general cast in defiant Bull Connor roles." And this battle could be as bad as any in American history: "Living in a world where 30 percent of the population—old, rural, and white—controls the destiny of a new and diverse generation of Americans can lead only to civil strife, and perhaps even to civil war." This, again, would be a "war between states," because the 70 percent would live in just fifteen of them.

History, to Mr. Taplin, is moving at blinding speed. Rural America is to urban America as the South was to the North—Paul Krugman has got us used to that. But Mr. Taplin, invoking states' rights, brings us to brave new ratios: As Bull Connor was to Alabama, Jerry Brown is, or was, to California; as the election of Abraham Lincoln was to the onset of the first Civil War, so the election of Donald Trump may be to the beginning of the second. History apparently cannot photocopy itself into the future without becoming more absurd than it was at first. And who are the people of the two sides so absolutely divided, so near to civil strife and even war? The urban side, according to Mr. Taplin, consists of people who desire "a low-carbon economy powered by solar and wind; a single-payer health care system; free community college; common-sense gun control." On the rural side, "As much as a quarter of our population might want to live in a coal-powered, open-carry Wild West society."

I think Mr. Taplin has taken a bigger bite than he can chew. He is too excited, too frightened, too angry, too inclined to oversimplification, and too sure of the Tenth Amendment as the solution of first resort. The idea that urban America, concentrated in fifteen states, can just pick up its feet and secede from the rural thirty-five is simple, but it raises complex questions, and perhaps some mysteries. Could 70 percent of our present population live off the land of fifteen states? Would they perhaps be willing to import necessary supplies from the thirty-five, and at fair prices? Or might the fifteen—so superior in population, money, and intelligence—be obliged to conquer the thirty-five, enslave the people, and force them to produce the necessary surpluses of goods, a recourse for which there are precedents? And where can one see a map showing the proposed boundary between the two Americas?

But why should anybody, at the appearance of a domestic or a human dispute, think *first* of crisis, civil conflict, and war? Might one not suggest, as an alternative to a quick divorce, as a beginning maybe of justice and peace, some effort at understanding? As a way to begin to understand the alienation between the two Americas, or between the two ends of the economy that has so far connected but not united them, I will suggest a thorough history, with accounting, of the coal economy in the mountains of Kentucky and West Virginia, saying finally what the costs and benefits actually have been, and to whom they have gone.

I am inclined at first to be amused at Mr. Taplin's extremities, but then, especially in considering his characterization of the people of the two sides, my amusement gives way to foreboding and sorrow too familiar, and I remember that Lee, not alone, thought the Civil War had been made by the hotheaded rhetoricians of both sides: the abolitionists of the North with their one-sin obsession, like the Prohibitionists and the pro- and anti-abortionists yet to come; and the aristocratic young horsemen of the South who thought themselves invincible and were, Sherman thought, the most dangerous people alive. Like those fanatics, Mr. Taplin sees all the goodness and innocence on one side and all the badness and stupidity on the other. And so in his mind and thought (not, I fear, his alone), we come again to the terrible swift sword, the allegory of absolutes that begins and sustains every war.

Unable, then, not to hear the drummer beating behind Mr. Taplin's words, I refuse the services of any drummer who would like to accompany my words. I want to try once again to speak only for myself, as I would try to do in conversation, let us say, with Mr. Taplin. Having been accused of wanting "to live in a coal-powered, open-carry Wild West society," what might an old, white, rural man be able to say in response?

Well, I have no ground on which I can stand and boast or utter a battle cry. My own poor state has a law permitting *anybody* to carry a weapon, for the freedom and safety of whom I cannot imagine. It also supports Mr. Trump and the Republicans. I am obliged to say also that we Kentuckians do not have an anti-coal party for which to vote. We have had also no assurance that either national party could have distinguished between the predatory coal companies and the coal *miners* who have taken the greatest risks, suffered the hurts, the deaths, and the economic jeopardies of their work. But I would ask Mr. Taplin to learn that for many decades some Kentuckians have opposed the coal companies and tried to speak in defense of the land and people of the coalfields, the most eminent of them being Harry M. Caudill of Whitesburg, whose books Mr. Taplin can read. We opponents of the coal companies have a score of zero, but we have at least kept alive the case against them. I suppose it is now impossible to know how many of us are carrying pistols, but I know that some of us are not. It would be fair and reasonable for outsiders to assume that some of us do not, and moreover that some of us were happier when carrying a concealed weapon was illegal. Some of us have intimate knowledge of the harm and the sorrow that can be wrought by pistols, and we want no more.

In the minds of Mr. Taplin and his like, the adjective "white" implies racism; "male," in combination with "white," "rural," and "old," implies sexism; "rural" implies backwardness, stupidity, and the degradation of "mind-numbing" physical work; and "old" implies political incorrectness on all accounts. It is not supposed that these qualities may vary in intensity or degree from person to person, but rather that they are absolute and fully descriptive of everybody. The only response to this that I can think of, that would not be of the same kind, would be this:

Come to see me. Follow a Kentucky backroad to my house. Shake my hand. Meet my family. Accept our welcome. Sit down at our table. Take part in our hunger, our food, and our thanks. Let us tell you about our country here, its history, its economic history. Let us show it to you, pointing out everywhere the signs of what is happening to it now. Let us introduce you to some of our people with problems, to some who are trying to help—to, especially, some of our good young people who are working in factories in order to keep their farms and their livestock and the work they are called to do. Let your visit be shaped by your questions, and let it last until your questions are answered so far as they can be, for here we live with many unanswered questions. You will of course make your own judgments and come to your own conclusions. But if, after such a visit, you could draw a line alongside us, stand on the other side, and look at us with fear and hate prefiguring war, I would be sorry, but I hope I would remember my good reasons for inviting you here. I would not start carrying a pistol.

Any urban American who might visit us, I hope, would trouble to understand the damage that continues to be done here by the interaction of two of the highest aims of industrial progress: to increase production per unit of work, and to do so at the least possible monetary cost, which means to do so with the smallest possible number of human workers and with the least possible respect for the places where the work is done. This depends upon an extremely simple way of thought, which excludes all concern for human well-being or for the well-being of the natural world, those two concerns being really the same. And the order of industrial processes also is extremely simple: a one-way passage from the mine to the smoke and the ash dump, or from the topsoil to the sewer.

Like the raw materials and the products of industrial manufacture, the industrial worker has always been predestined to disposability. But industrial agriculture, in addition to the always fewer living workers, must use life itself as a means of production. And so the simplifying forces, the straight line and the way of no return, propose to use as an inert, merely material "resource"—and thus destroy—an order, imponderably complex, unexplainably living, that is biological and ecological, in itself unwasting, self-replenishing, and utterly dependent on the principle of return.

Thus, producing (temporarily) more and more food with less and less human work, therefore with more and more technology, much of it toxic, therefore with less and less human affection and care, therefore with more and more waste, industrial agriculture is supported by an ever-enlarging debt to nature. It is operating, in other words, at a net loss that is incalculable, increasing, and unrepayable.

Our urban American visitors, if they come in time, will see the last abandoned and wasted houses and farmsteads that once belonged to diversified small farms where self-employed, self-responsible people earned, or tried to earn, decent livings from the land and their own work, and where, equally important, they raised their children in the knowledge of work and responsibility, also of the free pleasures to be taken from the fields and woods and waters they were native to. No visitor of course will see or remember seeing the houses and farmsteads of such farms that fire and decay and the bulldozer have now removed forever from the face of the earth.

Thus industrial agriculture has operated here also at a net cultural loss, also incalculable, unrepayable, and fearfully near to complete.

I have written these difficult paragraphs hoping to explain to our visitors what surely they will see: that (temporarily) more and more grain is being produced here to be made into more and more cheap food, cheapened by a radical reduction in the amount of farmwork (production *and* maintenance) by which people can earn a living here. In short, more food and less work gives us eroded and toxic fields and unhealthy people. The "best"—that is, the best paying and best paid—science and technology produce land-ruin, sickness, and ugliness. We are living now in the unhappiest, most costly chapter, so far, in the history of work.

15. On Education

If I seem to have been invoking our worn and almost compulsory belief that "education" or "better education" is the solution to every problem, then I need to make a correction. If education is the solution, that obviously prolongs the problem until later, which some find convenient. But I have no faith in the capacity of what we now call education to prevent or cure, even in the future, a national stupidity, particularly if the stupidity in question—that we can survive by wasting everything necessary for our survival—is scientifically accredited and publicly approved. I doubt that a required public school course in land stewardship would weigh effectively against "cheap food" as a fact of life or the belief that farmwork is degrading and farmers degraded.

I supposed for a while that a significant urban agrarianism, and thus an effective urban lobby for sustainable agriculture, might grow from the "food movement," but that so far has failed to happen. I welcomed the food movement. In principle and in general

I approve of it. On its own terms, it fails only when it fails to control production, and thus, as of old, throws individual producers destructively into competition with one another. But the acreage protected by the food movement—I mean by organic farming, community-supported agriculture, and the local suppliers of food stores, restaurants, and farmers' markets—is too small to be ecologically significant, or to affect the national food economy, let alone the national economy. Its *political* significance so far has been to distract attention from the enormous acreage still under the dominion of industrial agriculture. The surviving few critics of our "normal" food economy are regularly confronted by objectors who call their attention to the farmers' market of some large city. This is a bitter irony. The food movement, which the agri-industrialists would not have started and could not approve, now charmingly masks their continuing aggression against rural America. This sort of thing, and the great ignorance it comes from, account for the failure after many years of effort to establish a regional food economy for Louisville.

I still believe in the necessity for urban economists, journalists, and other "public intellectuals" to come to rural America on such a visit as I have described, but my own invitations and offers so far have been without result. There is, after all, no reason to question a conclusion already made and paved over, so long as it still bears a sufficient traffic of believers.

Though it seems unlikely to me that public schools, obligated as they are to please everybody, could effectively teach land stewardship, I can think of projects, best undertaken in schools, that would be materially useful to the human commonwealth. I would make these university projects, for I do believe somewhat in the trickle-down theory of education, if by education we mean the lived life and the pursuit of truth. One such project I have already suggested:

a history, with accounting, of the coal economy of Kentucky and West Virginia. This could not be taught or directed by specialists; it would employ the students as researchers; if well done, it would encourage other such histories, all greatly needed. But such a project could not be done in one of the great universities, which would be too concerned with intellectual fashions and with grants and endowments. We would need instead a small, poor, humble university, a ramped-up old teachers' college in one of the underpopulated states of rural America—let us say Wyoming. And let us think of it as the University of the End of Nowhere.

The project for that university that is dearest to my heart is one not likely to begin in my remaining years, but I love to think of it. It would be a course in Local Adaptation. Or, to touch it with the glamour of political correctitude, we could call it Local Adaptation as Multiculturalism. This would be a course taught by the whole university as its only course, and it would continue without interruption for the foreseeable future. There would be no division into semesters. There would be examinations and grades (honest judgments of the students' work so far), but no "finals." Students would be graduated from the course and the university upon their demonstration of competence in addressing questions raised by the human inhabitation of specific places: natural regions, watersheds, ecosystems, mining districts, shores, forests, farms, towns, cities. The focus would be upon actual problems of the present, and actual (past or present) solutions. There would be no more boundaries among "departments." All knowledge, all acknowledged ignorance, all questions would be brought to bear. There would be no more administrators than absolutely necessary. They would be paid no more than the teachers. Janitors and other maintenance workers would be paid as much as the teachers. Anybody with useful knowledge could teach. Anybody ignorant and curious could be a student. All the now-recognized disciplines and specialties would be needed so long as they proved useful to the curriculum of unavoidable questions and the search for answers. The ruling and ordering question would be: How can human beings live on *and from* any specified place on earth without diminishing its life and their own?

For those participating, this course from its beginning would invert the customary order of our thought about adaptation, and it would reverse the course of the modern history of human life in this country. Sometimes in the course of that history, settlers, in the true sense of the term, have come to a place intending to stay, to learn about it, to take good care of it, and to make themselves responsibly at home in it, thus adapting themselves and their ways of living to it. But predominantly our way of "settling" our country has been to require it to adapt itself to our preconceived ideas about it, to the kind of life we want to live in it, and, especially during the last century, to the capacities of our technology. "To think in terms of ideology rather than of geography," John Lukacs wrote in another connection, "accorded with inclinations of the American mind." That is a profound insight. It explains the inability, or the refusal, of our people in the West to adapt to the aridity of their region, the failure, relentlessly worsening, that so troubled Wallace Stegner, and others before and after him. But it explains no less our worsening failures in the better-watered and more forgiving East. It seems almost a joke to say that, even so mindless as we generally are, we live in our minds more than in our country, but it is true.

Living in our minds, believing we know what we are doing only because we don't know what we are doing, we have so far lived in our country, or upon it, by using it up. Against the good counsel of our own cultural tradition, we have inhabited our country by destroying everything in it that our life depends upon, even to our

426

moral character, so that we now can maintain a little self-esteem only by the discovery of other people's faults.

Our course, Local Adaptation as Multiculturalism, therefore would intend to turn American minds outward to where they are, the localities where they find themselves perhaps by chance of birth or where they have chosen to be. The teaching and learning, the asking and answering, the reading and writing, the *conversation* of the course would be directed to looking out and looking around, to examining the relationship between habitat and inhabitant. And so the teachers of biology and ecology would show by many examples that for nonhuman creatures, who do not import and export, local adaptation is a law as unrelenting as the law of gravity: They survive by the great accomplishment of belonging in their places. The anthropologists would show how certain peoples have survived and lived well by adapting to the conditions of their homelands, some of them extraordinarily demanding: the Bushmen or the Papago or the Australian Aborigines or the Inuit. The teachers and learners, the students old and young, would be brought to ask again and again if the cultures of the people were not validated by their adaptation, if a culture could be otherwise validated, if the world does not call out for a multiplicity of locally adapted cultures. Historians and ecologists would show how certain peoples and civilizations have failed by being wrong in what they have asked of their places, or by asking too much. Agriculturists, with the help of other disciplines, would show how farmers have failed, in the words of J. Russell Smith, by failing to fit their farming to their farms. And they would show, also with much help, the advantages of local adaptation, even on individual farms, of farmers, crops, and livestock. Teachers of the so-called fine arts would show that those arts, like the art of farming or cooking or house building or housekeeping, either sustain or fail to sustain the health of human dwelling places. And so on. This course, this conversation, in its ever-shifting parts, would be made formal by natural, mental, and disciplinary limits. At the same time, in its extent and duration it would be unlimited, for with so much knowledge and so much ignorance at play for such high stakes, its answers could never be conclusive, but would be always leading to more questions.

Thus in an actual poor place, in the poor outdistanced country of rural America, in the University of the End of Nowhere—which eventually we will call the University of the Beginning of Somewhere—a sort of counterspiral would begin to move. Some people would look out through their eyes. They would turn their heads and look around. They would start to ask questions that are obvious but rarely asked, never before in schools. The searching of the questions of local adaptation would necessarily begin with, and again and again return to, the ground underfoot, the university campus and its neighborhood. Where are we? They would find the coordinates on a map, the point of intersection. But where? What is here? What is here besides us? These questions begin a continuing sequence. What has happened here? What has happened here that should not have happened? What better thing should have happened? What should be happening here now? How would we know? What should be our standards of judgment? At some time early in this sequence of questions, the experts and specialists of the faculty would begin to widen their eyes and look at one another. They would shrug their shoulders. They would laugh. They would begin to speak to one another in common English, very good English of course, but common. They would become serious too, and humble, the words "seems" and "maybe" would become prominent in their vocabulary, for they would see that they have come at last to a real university, a common work of human survival and settlement upon the earth.

Eventually it will occur to them that we, who need and depend on our country, in our great good fortune of having a country, owe it a profound respect, even reverence. It will occur to them that we, who did not make this country, owe our thanks for its making and to its maker. They will be surprised one day by the thought that people who love their country want to live in it, to make for themselves in it a place that they will call "home." People who love their country will not call it "nowhere" or "the boondocks" or "rural America." They will see that if they put our country itself—its myriad of small places, each unique—ahead of their ideas about it and plans for it, then the course of its history turns around, first in their own hearts. They will realize that they haven't thought of their hearts in such a way in many years. But now they are compelled to that thought, for they know that the change they now desire must begin in the heart, if it is to begin. And so they foresee, and so they begin, a revision and a renewal of our work.

16. Patriotism, Nationalism, Antipatriotism

From here it is possible to come to further clarity on the present division between urban America and rural America. I will begin by repeating John Lukacs's perception that "to think in terms of ideology rather than geography accorded with inclinations of the American mind," from which it is immediately obvious that the anti-Trump or anti-rural urban American spokespersons do not think at all in terms of geography, which they wish to do without, but only in terms of the opposition between their own ideology and what they suppose is the ideology of rural Americans. To put a historical construction upon this difference, I return to my contention that, in the minds of those spokespersons, America has evolved from a country in which many different people saw a solution to their common land need into a nation without a country. And this, sad to say, aligns with my observation earlier that, in addition to its other oppositions, the Civil War opposed nationalism to patriotism. The North was nationalist insofar as it fought for the nationalist idea of union and for the conquest of territory. The South, on the contrary, was patriotic insofar as its people conceived that they were fighting in defense of their native homelands and homes, where they wished to "live and die." I see the difference, in short, as that between loyalty to a nation and loyalty to one's home, family, and neighbors, a war of conquest and a war of defense. This, complicated as it is by the South's defense of slavery as a part of its home defense, is a difference of enormous significance and portent, and I am glad not to be alone in thinking so. There is no assurance, obviously, and as I said earlier, that patriots will not serve a bad cause. But patriotism itself, as love of a home place and home country, is clearly a virtue. Though patriots obviously could support slavery, it is also obvious that slavery was not a result of patriotism.

For the French writer Georges Bernanos, the most disturbing and demanding event of World War II was the uprising over all the world of machine rule, as exemplified at last by the master machine revealed at Hiroshima. Civilization, once conceivable "as a refuge, a hearth," was now, as Bernanos saw it and I think correctly, under attack by the nationalist "modern state" or what he called "machine civilization." France, he thought, was "still a *patrie*, a homeland," which was "quite a different thing from the economic and political organization which tends to be confused more and more with the modern state." By contrast: "A homeland or fatherland is a moral being that has rights and duties." And: "Love of one's homeland, like love of God, is founded on the free gift of oneself."

Georges Bernanos died in 1948. In 1946 and 1947, he delivered a series of passionate speeches, published in English as *Last Essays*, in which he defended the idea and love of homelands against the growth of "despiritualized" and totalitarian machine civilization, as prefigured in the dictatorships of Hitler and Stalin and by "capitalist liberalism," which would seek to make humanity in its image, as only a species of machines, rather than the image of God. It is in its traditional spiritual or religious dimension that the "being" of the homeland is made whole: "What [the nationalist] loathes in the Christian idea of the homeland is that by it the human *patrie* is incorporated into the world of Grace and finds herself submissive to the law of Charity." In a time when "religion" and "religious" may be used as disparagements, such a statement might be accused of "tribalism," but that would make too provincial a thing of the law of charity. Bernanos saw all the traditional civilizations as connected to one another "by clear comparisons and profound similarities," whereas a machine civilization is one of a kind.

Bernanos's thinking refers particularly to persons and events of postwar Europe, and sometimes my ignorance impedes my reading, but in general I think he saw clearly the unprecedented great trouble that had come to all the world. Because he saw this from the standpoint of traditional patriotism, to which his commitment was firm and final, his almost ruthless truth-telling brings with it a certain comfort. And he offers again and again the steadiness of good sense. To those who think of equality as an invariable or absolute good, he says, "Totalitarian regimes are the most egalitarian of all: total equality in total slavery!" In case we think we have liberty because we so often say we do, he says, "There is no place for liberty in the gigantic mechanical factory which must be regulated like a clock." When he speaks of "the infernal cycle . . . of unlimited production for immeasurable destruction," some of us know exactly what he is talking about, and on the basis of a great deal more evidence than was available to him. I think we have to ask how completely, so far, his fears have been realized, and I think that even now there is more resistance to machine civilization than he foresaw, though the threat he identified certainly remains with us and grows stronger. I admit to taking much comfort from finding in these "last essays" several of my concerns in this book and elsewhere. On the subject of my present chapter, he says, "What [modern man] demands of these machines is the brutal destruction of the ancient, traditional, human rhythm of work." Yes. I have watched that happen here in my own homeland.

John Lukacs wrote in 1992 that "fifty years [after Hitler's National Socialism] nationalism still remains the most potent political force in the world." He followed Bernanos (and George Orwell) in distinguishing between nationalism and patriotism:

> When Hitler . . . in *Mein Kampf,* said that "I was a nationalist, but I was not a patriot," he knew exactly what he meant, and so ought we. Patriotism . . . is defensive, while nationalism is aggressive; patriotism is rooted to the land, to a particular country, while nationalism is connected to the myth of a people, indeed to a majority; patriotism is traditionalist, nationalism is populist. Patriotism is not a substitute for a religious faith, whereas nationalism often is; it may fill the emotional—at least superficially spiritual—needs of people. It may be combined with hatred. . . . "The ardent nationalist," said Duff Cooper, "is always the first to denounce his fellow countrymen as traitors."

Lukacs saw that the two sides in our Civil War conformed to this difference, the South being the side of patriotism and defense. But he saw too that this difference at least was quickly mended:

> Notwithstanding all of the bitterness between South and North that continued after the Civil War, no Southerner, after 1865, would advocate secession again . . . After the Civil War the South . . . became one of the most . . . nationalistic portions of the United States; and so it remained. The war against Spain in 1898 had the enthusiastic support of the South. Most of the American pacifists and anti-imperialists came not from the South but from the North.

This distinction seems to have become crucial to Lukacs's thinking, for he kept returning to it. He took it up again, with dire portent, in *Democracy and Populism: Fear and Hatred*, published in 2005. He died in May 2019, and so far as I know he did not write about the Trump presidency. But the following sentences seem to be a warning of what we had ahead of us:

> Since it appeals to tribal and racial bonds, nationalism seems to be deeply and atavistically natural and human. Yet the trouble with it is not only that nationalism can be anti-humanist and often inhuman but that it also proceeds from one abstract assumption about human nature itself. The love for one's people is natural, but it is also categorical; it is less charitable and less deeply human than the love for one's country, a love that flows from traditions, at least akin to love for one's family. Nationalism is both self-centered and selfish.

And on the next page he adds the thought that "old-fashioned patriotism" is "so often inseparable from gentlemanly behavior." In *A Short History of the Twentieth Century*, 2013, he returns again to that difference, and, as it appears from 2022, with the same foreshadowing: "When nationalism replaces older versions of patriotism . . . [the nationalists] seek enemies among their fellow citizens." I wonder what he would say, now, about the present division between liberals and conservatives, or Democrats and Republicans, both of which parties are seeking enemies among their fellow citizens, and neither is patriotic in the traditional sense of love of country or rootedness in the land.

From the point of view of a present-day agrarian whose homeland is in virtually defenseless rural America, it is thus pointedly tragic that the only truly patriotic defense of an American homeland against modern total warfare had to be a defense also of slavery. It is a further tragedy that the defeat of legal slavery entailed the defeat, far more conclusive and lasting than the defeat of slavery, of the traditional land-loyal patriotism embodied in Robert E. Lee.

It is arguable, I think, that Lee's patriotic devotion to a homeland in rural America has survived, marginally, until now in some descendants of slaves and in some white people, among them some like me, who are descendants of slave owners. That is odd. It is odd perhaps with the same oddity that some of the northerners who fought in the South to free the slaves went into the Indian country of the West to fight there a war of nationalist aggression and extermination.

But to understand fully our present division, we need to follow Lukacs a step further in his consideration of nationalism. He is speaking again of the legacy of World War II:

> What was startling and new in the twentieth century was the emergence of a certain antipatriotism in the name of nationalism. . . . Of course there always have been all kinds of people, from traitors through ideological revolutionaries to persecuted minorities, who would welcome the occupation of their country by another power. But what is remarkable is the appearance of such tendencies in the form of a certain ideological nationalism, which was the result not only of modern nationalistic indoctrination but also of those conditions of modern society which make it possible for many people to be nationalists without being patriots.

Lukacs is referring here to Hitler, an Austrian, who wrote that "Germany could be safeguarded only by the destruction of Austria," and also to Hitler's collaborators in other countries.

I am of course aware of the frequent use of Hitler's name to identify as deplorable almost anything that is deplored. But here Lukacs is calling attention to a drastically effective principle, or perhaps a vacancy, in Hitler's own character, and drastically serviceable to him in the character of others. I don't at all believe that there is a conscious line of thought from Hitler's nationalism to our own. But to realize from much evidence that, in the minds of the urban "real America" nationalists, America has become a nation without a country, and to know that the economy of urban America thrives *only* by extracting wealth from the country of rural America, is to see that American history is now in a dire chapter of antipatriotism.

The danger is plain enough. I have in mind the apparent tendency of enemy nations to become more like one another, and to follow one another into monstrosity. This seems to be the toll of war, and to be the reason that war does not lead to peace.

Though I could not then have called it antipatriotism, the willingness of so-called conservatives and conservatism to sacrifice the land to an interest alien to it has been clear to me since I first saw strip-mining in the coalfields of eastern Kentucky half a century ago. Such destruction could not have served the interest of the homeland of any people or any creature. It served what some are now calling "the real America," and of course it was justified as serving the national economy. The sight of a bulldozer exposing the coal seam by mangling everything above it—the trees, the topsoil, the subsoil, the loose rocks, the long tradition of land husbandry, whatever was in the way—declared unmistakably the establishment upon the land, upon any land anywhere, of the dominance of the machine civilization, another term I needed but did not then have. Then, though I understood the technological portent, I attributed the destruction, and the willingness to destroy, to "corporate greed," which had so far paid its way beyond the possibility of governmental stewardship. I already knew something of corporate greed from its damage to farmers and farming in my own homeland. Later I understood that corporate greed depended upon a national ignorance or indifference that implied a national permission. I still identified the greed and the willing destructiveness as "corporate," and I hoped for the eventual emergence of an anticorporate urban patriotism that would make the case for the defense of our homeland. It took the election of Donald Trump to convince me that the antipatriotism of the "conservatives" belonged equally to the "liberals." It was the national antipatriotism of a nation that defined itself as exclusively urban, and thus was content with its enrichment by the economic ruin of rural America.

That certainly does not mean that I am looking forward to the civil war predicted by Jonathan Taplin. I am as much opposed to the next civil war as I am to the last one. I suppose that, as long as life enough is in me, I will continue to oppose the great harms that have come to the land and people of this country, which of course includes the cities that have so much depended on it and so little cared for it. And I will continue to advocate, and to point out, better ways. If that requires repeating myself, as I often have done, so be it. But as I repeat myself, maybe I will continue to learn a little more and then a little more about what is wrong and what would be right. I mean at least to tell the truth, as I am able to know it, about the difficulty of our problems. And it seems to me that we have none greater than the opposition of nationalism to patriotism that accompanies and partly explains the opposition of urban America to rural America, as well as related oppositions.

To the extent that Americans are patriots, they take good care of their land—which mostly they don't do, and at present have no intention of doing. To the extent that Americans are nationalists, they depend on institutional or governmental solutions to all their problems. They depend unquestioningly upon the protection of the government, which, about in proportion to their wealth, they also hate because it is "too big" and they must pay taxes to it. They don't, in the way of patriots, care for their land and do everything to enhance its ability to support them. They don't make their neighborhoods safe by being neighborly, which would save a lot of spending on police and door locks. No, for them, safety now depends on purchases. Buy a pistol, a rifle, a dagger, a club, a system of cameras and alarms. This is "defense." The ultimate safety is in "national defense," which also must be bought. The national fear begins at the locked front door and builds upward into a great national industry and business of armed force. Americans are so frightened, or so frightenable, of dangers so indefinably great that they must purchase enough explosives and poisons to kill them all in their own defense. In the nuclear war that America and other "developed nations" have been preparing for since 1945, the country that can destroy the world only once will be soundly defeated by the country that destroys it twice. If the American people are breaking up into divisions that are geographic, racial, economic, political, sexual, even into one-member species each with "their" own pronoun, it may be that our "defense policy" or our "posture of preparedness" has been impossible to quarantine in the Pentagon or in Washington, but has broken out and maddened everybody.

It is hard to know what to make of this great concourse of people all so overtaken by fear and anger and the need for self-defense and national defense. They are defined as nationalists, I suppose, by their great commonwealth of money and various kinds of credit, their superfluity of consumer goods, their actual or imminent poverty, and their peculiarly passive consent to industrial violence, including war. Perhaps they can be identified also negatively: As nationalists, or anyhow as nationals, they do not have home places or homes that they are permanently devoted to and wish to live in all their lives; and they do not have neighbors with whom they will live all their lives and love as themselves.

A homeland, a home, a beloved neighborhood are not available to people who are afraid and therefore filled with anger and preemptive hatred. Nowhere among the most prominent voices now is there an appeal to love, not for God or neighbors or for the country. The word "love" is so disrespected by materialism and depreciated by overuse that it now has for most people little of the life and force that actually belong to it. Love nevertheless is the only possible motive for the good work that is the only possible solution to our problems. Only the established and honored practice of love can give us things so difficult as wholeness or goodness or beauty or truth or freedom, let alone that "sustainability" that is on everybody's tongue. Ananda Coomaraswamy said that the artist— anybody dedicated to the well-making of any good thing—works for "the love of the idea of the thing to be made." He spoke of the ancient Greek idea that things should be made well in order to be "fit for the use of free men."

Patriots, people who love their homes and homelands, and who live and work in response to that love, now are comparatively few and can increase only slowly. Only people who know their land can effectively love it, and only by loving it for a long time can they competently (though never completely) know it. There have been times, I think, when American patriots were more numerous than now. But there are some Americans now who are patriots, and there are reasons to believe there may be more. Love of country is not yet a possibility foreclosed.

I mentioned a few pages ago what I take to be the tragic coincidence of patriotism and slavery in the South at the time of the Civil War. Another such tragedy was the convergence of Calhounian civilization, as it survived the Civil War in both South and North, with the machine civilization that Bernanos saw emerging from World War II. The transformation of war technology to farm technology gave a powerful impetus to the industrial dream, promising incalculable wealth to those best placed to receive it, that *all* bodily work should be done by machines and chemicals. The total, the totalitarian, triumph of machine civilization was to be the industrialization of all the landscapes of agriculture and forestry. At last the fallen world of work and sweat would be put right. Not just a master class but *everybody* now would live, like the Calhouns, free of the degrading work of farming and land husbandry. But the old law remained in effect. That kind of freedom depends upon slavery. The machine civilization provided the means to enslave the natural world. Soon now, the earth, the water, and the air will be ever at hand, ever subservient to our wants. Supposedly.

And now, prodded by the fear of climate change, many of us wish to replace the old industrial dream with a "green" industrial dream. This would replace the dirty energy from the fossil fuels with clean energy from sun and wind. This will require filling wide horizons with armies of titanic windmills and covering immense expanses of our long-suffering country with solar panels. The supply of energy will be truly limitless this time, and the greenly blameless humans will continue wheeling along in their automobiles with push-button windows.

To those who accuse me of technological backwardness (as some have done), I can say that my wife Tanya Berry and I have installed on the hillside above our house three large solar panels. These are semi-permanent. They rest upon heavy pylons set in concrete seven feet in the ground. They do effectively replace fossil fuel energy with solar energy, and they often reward us by running our meter backwards. However, as my wife very soon required me to see, they are ugly. Though they gather the sun's heat and turn it to human use, there is nothing of human comeliness or warmth about them, and we do not love them. Their unignorable hard angles usurp the shapeliness of our beloved hillside, and for the rest of our lives we will look at them with some pride, for which we will be paying a semi-permanent sadness. The sadness is in knowing, by this and other signs, that the machine civilization will be changed only somewhat by its concession to green industrialism.

The industrialization of agriculture, as well as all other kinds of land use, was accomplished by the application of the official, the academic and governmental and bureaucratic, "gospel of science and technology" to all of rural America. This transformation, as Pete Daniel rightly said, came at a "staggering human cost." It is a continuing cost no doubt as unpredictable as officially unacknowledged. A part of that cost was the dispossession and displacement of millions of people, farming people, whose worth and whose wishes were as entirely discounted here in rural America as if they had been living in the Soviet Union or China.

Another part of that cost, equally staggering, at least equally significant, is the radical depreciation of work. This depreciation seems always to have come in two stages. First, the qualitative measure of the product must be lowered so as to require less art or artistry in its making, and the product must be standardized, which is to say that all traces of the hands of an individual maker must be removed from it. This reduction allows the product to be made by workers working as machines or machine parts in a process entirely mechanical. Second, the workers having been standardized by mechanical work and thus made replaceable by machines, are then replaced by machines, according to the predestinarian law of technological progress.

Not all the millions of farmers eliminated from farming by the industrial dream were good farmers. Not all of them wanted to continue farming. But in trying to understand the cost and the meaning of their elimination, we must keep the good ones in mind, for as farmers in 1950 they all were free to become good ones. There was in farming no built-in or mechanical limit on their aspiration or the quality of their work. As farmers, unlike factory workers, they were responsible and answerable for the whole of their work and the whole of its product. So far as the possibility was in them, they were motivated by love for their work, for the product, and for the farms where their work was done. And they were free in the sense of being unbossed, self-motivated, self-disciplined, self-judging, independent so far as they were self-supporting, and neighborly so far as they were in need of help and able to give help.

To transform such people into industrial workers, their work had to be strictly and forever separated from love, from vocation, from artistry, from pleasure or satisfaction, from wholeness, from personal responsibility. The reproducibility of the industrial products contradicts the beauty of things made by living creatures. The work, in short, is alienated from life and from the lives of the workers. Thus it becomes a kind of punishment and a kind of slavery. And so we have truly a new thing under the sun: an immense number of human beings who hate their work.

I have no idea how long the world may tolerate such a violation of its own nature and of human nature. But it is immediately a disaster in the fundamental economies of agriculture and forestry. That is because, in any work of land use, the primary standard is not set by the market. It is set by Nature. The standard, inescapably, is health: the health of the natural world, which is upheld by certain laws, certain things that the human land user absolutely must or must not do. When her laws are violated, Nature immediately begins to impose her penalties: waste, pollution, ecological degradation, sickness, unhappiness, insanity, eventually shortness of breath, hunger, and thirst. This means, in the most practical economic terms, that the products of the land-using economies may, as now, be as poor as the taste or tolerance or ignorance or the brute need of consumers will permit. *But*, if the world is to last, the quality of land maintenance or land husbandry must be virtually perfect—as near perfect as it can be made by the work, the artistry, the love, the land need, the pleasure, the satisfaction of the land users. The laws of nature and of human nature are absolute and unremitting. They cannot for a moment be safely shortcut or ignored.

I have just defined, obviously, the land's unending need for a settled, permanent, locally adapted, self-renewing, self-educating population of gardeners, farmers, ranchers, and foresters, and for an equally settled and adept population of workers in the trades, crafts, arts, professions, and small-scale value-adding industries.

17. Goodness

If the nation and the country (the country itself, the land) are conceptually, imaginatively, and emotionally divided, then the nation becomes antipatriotic almost as a matter of course. It will treat its own country as a foreign land, a Third World to be colonized and plundered. It has forgotten, so far as it ever knew, the kind and quality of the work that is required for the good health and long life of the economic landscapes and their human inhabitants. It will not, because it cannot, imagine that such work can be highly skilled, loving, pleasing, and continuously living in the home places of the earth, work that is beautiful in the doing and in the results. The nation will not support such work, or pay for it. Its unconsciousness will lie over the land like a cloud. It will unknowingly subsidize its "cheap food" and "cheap energy" by the ruin of the land and the land's people. It will give more thought and importance to outer space than to the country it lives from. And this, ordinary as it has become, surely is a great evil.

Though it divides us and scatters us, as it seems, in ever smaller fragments, this evil belongs about equally to all of us who are living in and from this great swath of the world. It belongs to all of us without regard to sex, race, place of origin, or place of residence. It identifies us all impartially as Americans. As I have thought of this evil during most of my life, I have seen more and more clearly that it cannot be corrected solely by power or politics or technology or money. Those things, on their own terms, having their own reasons, are as fragmented and scattered as ourselves. I believe that the correction must be love, and I mean the practical love-until-death of neighbors and country. Such love and nothing else could reverse the industrial "process" of separating everything from everything. Such love, even before it accomplished very much, could make us whole and free, with a wholeness and freedom that likewise would belong to us all. It would involve an agenda of learning and work, longer than our lives, that likewise would belong to us all. I am speaking as practically and as seriously as I can, for the fate of work and the fate of our country are the same. The wholeness of work is the same as the wholeness of the land and the people.

The conditions on which we live in this world are stern, unrelenting, unrelentingly demanding of human goodness. Shakespeare taught us—in *King Lear*, for example, or in *Macbeth*—that evil finally destroys itself, for it is the nature of evil to destroy everything. But, as he also taught us, on its way to self-destruction evil can destroy much else. The so far dominant machine civilization has increased unimaginably the power and the scale of evil, but not, obviously, the power and scale of goodness. The capability of goodness—goodness that is true and actual—does not extend far beyond the scale of the heart and conscience and physical reach of individual humans. Can human goodness, heavenly and eternal as I believe it to be but only human in scale and power, outlast the machinery of extraction and war? We don't know. We know only that it is futile—it is impossible—to employ the machinery and the attitudes of evil in the service of goodness. We know we have no right *not* to employ the forces of goodness—love, truth, beauty, beautiful work—in the service of goodness. We have no right to refuse, even in defeat, the happiness of good work in the service of love. We must never be seduced by the devil's logic of fighting death with death and fire with fire.

CHAPTER IX

~

Words

I have spent many years working over the grounds of an agrarian indictment of the industrial destruction of the land and of its natural and human life. It now appears to me that I could not even approximately complete that work without incorporating more fully the theme of racial division, with which I dealt incompletely in *The Hidden Wound* fifty years ago. If the difficulty of this writing is a reliable measure, I now may have thought the best I can, if still incompletely, about the past and present of race relations. Burdened as never before by the wish for neighborly human relations, which certainly would include neighborly race relations, I have been writing an essay, an attempt, which almost by definition is work for an amateur, a nonprofessional moved by love. As often before in my essay writing, in this book I have often been in water over my head, breathing through a tube. As always in confronting the past, the persistent trouble in this book is that of not knowing enough: the impossibility of gathering into one consciousness all that has been recorded, and the more daunting impossibility of knowing the experience that was never recorded, or never told.

At the beginning of this writing and much more as I worked, our historical theme of race and race relations has seemed to me to have been and to be extraordinarily complicated and therefore extraordinarily difficult to think about. And so I have never assumed that after some reading and some thought I could propose a solution to "the race problem." Having no such expectation, I have tried to adhere to my belief that the right model or the norm of human relations is a conversation in earnest and in good faith between two people. When enough conversations of that kind are taking place across the racial divide, I assume, the divide will be no more. On that assumption, I have tried to write what I could honestly consider my part of a conversation, in which one thought naturally would invite another thought, perhaps a counterthought, or one story would be a reminder of another story. In some places, my side of the conversation has been disagreement, pointed and plain, but expecting a reply equally pointed and plain, and with perfect willingness to argue face-to-face with my opponent. In fact I would like, and would relish, a good deal more response than I have so far received from my opponents—to whom I have never wished any harm.

The influence of slavery and of race prejudice upon the two races, upon the history of work and economic life, upon our attitudes toward the land we live in and from, and upon our land itself has been profound and always damaging. If our long history of race prejudice and unfairness could end at last in the establishment of peace and goodwill among all of our people, that would not repay the costs and restore the losses of so much bad history, but it assuredly would be a help to us all, and it would involve right relations between political opponents, between country people and city people, and between our people and our land. By "right relations" I mean chiefly the courtesy that is always possible between two persons out of uniform and meeting face-to-face.

Although I have no plan of numbered steps for bringing such a result, my work on this book has required me to give a good deal of thought, which has been at least careful, to assumptions and circumstances, habits of speech and individual words that appear to me to be obstacles to peace and goodwill.

Above all, good relations among people or races of people cannot be made by force. As I think too much of our history proves, nothing of peace can be accomplished by the terrible symmetry of eye for eye, death for death, or even tit for tat. Retribution now entails the "right" or the "justice" of retribution later. But this is the right and justice that prevail in a cockfight. Any combat or conflict that divides people into winners and losers really never ends but only keeps the problem alive. At this point in the writing of my own book, I think the profoundest sentences in *Walking with the Wind* are these that come from John Lewis's account of the lunch counter sit-ins:

> No one would claim victory, which was no problem for
> us. A fundamental principle of nonviolence is that there
> is no such thing as defeat once a conflict is justly resolved,
> because there are no losers when justice is achieved.

This calls for maintenance of a clear connection between justice and truth, also for a fine balance of humility and magnanimity in the characters of people. And always, I would think, there must be an understanding of the limits of public solutions. Solutions that are legal or institutional or governmental may be necessary and proper in securing for some the unalienable rights that belong to everybody. Though such solutions clearly are victories for everybody, they cannot end prejudice. They cannot make people virtuous.

For that reason, I think that in public discussion of race and race problems there is too much emphasis upon public solutions to be enacted by agencies or institutions. In public protests and demonstrations about racial and other issues, the message often seems to be that people will do the right thing only when instructed or compelled to do so by some higher authority. But we need to consider the evidence that, in relatively settled circumstances, ordinary people in their ordinary lives have sometimes been well ahead of any public or institutional prescription.

For example, in the farming neighborhoods of my part of the country, there was, and to some extent there still is, a practice known as "work-swapping," in which neighbors gather to help one another at harvesttimes and other times when crew work is needed. As I have experienced this, the rule was "Nobody's done until everybody's done," and there was no settling up. Everybody's work was prepaid by the assurance that when anybody needed help the others would come. I think it would be impossible to say how old this practice is, or when or how it began. As I knew it, it was both orderly and informal. It had no institutional sanction or instruction or appreciation. It was as Christian as you please, but it was not *of* the church any more than it was *of* the government. I feel pretty sure that if it had been institutionalized it would have been ruined.

Another example, I think, would be that of the 925,000 black farmers in the South who, in the fifty years of racist violence following the Civil War, acquired title to 16 million acres of land. This could happen, Pete Daniel says, because in rural areas, blacks and whites necessarily worked side by side, and despite white supremacy, friendly relationships developed across the color line. Industrious African American farmers deferred when necessary and earned the respect of their white neighbors.

Both examples testify to the importance of settled life, proximity, mutual knowledge, neighborliness, respect, affection, and the sense of "what is right." By "deferred" Prof. Daniel pretty clearly means that the black people, in dealing with their white neighbors, observed the etiquette of conventional prejudice. The deference indicates at least that the convention was mutually understood, dealt with, and surpassed. This suggests that, under the influence of these "friendly relationships," the need to defer might gradually have worn away if the rural communities had not been unsettled by more war, depression, and the onset of "social mobility."

In our time, the qualities of neighborliness, friendliness, and "what is right" are generally undervalued or overlooked, and are replaced by the resort to remedies merely legal or political. How such human qualities and their good results could have occurred following the Civil War in the same region and the same time as acts of extreme cruelty and violence I do not know. Nor do I know what may be the fate of human conscience, the prompting of the sense of what is right, now, when we are struggling to live merely a public life, after the loss of nearly all functioning local communities.

In public comments and confrontations concerning race and race relations, the words "equality" and "freedom" and "racism" are often used as if their meanings were simple, settled, and agreed upon for now and forever. But as I have worked my way through this book, it has seemed to me that their meanings, as they often are used, are questionable. Sometimes, as they are spoken in public, their meanings seem to belong privately to the speaker. Sometimes the words are offered merely as gestures. This, I think, defines a need either to avoid them or to use them in ways that particularly define them.

The first reference of "equality," I suppose, is to the Declaration of Independence. That all of us are "created equal," I further suppose, means that we are equal, or should be, in "the eyes of the law." That God sees us as equal is an article of faith. That we should be treated as equal under the rule of our laws is theoretically and even expectably enforceable. But we know that, among ourselves, equality exists authentically only insofar as we grant it to one another in our ordinary dealings. The word nonetheless retains its meaning with difficulty in present circumstances. What does it mean to be equal in a destructive economy, or in a society of degraded or destroyed communities? What can equality mean when life is understood as a race to the top, and when people of wealth and power see themselves as "winners" and all others as "losers"? When the economy is ruled entirely by the principle of competition, are advocates for equality asking in fact for a fair share of dominance?

"Freedom," it seems to me, is now more in want of meaning than "equality." In the public realm, which is now about the only realm we have, it appears that to be free is to be unrestrained. It is to be limitless. To many liberals, to be free is to be personally (sexually and otherwise, but above all sexually) "liberated." To many conservatives, to be free is to be untaxed and unregulated (free to make money at any cost). This gives us the Trumpian Ethic, a liberal-conservative hybrid, which may, God willing, prove sterile.

But freedom as limitlessness is the definition preferred by Satan in *Paradise Lost*. He wishes, in perfect simplicity, to be unsubordinate, undependent, and of course ungrateful—or, to use a term much favored by our contemporaries, he wishes to be autonomous. But as the poem reveals, his freedom is that of a quasi-being, a fragment, and his freedom is limited to the power to do damage.

By that example and by my book's title I am prompted to consider that our need to be free may be the same, or close to the same, as our need to be whole. I took my title from an interview in which Ernest Gaines spoke of his wish that his work might help the black youth and the white youth of the South to understand each other. He imagines a white youth saying of a black youth, "[T]hat is part of me out there, and I can only understand myself truly if I can understand my neighbor." (And how touchingly he recalls us to our traditional culture by his use of the word "neighbor.")

Thus one of our most thoughtful writers assures us that we cannot be whole alone—or, as I would now add, free alone. To be whole, then, is to know ourselves, but in order to know ourselves we must know other people. And then by going on to say that in order to know ourselves, "we must understand what's around," Ernest Gaines may have referred to another need that he has felt strongly and has confirmed by one of his own crucial choices. This is the need to be at home in a place and among people we know. In fact, when he was able to do so, Ernest Gaines went home, bought a large lot on the plantation where he was born, where his people worked as slaves and as hired hands, and built a house there. And so by his example he requires us to consider that to be whole and free we must be at home.

And now, reading Kat Anderson's book on the land knowledge of Native Americans, *Tending the Wild*, I have come upon a further, most moving testimony to this need. The anthropologist George

Foster published seventy-five years ago an account of a Yuki Indian's happiness in returning to his home ground where

> The rocks and the trees knew him, and were glad to have him back; they were friendly toward him. . . . It is best to die and be buried in the ground that knows a person, the ground that is waiting to receive home its children.

If to be whole and free is to know oneself in part by knowing others, and to be at home in a place and a community where one knows and is known, this implies the further need to be self-disciplined and reasonably self-sufficient so as to have both the wholeness in oneself that is health and also freedom from being a burden or a nuisance to other people. And so we can see how rightly, in his *Second Defense of the People of England*, John Milton defined freedom in terms of the traditional virtues: "To be free is precisely the same thing as to be pious, wise, just and temperate, careful of one's own, abstinate from what is another's and thence, in fine, magnanimous and brave."

Of the inescapable words relating to race and race relations, "racism" may be the one that has come to be most carelessly used. Until recently I too was using that word to refer to the whole phenomenon of race prejudice, but that now seems approximate and unfair. In the course of this writing I have been obliged to consider that race prejudice manifests itself in degrees or intensities too various and numerous to name or know. At one end of the scale is the avowed doctrine and program of white supremacy, and I call that racism with no hesitation at all. At the other end of the scale there is what? Something, perhaps, like unconscious race prejudice? Somewhere near that end, I suppose, would be people like me, born into customary race prejudice, who feel that they have got rid of the old reflexes, but who know better than to be sure. Also somewhere at the end of the scale opposite to the avowed and militant racists are those who recognize and oppose the race prejudice they find in themselves, and those who can see, through their prejudice, the right thing to do, and who then do it. And certainly it is wrong to label as racists whole categories of people, such as all rural Americans who voted for Trump, or all rural Americans.

And so as I have worked my way to here I have been more and more inclined to use the term "racism" only where I am sure it belongs, and elsewhere to replace it with "race prejudice."

In this as in several other books that I have written, I have had to deal repeatedly with the social agitation that we call "mobility." Whether upward or lateral, and upward usually is also lateral, mobility is affirmed, by some, as one of the achievements of the modern world, a freedom or a right. But whatever its worth to individuals, to human society as a whole, and to the human economy as a whole, it is extremely costly. Because we are so rootless, so virtually homeless, there are a number of problems we have that we cannot solve. Obviously, if there is no permanence of residence among a high percentage of our people, we can have no stable, self-conserving communities. Without stable communities, we cannot develop local economies fitted to the natural limits, requirements, and advantages of our home landscapes. Without stable communities, neither parents nor teachers will teach the children the history or the natural history or the free pleasures of their home places.

Because we are to such an extent strangers to one another and to the land we live on and from, because our communal memories are therefore so drastically shortened, we are now further than we have ever been from the task, ever more pressing and necessary, of adapting our economic lives to their sources in the natural world. It is curious that we are now conducting a national debate on immigration policy without ever a question or a mention, let alone knowledge, of the carrying capacity of our land with regard either to our population or to the demands of our extravagant economy, which subsists so far upon the fable of limitless natural resources. Hospitality and generosity are indispensable virtues, but what if you yourself are wasting or using beyond replenishment the goods that will be needed by your guests? Carrying capacity is a subject of immediate and urgent importance to every keeper of grazing livestock, but such people are now rare and endangered.

From whatever angle we approach our prominent and interrelated diseases—land abuse, poverty, public violence, pollution of the whole so-called environment, climate change, bad health—we will have to deal with the problem of mobility. And we certainly cannot avoid it when considering our old and continuing problems of race relations. Moving a problem from place to place, it seems to me, almost certainly makes it harder to solve. When black people and white people lived together, even racially divided, for some generations in the same places, usually farming communities, they were likely to know fairly competently both one another and where they were. They spoke pretty much the same language, consisting crucially of names—of people, places, tools and equipment, plants and animals—familiar to them both. Such common knowledge, given fairly stable circumstances and enough time, might have narrowed the racial divide or, given time, removed it altogether. I say "might have" because I don't speak for everybody, and because we will never know.

We will never know because our people in general have never settled in place long enough to achieve the necessary cultural convergence of local economy with local ecology. The apparently natural human inclination to settle and become responsibly at home has repeatedly been dominated and upset first by the westward movement and then by the migration of country people into the cities, also and increasingly by large-scale technological and economic changes.

Mostly, as I have said, the farming communities of my own part of the country were fairly settled, and had been for a long time, before the onset of World War II and the war economy. Though some people were poor, nobody was homeless or unemployed. There were some, expectably, who worked as little as possible. Some of the elderly had slacked off or mostly quit, but nobody had "retired." I knew some "disabled" persons of both races who kept vigorously at work. Our great social problem, which we did not then address and the white people did not acknowledge as a problem, was school segregation and the racial division of which it was the official presence. That problem would be officially solved in due time, but by then any such success would be qualified and obscured by the general disintegration of the rural communities.

One of the cruelest of our mass migrations was that of the economically obsolete, mostly black people from the farmlands of the South, and of the economically obsolete, mostly white people from the Appalachian coalfields, to the industrial cities of the North and Midwest. This was so cruel because there was nothing left to support them where they came from and no assured support for them where they went, because their obsolescence was sudden, because they were so numerously affected, and because the change was so drastic.

Country people who go to live in a city, especially if they go with no possibility of return and no foreseeable future, are as completely changed, probably, as humans can be and still live. Though when they arrive in the city they may meet people they have known before, they have come to a place that to them is new. Because they can arrive only as they were formed by the places they have left, they are new people in the places they have come to. They have lost their home places and their old neighbors, their work, their native histories and geographies, which are no longer necessary. Virtually all the contents of their minds suddenly are obsolete and useless. Above all, their old language, their home language, so poignantly filled with familiar nouns and names, also is useless, unintelligible to the people they now must learn to talk to.

Such were the changes suffered by all the obsolete migrants. If they were white people from the coalfields, they would face a prejudice newly prepared for their arrival, and they would be called "hill-billies" or "briars." They would pay penalties for that distinction. If they were black people they would face an urban version of the customary race prejudice they had faced at home. For all migrants the customary prejudices would be compounded by the fear and suspicion directed at strangers among strangers in a strange place.

Early in my life a great many black people lived in the country and were country people. Now nearly all of them live in cities and are city people. In the articles and comments I have read about the present version of "the race problem," I don't think there has been enough understanding of the difference between country people and city people, or of the greatness of the change of mind and life that must occur when country people move to the city. Because of that difference and the effects of so drastic a change, people who lived with race prejudice in the country, and who came to know one another and associate with one another, despite the prejudice, with an amity exceeding tolerance, must begin all over again to deal with the same prejudice, and now estranged by it, when they move to the city.

I have just described some of the unaccounted costs of mobility, costs payable only personally by individual people, one by one. Such costs undoubtedly will continue to be paid by individuals, to whom of course there can be no restitution. But the greatest cost, also final and unrepayable, will be paid by our country, the American land itself, which for a while will be increasingly used and abused by numerous people, fewer and fewer of whom will live in it or know anything about it.

Much of the great wrong to our land that all of us are doing now, and for a while must continue to do, cannot be undone. That is in accord merely with the way of this world and with the tragedy of our life in it. The rivers that carried the soil away will not bring it back. Eventually, given enough human love and will, enough time, and the blessing of Heaven, we may begin to heal the damage. But to do that, I believe, we will have to recover our now perishing traditions of land need, land knowledge, land husbandry, and homemaking. And we all will need more than ever to learn and take to heart the corresponding traditions, the true multiculturalism, of the people inhabiting this land, and ably caring for it, before 1492.

"Mobility," then, is a polite name for a ruthless process of individualism and selfishness for some, for others separation and loneliness. Its costs can be summarized as dismemberment from one another and displacement from any homeland, two effects amounting to a single great estrangement or exile.

Just in time, I have received from a friend the phrase "obedience to the unenforceable," which my friend attributes to Lord Fletcher Moulton, an English jurist. The "unenforceable" that must be obeyed is a body of ancient laws, inherited rather than legislated, originating in impulses of the heart, borne by traditions older than history: the trustworthiness and the trust, the kindnesses and mere decencies fundamental to community life. "Love thy neighbor as thyself" is a law, a stay against disorder and ruin, unenforceable but calling out to be obeyed. In a community or a society that is sufficiently at peace and reasonably secure economically, these unenforceable laws are remembered by enough people and often enough obeyed, even across social and racial divisions, so that the community coheres, functions, and survives. It seems to me that this unofficial, offhand lawfulness is more necessary and effective than the rule of law. But in times of public violence, of war, or of the unofficial violence that proceeds from war, this unenforceable obedience, which is no less than the practice of neighborly love and peace, becomes startlingly fragile. Fear and suspicion undermine the homegrown structures and habits of neighborhood—the generosities, the fair exchanges, the watching and the care, the courtesies, the good manners—leaving the people to live either with or without the protections and services handed down to them by law. Amid the disorders that multiply in the absence of willing neighborhood, the social current no longer moves toward kindness and community, but instead toward individuals, divided, threatened, and alone.

Such was the condition of the people of Kentucky during the Civil War and for many years afterward. In a small rural community like mine, time and mortality, a common culture, and the continuity of work and shared experience may have healed the divisions in a generation or two. In other places the forces and effects of disintegration may have lasted much longer. We have poor means of accounting such things, and certainly no means of setting an expiration date for our destructiveness. Who is to say if animosities and the habits of violence bred in Kentucky by the Civil War did not assert themselves again in the questionable election and assassination of Gov. William Goebel in 1900, or again in the Black Patch War in several western counties during the next decade?

Now our entire nation seems as picked apart by fear and anger, animosities political and personal, as Kentucky was during its long version of the Civil War. But that old disruption may have lasted in Kentucky no more than fifty years, whereas the present national one has been going on and growing always worse since the industrialization of rural America began in earnest at the end of World War II. The mobility that has dispersed our families and shaken our communities to their roots we now accept as we accept the lengths of days and years, or as we accept the dependence of our economy upon continuous war. War seems to have established the mode of our public thought. Our version of national good, "economic growth," is largely based upon a war against the earth, using the machines, explosives, and poisons that are the technologies of war. In our history we have too readily and too often resorted to violence, but never so much as now have we made violence the norm of our life, repeatedly solving our problems by applications of force while ignoring the further problems that inevitably result. As recently as the fateful spring of 2020, I heard yet another expert witness speaking of the human "war against nature," with no hint of a realization that Nature, on *her* conditions, may be our teacher and ally. We will eventually lose our war against nature, the expert prophesied, but we must keep up the fight as long as possible.

Because there are no effective social structures intervening between dispersed individuals and the general public, our appeals for remedies and solutions are directed mainly to the government. But if we are right in expecting the government to serve our wellbeing, we are wrong to expect it to do so more than somewhat. The rule of law offers us, never perfectly, certain protections and services, thus completing our citizenship and respecting us as sharers in the national polity and fate. But only those other laws that cannot be publicly enforced but must be privately obeyed can make us good neighbors to one another, and so help us to preserve this world and its human life.

Circumstances no doubt could be worse than they now are for the practice of neighborhood, though now they are bad enough. But the parable of the good Samaritan pointedly forbids any appeal to circumstances. It is in bad circumstances that neighborly love is most needed and required. But we should notice, even so, how the difficulty is increased by circumstances specifically modern.

However inclined one might be to follow his example, the good Samaritan's neighborly care is easy to imagine. Finding a man robbed and badly hurt lying on the roadside, the Samaritan stops, dismounts from his donkey, treats and binds up the man's wounds, helps him onto the donkey, and takes him to an inn where he can be cared for. The story is completely straightforward; the needed helps are all at hand. I have known that story all my life, and I have often had it in mind. But more than fifty years ago when I was living in New York, I was on the subway, having boarded the train probably at 193rd Street in the Bronx. It was about ten o'clock at night, the train was nearly empty, and I was sitting facing the doors in the middle of the car. At a stop far uptown, the doors opened, a man fell facedown into the car and lay without moving, the doors clapped shut, and the train moved on. What has made this unforgettable to me was my failure to do anything. I just sat there, as if paralyzed by my surprise, by my perfect awareness that this was, for the fallen man, an emergency, and by my inability to think of anything to do. The only other person in the car was a fairly young man dressed all in white as if for work in a hospital, and clearly more experienced in such things than I was. He promptly got up, grasped the man's arms, lugged him out of the doorway and onto a seat where he sat as lifelessly as a sack of laundry. The man in white clothes returned to his seat. Neither of us had said a word.

I was immediately ashamed of my failure to act. At least I could have helped to get the half-obliterated poor soul onto a seat. I am sure that, as soon as I could think, I was comparing my performance with that of the Samaritan. And I am still asking what I, or I and the man in white, should have done. The man in white had done a decent thing but not, clearly, a complete one. The fallen man obviously needed care that two men on a moving train could not provide. He was not fat, but he was not small either. Suppose we, his only neighbors, had managed to carry him off the train and up the steps to the street, what then? I might have thought of calling the police. If there was something more appropriate to do, the man in white might have known, but I certainly did not. Now I can see that the only really sensible thing would have been to hail a taxi and take our patient to the nearest emergency room. But I, for one, could not afford a taxi in those days, I was probably carrying only a few dollars in cash, and I did not own a credit card. I might have concluded, and maybe I did, that the world I was in had not been contrived with the possibility of neighborly help in mind. Now it seems to me that the work of Dorothy Day must have begun with the convergence in her mind of such calamity and helplessness with the imperious Gospel.

That convergence anyhow is an apt description of our situation now. Though we have still the old instructions, and though many of us still know them, or have heard of them, the old voices are not the ones we are listening to. The voices we are most likely hearing now are telling us how we come to ruin alone, or how we suffer according to category. Or we hear of the future in which the worst that has happened will continue to happen and get worse until, with a logic terrible and just, the End will come—*unless* the redemptive stroke of political power or political genius or a new miracle of science and technology comes first. And so by our protests and "activism," our editorials, columns, and comments, our banners, slogans, and political platforms, we sustain our wish to change the world without changing ourselves.

And yet in such quiet as we salvage from the news, the public noise, and the electronic whispering in our ears, surely we must suspect that the most needed changes are humble and obvious and old, and must be made in our hearts. For the responsibility even for global warming and global war finally descends upon us privately to question our lives and our ways of living. To replenish our shared life and the life of our land we have at last no recourse but to willing obedience to the laws that are oldest and best. For not obeying those unenforceable laws we can be forgiven, I hope, but we cannot be exonerated or excused.

One other word or concept that seems to me to trouble much of our thinking, and it certainly has troubled mine, is "human," the meaning of which is no longer reliable, but may change from one speaker, or one kind of speaker, to another. This matters because in our talk of race relations and other social problems we almost customarily use "human" or "humanity" as the most reliable standard of value and common denominator: "They are human just like us," we say, or "We all share the same humanity." But we are no longer sure what we mean by that.

The most immediate reduction of the concepts of "human" and "humanity" that we must deal with, the reducers must have understood as merely practical. If some people were too good to do bodily or "degrading" work, then there had to be other people to whom such work was appointed. This was a division of long standing in the Old World. For some of our ancestors this was reason enough to cross the ocean. In the New World the European migrants were comparatively free and equal. But at least some of them had brought the pride and sloth that informed them that some work was too degrading for the better people to do. To some of our ancestors, it was obvious that Adam's burden properly should be borne by black slaves. And so we revived the debilitating, the truly degrading, idea that some people were good only for doing other people's work. Thus the doctrine of "labor-saving" was established in the United States.

The first reduction, then, was from human in the full, fine sense of the term to the category of human-as-work-animal. Under the rule of industrialism, there was a further reduction to human-as-industrial-machine, and then, by a merely logical progression, to the displacement of the human-machine by a machine.

That reduction has been accompanied and abetted by another that I suppose we are obliged to call "scientific."

There was a time in the history of Western civilization when "human" or "man" was understood by everybody in about the same way. The order of *The Divine Comedy* comes from Dante's, and his readers', understanding of what a human is: a creature unique in creation and among the creatures, possessing certain characteristic powers and limits, capable of good and evil and of choosing between them, expected to choose good, and granted a unique and proper place in the order of heaven and earth—that is, between the animals and the angels.

Shakespeare's vision of humanity, and of the human place in the order of creation, three hundred years later was still about the same. When he wrote *Macbeth*, he had the old order closely at heart.

When Macbeth wavers in his intention to kill Duncan, the king of Scotland, in order to take his place, Lady Macbeth upbraids him:

> Art thou afeard
> To be the same in thine own act and valor
> As thou art in desire?

And Macbeth, though not enough convinced, replies with an idea surely central to our tradition:

> I dare do all that may become a man.
> Who dares do more is none.

Lady Macbeth fiercely contradicts him, but her contradiction itself affirms the ancient law:

> When you durst do it, then you were a man;
> And to be more than what you were, you would
> Be so much more the man.

As the play itself and too much of human history will demonstrate, for a man to attempt to become more than a man is to become not a greater man but a monster. For a mere human to appropriate godly powers in order to overrule the laws of nature or of human nature was traditionally the transgression most to be feared. In the classical branch of our heritage this was called "hubris," in the biblical branch it was called "pride" in the sense of extreme arrogance. The surplus or superhuman power, once appropriated by humans, can do only damage. The traditional definition of "human" is composed of limits as much as privileges. To be properly human, there are some things we must not do. The opposing creed, dominant in our own time, holds that there are no limits. Anything humans can do, they must do. Anything goes.

Humans in their proper place in the order of things, living within their prescribed limits, choosing good over evil, are admirable creatures. To do no more than "may become a man," as the great law says even in the mouth of the faltering Macbeth, clearly implies that a man, so doing, is a becoming or a comely thing to be. Human beings, so defined and so acting, embody not only the goodness or virtue worthy of divine favor, but also a share of sanctity itself. We could say that the traditional definition of humankind comes to us ultimately from Genesis 2:7:

> And the Lord God formed man of the dust of the ground,
> and breathed into his nostrils the breath of life; and man
> became a living soul.

The human record, "from man's first disobedience" until now, is fairly consecutively a series of insults given by humans to that old high definition. But as long as that definition remained culturally alive and present in our consciousness, we at least knew where our thoughts and deeds located us within the order of Creation, and according to the laws, natural and divine, by which we were ruled and judged. Toward the end of the eighteenth century William Blake could still speak confidently of "the human form divine," remembering that Adam and Eve were created in the image of God.

But, progressively, we put ourselves more and more fully in charge of defining ourselves, in order, as we seem to have thought, to become more comprehensible to ourselves. And so we removed from our origin all vestiges of miracle and mystery. We enlarged our estimate of our powers of reason and understanding. We began to comprehend reality scientifically—though always by reducing it to the size and the terms of our comprehension, understanding the darkness by subjecting it to brighter and brighter light. We became *Homo sapiens*, every one of us a "wise man." We began, by further reductions, to understand ourselves as rational animals, or as animals with "big brains," or as biological machines. And this reduction of the human being increasingly to a kind of puppet, ruled by biological or genetic or technological determinants, was sponsored, paradoxically and absurdly, by a romantic version of the human being, especially the scientist, as "free" adventurer, explorer, discoverer of virgin territories and new worlds. This vision lands with a jolt at last upon the lowly consumer who, enchanted by the arts of public relations and salesmanship, is foredoomed to pay for it all.

But that does not complete my account of the evolution of the human image in our time. I must notice also that to accompany the vision of *Homo sapiens* as the compelled fulfiller of a high human destiny yet to be revealed, there is among modern artists and intellectuals a powerful, persistent current of misanthropy. This is communicated as a mood or tone, a sort of tune often heard in the revived genre of end-of-the-world predictions. The tune, learned from a kind of old-time preaching, wishes us to know that the climate-change apocalypse or the nuclear holocaust or the triumph of the robots will be just exactly what we wicked humans deserve, the predictors clearly willing to suffer this justice themselves in order to see it suffered by the rest of us.

And so we have wound up somewhere near the end of an age of which we humans have put ourselves solely in charge, and in which we cannot at last arrive at a favorable opinion of ourselves.

The word "human," like the idea it stands for, has thus become a shoddy thing. It is a leaky vessel that we keep afloat by pumping day and night. It seems no longer able to draw the "all" of the Declaration, or two races of it, into the same thought. The wish to improve the lives of black people is now so tightly concentrated upon the plight of black people as to ignore the extent to which their plight may be shared by white people. Recently there has been an outbreak of articles, on paper and online, about discrimination against black farmers in the offices of the United States Department of Agriculture. The dozen or so of these articles I have seen appeared in 2019. These articles appear to have their headwaters in the work of Pete Daniel, whose book *Dispossession* I have already discussed at length. Prof. Daniel's report leaves no doubt that a bias against black farmers has been extensive, openly practiced, and ongoing for many years throughout the federal agricultural bureaucracy. That is not in question. But as a rural American and a member of the perishing remnant of a once-vital farm community, I find this gathering of articles remarkable for two reasons. First, they may comprise the most sustained public concern for the fate of *any* American farmers in the last half century.

Second, all of these articles are focused almost exclusively upon the land losses of black farmers. This matters because the failure of black farmers cannot be fully understood apart from the failure of white farmers at the same time. Whereas more black farmers failed, in proportion to their total number, than white farmers, unquestionably because of racial discrimination, the number of failed white farmers was much larger, the failures together amounting to a catastrophic departure from the land of farm families of all races who should have been its cherishers and caretakers. The departure of so many of both races, as I have shown earlier, occurred because of the government's "cheap food policy" and because of its unrevoked quasi-policy of "too many farmers" and the supposed need to reduce the farm population.

In his article "This Land Was Our Land," in *The Atlantic* of September 2019, Vann R. Newkirk II writes, "As the historian Pete Daniel recounts, half a million black-owned farms across the country failed in the 25 years after 1950," but he does not give Prof. Daniel's number for the failed white-owned farms during the same years. And he gives not a hint of Prof. Daniel's account of the anti-farmer bias that ruled the whole structure of industrial agriculture then and in the years following. Mr. Newkirk writes further that "the black population in Mississippi declined by one-fifth from 1950 to 1970, as the white population increased by the exact same percentage. Farmers slipped away into the night, appearing later as laborers in Chicago and Detroit." This implies that so many black farmers were replaced by so many white farmers, which is not true. The number of *all* farmers has been drastically reduced.

Exactly that incompleteness, the careful division of the fate of black farmers from the fate of all farmers and the fate of the farmland, is characteristic of all such articles that I have read. This, I believe, is because the prejudice against black people has, for the liberal writers of these articles, the status of a recognized prejudice, whereas the prejudices against farmers and farming and farms are unrecognized. And so these special or exclusive pleaders for black farmers leave out of consideration a number of things that urgently need to be considered. A competent evaluation of the present condition of farmers and farmland would be useful equally to farmers of both races, to the health of nature, and to consumers of food.

But such an evaluation cannot be conducted in the shallows of present racial politics. It would require a complete accounting of our present agricultural economy, tracking the money as it comes and goes, tracing the costs and benefits, determining the costs and who pays them, the benefits and who receives them. It would examine the several ways of using and caring for the land, and the different or divergent standards by which these ways may be measured. It would, above all, examine the effects of farm surpluses upon the national economy, upon the economies of farmers and farms, and upon the farmed lands and the waters flowing from them. Finally, I think, it would have to ask what would be the right kind and degree of farmers' dependence upon the government: If surpluses were controlled, and if farmers were paid fairly for their work—in land husbandry as well as food production—what might be the extent, then, of government subsidies to farmers?

Such critical work obviously needs to be done, but it is not likely to be done by any of the present political sides. Notwithstanding their uncompleted solicitude for black farmers, it seems to me that liberals in general agree with conservatives in general that farmers in general are not deserving of serious consideration. And the last thing that either party wants to hear about is the fate of the farmland, never mind that they are eating glyphosate in their breakfast cereal.

I have at hand a graph from Prosperity Now and the Institute for Policy Studies, showing "median household wealth by race/ethnicity in the United States (1983–2024)." In 1983, according to this graph, the median household wealth of white people was $102,200; for the households of black people it was $6,800. The "forecast" for 2024 is $122,366 for white households, and for black households $1,233. The two lines of the graph are wide apart all the way across. This graph exists to demonstrate the truly shameful economic inequality now existing between the two races. But the graph, like the several articles on the dispossession of black farmers, is statistically incomplete.

We are pretty obviously expected to assume that the top line of the graph represents a norm or baseline, and that racial justice or equality would be achieved if the bottom line were to be raised to the level at the top line. So far, this makes a kind of sense: It makes sense if the only interests involved are those of the white humans and the black humans, and if the only measure required is that supplied by our present economy, which is concerned only with the monetary worth or wealth of humans. And here is where we are betrayed and left in the dark by our reliance on "human" or "humanity" as a standard of value. From the standpoint of rural America, it is immediately apparent that an interest of major importance has been ignored: the interest of what Aldo Leopold called "the land-community," which is to say the land itself and all the creatures, living and not living, that constitute and preserve its life. Clearly this is a vital interest, and it is clearly superior in importance to the human interest, insofar as without the land-community humans cannot exist.

I don't know how the interest of the land-community might be represented in this graph or in such a graph—maybe that is not possible. But I was made aware of its exclusion by my wife's observation that if the bottom line probably is too low, the top line certainly must be too high. She meant that a high percentage of the household wealth of both races is derived from the abuse and often the permanent depletion of the health and wealth of the land-community—that is to say our enslavement of the land, the water, the air, and all the creatures living from them, including of course all of us humans.

The point, now, ought to be obvious: The earth that we are laying waste, presumably for our benefit, is neither human nor separable from humans. If we see our participation, at present ines-capable, in the abuse of the land-community as normal or accept-able, we forfeit our right to oppose the abuse of humans. If it was once arbitrary and wrong to count a Negro slave as three-fifths of a person, it is now arbitrary and wrong to count as a single citizen one mere human plus a gigantic overdraft upon the world's sources of energy, food, and other commodities, plus a gigantic discharge of toxic wastes and pollutants. This disproportion both causes and obscures a crisis in our understanding of equality, citizenship, and membership. We now measure those things by the quantities of monetary net worth, earnings, "purchasing power," expenses. Those measures are significant, but we need also an ecological accounting of our economic *practices*. And this, which would define our human responsibility, we have not begun to do.

And so we apparently have exhausted (temporarily, I hope) "hu-man" as a term of value or a standard of conduct, for it has been too long associated with our history of desecration. It draws too small a boundary, leaving too much of importance on the outside, enabling by now a nearly perfect divorce between our people and our land, and clearly prefiguring the ruin of both. We need a more capacious, more generous term that will enable and even require us to include all that should be included and to think of everything in need of our thought. It seems to me that the needed term is "life." And now that I must argue to that point, I am grateful that I don't have to find the way alone.

As my guide, to begin, I will need Martin Luther King Jr.'s great speech at Riverside Church in New York on April 4, 1967. I think he was always scrupulous, and exceptional, in his insistence upon the inclusiveness of Thomas Jefferson's "all." At first, necessarily, he focused his work and care upon the problems of institutional racism in the American South. And then there came a time when "all," for him, could no longer be so confined. In the Vietnam War he had seen this nation's racism magnified into an international nightmare, not to say an international absurdity. He had watched, he said, "Negro and white boys on TV screens as they kill and die together for a nation that has been unable to seat them together in the same schools." He had accepted the Nobel Peace Prize in 1964 "on behalf of all men who love peace and brotherhood." He had understood that award as a commission, "a calling that takes me beyond national allegiances." But he was mindful, above all, of his commitment to the great principle of love as taught and practiced in the Gospels, which he knew he had to accept as "a call for an all-embracing and unconditional love for all men."

He clearly was pushing hard at the boundaries and definitions that have divided us and enabled us to say "all but some" or "all but these." His commitment to nonviolence and neighborly love was final and unshakeable. He carried it as far as it could be carried within the most generous circumference of "the one blood" of which "God made all men." How much farther he might have carried it we cannot know, for he lived only one year past his speech at Riverside Church. That speech nevertheless is clearly the work of a mind unresting, still in motion, still reaching for the full extent not just of what Thomas Jefferson meant by "all," but of what we now must learn to mean by it.

That the great principles of nonviolence and neighborly love can and ought to be extended beyond the bounds of merely human concern he may have begun to feel. Or so it seems to me. In the midst of his Riverside speech there is a sentence that astonishes and moves me now in a way that it could not have done in 1967. "I speak," he

474

said, "for those whose land is being laid waste, whose homes are being destroyed, whose culture is being subverted." This sentence enlarges his concern and his charity so as to include, with the people, their land, their homes, and their culture. He saw in Vietnam what was not yet so visible in this country: that the destructiveness of industrial warfare, like that of industrialism itself wherever it acts upon the natural world, is total. To destroy the people or the land is to destroy both and also, in Vietnam, it was destroying the ancient culture by which the people had made themselves at home on their land. With only the difference that in Vietnam the land-cultures were older and more conserving than ours, the same destruction was already happening here. In 1967 it was happening here most visibly, to my own knowledge, in the Appalachian coalfields where the mountainsides were being destroyed by strip-mining, but such places were then as now not much known or noticed. In the intervening half century, the destruction has become widespread, and much or most of rural America is being "Appalachianized." Outside the affluent parts of the cities and apart from the wilderness preserves, it is all a "national sacrifice area." In Vietnam, and in other small countries, the power misapplied has been military force; here it has been economic force. Now, in the third decade of the twenty-first century, King's sentence about our total destructiveness in Vietnam in 1967 could be spoken reasonably and upon visible evidence by any advocate for the land and people of rural America: "I speak for those whose land is being laid waste, whose homes are being destroyed, whose culture is being subverted."

The enslavement of black Africans, like our dispossessions and our wars of extermination against the American Indians, was a result of oceanic navigation, which broke through the continental limits within which Europeans had so far been confined. It introduced into the minds of the European races the fateful and childish idea that what we don't have here, or what we use up here, or what we merely have heard of and want, we can get from somewhere else. It also put European "discoverers" into contact with people who looked enough unlike themselves that, again fatefully and childishly, the discoverers could define them as "wild" or "savage" or "uncivilized" or "heathen"—in effect, not human—and thus could blamelessly mistreat or kill them, or could exploit them as slaves, as they exploited other foreign merchandise. This was the beginning of what we now call globalism or the global economy, which is to say the worldwide hunt for cheap goods and cheaper labor.

The Trump administration fully revealed the conservative program, which is, with no regulation or restraint, to gouge, drill, scrape, scour, burn, and poison the earth until there is nothing left of it that can be converted to money. The liberal program is different only in asking for a few exceptions. Theirs is a rare fastidiousness that asks a wholly violent economy to interrupt its daily pillage in order to extend a political kindness to wilderness areas, women, and a selection of minorities.

I conclude that, not human life, but life itself is the only vessel that can contain all of us humans, however we may divide ourselves against one another—which it does by containing also the living world itself. To speak further I need now to take as my guide the musician, philosopher, physician, and Christian missionary Albert Schweitzer, who gave us the phrase "reverence for life," which resolved a crisis of his own thinking in 1915, and a century later is indispensable to these latter pages of my book.

The onset of World War I in 1914 seems to have affected Schweitzer much as the conclusion of World War II would affect Georges Bernanos. Schweitzer regarded it as "the downfall of civilization." Perhaps he owed something of the power of this realization to his African patients. It must have been bitterly clarifying to him to find that such massive and extensive warfare was incomprehensible or inexcusable to the Ogowe people, whom he nevertheless considered "primitive" or "savage." The war forced him "to acknowledge that public opinion . . . approved of, as opportune, inhumane courses of action taken by governments and nations." To the countries involved in the war, "*Realpolitik* . . . meant the approbation of a shortsighted nationalism, and compromises with forces and tendencies which had been resisted hitherto as hostile to progress."

Preceding the outbreak of war, Europeans had felt an optimism that was incomprehensible to Schweitzer: "It seemed to be assumed everywhere not only that we had made progress in inventions and knowledge, but also that in the intellectual and ethical spheres we lived and moved at a height which we had never before reached, and from which we should never decline." In Schweitzer's view, the generation before the war had believed that progress realized itself "in some measure, naturally and automatically" so that humanity "no longer needed any ethical ideals." Although the error of this had been proved by the coming of the war, Schweitzer clung to the belief that modern European civilization had produced a "will to progress" that was a new thing and itself evidence of progress. His discussion of this matter seems to me in a number of ways questionable. For example, he felt that this ideal of higher spiritual and material development of mankind was inherently unselfish. The modern European, he said, "is less concerned about his own condition than about the happiness which he hopes will be the lot of coming generations"—which we recognize now as the propaganda of totalitarian regimes, also as the "creative destruction" of our own apologists for industrial "development." At this point Schweitzer, maybe in some desperation, was keeping faith with "the man of modern Europe": "It is on his will to material progress, acting in union with the will to ethical progress, that the foundations of modern civilization are being laid."

I am dealing here with chapter XIII of *Out of My Life and Thought*, which was published in 1931. The ninety-one years from then until now have made it obvious that there was never a possibility that ethical progress would, or could ever, develop in union or in parallel with material progress. Material progress was never going to wait for ethics to catch up. It would only leave further and further behind the warning given to us in antiquity that we might "do all that may become a man," but not more and nothing else. The material progress that brought us to the wars of the twentieth century, and the twenty-first, merely took advantage of our long habit of ignoring the traditional warning.

Meanwhile Schweitzer was trying to find a concept that would carry his thought beyond the present failure of civilization, and he was stuck. Finally, in September 1915, he had to make a long river journey. He was still "struggling to find the elementary and universal conception of the ethical," but the revelation that came to him was not a result of his struggle. His account of it is exhilarating: "Late on the third day, at the very moment when, at sunset, we were making our way through a herd of hippopotamuses, there flashed upon my mind, unforeseen and unsought, the phrase, 'Reverence for Life.'"

After that, he seems to have been relieved of his fretting about progress. He saw that reverence for life was fundamental, not to be progressed from to anything better or different. He said so responsibly, clearly, and bravely: "A man is ethical only when life, as such, is sacred to him, that of plants and animals as that of his fellow men, and when he devotes himself helpfully to all life that is in need of help." He faced, though with regret, "the puzzling and horrible law of being obliged to live at the cost of other life." There is no sign in *Out of My Life and Thought* that he saw how this "horror" was mitigated by the ceremonial reverence, gratitude, conviviality, and thrift with which other life was used by people he would have considered "early" or "primitive" or "savage." But he relieves the horror himself by a measure of humor, when he comes to his book's epilogue, in a paragraph one is likely to remember:

> I rejoice over the new remedies for sleeping sickness, which enable me to preserve life, whereas I had previously to watch a painful disease. But every time I have under the microscope the germs which cause the disease, I cannot but reflect that I have to sacrifice this life in order to serve other life.

We owe this man great respect for the clarity and candor of thought that came to him after the transforming phrase flashed upon his mind. By his association of life with reverence, he set it conclusively apart from its commodification by genetic engineering. He saw how immediately and urgently it opened into mystery: "Who among us knows what significance any other kind of life has in itself, and as a part of the universe?" And from mystery it led—logically he seems to have thought—into religion:

The ethic of Reverence for Life is the ethic of Love widened into universality. It is the ethic of Jesus, now recognized as a logical consequence of thought.

As much as I admire Schweitzer, I am puzzled by his urge to crowd love and reverence for life into the category of "ethic," and then to make the ethic "a logical consequence of thought." In the story he told us about his discovery, it was only after deliberative thought had left him stranded that his great phrase "flashed" upon his mind. Schweitzer seems to have considered himself, first and last, a man of thought. For that reason, I daresay he thought of reverence for life as his own discovery and as a step forward for humankind, perhaps an increment of ethical progress. And though little has come of it, for the post-Renaissance European (and American), it was in fact a step forward. The minds of modernizing Europeans, when going about their great business of increasing human knowledge and human wealth, had been little enough distracted by reverence for anything. And so Schweitzer's "flash" of reverence for life was as greatly needed as it could possibly have been. The world was perishing for it, though among people so excitedly globalizing it could find no purchase.

But to another way of looking, Schweitzer's ethical step forward may be more a step backward to something that humankind had always known. Before and even during the reign of the mind that made World War I (et al.), there were a lot of people in the world for whom reverence for life was a daily practice, an ordinary *way* of life. For them, if it was religious—Schweitzer was right to associate it with religion or the specialty that we call religion—it was also economic. And so we have got to ask what it is about life, more than anything else, that causes humans to revere it.

So far as I know or can imagine, people who have revered life and those who still revere it would all give the same reason: that it has appeared to them to be a great miracle, unaccountable on the terms of available knowledge. To those who disdain the word "miracle," life is still a great mystery. That is because life—life itself—is not a substance. Air and light are oak and iron in comparison to life itself. For a good while now, I have been asking my scientific friends if any scientist has ever passed a dissecting blade between an organism and its life and then placed the lifeless body of the organism into one vessel and its removed life into another, so as to study the character and consistency of life itself. So far as I have discovered, life itself has never been isolated or captured or confined. The most principled materialist is a living creature who has never seen or heard or tasted or touched or smelled, let alone weighed or measured or priced, apart from his body, the life that so far has animated his body. He can only be amazed, like all his kind from the beginning until now, that life is something that in one moment creatures have, and in the next have had.

Because the age of global search and discovery now is ending— because by now we have so thoroughly ransacked, appropriated, and diminished the globe's original wealth—we can see how generous and abounding is the commonwealth of life in comparison to that merely of humans or humanity, and how fairly, we could almost say how democratically, it is portioned out among the creatures. A mouse, a horse, a butterfly, a fly, a microbe, any poorest or oddest human—each has as honest and sufficient a portion of life as a billionaire who owns a government. And now that we have so far "mastered" the globe, perhaps we can again see beyond its physical limits to its mysteries that we will never "discover" or explain.

Perhaps we can see how reverence for life—how even life itself as an acknowledged mystery, immaterial and immeasurable—undermines and shakes the modern structure of human prerogative and technological progress. As life is not isolatable, or empirically knowable, so it is not reducible; it cannot be made into anything that it is not. It is not something we can have only for ourselves, or something we can compete for and take away from others and so have more for ourselves. Our life can be made more abundant, as Jesus said, but not by any quantifiable amount. As the ecologists have been telling us for a long time, we cannot have life for ourselves alone but only in common with other living creatures, the significance of which, as Schweitzer said, we are unlikely to know. And so we may begin to see how, for Schweitzer, the word "life" as opposed to the word "human" attracts the adjective "sacred," and how it renews and enlivens such words of value and reverence and affection as I listed at the beginning of Chapter II: the crown or canopy of our language that materialism and determinism have lopped off.

Perhaps we can see also how this understanding of life as sacred mystery rejoins us to the traditional knowledge of our predecessors and ancestors, our true heritage, that materialism has dismissed as "mythology" or superstition. In a number of places not much attended to in our time, the Bible holds that *every creature* lives by sharing in the breath and spirit of God. Here, again, is Genesis 2:7: "And the Lord God formed man of the dust of the ground, and breathed into his nostrils the breath of life; and man became a living soul." And here from Psalm 104, a prayer of praise, is the thirtieth verse, which speaks of all the creatures, "both small and great beasts": "Thou sendeth forth thy spirit, they are created." Such

passages surely were on William Blake's mind long afterward, when
he proclaimed that "everything that lives is holy."

But now I need to hesitate a moment over the too narrow meaning I have so far given to "life." Some years ago I learned from my
friend Wes Jackson, who was following his friend Stan Rowe, of
the inadequacy of the word "biosphere," and the need to replace
it with "ecosphere." That is because creatures we think of as living
cannot live without creatures we think of as nonliving: light and
air and water and rocks. And so as my last witness I want to call a
Pit River Indian by the name of Bill. According to Kat Anderson's
book on the traditional land management practices of the California Indians, the anthropologist Jaime de Angulo was talking with
Bill sometime in the 1920s, when Bill told him:

> Everything is living, even the rocks, even the bench you
> are sitting on. . . . Everything is alive. That's what we Indi-
> ans believe. White people think everything is dead.

That seems to me, for one thing, to be a fairly complete criticism
of the European occupation of America so far—at least in its so far
dominant version. As evidence, we treat the soil of our farmlands
and working forests, not to mention all land to be "developed," as if
it were dead; we treat living farm animals in confinement as if they
are dead; we look upon whatever is unwanted or in our way, from
"fetuses" to technologically obsolete workers and farmers to mountains and forests, as if they are dead already or might as well be dead.

People true to the present time will conclude as a matter of
course that Bill was talking religion or, more likely, superstition.
But he was speaking merely of reality as he and his people knew it.
His knowledge would be better called "not modern" than "primitive." He was not an oddity or a special case. We have from several

sources the knowledge that we live in a world entirely living, in a commonwealth of living creatures interdependent and mutually sustaining, all of it inspired and animated by the mystery or miracle of life. From the same sources we are assured that this community of creatures—though clearly not biased in favor of human comfort or longevity—is orderly, beautiful, good, deserving of our love, forbearance, and care. We understand that we cannot live except by the sacrifice of other life, but we know that we cannot know either the portion of life that we may allowably take or the worth or significance of the taken life. From the mystery by which we are alive, from our irreducible ignorance, we readily deduce the terms upon which we and our kind must live if we are to live for very long: that we need to obey absolutely Nature's requirements to keep all of her places healthful and whole, and to waste nothing; that we need to use sparingly, carefully, kindly, and gratefully all that we must use. As we are not whole in our selves when divided from other humans, so we are not whole as humans when divided from all other creatures, so we are not whole as creatures when divided from the earth, from a home country and the landmarks and reminders of a home country. These connections we need to know, understand, imagine, and live out. Thus we complete our story as members and as persons. This is the wholeness that we long for, that we hear about from our forebears and our prophets. This is the work we are called to, individually and all together.

That or something near it, I think, is our original vision of our life in this world. "Advanced civilizations" always have had trouble keeping it in mind. I think that its influence survived and continued, here and there, now and then, in post-Columbus America, among the country people of all races, those who lived from the country they lived in and took care of, in a line of unbroken responsibility going back before history. It is not enough to think that we have adequately placed ourselves when we have bought pieces of the earth for ourselves alone. It is the placed community of ourselves together that we need and long for, as the old people in *A Gathering of Old Men* long for their lost community, the wholeness they once made of and for themselves in a place that was never their "property," that they owned just by their belonging to it. The old people of Ernest Gaines's book—like some of their generation of both races in my own country—were people, natural and traditional, whose minds were capably employed where they lived and worked, who did not work in one place with their minds in another or on quitting time. Some of the same kind were born and brought up to the old values here in my own home country in the twentieth century, but always fewer.

As a rule, our modern age of global plunder has rejected the old ways completely in favor of an economy of rapid extraction, consumption, and waste. But the survivals and reminders of our original vision, alongside the plain evidence of our failure, should tell us how petty and provincial has been our wish to divide ourselves as humans and kinds of humans and individual humans in competition against one another and against the earth. By imposing slavery upon the world, we have enslaved ourselves. Now all of us, rich and poor alike, are living as slaves of Mammon in a sickened world. As little as half a century ago, more freedom was available to us than we have now. Even so recently there were choices that we were free to make, which now cannot be made. Not now or for years to come can we choose to be free of filth and poison, or to be as healthy and whole as we naturally want and need to be.

We are now reduced to one significant choice. We can take our stand either on the side of life or on the side of death. This will never be presented to us as one large and final choice, but only as a succession of small choices, continuing to the seventh and the seven-hundredth generation. Because we have not forgotten all of our true heritage or lost all of its records, signs, and relics, we can begin to imagine how this would be. By a long persistence of human choosing, not of human life but of the world's life, which is both its and ours, everything would be changed: how we would live, how we would live together, how we would earn our living, how we would work. If we worked for the world's life, in good faith, with sufficient love, and knowing how, our work would become good. It would become beautiful. It would make us happy, and not with the future happiness of political promising. It would make us happy as soon as we began to do it.

Some Writings Related to This Book

————————————— ∿ —————————————

Adams, John Quincy, *Diaries 1779–1821* and *Diaries 1821–1848* (two volumes), edited by David Waldstreicher, Library of America, 2017.

Anderson, M. Kat, *Tending the Wild: Native American Knowledge and the Management of California Natural Resources*, University of California Press, 2005.

Belloc, Hilaire, "The Modern Man," *Who Owns America?*, edited by Herbert Agar and Allen Tate, Houghton Mifflin Company, 1936. Reprinted by ISI Books, 1999.

Bernanos, Georges, *The Last Essays of Georges Bernanos*, translated by Joan and Barry Ulanov, Henry Regnery Company, 1955.

Berry, Wendell, *The Art of Loading Brush*, Counterpoint, 2017. (Pages 8–9 for definition of agrarianism, and "The Thought of Limits in a Prodigal Age.")

Brady, Lisa, "The Wilderness of War: Nature and Strategy in the American Civil War," *Environmental History and the American South: A Reader*, edited by Paul S. Sutter and Christopher J. Manganiello, University of Georgia Press, 2009.

Brueggemann, Walter, *Tenacious Solidarity: Biblical Provocations on Race, Religion, Climate, and the Economy*, Fortress Press, 2018.

Carey, Graham, "The Majority Report on Art," *Temenos Academy Review* 19 (Ashford, Kent), 2016.

Catton, Bruce, *The Civil War*, American Heritage Press, 1971.

Chargaff, Erwin, *Heraclitean Fire: Sketches from a Life Before Nature*, Rockefeller University Press, 1978.

Thomas D. Clark Memorial Issue, *The Register of the Kentucky Historical Society*, Winter/Spring 2005.

Clark, Thomas D., "An Interview with Thomas D. Clark," *Plantation Society in the Americas*, Summer 1996.

Clark, Thomas D., *My Century in History: Memoirs*, The University Press of Kentucky, 2006.

Coates, Ta-Nehisi, "What This Cruel War Was Over," *The Atlantic*, June 22, 2015, https://www.theatlantic.com/politics/archive/2015/06/what -this-cruel-war-was-over/396482/

Coomaraswamy, Ananda K., "Education in Art," *Temenos Academy Review* 20 (Ashford, Kent), 2017.

Daniel, Pete, *Dispossession: Discrimination Against African-American Farmers in the Age of Civil Rights*, The University of North Carolina Press, 2013.

Daniel, Pete, "Farmland Blues: The Legacy of USDA Discrimination," https://southernspaces.org/2013.

Davenport, Guy, *Pennant Key-Indexed Study Guide to Homer's Iliad*, Educational Research Associates in association with Bantam Books, Inc., 1967.

Faulkner, William, *Novels 1942–1954*, edited by Joseph Blotner and Noel Polk, Library of America, 1994.

Fields, Mamie Garvin, with Karen Fields, *Lemon Swamp and Other Places: A Carolina Memoir*, The Free Press, 1983.

Flood, Charles Barcelen, *Lee: The Last Years*, Houghton Mifflin Company, 1981.

Flynt, Wayne, *Dixie's Forgotten People*, Indiana University Press, 2004.

Foote, Shelby, *The Civil War: A Narrative* (three volumes), Vintage Books edition, Random House, 1986.

Franklin, John Hope, *Reconstruction After the Civil War*, third edition, The University of Chicago Press, 2013.

Gaines, Ernest J., *A Gathering of Old Men*, Knopf, 1983.

Gaines, Ernest J., *Mozart and Leadbelly: Stories and Essays*, Knopf, 2005.

Gaines, Ernest J., *The Tragedy of Brady Sims*, Vintage Books, 2017.

Gaudet, Marcia, and Carl Wooten, editors, *Porch Talk with Ernest Gaines: Conversations on the Writer's Craft*, Louisiana State University Press, 1990.

Gaventa, John, "Power and Powerlessness in an Appalachian Valley—Revisited," *The Journal of Peasant Studies*, 46:3, 2019.

Gill, Eric, *A Holy Tradition of Working: Passages from the Writings of Eric Gill*, selected by Brian Keeble, Golgonooza Press, 1983.

Grimes, Mike, compiler and editor, *Lockport,* no publisher named, 2018.

Hall, James Baker, *Tobacco Harvest: An Elegy,* photographs by James Baker Hall, essay by Wendell Berry, The University Press of Kentucky, 2004.

Harrison, Lowell H., *Civil War in Kentucky*, The University Press of Kentucky, 1975.

Harrison Lowell H. and James C. Klotter, *A New History of Kentucky*, The University Press of Kentucky, 1997.

Hollander, John, editor, *American Poetry: The Nineteenth Century*, Library of America, 1993.

hooks, bell, *Belonging*, Routledge, 2009.

hooks, bell, *Outlaw Culture*, Routledge Classics, 2006.

Hubbard, Harlan, *Payne Hollow*, Gnomon Press, 1974.

Hull, William E., *Beyond the Barriers*, Mercer University Press, 2012.

Kennedy, David M., *Freedom from Fear: The American People in Depression and War, 1929–1945*, Oxford University Press, 2005.

Kibler, James Everett, Jr., editor, *Taking Root: The Nature Writing of William and Adam Summer of Pomaria*, The University of South Carolina Press, 2017.

Killebrew, J. B., *Report on the Culture and Curing of Tobacco in the United States*, Government Printing Office, Washington, D.C., 1884.

King, Martin Luther, Jr., *A Testament of Hope: The Essential Writings and Speeches*, edited by James M. Washington, Harper One/HarperCollins paperback edition, 1991.

King, Martin Luther, Jr., *Why We Can't Wait*, Signet Classics, 2000.

Kirwan, A. D., editor, *Johnny Green of the Orphan Brigade: The Journal of a Confederate Soldier*, The University Press of Kentucky, 2002.

Kleber, John E., editor in chief, *The Kentucky Encyclopedia*, The University Press of Kentucky, 1972.

LaDuke, Winona, "Prophecy of the Seventh Fire," Thirty-Seventh Annual E. F. Schumacher Lecture, Schumacher Center for a New Economics, 2017.

Langland, William, *Piers the Plowman*, translated by J. F. Goodridge, Penguin Books, 1966.

Lewis, C. S., *Studies in Words*, Cambridge University Press, 1967.

Lewis, John, with Michael D'Orso, *Walking with the Wind: A Memoir of the Movement*, Simon & Schuster Paperbacks, 2015.

Lovejoy, Arthur O., *The Great Chain of Being*, Harvard University Press, 1967.

Lowe, John, editor, *Conversations with Ernest Gaines,* University Press of Mississippi, 1995.

Lucas, Marion B., *A History of Blacks in Kentucky*, Volume I, *From Slavery to Segregation, 1760–1891.* The Kentucky Historical Society, 1992.

Lukacs, John, *Democracy and Populism:Fear and Hatred*, Yale University Press, 2005.

Lukacs, John, *A Short History of the Twentieth Century*, The Belknap Press of Harvard University Press, 2013.

Lukacs, John, *Five Days in London, May 1940*, Yale University Press, 1999.

Lukacs, John, *Last Rites*, Yale University Press, 2009.

Lukacs, John, *Outgrowing Democracy: A History of the United States in the Twentieth Century*, Doubleday & Company, 1984.

Lukacs, John, *Remembered Past: John Lukacs on History, Historians, and Historical Knowledge*, edited by Mark G. Malvasi and Jeffrey O. Nelson, ISI Books, 2005.

McPherson, James, *Battle Cry of Freedom*, Oxford University Press, 1988.

Meacham, Jon, *The Soul of America: The Battle for Our Better Angels*, Random House, 2018.

Merton, Thomas, *Disputed Questions*, First Harvest Edition, 1985.

Merton, Thomas, "Hagia Sophia," *The Collected Poems of Thomas Merton*, New Directions, 1977.

Milne, Joseph, "The Call of Justice," *Temenos Academy Review* 21 (Ashford, Kent), 2018.

Milne, Joseph, "The Heavenly Order and the Lawful Society," *Temenos Academy Review* 17 (Ashford, Kent), 2014.

Mosgrove, George Dallas, *Kentucky Cavaliers in Dixie: The Reminiscences of a Confederate Cavalryman*, Courier-Journal Job Printing Co., 1895.

Nagel, Paul C., *John Quincy Adams: A Public Life, a Private Life*, Harvard University Press, 1997.

Nathans, Benjamin, "Rewriting Human Rights," *The New York Review of Books*, December 5, 2019.

Newkirk, Vann R., III, "This Land Was Our Land," *The Atlantic*, September 2019.

Orwell, George, *1984*, A Signet Classic, with an Afterword by Erich Fromm, 1961.

Plato, *The Collected Dialogues Including the Letters*, edited by Edith Hamilton and Huntington Cairns, Bollingen Series LXXI, Pantheon Books, 1961.

Powers, Thomas, "The Big Thing on His Mind," *The New York Review of Books*, April 20, 2017.

Pryor, Elizabeth Brown, *Reading the Man: A Portrait of Robert E. Lee Through His Private Letters*, Penguin Books, 2008.

Riley, Franklin L., editor, *General Robert E. Lee After Appomattox*, The Macmillan Company, 1922.

Riskin, Jessica, "Just Use Your Thinking Pump," *The New York Review of Books*, July 2, 2020.

Roland, Charles P., *Reflections on Lee: A Historian's Assessment*, Stackpole Books, 1995.

Rosengarten, Theodore, *All God's Dangers: The Life of Nate Shaw*, Knopf, 1974.

Ruskin, John, *Unto This Last* and *Munera Pulveris*, The World's Classics, Oxford University Press, 1923.

Schelling, Andrew, *Tracks Along the Left Coast: Jaime de Angulo & Pacific Coast Culture*, Counterpoint, 2017.

Schweitzer, Albert, *Out of My Life and Thought*, translated by C. T. Campion, Henry Holt and Company, 1958.

Scott, James C., *Against the Grain: A Deep History of the Earliest States*, Yale University Press, 2017.

Skeat, Walter W., The Rev., *A Concise Etymological Dictionary of the English Language*, Capricorn Books, 1963.

Smith, Kimberly K., *African-American Environmental Thought: Foundations*, University Press of Kansas, 2007.

Smith, Page, *Trial by Fire: A People's History of the Civil War and Reconstruction*, McGraw-Hill Book Company, 1982.

Snyder, Gary, *The Great Clod: Notes and Memoirs on Nature and History in East Asia*, Counterpoint, 2016.

Solzhenitsyn, Alexander, *One Day in the Life of Ivan Denisovich*, translated by H. T. Willetts, Everyman's Library, 1995.

Stewart, Mart, "If John Muir Had Been an Agrarian," *Environmental History and the American South: A Reader*, edited by Paul S. Sutter and Christopher J. Manganiello, University of Georgia Press, 2009.

Taplin, Jonathan, "Rebirth of a Nation," *Harper's Magazine*, November 2018.

Tate, Allen, *Essays of Four Decades*, Introduction by Louise Cowan, ISI Books, 1999.

Tate, Allen, *Stonewall Jackson: The Good Soldier,* J. S. Sanders & Company, 1991.

Taylor, John M., *Duty Faithfully Performed: Robert E. Lee and His Critics*, Brassey's, 1999.

Tenney, Paul, "Seeing Through the Mirage of Localism," *28 Comments*, November 7, 2016.

Traub, James, *John Quincy Adams: Militant Spirit*, Basic Books, 2016.

Twelve Southerners, "Introduction: A Statement of Principles," *I'll Take My Stand*, Louisiana State University Press, 1977.

Uglow, Jenny, "What the Weather Is," *The New York Review of Books*, December 19, 2019.

Wallis, Don, *All We Had Was Each Other: The Black Community of Madison, Indiana, An Oral History*, Indiana University Press, 1998.

Warren, Robert Penn, *Jefferson Davis Gets His Citizenship Back*, The University Press of Kentucky, 1980.

Warren, Robert Penn, *The Legacy of the Civil War*, University of Nebraska Press, 1961.

White, Lynn, Jr., "The Historical Roots of Our Ecological Crisis," *Science*, March 10, 1967.

Whitman, Walt, *Poetry and Prose*, edited by Justin Kaplan, Library of America, 1982.

Wilkinson, Crystal, *The Birds of Opulence*, The University Press of Kentucky, 2016.

Wilson, Edmund, *Patriotic Gore: Studies in the Literature of the American Civil War*, Oxford University Press (New York), 1962.

Woodward, C. Vann, *Origins of the New South, 1877–1913*, Louisiana State University Press, 2013.

Woodward, C. Vann, *Reunion and Reaction*, Oxford University Press, 1966.

Woofter, T. J. Jr., and Ellen Winston, *Seven Lean Years*, The University of North Carolina Press, 1939.

Wright, George C., *A History of Blacks in Kentucky*, Volume 2, *In Pursuit of Equality, 1890–1980*, The Kentucky Historical Society, 1992.

Yellowtail, Thomas, *Yellowtail, Crow Medicine Man and Sun Dance Chief: An Autobiography*, as told to Michael Oren Fitzgerald, The University of Oklahoma Press, 1891.

Index

Index

About the Author

———————————— ～ ————————————

Wendell Berry is the author of *The Unsettling of America* and *The Hidden Wound*, as well as more than fifty other books of poetry, fiction, and essays. He has been awarded the National Humanities Medal, the Cleanth Brooks Medal for Lifetime Achievement by the Fellowship of Southern Writers, the Louis Bromfield Society Award, and most recently the Henry Hope Reed Award. He lives and farms with his wife, Tanya Berry, in Kentucky.